MIT

THE CAMPUS GUIDE

MIT

A HISTORICAL AND ARCHITECTURAL GUIDE BY
Douglass Shand-Tucci

PHOTOGRAPHY BY JOHN HORNER

PREFACE BY L. RAFAEL REIF
FOREWORD BY MARK JARZOMBEK

In memory of Rawson Lyman Wood and H. A. Crosby Forbes

PRINCETON ARCHITECTURAL PRESS
NEW YORK

PUBLISHED BY
Princeton Architectural Press
A McEvoy Group company
37 East 7th Street
New York, New York 10003
www.papress.com

© 2016 Princeton Architectural Press
All rights reserved
Printed and bound in China
19 18 17 16 4 3 2 1 First edition

SERIES EDITOR: Jan Cigliano Hartman
EDITOR: Meredith Baber
DESIGNER: Benjamin English
DESIGN ASSISTANCE: Jimin Park

SPECIAL THANKS TO: Nicola Bednarek Brower, Janet Behning, Erin Cain,
Tom Cho, Barbara Darko, Jenny Florence, Lia Hunt, Mia Johnson,
Valerie Kamen, Simone Kaplan-Senchak, Stephanie Leke, Diane Levinson,
Jennifer Lippert, Sara McKay, Jaime Nelson Noven, Rob Shaeffer,
Sara Stemen, Paul Wagner, Joseph Weston, and Janet Wong
of Princeton Architectural Press —Kevin C. Lippert, publisher

LIBRARY OF CONGRESS CATALOGING-IN-PUBLICATION DATA
Shand-Tucci, Douglass, 1941–
MIT : an architectural tour / by Douglass Shand-Tucci ; photography by
John Horner ; preface by Rafael Reif ; foreword by Mark Jarzombek.
    pages   cm.—(The campus guide)
Includes bibliographical references and index.
ISBN 978-1-61689-274-6 (alk. paper)
1. Massachusetts Institute of Technology—History. 2. Massachusetts Institute
of Technology—Buildings. 3. Architecture—Massachusetts—Boston—
History. 4. Boston (Mass.)—Buildings, structures, etc. I. Title. II. Title:
Massachusetts Institute of Technology.
T171.M428S53 2016
374.4'4—dc23   2014049070

Contents

How to Use This Guide

The rich history of MIT is generally divided into two eras, that of the first Copley Square campus in the Back Bay and the second Charles River Basin campus in Cambridgeport. This book presents the story through a set of chapters divided into two parts, "Global Portals: The Great White City of the Gods of Copley Square" and "Campus Walks: Inventing the Future on Boston's Left Bank." The first part explores the cultural and intellectual ideas developed in MIT's formative years. The second part presents the development and expansion of those ideas in an increasingly global context through exploration of the modern campus, at the same time helping the visitor experience certain coherencies within the campus layout.

Not to be missed is the MIT Museum at 265 Massachusetts Avenue, southeast of Central Square. This museum hosts collections of technology-related art, holography, artificial intelligence, robotics, kinetic art, and the history of MIT generally. There is a wide array of exhibitions and displays with related programming.

Also of interest is the MIT Press Bookstore at 292 Main Street at Kendall Square. In addition to its own distinguished list of books, it features a wide array of books about MIT by all publishers.

For more information:
on visiting MIT   http://web.mit.edu/institute-events/visitor/
on MIT campus art   http://listart.mit.edu/

Preface

MIT is a community of people unusually interested in knowing how things work. If you want to know how *we* work—and how the people of MIT have come to produce such a record of discovery and invention—you could start by reading the character of our campus.

MIT was founded—*is* founded—on a reverence for the core principles of science, engineering, and mathematics, principles as grand, elegant, and severe as the great limestone columns that center your attention on Killian Court. That timeless space is ringed by the names of the scientific giants whose work makes possible all of our modern marvels; knowing our debt to them keeps us humble! In the same way, working in close quarters with the laws of nature, we learn to take our work seriously, but not ourselves.

At our core is an irreverence too, the shared conviction that the status quo is merely the beta release. This is the playful, subversive spirit that inspires our long tradition of campus "hacks." You will find these quirky, witty, technically brilliant student pranks memorialized in the Stata Center with an MIT police car and an enormous fiberglass cow, each of which once made a surprise appearance on MIT's Great Dome. That sense of daring and play shows up in our architecture, from the Stata Center's cheerfully unpredictable facade to the permanent surprise of Simmons Hall's wild metallic grid. Combining our faith in the power of science with an appetite for unconventional ideas gives us a certain creative audacity—and an instinct to "hack the world."

Because openness is a central MIT value, our campus is open too. The vast majority of our buildings are open to the public and the campus has no visible perimeter; we are an aggressively ungated community that works around the clock and welcomes the world in. This physical openness encourages new intellectual connections: our buildings link so seamlessly that you often do not realize you have passed from one to the next, and we cross between academic disciplines just as freely, on a mission to find answers to the world's great challenges. And the people of MIT—the faces you see streaming through the Infinite Corridor between classes—reflect our meritocratic openness to talent, from absolutely everywhere.

The campus also tells you that MIT is hands-on. We believe in learning by doing—and by making, exploring, designing, inventing, and performing too. Much of the daily work of our faculty and students happens in extraordinarily advanced laboratories, in fields from cancer, brain science, robotics, and nanomaterials to alternative energy and astrophysics. But we also have our own machine shop, a wind tunnel, an aerospace research hangar, a research nuclear reactor, and a glassblowing lab. We like to make things—and we like to make an impact. Taken as a whole, our campus is a workshop for inventing the future.

Finally, you can tell a great deal about MIT by where the campus *is*—and where it is not. We are not in the woods or set apart on a hill. We are right in the heart of the city, the hot center of one of the world's most vibrant hubs of innovation and entrepreneurship. Hundreds of start-ups are founded by our faculty, alumni, and students every year, many right here in the neighborhood; it is not too much to say that you cannot tell where Kendall Square stops and MIT begins. We are minutes from an international airport, and a few hops on the subway from brilliant colleagues at neighboring universities and at some of the finest hospitals on earth.

In a sense, MIT's greatest invention is itself, a high concentration of unusual talent pursuing an inspiring mission—to advance knowledge, educate students, and bring knowledge to bear on the world's great challenges for the betterment of humankind. Grounded in scientific rigor, we are playful and open, we like to get things started, and we are very much connected to each other and to the world. We are a community of people relentlessly curious and restlessly creative—bold, ambitious, hands-on problem solvers unified in a mission to serve.

You see it in our campus and you see it in our faces.

Welcome to MIT!

Sincerely,
L. Rafael Reif
President

Foreword
Thoughts on the MIT Campus

Imagine that today is September 2, 1917; I am newly matriculated at MIT and I am on my way to my first class. I have left my hot attic apartment on Boylston Street and, dressed in my best shirt and jacket, walk down stately Commonwealth Avenue. I take a right onto West Chester Park (now known as Massachusetts Avenue). From the head of the Harvard Bridge my view opens to a wide panorama of the Charles River. The reeds and mosquito-infested mud flats that were there just a few years ago have disappeared. Instead, I see on the opposite shore a granite embankment, and behind it a modern motorway running along the river. But most remarkable of all is the new, white marble building stretching the length of more than two football fields along the river. It is not only wide, but also tall. The first floor is nothing less than seventeen feet high! The building has an impressive dome at the center, the likes of which I've never seen before. A wide, axially placed, paved courtyard opens to the river. I hurry across the bridge, walk across the great court toward an imposing, ten-columned Ionic porch, and enter through the massive front door with a sense of awe and pride.

The year 1893 saw the complete breakdown of the American economy. Railroads, mines, and banks had overextended their debt, and, when one bankruptcy led to another, it all came to a crashing halt. Unemployment rocketed to about 18 percent. Not a single building of any consequence was built in Boston or, for that matter, anywhere else in the United States. But with the economic revival in the following years, there was also a remarkable change of attitude in the architectural world. The hulking, Gothic-inspired architecture that was so admired in the previous decades was now out of fashion. The new style favored neoclassicism, which spanned a range of approaches from the light touch of the Italian Renaissance to the monumental look of ancient Rome. Boston, of course, had many excellent examples of that older style, especially in the Back Bay and none more weighty than Trinity Church (1877), designed by America's leading architect, H. H. Richardson. It was built of a pale-brown, roughly chiseled sandstone. Windows were tall and narrow, producing a sparsely illuminated interior; and rising from the midst of the composition was a broad-shouldered, turreted tower that for the uninformed could easily have been mistaken for a castle.

The new style was linked to the school of architecture in Paris known as the Beaux-Arts. Though its students had held firm to the ideals of neoclassicism during the nineteenth century, they had also embraced the changing times in a way that the neomedievalists did not. The Beaux-Arts welcomed steel, gas lighting, and broad streets that could accommodate urban traffic. In the United States, the greatest representative of the style was the New York firm McKim, Mead & White, which designed Pennsylvania Station in New York (1910) with marble exteriors and vast well-lit waiting rooms. The firm also designed the Minneapolis Institute of Art (1915) with simple proportions and a tall, porticoed entrance with six fluted Ionic columns. In Boston the firm designed the trendsetting Boston Public Library (1895). With its marble cornice, columns, and arches, it provided a stark contrast with Trinity Church on the other side of the plaza. The library is still today heralded as one of the finest example of Beaux-Arts architecture in the United States. Boston was soon graced with other buildings in the new style. These include the Museum of Fine Arts (1906–9), which featured a colonnade of eighteen imposing Ionic columns creating a generously scaled, if not somewhat cold, backdrop to the Fenway Gardens. But in siting and scale, nothing compared to the New Tech, designed by William Welles Bosworth, who was a graduate of both MIT (1895) and subsequently the Beaux-Arts. The building was clearly "a statement" that spoke to the modernizing spirit of the age.

The Great Dome, raised high above the mass of the structure so that it could be seen from across the Charles River, was modeled on the Pantheon in Rome (around 120 CE). The Pantheon was, however, not a familiar point of reference in the nineteenth century. Domes in the United States drew on English Renaissance models with their pronounced shape. They inevitably had a lantern on top and were ornamented with columns. The exception was the great "Rotunda" of the University of Virginia, designed by none other than Thomas Jefferson. All of these domes, however, were made of wood and plaster.

One has to remember that the art of using concrete, forgotten in the Middle Ages, was reintroduced into the building arts only in the late nineteenth century, which makes the MIT reference to the Pantheon and to concrete so important. MIT boasted, in fact, the largest concrete building in the world at the time. Today MIT's concrete is all but invisible behind dropped ceilings and thick clusters of pipes. But it has proven the test of time, for the building, now a hundred years old, has had to put up with massive amounts of use (and abuse) with hardly any overt signs of distress.

The New Tech contrasted with its immediate context, for when the area along the Charles River was drained, it was developed as a vast factory district. Behind MIT there towered dozens of smokestacks above boxy brick factories darkened with soot. Here one found piano manufacturers, furniture makers, ironworks, machinists, printing companies, automobile manufacturers, and even candy makers. Some of the first Model Ts were made in factories along Massachusetts Avenue. The noise of machinery and factory whistles could easily be heard at the New Tech; and even the various smells permeated the classrooms. There are still alumni who can recall the sweet odor of Necco wafers wafting through the labs. For almost a hundred years, it was a neighborhood of workers. Old-timers will remember the F&T railroad car diner, where one could get pastrami sandwiches or meatloaf with coffee or a beer and where fresh-faced students sat next to broad-chested mechanics. A few traces still exist. The MIT Museum, for example, at 265 Massachusetts Avenue, is housed in what was once the Cambridge Motor Company. Closer to MIT there is the enormous Metropolitan Warehouse (1917) with its thick, fireproof brick vaults that are still used today. But much has changed. The Necco Factory on Massachusetts Avenue was sold and refurbished by the pharmaceutical giant Novartis. The F&T and various factories were demolished in the 1980s when the land was sold to a developer. The area around Kendall Square is now home to sleek new buildings, cafes, and upscale apartments.

MIT's campus has also changed over the decades. The area to the west of Massachusetts Avenue, which was largely open land, now houses sports buildings and dormitories. In the 1950s, following the Second World War and the subsequent soul-searching about the nature of technology, MIT brought in the Finnish modernist architect Eero Saarinen to design a chapel and auditorium, which stand as some of the best examples of early modernism in the United States. The great white billowing roof of the auditorium is now invisible under the heavy-looking, copper sheathing of the recent "restoration." But the Chapel has remained intact. It is a lesson in under-stated brilliance. Over the decades, as MIT grew new buildings were added, mostly with only a casual reference to the larger idea of what a campus is or should be. And yet, despite the resultant jumble, the unique density of buildings gives the contem-porary campus a sense of compression, most palpable along the "Infinite Corridor," as it is called, that links the entrance of MIT on Massachusetts Avenue to the center of the campus.

Traveling along the corridors requires a special cognitive ability that can easily confound newcomers. The Main Group, as Bosworth's buildings are called, is made up of Buildings 1 to 10; the entrance on Massachusetts Avenue, though offi-cially the Rogers Building—named after MIT's founder, William Barton Rogers—is usually known simply, and somewhat mysteriously, as "Building 7." Somewhere there is E15, NW14, and W25. The origin of the nomenclature is not known for certain, but it was first used during construction to number the various parts of the massive building. "Building 1" is not a "building," in fact, but part of the giant mass of the Main Group that is on the corner of Massachusetts Avenue and Memorial Drive. "Building 2" is its partner, across the central axis, and so forth. The Great Dome, the icon of MIT, is simply known as "Building 10." The School of Architecture and Planning has offices in Buildings 3, 5, 7, 9, 10, E14, E15, and N51! And, indeed, for me to get to my office, I walk down a corridor that houses faculty offices of a different department, a student lounge, a tech support center, a seminar room, and even a high-end textile lab where they invented artificial skin; but one would never know it from the modest black door and the spent liquid hydrogen tanks in the hall. Unlike other campuses, there is no Chemistry Building or Engineering Quad. Such things—until recently—have been foreign to MIT.

So how did this come about? The explanation begins not in Cambridge, but at MIT's first campus, which was in Boston's Back Bay.[1] Like Cambridge, that area of town, with its fabulous row houses and wide shaded streets, had also been trans-formed from a swamp. It was planned as the home to Boston's expanding mercantile class. At its heart was Copley Square, which was designed to host a set of new institutions, the most remarkable of which was MIT. The building, sited on Boylston Street (and demolished in the 1950s), opened in 1863 and spoke to a dramatic transformation in the sciences. In the 1860s, one has to remember, fossils were still thought by some to be God's mistakes; the idea that the earth had a crust was not yet discovered, and *On the Origin of Species* by Darwin had only just been published, in 1859. The input behind the creation of MIT reflected not just new and controversial attitudes toward science, but also, just as importantly, the changing reality of the Industrial Revolution. Though the revolution's origins were in Europe, the core energy of it was shifting to the United States, where a series of inventions began to reshape the foundations of how things were made and produced: the mechanical grain reaper was invented in 1834; the steam shovel in 1839; the sewing machine in 1851; the shoe-making machine in 1860; the elevator was patented in 1861; the Porter-Allen steam engine was introduced in 1862.

Sensing the drastic shift that was taking place, Rogers (1804–1882), a progressive intellectual and scientist, worked tirelessly for over the better part of a decade to convince the state of Massachusetts to fund a home for scientific learning. His efforts paid off. And even though he is largely unsung in the annals of nineteenth-century intellectuals, he certainly deserves greater recognition. At least at MIT, his name is proudly etched in the entablature of the 77 Massachusetts Avenue portico.

The Institute started with just four departments, each speaking to an important sector of the emerging economy: 1: Agriculture; 2: Natural History, Geology, Chemistry; 3: Mechanics, Commerce; and 4: Fine Arts and Architecture. But this initial set of divisions proved to be too modest. By the 1880s technologies were developing at a rapid pace, professional societies were springing up, and industrialization was expanding. New faculty members were added and new courses created. The School of Mechanic Arts was established in 1876, and in the same year, the Women's Chemistry Laboratory. The Department of Electrical Engineering was created in 1882, the Department of Chemical Engineering in 1888, and in the 1890s, the Department of Sanitary Engineering was established and the Department of Mining Engineering separated from Geology. By 1900 MIT had grown from four departments to thirteen. Graduate programs in the various sciences also came into existence. By the late 1890s, the original cast of 10 faculty and 70 students had ballooned into 150 faculty and 1,300 students.

The unrelenting demand for ever more space resulted in buildings that were spread out over numerous city blocks. For students and faculty, the dispersal of the various facilities was time-consuming and inconvenient. As Bosworth recalled, "Just going from the old Walker building to the old main building for different classes, without an overcoat, in winter, was cruel."[2] The absence of dormitories contributed to this sense of diffusion. Students lived in their own apartments or with relatives. Wealthy students joined social or dining clubs; poor students rented spaces in nearby attics or basements.

Even though MIT had made every effort to deal with its own success, the campus by the turn of the century was not only inefficient, but also out of step with contemporary demands for a cohesive collegiate atmosphere that required on-site dormitories, sports facilities, libraries, and adequate student unions. Universities like Princeton, Columbia, West Point, Stanford, and Wisconsin had already set a standard in this respect. Designed by the top architectural firms of the nation, they were embedded in parklike environments with plenty of room for expansion. With the Land Grant Act of 1861, state universities were springing up across the nation, many with excellent laboratory facilities. It is safe to say that the expansion of academe during this period placed a unique stamp on the American consciousness, one that defines it still today.

Back at MIT, with pressure mounting to address the situation, a new president was chosen, Richard Cockburn Maclaurin (1870–1920), a Scottish-born New Zealander, who was given the mandate to tackle the problem. Educated at Cambridge University, he was at that time teaching physics at Columbia University and was also serving as the chair of the Department of Mathematical Physics. He was inaugurated on June 7, 1909, at age thirty-nine. He was a man of enormous energy and an excellent orator, able to put into plain language what, according to him, MIT's vision of itself should be. The core of his message was that the mechanical age of old had given way to a new age, the age of research. The "great problem," as he saw it, was not simply "to organize our knowledge [but] to organize it in such a way as to make it as effective as possible in industry."[3] MIT's alumni journal, the *Technology Review*, echoed Maclaurin's sentiments, noting that in this "era of business and great business development," MIT appreciates "the necessity for a different sort of education to meet changing conditions in the United States."[4]

Despite Maclaurin's grand aspirations, MIT was in difficult financial straits. Harvard had made several offers to buy the Institute, offers that the MIT faculty rejected. Restoring its financial footing and moving an institution as big as MIT was practically unheard of and probably no one at MIT could even yet envision what it entailed, but there was no stopping the process. The site that was finally chosen was across the river from Back Bay, in Cambridge on a flat, fifty-acre field on the Charles River that had only recently been nothing more than a swamp. Architecturally speaking, the site was not for the faint of heart, since it was exposed to the gaze of the Bostonian elites, who could view it from the bay windows of their apartments. Maclaurin was well aware of the challenge: "We have a glorious site and glorious opportunities, but our task of design is not made more easy by the great expectations of Boston."[5] He was determined that the result should not disappoint:

> If we do not rise to the level of this great [architectural] question we will commit a crime against Technology students for generations to come and a crime against the whole community in which they live and move.... What is that impress to be? Will it adequately express the ideals of the Institute, the nobility of its purpose and the dignity of its work? Will those ideals be presented as impressively and as beautifully as by the towers and spires and other architectural features characteristic of the great churches of the Middle Ages? If they do not, it will be a permanent slur on our intelligence and on our taste, for the idea of education for which the Institute stands is as noble an ideal as any that can be expressed by form, and it is pre-eminently the ideal of the thoughtful section of the American people today.[6]

Without that powerful statement, the design for MIT would not have been as successful. But the eventual building, with its innovative design and majestic court-yard and dome, almost did not come about. It took a while for MIT to figure out how to translate its understanding of itself into a building. It took a while to find the right architect and engineer. It also took a while to find a donor. It was George Eastman of Eastman Kodak who came to the rescue with a $2.5 million check that in one fell swoop changed MIT from a public institution to a private one.

The building was a success because MIT, by the time it commissioned the building, knew what it did not want as much as what it wanted. It did not want a Harvard-style campus of independent buildings. It wanted a megabuilding that was flexible on the inside and that could be expanded on the outside. And of all the major campus commissions in the United States from that era, and there were indeed a goodly number, MIT was unique in its vision. Most campus architects favored a Gothic style (Princeton and Chicago) or the bricks of neo-Georgian (Harvard). MIT's austere classicism stood out as unusual. But as the twentieth century progressed, attitudes about MIT's buildings shifted with the changing needs and fashions. The coherency of the original vision began to erode. Some buildings were designed to be purposefully functional and prosaic, but fortunately, there was always an under-current of quality. Baker House (1949) by Alvar Aalto, the Charles Hayden Memorial Library (1950) by Voorhees Walker Foley & Smith, and the MIT Chapel and Kresge Auditorium (1955) by Saarinen are world-class buildings and classics of midcentury modernism.

The formidable I. M. Pei had a huge impact on the campus with the Green Building (1964) and the Dreyfus Building (1967). He, more than other architects, understood the principle of connectivity to the MIT campus. Somewhat more generic were buildings 36 to 38 on Vassar Street designed by Skidmore, Owings & Merrill; more monumental was the Stratton Student Center (1968) with its massive external staircase and huge glass windows.

In the opening years of the twenty-first century, MIT sought to update a campus that had grown stale and complacent. A group of leading architects soon made important contributions: Simmons Hall (Steven Holl, 2002); Zesiger Sports and Fitness Center (Kevin Roche and John Dinkeloo & Associates, 2002); Stata Center (Frank Gehry, 2004); Brain and Cognitive Sciences Building (Charles Correa and Goody, Clancy and Associates, 2006); the New Media Lab Building (Fumihiko Maki, 2006); the Koch Institute (Goody Clancy & Associates, 2010); and most recently the new building for the Sloan School of Management, known as "Building E62" (Moore Ruble Yudell).

These buildings forced MIT to take a new look at the campus and to begin to think about the weak links in the campus, namely the area around Kendall Square. Once a rather seedy boundary between MIT and the old factory district, it is now the site of research laboratories of the world's leading pharmaceutical and medical industries—it is the access point to one of the world's great institutions of learning. In a sense, if MIT's old entrance was along Massachusetts Avenue, its new entrance is going to be Kendall Square. But what will it look like ten years from now? Will it have a vision that speaks to our age, just as the New Tech spoke to its age back in 1916? Time will tell. But it is clear that an institution as important as MIT will continue to grow and will thus continue to be a campus that struggles to shape its identity as much as it is being shaped by the changing times.

Mark Jarzombek
Professor of the History and Theory of Architecture

1 For a full account of the first campus and the move to the new one, see my book-length study: *Designing MIT: The Architecture of William Welles Bosworth* (Boston: Northeastern University Press, 2004).

2 Bosworth to Miss Schillaber, April 19, 1954, MC 612, Box #77, 93. Correspondence, Fassett with Bosworth, MIT Archives.

3 Richard Maclaurin, "University and Industries," *Journal of Industrial and Engineering Chemistry* 8, no. 1 (1916): 59.

4 Richard Maclaurin, "President's Speech at Annual Banquet," *Technology Review* 13, no. 4 (April 1911): 227.

5 "The Growing Influence of the Alumni," *Technology Review* 15, no. 2 (February 1913): 151.

6 "Alumni Preparing for a Supreme Effort," *Technology Review* 14, no. 3 (March 1912): 154.

Author's Acknowledgments

My purpose in this book is to give MIT a richer—and perhaps deeper—sense of itself, historically, to share with visitors in all its orbits, metropolitan, national, and global. I have in mind not so much a sense of *what* the Institute has become—the best scientific university in the world (unless it be Britain's Cambridge)—as *how* this prize was grasped, grasped by the Gods of Copley Square in the Great White City on the Charles that they conceived and built more or less a century ago, beginning in 1913–16.

An important subtext of this aim, reflected here in the sort of "disruptive scholarship" I am prone to—which the High Tech world has happily taught us can be more positive than negative—is the way New England intellectual and cultural history over the last 150 years has been so formative an influence in creating MIT. In creating it, moreover, not as one of the great Boston institutions of today, but, in fact, as one half of what is perhaps now the single greatest and most characteristic Boston institution. That is something called "Harvard/MIT"—including on the Harvard side of the equation Harvard Medical School and the Massachusetts General Hospital, around which stand the whole medical and life sciences centers of the Back Bay Fens and Longwood and East Cambridge areas, a constellation superbly symbolized by the new "Ragon Institute of MGH, MIT, and Harvard" in Kendall Square, where this book ends.

This may seem too large a claim. Certainly it is true that the Boston city-state cannot in any period be reduced to a "one-company town," even if that company is Harvard/MIT. Such a claim seemingly diminishes the claims of Boston's Museum of Fine Arts or, for a more recent example, of WGBH Educational Foundation, standard bearers in their own fields of world stature. Yet at various periods in American history I would be prepared to advance the same arguably too-large claim for other institutions. Harvard in the seventeenth century stood unrivaled. So too Trinity Church, Copley Square, in the era of Saint Phillips Brooks and H. H. Richardson; as well the *Liberator*, in the hands of William Lloyd Garrison, prophet of the Abolitionist Movement. The Boston Public Library, the first tax-supported, big-city circulating library in the world open to all and an epochal development in Western history, is an example of the 1850s. So too Massachusetts General Hospital when it was the first venue in the world for the public use of *anesthesia*—the word was coined by Oliver Wendell Holmes Sr.—a development without which modern medicine would hardly be possible.

Perhaps this is why an institution like the Boston Symphony Orchestra, the first professional musical organization of its kind anywhere, does not seem diminished either by calling Harvard/MIT Boston's greatest and most characteristic institution of today. Nor the several academic siblings of MIT in the late nineteenth century—some Boston Brahmin in origin, some not—Tufts, Boston University, the Perkins Institution for the blind in Wellesley—all famous in their own right now, all such bright stars in Boston's present-day galaxy of institutions.

History is noisy. It is important to be able to detect the signal through the noise, and because history is always about change, that is the signal to listen for. The French poet Paul Valéry insisted that "history is the science of what never happens twice," to which Brandeis historian Morton Keller added that this was "one of the ways by which historians are supposed to be distinguished from antiquarians, who… are above all interested in changelessness." MIT is fortunate that one historian in particular has listened quite acutely, Mark Jarzombek of the School of Architecture and Planning, to whom I must convey my greatest debt. An old friend and colleague, and my first teaching assistant when I taught at MIT thirty years ago, Mark has been for me the exemplary scholar, proof that scholarship can be done and done well— not least in *Designing MIT: Bosworth's New Tech*, the book that first took up the subject and aroused my interest in 2004.

My second debt is equally clear, for President L. Rafael Reif declared very pointedly to me at our meeting to launch this project that he too thought William Welles Bosworth's work was still the MIT standard one hundred years later. On the day of our meeting in the handsome presidential office Bosworth designed, I knew I could write the book that needed to be written, certainly not scanting post-Bosworth MIT—no one loves Aalto's Baker House or Saarinen's chapel more than I, nor more admires I. M. Pei's Heroic Concrete design—but grounding it all in Bosworth's spectacular Great White City and in the context of the broadest possible cultural history, very much in the spirit of my Harvard guide, the first Princeton Architectural Press book I did, in 2001, for Jan Cigliano Hartman's innovative Campus Guides series.

Of the photographer for this project, John Horner, enough cannot be said. His job, from my point of view, was not just to illustrate my text but also to inspire me. He has done both. We agreed early on that the dignity of his photographs, as of my text, depended on fewer photographs but every one always a full-page or two-page spread in size. No postage stamps for MIT! This became our mantra. I am especially grateful to John for the gorgeous mock-up Mark insisted on, and which John took the lead in creating as a model for the final design of the book. Carl Lostritto's delightful maps herein speak for themselves. They are both clear and striking, no easy balance to achieve.

The focus of this story is on MIT's first campus on Copley Square and its present one on the Charles River Basin. But the full story of the Gods of Copley Square, the triumph of the nineteenth-century Boston Brahmin Ascendancy on the eve of its decline and fall, has yet to be told. I hope it will be the subject of my next book, for the Acropolis of the New World—as it was called for a brief, crucial half century from the 1860s to the 1910s, from its cornerstone of MIT to its apotheosis in the Boston Public Library—is a tale of no small consequence. It marks the dawn of the modern American experience, not just in the Institute and library but in other chapters: Richardson's revolutionary design of Trinity Church; the construction of the world's first purpose-built public art museum, Boston's Museum of Fine Arts; and the start of four-year medical education at Harvard Medical School; never mind the careers of John Singer Sargent and Maurice Prendergast, the birth of the Boston

Marathon, the evolution of the Boston School of Psychotherapy, and the beginnings of Asian art studies in this country. One could go on, and if one did, the historic debut of Darwinism in America and the advent of the telephone and the idea of laboratory instruction, all to MIT's credit, would certainly have their own long chapters.

This book has its most immediate origins in some parts of this larger tale that were published in a distinguished online arts and literary journal, *Open Letters Monthly*, in 2012, including one that made plain my admiration of and fascination with MIT's founder, William Barton Rogers. He is a man whose measure we have not yet, I think, fully taken; nor indeed have we of his wife, Emma Savage Rogers, a cause I'm glad to say I've sensed a distinct interest in at the Institute. I say this particularly in light of my experience of Israel Ruiz, the Institute's treasurer and executive vice president. The third person present at my meeting with President Reif, Israel first disclosed to me then how fiercely ambitious for MIT's future its leaders still can be. It was an inspiring moment. And his support and counsel in matters large and small ever since has been invaluable.

Another large debt is owed to Philip Alexander. We disagree about a great deal, but MIT is very lucky in the author of its in-house history, *A Widening Sphere*, published by MIT Press in 2011. I have relied on it in a thousand ways. That said, I have still been rescued several times by MIT Museum curator and historian Deborah Douglas, who has been kind enough to ask me to be a visiting lecturer in her class. It was also a particular pleasure to discover a most excellent archivist I have worked with before who is now at MIT, Nora Murphy, who has answered my every request for access to sources and made me very welcome in the Institute's archives. Another old and valued acquaintance presented himself in the Boston architect Nader Tehrani, head of MIT's School of Architecture and Planning. Nader answered my every question and left no loose ends. I am grateful, too, for a long interview with associate provost, Professor Philip Khoury. Pamela Delphenich, director of campus planning and design, and Thayer Donham, senior campus planner (to both of whom I was introduced by Ruiz), played an especially useful role in my earliest gropings toward the book's structure.

As various issues arose the following never disappointed: Gary Torndorf-Dick, program director of the Department of Facilities; David Fixler, a member of the team that restored Baker House; Leila Kinney, executive director of arts initiatives; and Gary Van Zante, MIT Museum curator. I am also grateful at the Vendome end to Robert Johnson and at the MIT end to Dineen Doucette, Anne Deveau, and Maureen Jennings for making the life of a visiting scholar go so smoothly.

Finally, to my IT guru, Abe McLaughlin of the *Christian Science Monitor*, and to the friends I asked to be my readers—Keith Morgan, professor of American and European architecture and director of architectural studies at Boston University, and Peter Kadzis, senior editor at WGBH News—endless thanks and praise. And to Jordan Kauffman, who dealt with the digital mechanics of the editing process with Princeton Architectural Press, many thanks. He deftly managed both authorial and editorial privilege.

Anyone who reads this book as ideally it should be read, from beginning to end, from front to back, will notice in places a repetition of certain material. This is deliberate. A book like this is very apt to be read in sections—perhaps "Part Two" and not "Part One," or just one or two tours—by readers with specific interests or visitors with particular goals. The repetition is meant to ensure that, whatever parts are read in whatever sequence, the pertinent background material will always be available.

Douglass Shand-Tucci

PART ONE

The Great White City of the Gods of Copley Square

Cornerstone

William Barton Rogers: Brahmin Acropolis, Immigrant Dreams

The son of an Irish patriot who fled British-ruled Ireland to America, William Barton Rogers himself fled the American South of slavery, anti-Semitism, and anti-Catholicism, giving up a professorship at the University of Virginia to relocate to New England. "All roads led to Boston for Rogers," one later MIT president said of the city in which liberal and intellectual bastion Rogers was determined to found what became the Massachusetts Institute of Technology.

Cornerstone

William Barton Rogers: Brahmin Acropolis, Immigrant Dreams

> The early Boston Brahmin was very global, as we'd say today. Characteristically, he
> set sail for the furthest possible horizon; and he did it in the right way: never forgetting
> where he came from, but never shrinking either from what he might become; ever alert
> as well to those whose own horizon might be the Brahmin's point of departure.
> —H. A. Crosby Forbes

"Our architecture reflects us, as truly as a mirror." So the most illustrious alumnus
of MIT's architecture school, Louis Sullivan, wrote in *Kindergarten Chats*. He didn't
mean past architecture, his or ours, whereas our subject is 150 years of building
MIT, a place famously not beguiled by the Muse of history. The very future-oriented
Sullivan probably shared the view, widespread at the Institute still, that studying
what is over and done with is more or less a waste of time for those whose minds
are intent upon the future. To that charge, however, the philosopher William James
made sure response. In *Pragmatism*, he asserted, "We live forwards...but we understand backwards." It is a pronouncement of special interest to us here, because the
philosopher first made it in 1907 at MIT, where at the first Rogers Building in Copley
Square, James delivered the Lowell Lectures, from which his great book was drawn,
launching Pragmatism as a public movement—the first major American contribution
to Western philosophy, many have said.

   "The present," James went on to explain quite simply, "sheds a backward light."
Or, as James scholar J. Michael Tilley puts it, "All attempts to understand ourselves,
God, and the world depend on our experiences." Yours and mine. In every generation.
My old mentor, the Anglican theologian John Macquarrie, Lady Margaret Professor
of Divinity at the University of Oxford, pointed out in his book *Christian Hope* that
in the same way we now know that to look into the night sky is to look not only "into
space, but into the past," so also "though one cannot change the facts of the past,
the value of those facts can be changed and often is changed." That is perhaps the
scientific way of perceiving the value of James's "backward light."

   How we take advantage of this truism as James saw it determines much.
The critic Walter Benjamin famously insisted in his studies of the arcades of Paris
on what I see as the best way: "The true method of making [past] things present
is to represent them [our ancestors] in our space, not to represent ourselves
in their place." Imagine William Barton Rogers, MIT's founder, who died well over
a century ago, "in our space" on a jetliner today flying across the Pacific from
Singapore to Boston.

   An absurd thought. Until one recalls the hopes that Singaporeans have
today—never mind MIT's hopes—of something called the Singapore-MIT Alliance
for Research and Technology. It is no bolder an idea than Rogers's in the 1850s for a

great scientific institute in Boston that would, in his words (in his proposal of 1845 to the Boston philanthropist John A. Lowell Jr.), "overtop all the universities of the land." No bolder either than that of Singaporeans today to be "the Boston of the East, an incubator of ideas"—this quoted in 2010 from the *Times of India*, in which Hemali Chhapia editorialized, "Singapore, not quite Boston." But do not doubt that MIT's founder—if in our space today—would be quick to fly over the Pacific and change all that, as Singaporeans may yet change it on their own.

Dreamers, especially immigrant dreamers, are like that. One of them was Rogers's father. Dr. Patrick Kerr Rogers was a little too ardent a supporter of the Irish Rebellion of 1798, and when his anti-British activities dictated a swift departure for America, he proved to be a bold enough immigrant. He wrote to another and more notable revolutionary, Thomas Jefferson, to ask about a faculty position at the University of Virginia. As it turned out, it was not Dr. Rogers but his son who would become a UVA professor. The son would also be an "immigrant" of dreams. In his case, he left the South and settled in "Glorious New England," as Rogers called what was a very different country from the American South. Virginia's racism, its anti-Semitism, its anti-Catholicism, and above all its anti-intellectualism drove MIT's future founder to New England as surely as the British drove his father to America.

Throughout his life's journey, Dr. Rogers did not lose touch with Jefferson. We have the testimony of Jedediah Hotchkiss—who spoke at Rogers's memorial service at the Institute's Society of Arts—that Dr. Rogers once took his son to Monticello to meet the American founding father. "The quick eye of the philosopher instantly saw that no ordinary man was before him," Hotchkiss recounted, emphasizing how Jefferson at once began to quiz young William as to his knowledge of natural science. "That done, he turned to the father and spoke to him of the son who had a future full of promise." It was a predictable report, the sort of anecdote that tends to be told about all great men in their youth, an anecdote especially appropriate to recount at a memorial service. But it is true: Rogers, the creator of an institution as American and as revolutionary in his own sphere as the larger creation in which Jefferson had taken such a lead, certainly wasn't at all ordinary. Nor would there be any more characteristically American or revolutionary an institution than the Massachusetts Institute of Technology. The author of the Declaration of Independence was not wrong about the future founder of MIT.

Here is a key portal, one that like all portals (as most well-informed fans of science fiction will not need to be told) is "always bidirectional...otherwise astrophysicists call them *black holes*," as I was informed by an MIT official. Indeed, if you type "What is a portal?" into the Google search box, you will find yourself on something of an adventure in realms not always very scientific. You will learn, for example, that negotiating a portal is from one point of view an ancient alchemical activity.

I paused at that one, remembering that a major work of the Catalan sculptor Jaume Plensa, *Alchemist*—consisting of mathematical symbols wrought into the stainless steel form of a thinking human being (one you can actually enter)—stands across from the portico that marks MIT's main entrance at 77 Massachusetts

Copley Square, a New World Acropolis of new learning—Faith and Learning, Arts and Sciences—MIT its cornerstone, Trinity Church its centerpiece, and the Boston Public Library its apotheosis, the whole the triumph of the Boston Brahmin Ascendancy at the dawn of the American century. ABOVE: Looking west from MIT past Trinity and the new Museum of Fine Arts toward Dartmouth Street and the public library, the Harvard Medical School, and the Old South Church. BELOW: Looking north, left to right: the three towers that originally dominated the square before the later introduction of tall office buildings: Old South Church, Trinity Church, and Brattle Square Church

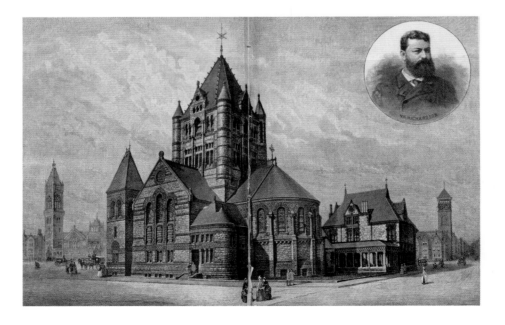

ABOVE: Looking westward down Boylston Street to the Old South tower, in the foreground is the MIT block, centered on the twin classical buildings designed by William Gibbons Preston, a leading Boston architect of the era, and both built by Rogers—the first Rogers Building and the Museum of Natural History. The museum moved from Copley Square to the Charles River Basin in later years, where it changed its name to the Museum of Science. BELOW: Looking eastward, Trinity Church to the right, the MIT block to the left, and the Boston Bicycle Club arrayed in front of Trinity

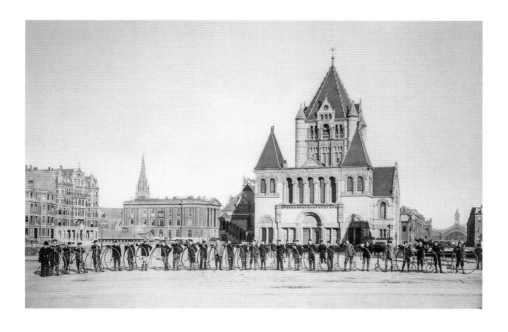

The diorama in the lobby of the old New England Life Building on Boylston Street depicts the first stage in the development of Boston's Back Bay. The two twin classical structures of the MIT block are there, showing either direction for blocks in the mid-1860s. The Museum of Natural History is finished and the first Rogers Building is still under construction.

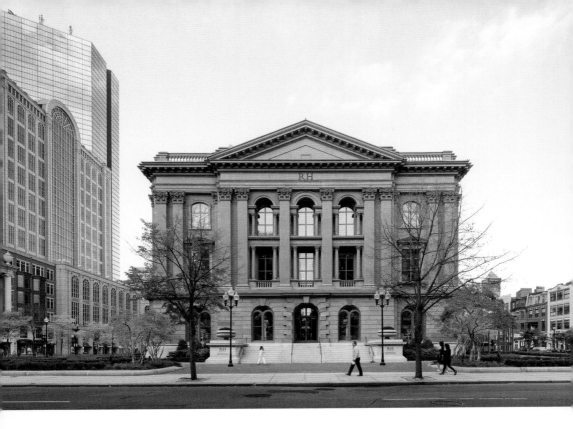

The Museum of Natural History is all that is left of the MIT block today. Louis Sullivan, the most famous alumnus of the Institute in the nineteenth century, wrote in his autobiography of rushing from the Rogers to this building for class in an era when classes were also open to students of BU, allied then to MIT and thus involved in Copley Square from its early years in the 1870s. BU, although not a Brahmin foundation, would later become based in Copley Square, in the early 1900s.

Avenue. The sculpture commemorates the Institute's sesquicentennial, and just as certainly *Alchemist* pulls us 150 and more years backward. We live forward, but we understand backward. Especially revolutions of the sort the founding of MIT precipitated when it opened its doors on what would become Copley Square in the mid-1860s.

    Revolutionary is not a word most would associate today with that locale. Yet Michael Cannell, in his 1995 biography of the architect I. M. Pei, had certainly heard, as he put it, of "the Acropolis of the New World, as Bostonians boastfully called Copley Square" in the nineteenth century. Not only Bostonians: in 1894, in a story on September 13 about the opening of the new Boston Public Library, the *New York Times* declared, "Copley Square...contains as large a proportion of the fine structures in modern Athens as the Acropolis did in ancient Athens."

    By Cannell's time in the 1990s, most had forgotten the square's role as the seedbed of so many of Boston's great galaxy of institutions of Faith and Learning, Arts and Sciences. By then all but two of the constituent parts of that Acropolis had dispersed, in search of institutional expansion, scattering themselves all over

Greater Boston. But in one field, Pei's biographer found, the square still held its own. Architecture. Describing the design of "H. H. Richardson's Trinity Church... [and] McKim, Mead and White's serenely classical public library, the largest of its kind in the world," he hymned these "two great public edifices [...] faced each other across one of America's most celebrated public spaces." Reminders today of the square's nineteenth-century stature include the church and library that originally were, respectively, the centerpiece and apotheosis of the Acropolis. Its cornerstone was MIT.

Details of how all this came about are hard to come by. Real estate machinations obscured the entire process. There was something called the Committee of Associated Institutions arguing for grants of land "for the use of such institutions as may associate together for the public good." But the sequence remains difficult to sort out. There was at first "a question concern[ing] the location of Copley Square. Although some kind of open and planted area was envisioned in that neighborhood as early as 1860, its shape, location, and name were changed several times," according to Bainbridge Bunting's 1967 book on the Back Bay. But there seems to have been no question at all about the Acropolis, several blocks being set aside for public buildings in the 1860s and 1870s.

State grants to MIT and the Natural History Society in 1861 led to the opening of MIT's first building in 1868, followed within two years by another state grant in 1870 to the Museum of Fine Arts and the erection in 1872–73 of Trinity Church and the New Old South Church. Thus five of the seven major landmarks of the future square were underway within five years of the MIT building's opening. All were completed by 1876. A third state grant for the Boston Public Library came four years later, in 1880, and the erection of Harvard Medical School in 1883 was followed at once by the taking of the land between all these landmarks for the square itself. A projected MIT building in 1884 right in front of Trinity Church seems to have precipitated matters (probably deliberately). I leave it to the reader to imagine what was going on by reading between the lines of Walter Muir Whitehill's account of MIT's role in the siting of the Museum of Fine Arts, wherein what might be called the entrepreneurial origins of Copley Square are as clear as its cultural origins:

> Matthias Denman Ross, a businessman... pointed out to the Legislature the financial advantages of reserving certain areas in the Back Bay for open spaces or the use of public institutions.... In accordance with this logic the Legislature in 1860–61 granted land on Boylston Street... to the Boston Society of Natural History... [and] to the Massachusetts Institute of Technology, of which Ross had been one of the founders. Through the work of Ross the Boston Water Power Company had been persuaded to convey to the city in trust the land subsequently awarded to the museum to be used either for an Institute for Fine Arts or for an open space. The... lot was conveyed to the [art] museum trustees... [on condition] that the museum should be open free of charge four days of each month. Matthias D. Ross was, incidentally, one of the first three trustees appointed to the Museum board by the Massachusetts Institute of Technology.

Another example of the interlocking interests: William Endicott, a wealthy Brahmin merchant, was MIT's treasurer in the same period (1867–72), as he was an art museum trustee and chair of the museum's fundraising committee.

Life and Letters of William Barton Rogers is quite forthright about the result of all this, if not the details. Of Rogers's proposal to the state legislature seeking land in the Back Bay for the new Institute in the 1850s and 1860s, it says that the proposal "must be regarded as foreshadowing the establishment of not only the Massachusetts Institute of Technology, but also of that noble group of buildings now occupied by the Boston Society of Natural History and by the Boston Museum of Fine Arts, as well as, more indirectly, Trinity Church and the Boston Public Library." Erected at what would become the northeastern corner of the embryonic square, the MIT block, furthermore, was from the first the cornerstone of a civic aspiration as noble as its coming architecture. An Acropolis with a mission.

Bostonians were determined to shape their country's future, as they felt only their city could—that city famously "built upon a hill." This image of Puritan Boston was so powerful it was later appropriated for the nation as a whole by President Ronald Reagan. Real estate development was meant to be profitable but in Copley Square it was distinctly in aid of a much larger cause, the promotion generally of Faith and Learning, Arts and Sciences. It was all encoded with the values of what Notre Dame historian James Turner called "the closest thing to an American aristocracy, the Brahmin class of Boston." And nothing was plainer from the start than that, although Faith might be ceded the place of honor, Learning held the upper hand in this Acropolis. Ever since the founding of Boston Latin School in the 1600s and—to give Latin graduates someplace to go, it was said—Harvard College, also in the 1600s, learning had become Boston's passion and its Brahmins' vocation.

The Brahmin ruling caste arose in the early nineteenth century as the third iteration of a continuum of Puritans-become-Patriots-become-Brahmins (who were almost invariably Federalists politically and Unitarians philosophically) that originated in clerical and mercantile New England. The name originated when Ralph Waldo Emerson's transcendentalism earned him, according to Paul Brunton, author of *Indian Philosophy and Modern Culture*, the appellation "the Boston Brahmin." Oliver Wendell Holmes Sr., writing in the *Atlantic Monthly* in 1861, applied this allusion to India's learned caste to the whole of Boston's learned rulers. The title stuck. When he "met with the British viceroy in 1930...Gandhi took some duty-free salt from his shawl and said, with a smile, that the salt was to remind [him] of the famous Boston Tea Party." (The tea that had been tossed into Boston Harbor was East India Company Tea.)

By the late nineteenth century Boston's Brahmins were somewhat disillusioned with, on the one hand, Gilded Age money-making values and, on the other, increasingly corrupt political values. Both were losing games for aristocrats, whose memory of both mercantile and immigrant needs had fast receded as they rose to preside over what I call the Brahmin Ascendancy. Boston's Brahmins turned their back on post–Civil War values, as they could afford to, sure that their values were superior. Arguably, they were.

Specifically modernist values were no one's cause originally and were never explicit. But, as I wrote in "The Boston Religion: The First American Modernist," the fact that such values quickly emerged can have surprised no one. Unitarians were pioneers of a modernist synthesis, one that demonstrated "the characteristic features of modernism…capitalism, theism, liberalism, and optimism." William R. Hutchison wrote in *The Modernist Impulse in American Protestantism* that while Unitarians may not look or sound a lot like cutting-edge modernists, that's just what Boston's ruling-class leaders were. Witness the close watch the historian Henry Adams kept on Trinity Church while it was under construction. Whether or not Adams entirely understood rector Phillips Brooks's new theology or Richardson's new architecture, scholars now see those purposes as no less modernist or proto-modernist than MIT's, though in a different way. Ideas that Richardson (arguably the first great American-born architect) inspired in MIT's Louis Sullivan—and Sullivan in turn in Frank Lloyd Wright—though they were just the beginning of the square's mission, were also the beginning of the modern American experience, in the dawn of which, on its cutting edge, Copley Square would play the seminal role.

The ideas *behind* the architecture were equally momentous. Trinity was a radically different kind of national cathedral ("the glory of America forever," its founding rector called it) from the more conventional one later built in Washington. It was conceived as the transatlantic religious mecca of the followers of Saint Phillips Brooks, so powerful a religious leader that he was later canonized by American Anglicans. Likewise, Boston's new Museum of Fine Arts, which would open next door to Trinity in 1876 (facing MIT diagonally across the emerging square), was no adapted royal palace but arguably the world's first purpose-built public art museum. ("Museums to house great art collections, of course, existed in Europe… [and] even in nineteenth-century America the picture gallery and Academy of Fine Arts were not unknown by 1870. Yet these institutions," the architectural historian Margaret Henderson Floyd wrote, "should be distinguished from the great museums of the nineteenth century." The first of these comprehensive and wide-ranging treasure palaces was the Boston art museum, closely followed by New York's.) Nor was the museum's late nineteenth-century achievement in Copley Square less creative than MIT's or Trinity's. The art critic Sebastian Smee, for example, has rightly compared the development of the museum's Asian collections to the writings of the Transcendentalists in the nineteenth century and the surge of new music fostered by Serge Koussevitzky's Boston Symphony Orchestra in the early twenti-eth. All are undoubted glories of the history of the arts in this country.

Then there was Harvard Medical School, erected on the other side of the embryonic square eight years after Trinity, next to where the Boston Public Library would be built. Designed as the spearhead of the revolution in American medicine that would be led by Charles W. Eliot's Harvard, and rivaled only by Johns Hopkins in Baltimore, it was the crown jewel of Eliot's modern Harvard. That MIT was not the

One of MIT's founding professors, in 1861, Charles W. Eliot was elected president of Harvard in 1869 and built the crown jewel of modern Harvard in that era—Harvard Medical School—on the western side of Copley Square in 1883. It was designed by the firm of William Ware, the head of MIT's architecture school (on the square's eastern side) and also the secretary of the School of the Museum of Fine Arts (on the southern side), an institution of which MIT was one of the three founders in 1876. All this is evidence of the interlocking relationships of the square that made it so fructifying as an intellectual and academic center.

only bastion of science in the New World Acropolis is often forgotten, never mind to what extent the two Copley Square institutions paced each other. President Rogers's opposite number at Harvard Med was his old MIT colleague President Eliot, but the medical school's actual leader after Eliot's retirement was Henry P. Bowditch, a Boston-born Brahmin who, after Harvard, studied in Europe. According to Marc Rothenberg's *The History of Science in the United States*, "In 1871 President Eliot… invited [Bowditch] to return home 'to take part in the good work of reforming medical education.'" The result was "the first lab for experimental medicine established in this country.…With [his] enthusiasm and inspiration, almost every scientific interest of a complete modern medical school was stimulated." In 1883, when the new Copley Square facility opened, Bowditch was named its dean by Eliot.

Designed, significantly, by the partner of the founder of MIT's School of Architecture, the medical school fostered rapid change. At once the "four years required course was adopted.…A further significant innovation was the calling of outstanding men from other universities to assume positions in the school." The same emphasis on lab work as at MIT is evident in this report from the Center for the

History of Medicine: "Harvard's reformation in medicine took physical expression in the Medical School's construction of a new building.... As the school moved into its new quarters at Boylston and Exeter streets...Bowditch was principally concerned with the research aspects of medicine...and the Boylston Street facility with its five separate laboratories mirrored [his] interests."

Leadership like that was decisive in the evolution of the New World Acropolis. The Brahmins had their share of reactionaries, but the caste's leadership was conspicuously progressive. If particular places can have archetypes, Boston's—certainly Copley Square's—has historically been the reformer. Within a decade or two, so widespread was President Eliot's influence that he would be called "America's headmaster." As the representative figure of a metropolis that was consolidating its role as the nation's intellectual capital, Eliot would take his place alongside J. P. Morgan, the New York archetype of the tycoon, representative of the emerging national financial and media capital, and Theodore Roosevelt, the statesman archetype of Washington, the national political capital. (When Cecil B. DeMille, the archetype of the movie mogul, appeared on the scene in the new century, and Los Angeles came to be seen as the country's entertainment capital, it could be said that the four national capitals of the modern American experience were in place.)

Rogers was another such reformer, and his goals as the founder of MIT were not less ambitious. Nor would they resound any less grandly than Eliot's in the "American century," as the twentieth century would be called time and again. About this Rogers was very clear. Remember his vision of MIT: a scientific university, as it would become, that would "overtop all the universities of the land." *All.*

More than a century and a half later and halfway around the world, the historian of science Steven Shapin, writing in the *London Review of Books* in 2003, pointed out how brilliantly Rogers succeeded: "The self-consciously hybrid creation" the Institute was created to be—"combining elements of research university, polytechnic and...liberal arts teaching college"—would become "the first entrepreneurial university and a model for others, notably Stanford [founded 1891].... MIT saw High Modernity coming, embraced it, and it did more than any other American educational institution to hurry it into being." Richardson's architecture at Trinity, art for the masses in the first purpose-built art museum, and the new medicine at Harvard Med all paralleled in their own way MIT's "High Modernity." The Acropolis would be as modernist as its academic cornerstone.

How so? Listen to Emerson, in *Life and Letters in New England*, pronouncing late in life what struck him about the late nineteenth century: it seemed to him that "the mind had become aware of itself." Hence the significance of historian Robert Richardson's observation that "[William] James was a major force in developing the modern consciousness at the same time Freud was developing the modern concept of unconsciousness." To look to each man, one in Boston, one in Vienna, is to see what would be as central to the modernist experience throughout both Europe and America as it was in Copley Square, which soon enough became a notable station on that transatlantic continuum.

The houses of many of the leading figures in Copley Square in the residential portion of Back Bay often suggest other interlocking relationships. The town house of James Pickering Putnam, a leading professor at Harvard Medical School and the foremost American Freudian—he and Freud conducted an historic correspondence—lived diagonally across Marlborough Street from William and Emma Rogers, whose town house is visible further down the street on the right.

And here opens in one sense the widest and most physically obvious global portal, for which Boston Harbor then (perhaps like Logan International Airport now, even in the age of the internet) was the well-worn channel. Quite aside from Boston's historic links across the Pacific to an emerging Asia, the absolutely most vital links then were across the Atlantic. The UC Berkeley historian Mark Peterson declares in *The City-State of Boston: A Tragedy in Three Acts, 1630–1865* (forthcoming), that already by 1865 "Boston was the entrepôt, the material and cultural broker, for virtually all relations between Europe and North America." Nor did this passageway close up in the 1860s. Harvard Medical School historian and William James scholar Eugene Taylor has written in the *New York Times*:

> With a handful of colleagues in the US, France, Italy, and Switzerland, [William] James also helped inaugurate experimental psychopathology. Their efforts made Boston

the center of developments in scientific psychotherapy in the English-speaking world from 1880 to 1910, long before psychoanalysis became prominent....James...was the first to introduce the work of Josef Breuer and Sigmund Freud to Americans in 1894. Eventually, James and the so-called Boston School of Psychotherapy would become the taproot for developments in personality and in social, clinical, and abnormal psychology.

Similarly, Dr. James Jackson Putnam of Harvard Medical School and Massachusetts General Hospital would publish the first paper in English on Freudian psychoanalysis in 1906 in the *Journal of Abnormal Psychology.*

MIT was distinctly a part of this through the Lowell Institute (on which more soon). Based in the Rogers Building, the Lowell Institute was so integral to MIT's role in Copley Square that in the 1893 catalog prepared for the Chicago World's Fair explaining Tech's program, the Lowell Lectures were fully discussed. At MIT in that series, William James gave two significant courses in this area: The Brain and the Mind in 1878, later to become major chapters of his *Principles of Psychology,* and Exceptional Mental States in 1896, the latter of which Eugene Taylor famously reconstructed and published. Of the earlier Lowell course, academic psychologist Susan Gordon wrote in 2013: "James and his medical colleagues, James Jackson Putnam and Henry Pickering Bowditch, had been conducting the first investigations of brain neurophysiology in the United States in Bowditch's laboratory at the Harvard Medical School, and out of these endeavors James had assembled the first laboratory in experimental psychology in America for student instruction...[begun] in conjunction with a new course taught by James,...the first course in physiological psychology to be taught in an American university." Later Dr. Putnam also gave an important series of Lowell Lectures in this area.

Modernist gods. Modernist Acropolis. How modernist? Very quickly Copley Square's intellectual life became of international significance, and MIT was at the center of it. Historian Nathan G. Hale Jr. wrote in *The Rise and Crisis of Psychoanalysis in the United States: Freud and the Americans, 1917–1985* that "Putnam and a small circle...between 1890 and 1909 developed the most sophisticated psychotherapy in the English-speaking world." In 1909, when Freud accepted an invitation to lecture and receive an honorary degree at Worcester's Clark University, a bastion of the Boston School of Psychotherapy (its president, G. Stanley Hall, had studied under James at Harvard, receiving the first psychology doctorate awarded in America), it meant the Boston School was endorsing Freud. "Near Boston, to give a series of lectures," Freud wrote to a friend triumphantly; knowing this would "annoy some people in Berlin as in Vienna. That cannot do any harm," he concluded drolly, crowing that it was his psychoanalytic school's "first official recognition" anywhere.

Putnam was key to it all in the wake of James, who also attended the lectures. Both were discreet. Although the *Boston Evening Transcript,* then Boston's newspaper of record, fully reported Freud's visit to Greater Boston, the *New York Times* apparently heard nothing about it. And just as he had sponsored Freud not at the Harvard Medical School in Copley Square but at outlying Clark, Putnam then entertained Freud over the weekend, not at his home on Marlborough Street in the Back Bay but at his Adirondack camp. Although he parted company with Freud on the matter of the Viennese doctor's atheism, he sponsored Freud, but cautiously. Putnam supported the Emmanuel Movement, founded by the Emmanuel Church on Newbury Street to combine religion and psychotherapy, which Freud attacked during his American visit in a famous interview given to the *Transcript*.

The Viennese doctor and the Boston Brahmins needed each other. Putnam, Alan Lawson writes, "belonged to [one of] New England's most prominent families and acted within an open democracy. Freud's circumstances were much more limiting. Freud was a nonreligious Jew living in an increasingly anti-Semitic, decaying aristocratic society [socially aristocratic, not intellectually aristocratic] that he was moved at least once to call a 'prison.'" The correspondence between Freud and his main American ally, Putnam, strikingly reveals the gap in status. The alliance proceeded as much out of Boston's intellectual history as that of Vienna or Paris. Writes Lawson:

> Three major factors in the American situation at the time of the Clark Conference prompted a favorable response to Freudian concepts. First, Freud's call for psychologists to help free people from repressive religious and sexual taboos....Second, Freud's emphasis on the subconscious, on the will, comported with the American effort, led by James...toward consideration of subjective mental states. Finally...James and Putnam favored the subjective side of psychology [, which] fitted with the religious and transcendental beliefs [of]...Emerson....Out of that combination of American attitudes and Freudian guidance grew what was called the Boston School of Psychotherapy.
>
> As early as in 1904...Putnam had declared [Freud's] psychoanalytic method far from useless. His sympathetic reading of Freud had been the first real opening for [Freud's] ideas in the American medical establishment.
>
> The Freud-Putnam alliance thus forged is regarded by more than one scholar as the most lasting legacy of Freud's visit to America, a country he actively disliked. Putnam was an exception. Freud wrote Putnam in 1911 asking him to be the first president of the new American Psychoanalytical Association. "Only you and only in Boston," Freud wrote, according to George Prochnik, "could be the starting point."

Freudianism was not the only face of high modernism at Harvard Medical School, an institution that paced MIT. (The medical school, by the way, was designed by the head of Tech's architecture department.) Another star of Copley Square medicine was Harvey Cushing, an Ohioan who is today regarded as the father of modern

Though Freud, an atheist, was chiefly the guest of Dr. Putnam, a devout Christian Unitarian, during his visit to Greater Boston, he gave an important interview to the *Boston Evening Transcript* attacking the Emmanuel Movement, a specifically Christian attempt at healing mental illness. OPPOSITE: Emmanuel Church on Newbury Street

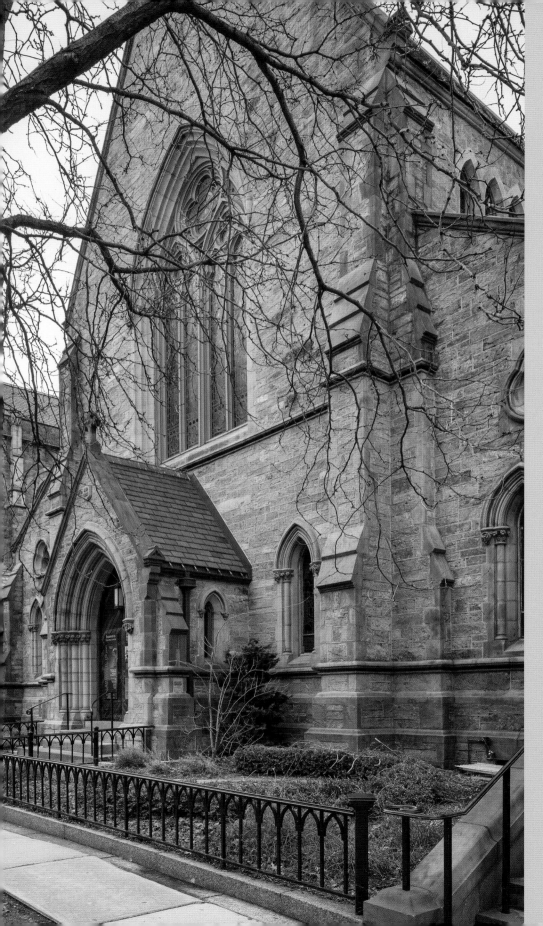

neurosurgery, a member of the Harvard Med class of 1895. Perhaps his best friend in his Copley Square days was Elliott P. Joslin, a pioneer of diabetes research. Joslin, who began his practice in his parents' town house at 517 Beacon Street after graduation and continued for fifty years at 81 Bay State Road, was the inspiration for Boston's Joslin Clinic, the world's first center for the care of diabetes.

How deep MIT's involvement was in these currents of thought coursing through Copley Square is clear in the fact that the feminist pioneer who established the Women's Laboratory at MIT, Ellen Richards, the Institute's first woman graduate, was described for her work in the equally revolutionary field of sanitation and human resources by the *Vassar Miscellany* in 1912 as "a seer…who lived a generation ahead of her time [according to] principles that today are popularly attributed to the Emmanuel Movement."

One does not have to look far for an equally significant artistic aspect to Copley Square's modernity, one that involves MIT even more closely. Bruce Smith and Alexander Vertikoff point out in *Greene and Greene: Masterworks* that the famous architects Charles and Henry Greene, Cincinnati natives and masters of the new "bungalow," were first "exposed to Japanese art and culture during their university years in Boston, where they attended the Massachusetts Institute of Technology. Lectures on this newly opened Asian country were often presented in the city.…The Museum of Fine Arts [then in Copley Square] held the country's major collection of Japanese pottery and art." Thus fortified, these designers, who would become to California what Charles Rennie Mackintosh was to Glasgow and Frank Lloyd Wright was to Chicago, went on to achieve such a level of work that in 1952 they were cited by the American Institute of Architects as "pioneers of modernism" in America.

Whether they were scientific luminaries like Putnam or artistic ones like the Greene brothers, most of the Gods of Copley Square were modernist gods. Even those in waiting. In that category, for example, was T. S. Eliot, whose first vision (while a Harvard student) of *The Waste Land* was south of the square in the South End slum. As did the "aristocratic rectangle" of the Back Bay north of the square, it bookended and fed Copley Square, which needed waiters as much as professors, artists' models as well as Brahmin aesthetes and painters. The intimate interrelationship between all these things, moreover, was evident as far away as Stockholm and as far ahead as 1948, when Eliot's Nobel Prize citation read: "Born in the Middle West, where the pioneer spirit was still alive, raised up in Boston, the stronghold of Puritan tradition, you came to Europe.…The position you have held in modern literature parallels a comparison with that occupied by Sigmund Freud [and]…the novelty of the therapy which he introduced with psychoanalysis would match the revolutionary form in which you have clothed your message."

Rogers's "revolutionary form"—insisting that hands-on laboratory work was as important as scholarly study—is what entitles him to stand so high in such company. Furthermore, "Thanks to early textbooks," David Kaiser has written, "like [those of] MIT physics professor Edward Pickering, published in 1873—the earliest known physics laboratory manual published in the United States—Rogers's innovative approach became a model for scientific teaching elsewhere."

Yet MIT's founder was far from envisioning a technical school, however superlative. "Rogers kept pushing the big tent view," Philip Alexander writes, "over and beyond what the Institute already offered in William Atkinson's English and history courses." Atkinson would teach at MIT for twenty-one years, starting in 1869. "In 1871 Corporation member Joseph White, secretary of the state board of education, suggested inviting outside lecturers to speak…so that the Institute might further meet the 'obligation…to give its students a liberal as well as a technical education.'…These sentiments were echoed in the public press." The tension over the role of the humanities and social sciences would linger, yet its presence in the very first decade of MIT's existence should be noted. As should its high profile. In a paper given in 1873 at a national convention, published in *Popular Science Monthly* that November, Atkinson, himself classically educated at Harvard, argued for a "scheme of liberal education, applicable to a whole free people, which shall use that people's own language on the one hand, and the great instrument of modern science on the other, as its chief disciplinary instruments, in lieu of the obsolescent scheme for a liberal class education, based on the study of dead languages."

The argument was not whether the liberal arts belonged in technical education, but *how* they belonged. Atkinson's paper "The Liberal Education of the Nineteenth Century" was so celebrated that it was republished nearly a half century later by another MIT professor of English, Frank Aydelotte, in *English and Engineering,* along with buttressing essays by a whole raft of worthies, including Emerson, Newman, Carlyle, Ruskin, and Rogers's successor, President Francis Walker. In a speech at McGill University in 1893, Walker "acknowledge[d] that those who direct many technical schools have made a mistake in altogether, or nearly so, omitting from their curriculum philosophical as distinguished from scientific, liberal as distinguished from exact, studies."

By the 1890s Walker (personally chosen by Rogers to succeed him) had consolidated MIT as "no mere technical institute; a university, rather, polarized around science and engineering," in Alexander's words. And if one studies the MIT catalog for the 1893 Chicago World's Fair, much of what Walker talked of is reflected in what are called the "characteristic features" of the Institute, all five of which MIT still proudly claims in the twenty-first century.

In addition to quality of the faculty, the high standard of scholarship, and the "high grade of thesis work," the catalog highlights both scientific *and* liberal studies. MIT was "the largest scientific and technical school in the United States and one of the largest in the world," the text states, "the number of students 1060…from thirty-nine states…and from seventeen foreign countries." The "laboratory principle" is stressed: "Here the first laboratory of general chemistry was organized by Eliot and Storer. Here the first laboratory of general physics was planned by President Rogers and organized by Professor Pickering.…In 1873 a mechanical engineering laboratory was opened…believed to have been the first engineering lab ever established.…The laboratory of electrical engineering…was the first established, at least in the United States." Finally, it declared that while "in some, perhaps most, scientific or technical schools, there are no 'liberal studies' aside from those of a professional character,… [the] Institute of Technology [has]…maintained the position that some degree of philosophical study should be combined with scientific work."

MIT insisted, unusually, on the liberal arts playing a worthy role in the "new education," and the Acropolis it was a part of insisted on taking science seriously. Wrote Boston University (BU) historian William Vance, his mind's eye surely fixed on the two allegorical statues of Art and Science that presided so grandly (and still do) over the square from the podium of the Boston Public Library:

> In higher education also, Bostonians sought to set standards unrivaled in modernity, quantity, quality, and accessibility. The founding of the Massachusetts Institute of Technology in 1861 constituted a decisive challenge to older conceptions of higher education, based upon letters rather than science, upon liberal rather than applied knowledge, upon abstract and general truth rather than the indicative and particular. Laboratory teaching was one of [MIT's] novelties.…The Institute shared a block… with the Boston Society of Natural History…with which it was allied. Together their three large buildings testified that the contemporary scientific interests and values were no less important to the city than those represented by Trinity Church and the Museum of Fine Arts.

About science the art museum ventured no opinion, but Trinity Church, best described in its early days as contested ground between liberal Episcopalians and progressive Unitarians ("the Boston religion"), again stood out as MIT's strongest, if perhaps most unlikely, supporter. Rector Phillips Brooks, an ally of Rogers and a member of MIT's governing Corporation, and nothing if not a modernist, "did not oppose the discoveries of modern science; he did not defend them; he simply assumed that the Christian was a lover of Truth, wherever it would lead," Bishop William Lawrence wrote. A Brahmin to his fingertips, rector Brooks was akin to Harvard Medical School dean Oliver Wendell Holmes Sr. across the square, who, if he was not exactly a pioneering poet, was certainly a pioneering medical school dean, and in that respect decidedly a modernist.

Holmes "named the Brahmins and described their function," wrote the critic Van Wyck Brooks, "as leaders of learning and bearers of light. It was he [Holmes, as dean of Harvard Medical School] who spread the gospel of science." Brooks added, "[As] the mind halted between the two opinions, the old classical systems and the new technical system, the opening of the Massachusetts Institute of Technology was the most notable symptom." Lewis Mumford, in retrospect, saw this too, believing it was key to the New World Acropolis. In 1969 in *Back Bay Boston: The City as a Work of Art*, he wrote, "[It was] in the Back Bay [e.g., Copley Square] that Boston first established itself as one of the centers of world culture in the arts *and sciences* [emphasis added]."

An aside: just as MIT would eventually need to move to the nearby Charles River Basin to expand, so too would its Copley Square neighbor, the Museum of Natural History (dropping the "Natural History" from its name in favor of "Science"). According to onetime Smithsonian Museum head Leonard Carmichael, Boston's new Museum of Science became "the first major museum anywhere to bring all science under a single roof—natural, physical, applied, and a planetarium." Today its attendance figures rank it sixth among all the science museums of the world, after Paris, London and Taiwan (tied for second), Shanghai, Chicago, and Seattle.

The arts would always remain the very essence of the Acropolis, both in curatorial mode at the art museum, where the acquisition and study of the greatest Japanese art collection in the Western world was ongoing by the late 1880s, and also in the creative mode, as in the case of the painter Maurice Prendergast, who became the first great American modernist master. Prendergast passed his formative years in Copley Square, which had as many art schools as bastions of science, most notably the School of the Museum of Fine Arts, which helped spark not only Boston's introduction into the United States of French impressionism, then at the cutting edge of Western art, but also the development of its American offshoot, called at first Boston impressionism.

The square signified a shift in Boston from the literary to the visual arts, illustrated by the move of novelist William Dean Howells from Boston to New York, for example, and the move of the architect H. H. Richardson—and landscape architect Frederick Law Olmsted too—from New York to Boston. (Indeed, add Henry Adams's move from Boston to Washington and you can see at a glance that the financial and media capital of New York, the intellectual capital of Boston, and the political capital of Washington were consolidating.) But science was less and less the junior partner in the New World Acropolis. Karl Wide and Nilo Lindgren recount in their history of MIT's electrical engineering department:

> Chance brought [Alexander Graham Bell] to Boston, which perhaps more than any other city in the world provided the proper intellectual, technical, and economical environment for the invention of the telephone….Bell had come to the intellectual and scientific center of the United States already thoroughly trained….Bell's contacts with the Boston scientific community steadily widened and his acquaintance with [MIT professor Charles] Cross…at MIT ripened….These contacts led to an invitation to Bell to address the MIT Society of Arts. Apparently it was that lecture on April 9, 1874, that prompted Cross to offer Bell free access to the Institute of Technology….Bell excitedly accepted the offer and began immediately doing experiments at MIT that would lead him within the next two years to invent the telephone.

A lecture at MIT on May 25, 1876, concluded with what Bell's biographer R. V. Bruce called "probably the first demonstration of electronic speech in the world." Only in its ninth year of operation, MIT was enjoying its first moment on the world stage—or, more strictly then, the transatlantic stage. And the square's, too.

One historian speaks of the "momentous threshold" Bell crossed over in his research at MIT on the telephone, and this was true as well of both square and cornerstone. We live forward. We understand backward.

Nearly a century and a half later, even in the face of the creation of the World Wide Web Consortium; or the sequencing of the first-ever map of the human genetic code; or the design and development of the guidance, navigation, and control systems that allowed humans to walk on the moon—in all of which MIT played a leading role—Bell's work in the Copley Square labs of the Institute in the 1870s, and his first demonstration of the telephone to the world at his MIT lecture in May 1876, remain epochal.

BU funded Bell while he was doing his research—a reflection of faculty-level alliances between it and MIT. Not only Bell's achievement but also the details of his "inventing" continue to attract attention. Some of the most recent work on the subject is by veteran science writer Seth Shulman, published in 2008 in *MIT Technology Review* in advance of his book *The Telephone Game*. His research was undertaken

LABORATORY WITH ELECTRICAL APPARATUS — PHYSICAL DEPARTMENT.

The MIT laboratory in the first Rogers Building in Copley Square, in which BU professor Alexander Graham Bell labored over the invention of the telephone. When Bell saw MIT's first building, he was inspired by how splendid it looked, as the only permanent building in the middle of nowhere.

at MIT's Dibner Institute for the History of Science and Technology. Although Shulman's research decisively uncovers Bell's debt to another inventor, Elisha Gray, MIT's role is more than confirmed, especially as to Bell's May 1876 performance before what Shulman calls "a good-sized audience at a meeting of the MIT faculty." Handwritten minutes from the MIT Archives "reveal that Bell carried on an unprecedented public conversation over the new fangled contraption," fully reported the next day in the *Boston Evening Transcript*. "The choice of MIT as the venue for the worldwide introduction of Bell's speaking telephone," Shulman writes, "couldn't have been more fitting." He continues: "MIT...had recently opened the Rogers Laboratory of Physics...on Boylston Street. The facility was the first of its kind in the United States....[Professor] Cross...granted [Bell] unfettered access....Bell seized the opportunity." The telephone and MIT, it soon transpired, were, so to speak, made for each other.

Which brings us back to the role of capitalism. Copley Square was overwhelmingly about Faith and Learning, Arts and Sciences. But it was also about entrepreneurship. Brahmins were very practical people of long-standing entrepreneurial habit. Indeed, in *Media, Culture and Society*, Paul DiMaggio titled his discussion of the founding of Copley Square's art museum "Cultural Entrepreneurship: The Creation of an Organizational Base for High Culture in America." The creation of which coincided in the square with the breakthrough of 1897, when MIT's engineers forced open another door to the coming twentieth century: within sight of the MIT block on the square's eastern periphery, just beyond Arlington Street, they broke ground for America's first—and the world's fourth—subway.

It was a telling symbol: an Acropolis on the subway, from which more or less continuously one trolley car after another emerged onto the surface and into the square. Prendergast loved painting them. They served professors and students, museumgoers and churchgoers, office workers and tourists and shoppers too, for by the 1890s, in between the accumulating landmarks, commerce had sprung up everywhere, including two grand hotels, the Brunswick (just opposite MIT on Boylston Street) and the Vendome (on Dartmouth just beyond Newbury Street). Guests in the latter in the 1880s famously included Sarah Bernhardt and Oscar Wilde. Glamour had its place.

Entrepreneurship was everywhere evident, particularly at MIT. It took its cue from the enabling Brahmin culture and set the pace as well in a square where many exhibitions at the art museum, for example, were of contemporary artists being actively collected. According to the 2009 book *Entrepreneurial Impact: The Role of MIT* by Edward B. Roberts and Charles Eesley, in its early years in the 1870s and 1880s, "MIT was seen as virtually alone as a university that embraced rather than shunned industry....From its start MIT had developed close ties with technology-based industrialists like Thomas Edison and Alexander Graham Bell."

Copley Square's architecture disclosed how it romanticized commerce. The Acropolis was also an agora. One of its most important early landmarks was Pierce Hall, erected in 1888 and significantly Hanseatic in style, recalling the trading city-state of Hamburg. Reports in the *Boston Daily Advertiser* on July 9, 1886, and April 9, 1887, document the diversity of Pierce Hall's life:

> The entire lower floor, which has a somewhat elaborate front with arched [display] windows, will be occupied by SS Pierce and Company, the noted grocers. The second and third floors will be dedicated to large dancing and banquet halls….These will be leased to Augustus L. Papanti. The remainder of the building…will be cut up into office suites and apartments….The architect is Mr. Edwin Tobey….The basement will be used as a wine cellar for Messrs Pierce and Company. All…will be lighted by electricity.

None of this, one imagines—just across the street from the new Museum of Fine Arts—was entirely out of mind when Professor James gave his course of lectures on Pragmatism. "James was anxious," Bruce Kuklick wrote in his introduction to the philosopher's work, "to uncover what true beliefs amounted to in human life, what their 'Cash Value' was as philosophy." That was something the ruling caste understood. And "it made survival the test of intellectual as well as biological fitness." This "pragmatic theory of truth applied to Darwinian ideas" was also something, as we will soon see, that Rogers identified with. It was clearly modern, obviously commercial, and in both respects attractive to a broad cross-section of the booming, growing American metropolis that Copley Square arose in.

From the very first days of Copley Square, not only religious but class and ethnic divisions were trumped so thoroughly by all this that one might say it had been conceived by Boston's working classes as much as the ruling class, for immigrants as much as for patricians. As DiMaggio puts it in his clear-eyed way, "Alongside and complicating the Brahmins' drive toward social exclusivity was a conflicting desire, as they saw it, to educate the community." In Copley Square that drive achieved its full force, while at the same time the conflict it engendered, however genteel, proved very fructifying on all sides.

This was conspicuously the case with the second generation of the masses in the case of the square's cornerstone. At MIT, as Philip Alexander has documented, "Rogers brought sons of factory workers, laborers, blacksmiths, janitors, and hackney drivers together with upwardly mobile offspring of bank clerks and factory managers, together with heirs of vast family fortunes, privileged Brahmins."

But what Alexander insists on for MIT "was a true melting pot, the American fantasy," a place where "shared professional values overrode social, ethnic, and religious prejudices." That was also true of Copley Square as a whole, again a reflection of the Brahmin educational mission that so attracted Rogers. It was a value system applied to the very first generation of immigrants, for instance, diagonally across from MIT at the new Museum of Fine Arts.

The novelist Margaret Allston, in her 1899 account of the Copley Square art museum, painted a scene more picturesque than aristocratic. In *Her Boston Experiences*, she wrote of "the great number of Italians who congregate of a Sunday afternoon there when there is no admission fee." She describes "Italian women in gay

THE GLOBE EXTRA!

LATEST

FIRST CAR OFF THE EARTH.

Allston Electric Goes Into the Subway on Schedule Time.

THE CROWDED FIRST CAR AT THE SUBWAY ENTRANCE

Over 100 Persons Cheer for Allston, the Motorman, the Conductor and Themselves—Trufant and Reed, Faithful Employes, Had Charge of the Car—One-Third of the Early Passengers Were Women—Everybody Was Good-Natured, and the Historic Trip Was Pronounced a Great Success.

The invention of the telephone by Bell in MIT labs, and the design and construction of America's first subway system in the 1890s by MIT engineer Howard A. Carson, chief engineer of the Transit Commission, were perhaps the two most obvious technological advances that marked Copley Square's early history in the sciences. This was in tandem with the artistic creation Trinity Church, that church being the first mature American architecture and a cultural revelation.

Progressive Boston did not hide its loyalties: thus one of the chief sculptural images in enduring stone that was carved into the campanile of the famously liberal Unitarian Brattle Street Church was that of Giuseppe Garibaldi, whom even Henry Adams seemed to approve of. In this present-day view the Charles River Basin campus of MIT is visible along the river in the background.

garments, others in plain, dark clothes, invariably brightened by a brilliant handkerchief or scarf." The museum's response to these first-generation Italian immigrants, largely illiterate in English, was what? According to Whitehill's centennial history of this august Brahmin institution, the response was to immediately hire "an Italian-speaking guide."

The significance of all this did not go unnoticed at the time. It got to the point, in the words of the historian Jane Dini, where the Brahmin *Transcript* "commended Italian immigrants for their regular attendance at the art museum" while chastising the ruling class, pointedly noting that "the [immigrants] far outnumbered all other visitors, including the patrician Back Bay." The square offered these immigrants a warmer welcome than might be imagined today. Of the three church towers that dominated Copley Square before various tall modern buildings intervened, that of the Brattle Church boasted a sculpture (circa 1872) of the Italian freedom fighter Giuseppe Garibaldi alongside one of Lincoln.

In a few cases already the welcome was at the highest level. At MIT one of the leading professors in the 1870s was Gaetano Lanza, the engineer son of a Sicilian immigrant to America. More usual was the tentative ticket to success of President John F. Kennedy's grandfather John F. Fitzgerald, who was a student at Harvard Med and only redirected his energies toward politics when family finances dictated a career change. Dennis P. Ryan wrote in *Beyond the Ballot Box: A Social History of the Boston Irish, 1845–1917* that Harvard Med dean Holmes Sr. "helped promote the careers of promising Irish medical students."

Another example of diversity at the highest level was the Irish American poet and editor John Boyle O'Reilly, a founding member of one of the square's most prestigious Brahmin institutions, the Boston Athletic Association. It was housed in a luxurious palazzo of superbly equipped gymnasia and Turkish baths, built just behind the public library on Exeter Street. In 1896 the BAA dramatized the square's diversity in connection with the revival in Athens that year of the Olympic Games after a hiatus of more than fourteen hundred years. It was deemed highly appropriate that an institution of the New World Acropolis should send a team. It ended up the de facto US team, there being no official one, and the BAA group made up a majority of the Americans who competed. The group's track and field athletes won six of the eleven first-place (today's gold) medals accrued overall by the Americans competing.

MIT played a leading role in all this. In 1889 the Boston Conference on Physical Training—"mark[ing] the beginning of the physical education profession in the U.S.," in the words of the historian John Lucas—was held at the Institute, the sort of thing the dynamic President Walker was apt to get involved in. At this conference, Baron Pierre de Coubertin, founder of the modern Olympics, spoke in "unvarnished praise of English 'muscular Christianity,'" asserting strongly the superiority over German and Swedish gymnastics of "the English athletic system as understood and explained by the greatest of modern teachers, Thomas Arnold of Rugby." Seven years later, de Coubertin's plans reached fruition in Athens.

MIT alumnus Thomas Pelham Curtis, a San Francisco–born Boston Brahmin electrical engineering student (class of 1894), won first prize in the 110-meter hurdles, and with the other BAA athletes was welcomed back to Copley Square with a huge rally and fêted at a great civic banquet at the Hotel Vendome. MIT also played an important role in the history of the Boston Marathon, first run in 1897, just a year after the revival of the modern Olympics. Not only Curtis but the whole BAA team

INCIDENTS OF THE MARATHON ROAD RACE.

THE START

A SPURT

THE AMBULANCE CORPS

A STRAGLER

JOHN J. McDERMOTT FINISHES AHEAD

The New World Acropolis was naturally Greek themed. The Boston Marathon, its finish line at Copley Square, reflects Boston's role in launching the first modern Olympic Games at Athens in 1896, where a team from Harvard, MIT, and BU did so well it inaugurated the domination of the games in the modern period by the United States.

had been much moved and impressed by the Olympic marathon, and the Bostonians were determined to create an American version of it, the distance the same and Copley Square the finish line.

A patriotic twist was added when it was decided to hold the Boston Marathon, as it came to be called, on Patriot's Day (celebrating Paul Revere's ride). The twist was magnified by the association of the race with the New Old South Church on the square's northwest corner, in whose original meetinghouse the Boston Tea Party had been planned, and whose gorgeous new Ruskinesque Victorian temple in Copley Square featured a tall campanile, the sight and sound of which marked the race's climax.

Above all, however, the fact that elite education conspicuously partnered in the New World Acropolis with mass education was a critical aspect of Copley Square's diversity. Again MIT was in the lead. Consider this report in the *Boston Globe*, which focused on the allied trio of MIT, the Natural History Museum, and the Lowell Institute, forerunner of university extension in America (and eventually, as we shall see, of educational television):

> One of the great forces in free education by lamplight [e.g., night school] in Boston is the Lowell Institute, which maintains an elaborate free lecture course at the Rogers building, Institute of Technology, and various free classes for workers [, including] a class of instruction for industrial foremen under the direction of Professor C. F. Park of the Institute of Technology…given in [MIT] Engineering Building A in Trinity Place… [and] intended to bring the systematic study of applied science within the reach of young men who follow industrial pursuits by day. Another Lowell Institute class is the teachers school of science under the direction of Prof. G. H. Barton, curator of the Natural History building…embrac[ing] field talks on botany, zoology, and geology. Laboratory lessons are also included.

Where MIT led, others followed. BU, notably not a Brahmin institution but middle-class Methodist in inspiration, was very progressive in its proclaimed gender equality and Germanic graduate school emphasis. Though not based in the square until the 1900s, BU was involved in it from the beginning, being affiliated in the 1870s with MIT, which offered all of BU's science courses for years. Northeastern College (soon to be a university)—an almost completely working-class school originally— began across Boylston Street from MIT at Copley Square's (and America's) first Young Men's Christian Association. Similarly, Emerson College was drawn to the square. So too what is now the Massachusetts College of Art.

The first permanent home of the venerable American Academy of Arts and Sciences, founded by John Adams himself in the eighteenth century, was built on Newbury Street in the block next to the MIT block in the 1900s. William Barton Rogers was in his time a leading member of this distinguished institution, now based in Cambridge north of Harvard Yard.

MIT's most famous architecture graduate, I. M. Pei, attended classes at the Copley Square campus and first heard Le Corbusier lecture there in 1935. A half century later, long after the School of Architecture was moved to Cambridge, he endowed Copley Square with its third masterpiece, adding to Trinity Church and the Boston Public Library a work in the twentieth-century modernist mode, the John Hancock Tower.

The elite side did not wince and wither in response. As late as 1910 the elite side of the equation was given a tremendous boost when a handsome headquarters building was erected near the MIT block on Newbury Street by the American Academy of Arts and Sciences, the venerable and prestigious society established by American founding father John Adams.

This contrast between elite and mass Learning and its consequence—the larger contrast between aristocratic and populist culture—was always somewhat obscured, however, by the fact that if MIT was indeed the cornerstone of Copley Square, the Institute was *not* its centerpiece. Nor, architecturally, was Learning. The Acropolis took its character at once and overwhelmingly from Trinity Church from the minute that first American "cathedral" was completed in 1875. The art historian James O'Gorman has rightly likened Trinity, clones of which sprouted over the next decades all over the country, to the work of the novelist Mark Twain, the poet Emily Dickinson, and the painter Winslow Homer in that the church "represented the coming of age of the American generation." Visually, Faith seemed to trump Learning in the square because of Trinity's prominence, even as, because of the museum's prominence, Art seemed visually to trump Science, never mind elite over mass education.

Finally, however, the balance was righted—tilted even—when in 1888–95 the apotheosis of Copley Square, the Boston Public Library, arose in all its glory on the square's western side, until then largely vacant. The library changed everything. Not just in Copley Square was it telling. In his history of American and European architecture, the British historian David Watkin remarked, "This imposing monument of plain white granite established Boston as a centre of world culture." Magnificently fusing both the square's aristocratic and populist traditions, the library, an epochal institution in Western history as the first tax-supported big-city public circulating library in the world, also blazed a path in art and architecture that finally dethroned the Richardsonian Romanesque of Trinity in favor of what scholars now call, fittingly, the American Renaissance. This new classicism, with the "City Beautiful" movement in tow, spread across the nation as the finale of the New World Acropolis as surely as had its beginnings two decades earlier, when Trinity Church's Romanesque profile was everywhere seen.

The Gods of Copley Square I have called the creators of all this, with Rogers in the vanguard. But gods wax, they don't wane. Their creations expand. They do not contract. Yet there was only so much room, which explains the dispersal, begun just after 1900, only five years after the completion of the public library consolidated the square's stature worldwide. First Harvard Medical School departed the square for Longwood, then the Museum of Fine Arts moved to Fenway, both complexes bigger than all of the square taken together. These were the neighborhoods closest to the Back Bay to the west.

And MIT, determined to stay close to the heart of things, chose the neighborhood nearest to the Back Bay to the north (albeit across the Charles River), Cambridgeport, building there a "Great White City," as the architecture critics called it. The site was Boston's grandest new stage, the Charles River Basin, overlooking downtown Boston, the harbor, and the Back Bay: "in the heart of greater Boston," the Institute's then president wrote to his chief donor. The intent was, he declared, "to command the public view for all time," to preside forever over the hub of the metropolis and its global portals.

Of all that, much more later. Suffice it now to bring again to mind Cannell, Pei's biographer. He was so interested in Copley Square in our own day, a century later, because it fell to Pei and to his partner, Henry Cobb, to add to what could never move from the square. They ensured that even as business advanced on education and culture, the square's original stature would never be entirely forgotten. To its twin architectural masterworks of church and library, they added a modernist, third masterpiece: a skyscraper.

In the 1960s Pei reported, "Harry and I came to the conclusion that [what] Copley Square, in spite of these two great buildings by Richardson and McKim, Mead and White...needed was a twentieth-century addition to create a new space." A third masterwork! "So we decided to go ahead and do it." After several false starts, and in the face of huge opposition and one crisis after another, the deed was finally seen to be well done after all. How audacious was that? How MIT!

Some would say the result is best seen not in the square itself but from MIT's Cambridgeport campus along the river. Certainly at least one MIT faculty member sees significance in the fact that the Hancock Tower's angularity points directly to MIT's Cambridgeport dome. Carter Wiseman describes it in another book about Pei's work: "[Seen] from the riverbank in front of the MIT buildings today," a vantage that left Wiseman fairly awestruck, "Hancock has an almost unearthly presence...impossibly thin, dominating its surroundings with [an] icy elegance...[it is] one of the most arresting skyscrapers of the modern era."

That's the aesthetic message. Historically, the message is that a century after MIT was Copley Square's cornerstone, the Institute was still a player through the Pei office building in the square, forcing its modern-day transformation. Always MIT's formative institutional memory, Copley Square had already been reasserted on the Back Bay skyline by the earlier Prudential skyscraper, providing an axis for a new building in Cambridgeport by Pei himself. A decade later, the Hancock Tower, a triumphant final touch to the Back Bay skyline (which the Prudential Tower had heralded with much less distinction), underlined the square's reassertion on the skyline with redoubled power. Suddenly Copley Square was not just a formative memory but a newly compelling vision, beyond memory, newly dominant from one end of MIT's campus to the other.

Foundation

The Boston Money Tree

The grand Ionic portico facing Killian Court was
designed by William Welles Bosworth in 1916.

Foundation

The Boston Money Tree

It is time to discuss the Boston money tree. The subject should be required study for all students of the history of MIT, given that the original goals involved applied as much as pure science, "lab work" as much as "book reading," and entrepreneurship as much as learning. MIT was founded in 1861 as a catalyst for industry and business as well as for science. Steven Shapin explains all this in documenting his assertions about MIT's "High Modernity," which I quoted in the previous chapter. According to Shapin, from the beginning, in the late nineteenth century, "MIT most clearly envisaged a future in which academia and industry marched in lock-step.... It was designed to train industry leaders—...men 'who would become top executives rather than end up working for Harvard graduates'—and produce the sort of large-scale innovations that would spawn entirely new technology-based industries for the Boston region. [MIT] became the first entrepreneurial university." About this Shapin is clear: "From early in the twentieth century, MIT's faculty functioned as industrial consultants. Administrators had few worries about conflicts of interest since MIT saw itself as designed for public service, and the best way to serve the public was to get the knowledge into the factory and then on the market." (Actually, there was much worry, and controversy too, but the entrepreneurial principle always won.)

Shapin's observations came in a review of yet another tome on this subject, Henry Etzkowitz's *MIT and the Rise of Entrepreneurial Science*, in which Etzkowitz explains that by the mid-twentieth century, MIT's role in aiding technology transfer as a public service "extended to its role in founding the first venture capital firm in 1946." President Karl Compton, "drawing on his contacts among Boston's banking Brahmins, cobbled together a coalition with Harvard Business School to establish American Research and Development (ARD), designed to fill the gap between MIT's academic research and new firm foundation." Shapin believes that MIT repeatedly spurned Harvard's merger offers because "it was afraid that its entrepreneurial culture might be diluted."

A vital portal was the downtown Financial District, which has always clustered about Boston Harbor—itself a wider cultural portal. As the visitor gazes at the Financial District skyline from Cambridgeport today, it will be useful to think of just one tiny room on Congress Street, a room where in 1942 the ARD Corporation first opened for business. Its prosaic-enough-sounding idea was to channel funds from insurance companies and investment trusts through a development corporation in which MIT invested, as did the Massachusetts Investors Trust ("the other MIT," it has been called).

Prosaic? Russell B. Adams (about whom more shortly) observes, "It was an imaginative prescription—there was nothing like it in the country—and it was one

In *The Boston Money Tree,* Russell B. Adams begins MIT's history not in nineteenth-century Back Bay but in Boston Harbor in the eighteenth century, in the spirit of docks crowded with clipper ships, the greatest of which were designed by Donald McKay of East Boston and which circled the globe. Adams sees in MIT the principal carrier through history of "the Boston spirit." Wrote Samuel Eliot Morison: "*The Flying Cloud* was our Reims, the *Sovereign of the Seas* our Parthenon."

that Boston, with its great stores of intellectual and financial capital, was ideally suited to fulfill." State Street is often called the Vatican of high finance, so extensive are the funds held in trust there.

Not only MIT factors in here. The treasurer of ARD was also MIT's treasurer, Horace Ford, and its chairman, a key founder of ARD, was Merrill Griswold of the Massachusetts Investors Trust. ARD's president was Harvard Business School professor George Doriot. "Together," Adams attests, "the three represented that great triple-threat combination that helped provide the strength for Boston to pull itself out of its long sleep [in the early twentieth century]: the Harvard Business School, MIT, and the Financial community."

This is an even older story than either Shapin or Etzkowitz tells. It is a story that begins not in the nineteenth but in the eighteenth century. To understand the history of MIT from its founding is to take note of historian Mark Peterson's assertion in *The City-State of Boston* that "the best way to understand Boston's history from its founding is to think of it as a quasi-independent city-state, not unlike Venice, with its own hinterland and with a large and complex network of international trading, political and cultural connections." I would argue that while Harvard has historically been the standard bearer of this powerful city-state, MIT became the icebreaker. Significantly, Harvard's eminent twentieth-century historian Samuel Eliot Morison would find the poetry of it all less in Harvard Yard than in all those tall trading ships thronging Boston Harbor. Perhaps there is no better way to understand MIT's culture still—beautiful so often in its practicality—than to consider the clipper ship.

Morison was not thinking of Frank Lloyd Wright when he likened only one American architect "to a cathedral builder of the thirteenth century [to whom] came visions transcending human experience, with the power to transmute them into reality." He was referring to the greatest of the nineteenth-century naval architects, the East Boston builder of clipper ships, Donald McKay. "*The Flying Cloud* was our Rheims," Morison wrote, comparing that clipper to the coronation church of French kings, "the *Sovereign of the Seas* our Parthenon."

You can see the American Rheims in MIT's Hart Nautical Gallery, which has a splendid model of *The Flying Cloud* always on exhibit. It is the most famous of McKay's designs. Close by it is a work of art comparable to the finest ships' figure-heads of the period, a City of Boston seal salvaged from an old East Boston ferry, superbly carved and painted to show Beacon Hill's steeply built-up hillsides topped by the golden dome of the Massachusetts State House, with sailing ships in the foreground below. It calls to mind Morison's opening passage from *The Maritime History of Massachusetts, 1783–1860*: "A summer day with a sea turn in the wind. The Grand Bank fog, rolling in wave after wave, is dissolved by the perfumed breath of New England hay fields into a gentle haze, that turns the State House dome to old gold, films brick walls with a soft patina, and sifts blue shadows among the foliage of the Common elms. Out of the mist in Massachusetts Bay comes riding a clipper ship with the effortless speed of an albatross."

A memorable scene. But now let us abruptly about-face in Jamesian mode and transition toward what is surely the equivalent symbol of today, the spaceship. Pertinent here are the words of Hart Nautical Gallery curator Kurt Hasselbalch about the clipper ship that his collection first celebrated (a gift to MIT from Captain Arthur Clark, who shipped out of Boston on one such ship at age seventeen). The clipper, Hasselbalch writes, "represents a powerful symbol of American ingenuity and entrepreneurship. In the midst of the Industrial Revolution the clipper ships set many records for speed and profit, critical elements in the early decades of a fast-expanding global economy." Which explains perhaps why Adams, a writer for Bloomberg's venerable *Businessweek* and the head for some years of its Boston bureau, begins the history of MIT not in 1861 but in 1790, in *The Boston Money Tree*:

> Fresh from its great voyage of merchant adventure, the ship *Columbia* had been hailed by a cannonade of thirteen guns when it sailed home [from China] into Boston Harbor in 1790 to the cheers of citizens come to greet the tea-laden vessel at dockside. Plowing

The thesis of *The Boston Money Tree* is documented in a striking visual way by ship models at MIT's Hart Nautical Gallery. *The Flying Cloud*, "the clipper ship," the Hart's curator writes, "represents a powerful symbol of American ingenuity and entrepreneurship."

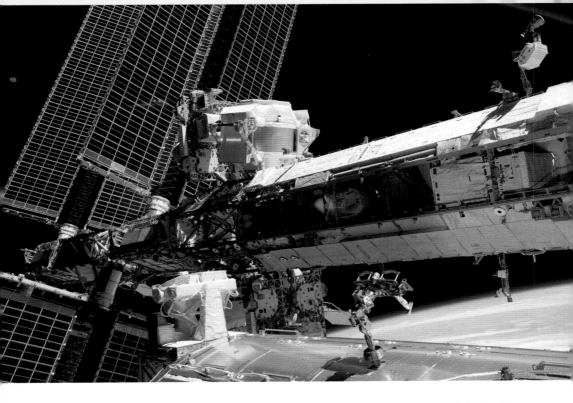

Another witness to Adam's thesis is the history of the Boston Brahmin Cabots at MIT. A family of many clipper shipmasters out of Boston, the Cabots were early supporters of MIT in the 1870s. Samuel C. C. Ting, Thomas Dudley Cabot Chair, headed the team that built the Alpha Magnetic Spectrometer in 2011.

speak only to the Cabots and the Cabots only to God," there was no nonsense about God's part in the conversation; the *Times* merely discoursed on Cabot's storied ancestry in general.

That the family's latest champion built the family firm into a "multinational behemoth" was only to be expected; likewise that he had bequeathed to the Institute the next generation to sit on MIT's Corporation, Louis Wellington Cabot, a life member emeritus at this writing. But most importantly, the distinguished capitalist and philanthropist endowed the Thomas Dudley Cabot Chair in 1960. A holder of that chair is the Nobel laureate Samuel C. C. Ting—a Chinese American, to make this history ring even louder—who headed the team that built the Alpha Magnetic Spectrometer for detecting dark matter that the space shuttle *Endeavour* flew to the International Space Station in 2011.

Two families, four generations: from clipper ships to spaceships. Thomas Dudley Cabot, late twentieth-century space-age great-grandson of clipper ship–era China trader John Murray Forbes, was named after the colonial governor of the Massachusetts Bay Colony, Thomas Dudley, who in Boston in 1650 signed the charter under which Harvard still operates nearly four hundred years later.

The larger point here—about *how* the very "spirit of Boston" came to be invested (according to Adams) in MIT—also explains *why* Boston's Brahmins made that conspicuous investment. In Adams's words, "Although as such matters are often reckoned in Boston, MIT was something of a brash newcomer, the civic jubilee attending the dedication of its new quarters in 1916 was brilliant testimony to the school's rapid rise *to nearly the same state of social and cultural grace as Harvard in the Boston scheme of things* [my emphasis]." Mark those words.

The MIT founder's ideas were only briefly fantastical. In his *William Barton Rogers and the Idea of MIT*, A. J. Angulo observes, like Adams, how quickly Tech pulled abreast of Harvard, citing historian David P. Tyack's study of Boston Brahmin Harvard professor George Ticknor as suggesting the reason. Tyack argues that because the Brahmin caste, even during the very early nineteenth century, "had difficulty translating its economic, social, and intellectual authority into political power, [it] sought to bypass [politics] and to influence the cause of the nation in other ways, [seeking] to control institutions—schools, churches, libraries, the legal system, the republic of letters—which would stabilize society." MIT was a stellar example. Another example of the Brahmin educational push of the period was Wellesley College, where in the early 1870s its head, Alice Freeman Palmer (a private student, by the way, of the philosopher George Howison when he was at MIT), shared the Brahmin goal of liberalizing Puritan educational ideals but not abandoning them.

The scholar Martin Green, more negative about late nineteenth-century Boston history, believes that politics actually trumped education and culture in the Brahmins' value system. He sees their institutionalism as a reluctant and angst-filled retreat from immigrant ward-boss politics. I disagree but think he did catch hold of an important truth easily missed in my more triumphant reading of Brahmin institutionalism. Admittedly, the Boston Brahmin, like his or her Puritan ancestor, did seek a holistic, totally integrated civic society that included politics. But I believe the loss of that holistic possibility only made the Brahmin investment in institutionalism all the more intense.

This registered especially in Copley Square, where MIT and the art museum were the first institutions standing and the first intellectual forces brought to bear. Thus when Green pronounces Copley Square "the world capital of the aesthetic movement," and does so because he sees the Brahmin invested so solely and so heavily in it, he is right to say that "in no other city in the world was the aesthetic movement such a dramatic event, because in no other city was it so obviously involved with politics and history." One thinks of the dominance of Jews in Vienna's intellectual and cultural life in the same era, the result of their being banned from Austrian politics.

Overall, however, notice that these Brahmin institutions were themselves conspicuously progressive, perhaps more so than a comparable politics could ever have been, Brahmins having remained mostly Federalists long after that party's decline. This was true of MIT, Rogers's idea of which was so radical that it encountered many more difficulties in fund-raising during the same period than, for instance, Louis Agassiz's Museum of Comparative Zoology at Harvard, even though "Rogers and his circle," Angulo writes, "struggled to raise a mere pittance by comparison." Still, when it was done, it was easy to see how the Institute benefited from this Brahmin propensity for institution building over politics.

One often encounters evidence of MIT's early parity with Harvard in contemporary letters, for instance, one from August 25, 1891, written by William James, perhaps foremost of Harvard professors at the time, published in his collected correspondence. He was writing to a friend of meeting "a really charming young North Carolinian educated at our Institute of Technology," a distinctly warm and almost proprietary way of referring to MIT. Then too there is contemporary literature, in which, of all the examples available, the one that stands out in my mind is *Miss Theodora: A West End Story* by the Radcliffe-educated author Helen Leah Reed, a delightful fin de siècle novel of old Boston in which MIT plays a large role. This story about the ups and downs of a Brahmin family turns on a widow who brings up her nephew Ernest to follow five generations at Harvard, where he dutifully goes to please his aunt, despite pining for MIT, where his best friend is studying Ernest's first love, science. Ernest in fact enjoys Harvard too much. His alert aunt begins to notice that he is becoming a tad dissipated because his studies are failing to sustain his interest and he is partying too much, all the while "frankly env[ying] his friends' opportunity for studying science" instead of Greek.

Sensing his predicament, the aunt allows Ernest to transfer to MIT, where he becomes at once very studious and industrious. It's a more interesting narrative by far than just this, but that theme does make plain how the best families in Boston came early to see the Institute—"'Tech' in boy's talk"—as a necessary and sometimes more desirable alternative to Harvard. At one point young Ernest, still at Harvard, is depicted as striking out somewhat with a woman, and they have this exchange: "'Oh, I used to think you would be an inventor, or—something. But now—.' 'I am nothing but a Harvard freshman,' he broke in, laughing."

In this popular late nineteenth-century novel, the Boston Brahmin boy loses the Boston Brahmin girl because he opted for Harvard and not the more adult-seeming MIT. In nonfiction, the story is much the same. The classic text is Cleveland Amory's *The Proper Bostonians*. Amory, scion of a noted Brahmin family, was the son of a Harvard graduate who had also studied at MIT.

Lectures on Architecture
by Wm. R. Ware
Prof of Archte Mass. Inst. Techy.
Season of 1870 + 1871

Design — *Nov. 9, 1870*

Lecture 1 –

Shape of rooms

Oblong rooms the long side =
diag – of sq of which the short
side is the side of the sq –

The height to be = ½ long side

Mean proportional easily got by
numbers 5 – 7 – 10

Diff. sized room made to look
proportional thus —

A nineteenth-century MIT student's class notebook.

Laboratory

Charles Darwin,
Alexander Graham Bell,
Louis Sullivan

Periodic Abstraction, by Felice Frankel, 2005, Dreyfus Building lobby

Laboratory

Charles Darwin, Alexander Graham Bell, Louis Sullivan

The heart of MIT still, because it is closest to founder William Barton Rogers in his public role as scientist, is the noble old landmark (now a very grand Back Bay home furnishings emporium) that was part of the original MIT block of the early 1860s: the old Museum of Natural History at the corner of Berkeley Street and Boylston. It is the stately twin of the first Rogers Building, now replaced by an insurance company behemoth. Those blessed with historical imagination might look at the old museum's broad front steps and think of Louis Sullivan—perhaps MIT's most famous graduate of the nineteenth century, the father of American architectural modernism—dashing up those steps to class on blustery winter days in 1872-73. MIT students, as well as BU students, took their many science courses in the museum, which for years functioned as the Institute's teaching annex.

It is the only building anywhere now standing that MIT's founder oversaw the construction of himself—Rogers was an influential member of the building committee. It was under the auspices of the Natural History Society that Rogers mounted his historic defense of Darwin's theory of evolution, during a fifteen-month period between late 1859 and early 1861. His pro-Darwin stance considerably heightened his public stature just when his battle to secure MIT's charter reached its successful climax.

"In the same month in which Darwin published *Origins*…[Rogers began his] evolution-related debates," writes A. J. Angulo, Rogers's effective biographer. Rogers's opponent was the leading American scientist of the era, Louis Agassiz of Harvard, never a Darwinian. Rogers was perhaps not so eloquent as Agassiz. But he was keener and more logical in argument, famous for his striking habit at crucial points of "turn[ing] his eagle eyes hard apart." By most accounts, Rogers won the argument at their series of public debates. Says Edward J. Pfeifer in his chapter in *The Comparative Reception of Darwinism*:

> Nothing like these debates occurred in the other countries surveyed in this volume. Nothing like them occurred in any other American scientific society, either. Clearly the reason that they took place in Boston was Agassiz's presence. The real issue at stake was whether Agassiz or Darwin's principles would guide future scientific research.…In this clash of world views the success of [Asa] Gray [Rogers's ally, another eminent Harvard scientist and Darwin's close friend] and Rogers certainly did not establish Darwin as right. Their success did, however, show that Darwinism would not collapse…even under the wrath of Agassiz.

Standing before this historic building today, if one looks eastward, up Boylston Street, the present-day skyscrapers overlooking Boston Harbor are visible in the far distance, as global portals.

The shock waves set off by Rogers's defeat of Agassiz—which is to say, the embryonic MIT's triumph over mighty Harvard—were significant for the stature of the coming Copley Square Acropolis, of which MIT would become the cornerstone in more than just an architectural sense. More and equally provocative sparks flew in American higher education when in 1869 the *Atlantic Monthly* published an article arguing forcefully for the practical training and laboratory idea so crucial to the thesis of MIT's founder. The article was not, however, by Rogers. It was by Charles W. Eliot. In the history of MIT *and* Harvard it is important to remember that the founder of modern Harvard was, before that, a founding professor of MIT.

The Harvard historian Louis Menand, writing in his prizewinning book *The Metaphysical Club*, is very explicit about this. "Harvard," he writes of Eliot's later election as president, "picked Eliot because it wanted to be reformed." And where did it go to find its reformer? To MIT. Eliot, Menand notes, because he had previously been spurned by Harvard, "was on the faculty of the Massachusetts Institute of Technology, which had recently been founded in Boston as a school to prepare students for the scientific professions." Eliot's election to Harvard's presidency was an absolute about-face for America's oldest institution of higher learning, "a recognition that science, not theology, was the educational core of the future—and that Harvard was in danger of losing its prestige."

About the subsequent effect of all this, Rogers's biographer also does not mince words. "Charles W. Eliot took the laboratory ideal to Harvard.... At the start of his presidency...Eliot reminisced about Rogers's 'example,' confessing, 'I received from [his] School much more than I ever gave.'" That was not totally true; Eliot and Frances H. Storer's first-in-the-nation physics manual greatly benefited MIT's early and growing reputation. Eliot would later be noted for using his scientific vocabulary at Harvard, calling the Fogg Museum a "well-fitted art laboratory" where, as Caroline A. Jones put it in *Modern Art at Harvard*, "art could be analyzed and compared, rather than a treasure house built to enshrine a cultural legacy."

The idea, once let loose, achieved wide currency. There had been good reason for Rogers, when founding MIT, to take pains to recruit Eliot. According to Angulo, "Once installed in Harvard's bully pulpit, Eliot preached the gospel of the laboratory....The spark of reform leaped to the desk of Princeton president John McCosh....[At Yale] faculty began transplanting the [laboratory idea] of the scientific school to the college proper....John Le Conte of the University of California, Berkeley, asked Rogers about MIT's laboratory method....By means of its example the idea of MIT became part of the broader discourse in American higher education."

Eliot in his 1869 *Atlantic Monthly* article "laid out more comprehensively even than Rogers himself the argument for separate institutions to train those interested in the practical applications of science," the historian Bruce Sinclair writes in his chapter of *Becoming MIT*. Good Unitarian progressive that he was, Eliot mounted "an argument reminiscent of Ralph Waldo Emerson's *American Scholar* address," Sinclair writes, "claim[ing] that technical schools ought to entirely [Americanize] national experiences and concerns....Political liberty, social mobility, and a wealth

MASSACHUSETTS.—INSTITUTE OF TECHNOLOGY, BOSTON.—THE

LABORATORY—CLASSES AT THEIR STUDIES.—See Page 228.

Charles W. Eliot, so well known as the founder of modern Harvard (elected president there in 1869), is less well known as a founding professor and ally of William Barton Rogers in launching MIT's revolutionary educational ethos, an ethos at the heart of Eliot's reforms at Harvard. ABOVE: Eliot teaching an evening Lowell Institute course in the first Rogers Building.

of natural resources gave the United States great advantages among the nations of the world, and Eliot imagined a comparatively grave responsibility for the country's educational institutions." (Eliot, interestingly, focused on the educational repercussions of Emerson's address. As we shall see later, Oliver Wendell Holmes Sr. concentrated on the social repercussions in his own *Atlantic Monthly* article, also in the 1860s, on the Boston Brahmins.)

Eliot maintained a lifelong view that a merged MIT and Harvard would do this best. Rogers's contrary view that it was best done independently by two institutions explains why many proposed mergers failed. That modern Harvard's founder should have come from MIT, however, shows their intellectual affinity and closeness. A reflection of this was, in Russell B. Adams's words, that "from the very start MIT had been clearly twined with Harvard and Harvard's wealthy stalwarts," both schools being ardent Brahmin causes, one privileging the liberal arts, the other science and technology.

The creation story of each institution is key. Both were founded as state schools, really. "This Society of Scholars founded in the year of our Lord 1636 by act of a Great and General Court of the Company of Massachusetts Bay convened in Boston by the 8th/eighteenth of September of that year" is how Harvard described its beginnings in its tercentenary announcement of 1936. MIT's birth narrative is very similar sounding: "In the year 1861 [by an] act to incorporate the Massachusetts Institute of Technology and to grant aid to said Institute and to the Boston Society of Natural History [it was so] enacted by the Senate and the House of Representatives in General Court assembled."

So the state that in the seventeenth century launched what would become the standard-bearer of American education—Harvard—would in the nineteenth century launch what became the icebreaker of the New Education, MIT. It is two acts of the same play. The historical continuity of the founding ruling class in question. Consult Oxford historian Diarmaid MacCulloch's *Christianity: The First Three Thousand Years*, a book of global reach, in which the author documents his assertion that Harvard was the star of what he calls "the Religion of the Book," and as such the chief ornament of "possibly the most literate society in the world." An astonishing accolade. And it was *exactly* that repute that drew Rogers to Boston two hundred years later. In 1846 Rogers wrote to his brother from the University of Virginia:

> Ever since I have known something of the knowledge-seeking spirit and intellectual capabilities of the community in and around Boston, I have felt persuaded that of all the places in the world it was the one most certainly to derive the highest benefits for a polytechnic institute....I doubt not that such a nucleus school would, with the growth of this active and knowledge-seeking community, finally expand into a great institution comprehending the whole field of physical science and the arts, with auxiliary branches of mathematics and modern languages, and would soon overtop the universities of the land.

With the exception of small, outlying Tufts College, founded by the Universalists in the 1850s in Medford, Massachusetts, MIT was the first of the great galaxy of present-day universities founded in Boston's orbit since Harvard itself in the seventeenth century. And very much its scientific and technological complement, as it turned out, in the wake of Harvard's own failure to generate such an institution internally (as, for instance, it did with its medical school).

There does remain in Copley Square today a beautiful if largely unrecognized reminder of the scientific pioneering spirit of MIT. It is one of the nine great allegorical murals of the Boston Public Library's Grand Staircase painted by the French Symbolist master Puvis de Chavannes and installed in 1895–96. Titled *Physics*—it is one of a series on different fields of learning—it depicts two figures representing, respectively, good news and bad, one in white with laurel, the other more darkly clad and covering her face, each riding electrical wires stretching between electrical poles. The modernity of it stands out in a mural cycle mostly depicting ancient Arcadian scenes. Herbert N. Casson, in *The History of the Telephone*, waxes positively lyrical about it:

> When Bell invented the telephone he surprised the world with a new idea. He had to make the thought as well as the thing. No Jules Verne or H. G. Wells had foreseen it. The author of the Arabian Nights fantasies had conceived of a flying carpet but neither he nor anyone else had conceived of flying communication....
>
> The telephone remains the acme of electrical marvels....Already, Puvis de Chavannes, in one of his superb panels in the Boston Library, has admitted the telephone and telegraph to the world of art.

What is significant to us here about this mural, a mural so strongly related to Copley Square and MIT, is that it seems to be an entirely unconscious tribute to both square and Institute in their earliest days, not solicited by either nor even understood as related to either by the muralist, who was apparently unfamiliar with the details of the history of the telephone. His description of what was in his mind while conceiving this mural never mentions it. This invention, developed in MIT's Copley Square laboratory and first introduced to the world at the Institute in Copley Square in 1874, is depicted for the first time in the history of art in the Boston Public Library mural, a telling reminder of one of early MIT's—and Copley Square's—first moments on the world stage.

Returning to Rogers's bold lead in aid of Darwin's epochal theory: it not only vitalized the primary scientific mission of the embryonic Institute but also affected its arts side, which from the beginning was hardly less important because of Harvard's deficiency in the arts (such was the senior institution's allegiance to classicism and theology). The appointment at MIT of a professor of architecture in 1865, and the initiation of the first courses offered in that artistic as well as mechanical subject a few years later, opened up a whole new world of study in this country.

Although Louis Sullivan's legacy—"form ever follows function"—has equaled Darwin's theory in its effect, dominating design generally in the twentieth century, Sullivan enjoys a much more limited fame among the public. Hence a long leap forward chronologically becomes necessary here—a digression, it may seem—until the "Pediment" portal (pp. 114–25).

Sullivan was a young student at MIT in 1872–73, and we have his word for it that the school taught him to draw and to draw well, if little else. But most importantly, it positioned him to confront the work of the first great American architect, H. H. Richardson, whose masterly new Brattle Square Church tower he could just see out the Rogers Building windows.

Louis Sullivan, the father of American modernist architecture and the only man Frank Lloyd Wright ever called master, learned most at MIT while gazing out the window at the rising architecture of H. H. Richardson, who became his hero. The Brattle Tower of what is now the First Baptist Church, across Clarendon Street from Trinity's Rectory, exerted a lifelong influence on Sullivan.

Sullivan's genius went unnoticed, so far as I can tell, in the corridors of the early architecture department. Today it is a different story. His famous pronouncement in "The Tall Building Artistically Considered" (*Lippincott's Magazine*, 1896), "form ever follows function," is the mantra and credo of the modern movement in architecture in the twentieth century. The words perhaps belong on some architrave in Copley Square. But Sullivan was not a God of Copley Square. Not in the sense that Rogers was, or Alexander Graham Bell, whose achievements endowed the New World Acropolis with such great distinction. Rogers immigrated from the American South to Boston, Sullivan from Boston to Chicago. Nevertheless, as with T. S. Eliot in the square's environs, the briefest time can be formative, and Sullivan's surely was. He is an excellent example of how Copley Square helped shape high modernity so very far afield that it has a good claim to have presided over the dawn of American modernism.

Sullivan became Richardson's man the moment he saw the Brattle Square Church tower, motifs from which, as well as from Trinity Church and Trinity Rectory,

This stairwell mural in the Boston Public Library celebrates the transmission of words over wires via telegraph and also the telephone after 1874 when Alexander Graham Bell first demonstrated the telephone at MIT in Copley Square in 1874.

kept appearing in his work for the rest of his life. He learned larger lessons as well. Indeed, insofar as the exterior is concerned, Sullivan's Anshe Ma'ariv Synagogue in Chicago, inspired by Trinity Church, is even better, to my mind: stronger in mass and bolder in form.

Nor is the Sullivan-Richardson connection the half of the tale of the history of modernism in America. Why does no one remember that Frank Lloyd Wright was Unitarian in heritage and outlook, absolutely in the Emersonian mode? Hence Unity Temple in Chicago of 1905, the grandfather of which, Joseph Siry suggested in the *Art Bulletin* in 1991, was James Freeman Clarke's Church of the Disciples in Boston's South End of 1868. And why does no one remember what was thankfully high-lighted recently in an exhibition sponsored by the MIT Museum, *Boston Grads Go to Chicago*? In the accompanying notes, the museum curators had this to say: "The initial core of what would become the Prairie School consisted of Frank Lloyd Wright and three MIT-trained friends who shared an office loft in Chicago's Steinway Hall, a core group soon joined by Walter Burley Griffin and Marion Mahony Griffin." The latter was also an MIT grad, and Wright's designer and chief renderer. It has been argued, I think correctly, that she was "the public face [i.e., the superb renderer] that helped Wright's work command attention throughout the world."

The MIT Museum exhibition also touched on the skyscraper, the aesthetic of which is identified with Sullivan. The curators point out, "Influential in the formation of the skyscraper aesthetic were [three architects, Richardson, William Le Baron Jenney, and Sullivan], each schooled in the Boston area." The reason why such facts often go unremembered is that when one is dealing with educational and "cultural cradles," or "mother cities," to use the town planning term, it is not sufficient to explore its "home game"—in this case what happened in Copley Square. One must follow the Louis Sullivans of the world to their destinations of achievement, and thus not lose track of the "away game," whether that be in the "near" away—one of Boston's satellite cities, like Worcester, Massachusetts, or Manchester, New Hampshire—or the "far" away, like Chicago.

In terms of early Boston modernist architecture, outstanding examples of both games are associated with a giant Boston firm, the United Shoe Company, whose splendid Art Deco skyscraper still stands in the city's downtown Financial District. Referring to the company's earlier factory in the North Shore suburb of Beverly, designed by Ernest Ransome in 1903–6, the critic Reyner Banham writes, "Even on the score of stylistic modernity…[this factory] is the match for anything built anywhere in the world at the time." Its "decorum and puritanism" seem to Banham very self-assured. It was restored and opened to the public in 1997. Le Corbusier visited MIT's architecture school in Copley Square and found it an abomination, but United Shoe's Beverly factory was an inspiration. Banham says, "Whereas for Gropius [such work was] simply [an] exemplar for a better modern industrial architecture, for Le Corbusier [that work] had become—like the Tempietto of Bramante—[an] exemplar for all architecture forever."

As an example of the "far" away game: the prime investor in the famous Fagus factory in Germany, which made Walter Gropius's reputation when he designed it in 1911, was the Boston shoe firm, and Banham suggests it was the "American connections" that supported the modern aesthetic for which Gropius is so celebrated. "It now seems likely," he says, that "the preferred flat-roofed silhouettes of the International Style derived to some significant degree from the fact [that] the American industrial buildings the [European modernists such as Le Corbusier and Gropius] knew from pictures had flat roofs."

All this highlights, of course, the role of investors and entrepreneurs, who must await another, perhaps equally interesting, exhibition. In our context here, the stars of that exhibition would undoubtedly be the brothers Peter and Shepherd Brooks, about whom the historian William H. Jordy predicted as long ago as 1972: "For those who take an overly provincial view of the Chicago achievement…how puzzling that two of the principal clients for Chicago commercial buildings were the Boston financiers Peter and Shepherd Brooks." Ada Louise Huxtable picked up this intriguing theme in *The New Criterion* in 1982, when she published a letter that Harvard professor John Coolidge had unearthed, which documented the Brooks brothers' direct involvement in design.

Meanwhile, *Kansas City Star* critic Donald Hoffman, in the first biography of the Chicago architect John Wellborn Root, completely reshaped scholarship in the matter. It turns out that the brothers, one of whom had made a special study of architecture, and both of whom lived within four blocks of Copley Square, were admirers of Richardson. "Plain massiveness is often most as effective," Peter Brooks wrote to his Chicago agent directing the architects working on the Monadnock Building, "as frequently and happily shown in Richardson's exteriors." Hoffman demonstrates time and again that "Brooks's concern about ornament [in the Monadnock Building] seems to have derived from aesthetic and functional considerations, rather than from consideration of cost." And the Monadnock Building's lack of ornament and smooth, flowing walls make it one of the seminal buildings in the development of modern architecture.

Before Harvard's art museum became a laboratory for art, MIT's architectural school was a laboratory for architecture.

Factory

Industrial Revolution,
Entrepreneurial Vistas

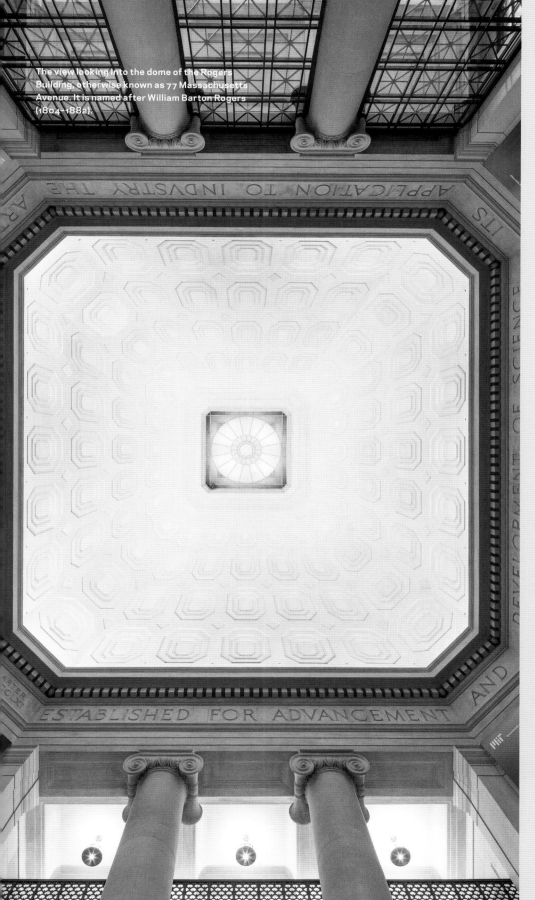

The view looking into the dome of the Rogers Building, otherwise known as 77 Massachusetts Avenue. It is named after William Barton Rogers (1804–1882).

Factory

Industrial Revolution, Entrepreneurial Vistas

Boston's age-old passion for education is what drew William Barton Rogers to the New England capital in 1853, but it's not what made his founding of MIT possible within eight years of his settling there. It was, rather, the way in which Boston's Brahmins were increasingly changing their ways at the time. They had introduced the Industrial Revolution to America and accumulated thereby huge fortunes, even greater than those of the China trade. But within only a few generations they were starting to repudiate that mercantile lifestyle, concentrating their city's resources more and more so as to consolidate its Athenian stature and further privilege education and culture. Never mind if this change in values meant ceding financial and media leadership to New York.

"History is about change," the Harvard historian Drew Gilpin Faust states, "and understanding how change happens, what leads people to embrace change, what leads people to reject change." Of all the periods in Boston's history, rarely is this more evident than the dynamic midcentury moment when Rogers and his wife, Emma Savage Rogers, settled in Boston.

The usual depiction of this period is that just as the Brahmins were retreating to a reluctant institutionalism in the face of surging immigrant politics, so were they losing financial clout to a booming, multiethnic New York. In reality, the terrain of the battlefield was very much otherwise. Quite a few historians—the more careful ones—have pointed out that in the early nineteenth century, even before the earliest of the immigrant waves, Boston's ruling class, politically Federalist and philosophically Unitarian, was already having difficulty (to repeat David Tyack's words) "translating their intellectual, social, and economic authority into political authority" in the face of the growing opposition of lower-class native Protestants, Yankees all. It was a difficulty their Puritan ancestors had also had.

The ceding to New York of financial leadership did have some clear economic benefits. There was clarity in the sorting out of New York, Boston, and Washington, D.C., as, respectively, the economic, intellectual, and political capitals of the country (soon to be joined by Los Angeles as the entertainment capital in the early twentieth century). But also, eventually, mostly *non-Boston* money was drawn into financing many Brahmin projects, including the building of a good deal of Boston's formidable new academic infrastructure in the twentieth century. For example, New York money—mostly J. P. Morgan's—built the first institution to depart the square in the early 1900s and expand elsewhere: Harvard Medical School, to Longwood. Another example would be MIT, whose new campus on the Charles River Basin would be paid for mostly by the du Ponts of Delaware and George Eastman of New York.

This reordering of resources has been misunderstood, many seeing Boston's financial decline in the early twentieth century as the result of a sudden failure of nerve or some kind of exhaustion. It's often said to have been reflected in archconservative "spendthrift trusts," for example, that did not encourage Boston money to risk much and tended, in the words of the historian Bainbridge Bunting, "to divorce business and the Brahmins" to such an extent that Boston lost one economic battle after another to New York.

Dartmouth College cultural geographer Mona Domosh has pointed out, however, that the battle was *not* chiefly between New Yorkers and Bostonians. Rather, it was between two different groups of Bostonians, both largely Yankee: on the one hand, the newer mercantile class drawn from the Yankee lower class and, on the other, the established Brahmin ruling class.

An important locale of the battle, moreover, was the Back Bay itself. As Domosh shows in her *Invented Cities*, the more aggressive, newer merchant class did agitate to compete more strenuously with New York by increasing, for instance, Boston's port capacities. It envisioned—imagine!—the Back Bay as a wet dock area after the model of Liverpool. We forget today what the Back Bay was the back bay *of*: Boston Harbor, which was not then separated from the Charles River by the turn-of-the-century dam that created the Charles River Basin.

But the Brahmins wanted nothing of Liverpool wet docks, not within sight of Beacon Street! "Their interest in improving their city," Domosh writes, "had shifted from economic to cultural improvement." Despite the fact that the Brahmin idea of a high-class residential and cultural Back Bay could be viewed, as its opponents pointed out, as likely to benefit only the few, they persisted in their cause, insisting on a grand new civic quarter of Parisian ambition, which would possess not only residential grandeur (Commonwealth Avenue) but institutional grandeur as well (Copley Square). Between what Domosh shows to be these "two distinct economic groups with different visions of the future of Boston," the Brahmins won.

What was going on is explained by Harvard historian Arthur M. Schlesinger Jr. more than a century later in a 1946 interview with Robert van Gilder in the *New York Times*. Schlesinger pointed to the historical "distinction, not wholly fictitious, between the aristocracy and the plutocracy; that is, between a ruling group which because of possession of land or some other long-settled status in the community, has some sense of social obligation, and a ruling group that is interested primarily in cash profit to the exclusion of other values." Crucially, Schlesinger continued, "the British ruling class has shown this capacity and I hope I am not sentimentalizing when I say that in a place such as Boston, members of the old ruling family group have value and some sense of the community as a whole."

Russell B. Adams documents in *The Boston Money Tree* what was Schlesinger's surmise, noting how this was reflected in changing Brahmin attitudes, which crystallized in the mid-nineteenth century. He describes the financier Henry Lee Higginson of the post–Civil War generation, for example, as "see[ing] Boston's attitudes toward the time-honored pursuit of wealth, *no matter how creditably conducted* [emphasis added], change from approbation to scorn." Charles Francis Adams's scorn for New York robber barons, who bested him in business dealings by tactics (he felt) he could not honorably counter, also comes to mind.

According to Paul Goodman in "Ethics and Enterprise: The Values of a Boston Elite, 1800–1860," these qualms were already surfacing even when Boston was at its economic height. "During the first half of the nineteenth century, as a group of Boston businessmen were transforming their region's economy, they were also elaborating a value system," Goodman writes. "Rejecting the single-minded pursuit of wealth, Bostonians claimed to prefer the balanced personality that tempered the quest for wealth with standards of gentlemanly decorum and the purifying influences of culture *and stewardship* [emphasis added]," all in the conviction that "by pursuing culture, the businessman might broaden his sympathies, refine his sensibilities, and *escape the moral dangers of a consuming thirst for gain* [emphasis again added]."

There is always another side to the story, but certainly two dispassionate foreign contemporaries and observers with very different perspectives—Alexis de Tocqueville and Charles Dickens—saw it this way already in the early to mid-nineteenth century. Tocqueville found Boston Brahmin manners "distinguished" and felt that because Bostonian "conversation turns on intellectual matters, one feels oneself delivered from those commercial habits and that financial spirit that render the society of New York so vulgar." Dickens more or less agreed, adding the famous remark in his survey of American cities that in Boston "the almighty dollar sinks into something comparatively insignificant amidst a whole pantheon of better gods."

The results of such qualms? Witness Henry Lee Higginson, who "at the peak of his business career" judged "material success as a corrupter of his generation," writing in 1878 to his literary cousin Thomas Wentworth Higginson. This is according to historian Adams. He concluded, despairingly, "I have become a money-getter." What Thomas did for literature, however—namely, discovering the poet Emily Dickinson—Henry did for music by founding the Boston Symphony, an achievement that even the New York musicologist Joseph Horowitz, who so misunderstands the Brahmin psyche, admits made Henry "a colossus, an American hero." And so was Rogers, for founding MIT. The reassertion here of Puritan ancestral values, which Rogers certainly bought into, is clear. I repeat Domosh's assertion—"The Boston elite developed an ideology that commercial pursuits were moral only if they contributed to cultural pursuits"—and include her droll addendum that it did not hurt that "through the channels of culture the [Boston] elite were able to express their distaste for the new industrialists."

Boston's ruling caste—ever global, which meant, first, national, in its interests—had its sights on bigger prizes than the inevitably entirely local prizes of immigrant politicians. The historian Peter Dobkin Hall argued in "Learning to Be Civic," "President Eliot's educational vision incorporated important elements of Unitarian and Emersonian ideas about character development, while continuing to embrace centralizing metropolitan conceptions of leadership." Eliot's goals were characteristic in being quite far-ranging. There was in Brahmin institutionalism a national and then an international dimension, as one might have expected, more than a local one. Boston-centric global studies were never more evident. Writes Hall:

Harvard's conception of leadership [under Eliot] was based on the idea of expanding Boston's national influence through its economic and cultural institutions, and doing so by recruiting the best and the brightest…who, imbued with the values of the emergent Brahminate, could be entrusted with the task of creating a national institutional culture on Boston terms. Within the framework of Eliot's "new education" [the *Atlantic Monthly* article defending Rogers's concept at MIT], Harvard's curriculum became a mechanism for leading students to discover specialized callings.…Combining the highest level of expertise with the highest values of public service, the university's graduates, as Eliot's protégé, Herbert Croly (Class of 1889) would put it forty years later, [were too] "perfect themselves as instruments for the fulfillment of the American national promise."

It was, so to speak, a charter for the American century, one President Eliot would lecture the brother of the German Kaiser about in his speech of welcome in Boston during that prince's visit to the United States in 1902.

From today's perspective, one can see Eliot's point of view more clearly in his suggestion that Boston's more liberal aristocrats would outlast the imperial Hohenzollerns. And while he was only somewhat right about that, even Bunting's "arch-conservative" and risk-hampering family trusts turned out to be rather vision- ary. James C. O'Connell remarks in *The Hub's Metropolis*, "Boston's specialization in money management"—that's what we call it now—"originated with the conservative family trusts and evolved into the mutual fund, the pension fund, and insurance industries and the rise of Fidelity, Putnam Investments, State Street Corporation, Liberty Mutual, and John Hancock." The historian Walter Muir Whitehill went so far as to assert that "the blending of scholars with an endlessly renewable supply of literate and responsible trustees and treasurers has done more than anything else to make Boston a center of civilization."

Rogers knew that—his father-in-law was a leading Brahmin banker—and that may have been one reason why he did not mistake the maturing and ripening of Boston for any overall decline in civic vitality. He saw it, rather, as a deliberate if gradual shift in direction. After all, from the beginning of the nineteenth century, advancing apace with industrialism of the Boston area, was an equally distinctive sense of what we would call today progressivism, or liberalism. We do not see the connection now—though Dickens did then—as clearly as we should, because in obscuring Brahmins we also obscure Brahmin liberalism.

But a later MIT president, Susan Hockfield, saw that portal plainly enough. In her speech marking the 150th anniversary of MIT's founding, she pointed out that for Rogers the reason "all roads led to Boston" was twofold. First, Brahmins, confident enough by then in their industrial success, were able to afford a shift to institutionalism given that the city had become the American industrial engine. In *Cities in Civilization*, for example, Sir Peter Geoffrey Hall focuses on the six pioneer- ing capitals of the Industrial Revolution. "The stories of Manchester, Birmingham, and Glasgow on one side of the Atlantic," he writes, "are paralleled by those of Boston, Pittsburgh, and Chicago on the other side," putting Bostonians in perhaps

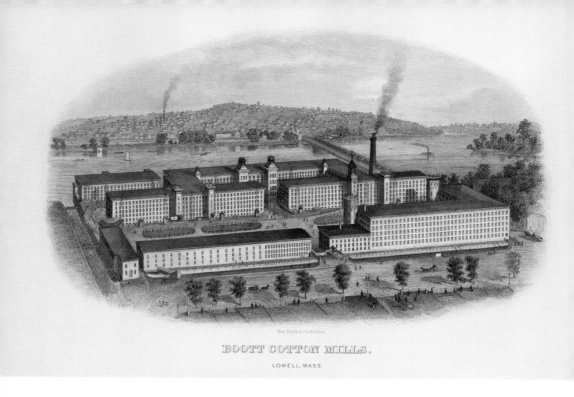

BOOTT COTTON MILLS.

LOWELL, MASS

Just as Cambridge was "Academic Boston" and Brookline "Horticultural Boston," Lowell was "Industrial Boston" and eventually the centerpiece of the American Industrial Revolution, launched at the beginning of the nineteenth century by the Boston Associates. As much as Boston's liberalism, this drew William Barton Rogers to the New England capital.

less refined company than they like to keep, historically. It's the reason why Boston built the satellite city of Lowell at some remove from core Boston, textile mills being no more welcome than wet docks in the heart of town. Calling Manchester, England, "the first and greatest industrial city of the world," Hall pairs it with what American city? Boston, of course, though you will never hear the Athens of America described among Americans as the Manchester of America.

Yet how can we overlook something so important? The historian Dan Yaeger wrote in 2010 in *Harvard Magazine*: "Few individuals have influenced economic history as did Francis Cabot Lowell....Born as American colonists struggled for political independence, he helped lay the groundwork for the new country's economic independence with his idea for an integrated textile mill. That concept eventually transformed the United States into a world trading power and put into play forces of technological innovation that continue today." Lowell, a keen observer, missed nothing on a carefully planned tour of Britain. Back in Boston he hired an engineer, Paul Moody, who, "with Lowell making the complex calculations," re-created the necessary machinery to establish what Yaeger calls "the first fully integrated mill in the world." Lowell himself "possessed a combination of ability, ambition, wealth, connections, and risk-taking that would come to define later generations of American entrepreneurs. Like Edison, Ford, and Gates, Lowell not only created products, he created a market where none existed."

Moreover, as a Boston Brahmin, he consolidated what would become a unique aspect of such an aristocracy, showing that the clerical and academic priorities of the Boston elite could be combined with more worldly skills. "He helped inaugurate a culture of innovation," Yaeger writes, "that has driven the world economy ever since."

Hockfield emphasized the importance of all this to MIT when she recounted in her speech that "by 1840, Boston's satellite cities contained the greatest concentration of American workers in the nation," stressing equally that Francis Lowell's textile city was also a direct attempt to reform the English factory city town. Dickens had seen this too. (Yes, the attempt foundered in greed soon enough. But is that more important than that it was made in the first place? And where else was such an attempt made?) That was the second reason why "all roads led to Boston" for Rogers: the region's increasing liberalism. Hockfield cites as evidence of this William Lloyd Garrison's antislavery agitation, Margaret Fuller's publication in Boston of "the first major feminist work in the United States," and Horace Mann's championing of the public school.

It surfaced in both the Patriots and the Puritans before them, this liberalism, and perhaps it was one of the reasons why Puritans and Brahmins had that difficulty with politics. Certainly it was easier to sustain at Harvard. The historian of science Edward J. Pfeifer traces it all the way back to the mid-1660s with the "American [which is to say Puritan] acceptance of new scientific thought—for example, Galileo's at seventeenth-century Harvard." It was only a handful of generations from the sixteenth-century scientific revolution of Galileo, Copernicus, Newton, and so on (John Harvard was a contemporary of and may have known William Shakespeare) and the discovery of the scientific method, to the emergence of the fields of chemistry, biology, and engineering, and what Justin Ervin and Zachary A. Smith calls "the most important social transformation in human history, the Industrial Revolution."

That revolution, led by the American Manchester, arrived on the eve of MIT's conception and founding. Ervin and Smith add, in connection, "Technology is and always has been the central catalyst making globalization possible." Boston's leadership in the Industrial Revolution certainly fueled the city's liberalism, and it would be hard to say which was more attractive to Rogers.

Brahmin liberalism was a very aristocratic liberalism. As was that of the first, more liberal Puritan—yes, liberal Puritan—congregation of Boston's Brattle Street Church. Its members in the late eighteenth century included Patriot-becoming-Brahmin descendants of the Puritans, such as John Adams and John Hancock—conservative both, but revolutionary enough. Rogers, of a little later generation (recall his father's connection with Jefferson) was of a similar ilk. However slow MIT was to admit women in his day, when he apparently felt forced to compromise its integrity by the need to placate businessmen donors who tilted conservative, by the 1890s the Institute seems to have been more welcoming by far to African Americans, although records are very rudimentary indeed in this respect.

Two aspects of the African American experience are particularly important. First, his abhorrence of slavery was a key reason why Rogers migrated from the

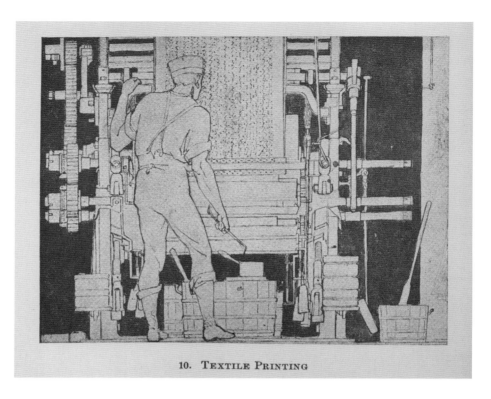

10. TEXTILE PRINTING

If the Lowellian phase of the Brahmin Ascendancy in Boston attracted Rogers as much as the mid-century Emersonian phase, it was the final Eliotic phase of which MIT was so conspicuous an ornament. The murals by Paul Nefflen in Huntington Hall date from the Eliotic period but celebrate the Lowellian period. This mural was entitled *Textiles*.

American South to New England. Second, the racist repute of Boston in recent decades is the result of racial and ethnic tensions of the late twentieth century that played out in the busing controversy entirely within the working-class neighborhoods of the small core city of Boston, as distinct from the real Boston, the huge metropolis of city and satellite cities and suburbs, which were arbitrarily spared the social disruption because of the accident that they are politically—but not socially, economically, or culturally—independent. At early MIT, during the time of the Boston Brahmin Ascendancy in the middle and late nineteenth century, Boston was very much at the heart of the movement for the abolition of slavery. As such, it was a beacon for African Americans everywhere.

That said, it was not until after Rogers's death—and twenty-five years after Lincoln signed the Emancipation Proclamation (earning him the "impassioned support" of MIT's founder, according to Philip Alexander)—that, so far as is known, the first African American student, Robert R. Taylor, enrolled at MIT. The president at the time, Francis Walker, counted among his many strengths (the very conspicuous weakness) that he was a flagrant racist. Nevertheless, Taylor did very well at the

Institute. At a time when seven hours of classes a day for four years was required to earn the MIT architecture degree, Taylor, "by his own account," in the words of Ellen Weiss in her biography of him, was "the first or among the first colored graduates" of the Institute. According to the author of the book's introduction, Henry Louis Gates Jr., Taylor was "the first professionally educated black architect in the United States" and "at or near the top of his class." Taylor was the product of a relatively privileged background—his father was a builder—and lived on Beacon Hill in the African American quarter on the North Slope, and later in the South End and in Bay Village. He won a scholarship for his last two years.

The cosmopolitan scene in Copley Square certainly would have helped to make Taylor feel somewhat less conspicuous than might have been the case else-where. The grand hotels, for instance, and the long-distance deluxe trains boarded at Back Bay Station were totally staffed by African Americans, who lived along prosperous stretches of nearby Columbus Avenue in the South End, or were butlers in the town houses of Commonwealth Avenue, all jobs then highly prized in the African American community. One prominent African American family, that of Judge George Lewis Ruffin, regularly attended Trinity Church and sang in the choir. Weiss notes in her biography of Taylor:

> Race may have been less of an issue at MIT than elsewhere because of the many international students. One year near Taylor's class included young men from Brazil, Bulgaria, Canada, France, Guatemala, Hawaii, Japan, Mexico, Panama, Peru, Puerto Rico, Trinidad, and Turkey.... As a student in the colorful class of 1888 put it, failing to fine-tune categories to the absolutes that effective racism requires, "Sixty-seven percent were light-complexioned, thirty percent dark. Eleven percent wore eyeglasses; one was color blind; and fifty percent thought they had mustaches."

While at MIT, Taylor made the acquaintance of Booker T. Washington, the charismatic African American leader and founder of the Tuskegee Institute (now Tuskegee University) in Alabama. Washington visited Boston twice, where he was made more than welcome in Brahmin town houses and his cause generously sup-ported. Washington was impressed with the young MIT student, it would seem, and Taylor was promptly recruited.

Tuskegee was itself an example of MIT's growing national influence, and Taylor's career there would be another. He spent virtually all his life on the faculty and as architect to the institute, designing many buildings. Proud of his MIT degree, Taylor returned to Boston in 1911 to speak at the Institute's fiftieth anniversary celebrations. And MIT returned the regard. According to Philip Alexander, the one place where Emma Savage Rogers (Rogers's wife) allowed herself to take up a prominent public role was in her support of the Tuskegee Institute.

MIT's first African American graduate, in 1888, was probably Robert Taylor, who was certainly the first professionally trained black American architect, shown here in class.

Keystone

MIT's Cofounder: Emma Savage
Rogers's Passion for Science

The support of the über-Brahmin Savage family that Rogers married into was key to MIT's founding. This family group shows William Barton Rogers and his wife, Emma Savage, standing behind Emma's father, James Savage, a wealthy Boston educational reformer, and his son, James Savage Jr., a casualty of the Civil War.

Keystone

MIT's Cofounder: Emma Savage Rogers's Passion for Science

Every women's room at MIT has historical significance. The first such facility at MIT, created in 1882, was the determining factor in a great controversy. In that year, the Institute decided to install women's "toilet rooms" in the newly erected Walker Building. This was the direct result of a plot by many of Boston's most blue-blooded figures, presided over by Emma Savage Rogers, wife of William Barton Rogers.

Rogers's Bostonian wife and in-laws represented, A. J. Angulo tells us, "the reformist spirit Rogers longed to see in the South. Among Boston's Brahmins they were known for their hatred of intolerance and bigotry and for helping to initiate the state's first public system of primary education." A statement of fact, merely, yet it marks a rather more positive note than has been usual among MIT chroniclers in dealing with the Savage family. Why has the Institute's first First Lady, never mind her father, not been taken more seriously by MIT's own chroniclers?

For example, the author of what is by far the best of the recent crop of MIT histories, *A Widening Sphere*, is content to describe the Savage family as "members of Boston's creamiest social elite"—whatever *that* means—thus greatly obscuring the "social, political and financial network that promised to give [Rogers's] educational plans a lift." More like any hope at all! Emma Savage Rogers, moreover, is hardly given her due. "Emma's life," we are told, "revolved around her three men." She was "their constant companion and looked after their every need with the help of an entourage of retainers." She is said to have been of "a type of New England womanhood" combining common sense, charm, and tact, who "used her winning ways to balance the clashing temperaments of her men folk." Of her intellectual capacity or mental force, or her educational or leadership capabilities, nothing is said, really. Nor is there any discussion at all of the fact that she was clearly identified by contemporaries as a "star" of perhaps the most radical educational experiment of the Anglo-American world of her time—an experiment not without significance to Rogers's own at MIT. This profile of her is as problematic as the placement of her portrait: near a distinctly downplayed private dining room that bears her name in the third-floor corridor of the building in which her husband's bronze visage is to be found in the first-floor lobby. It is all very distorting.

Better to read MIT biologist William T. Sedgwick's obituary in the *Boston Evening Transcript*: "Mrs. Rogers was herself the maker of the Institute." After the marriage in 1849 of Rogers into the very progressive and wealthy Savage clan, it was "the leisure which was now his [that] gave Professor Rogers time to develop and carry out the plan...[of] the Massachusetts Institute of Technology." Sedgwick asserts that "from her father [Emma] inherited a strong and original mind and a profound love of accurate scholarship" and with "her distinguished husband shared a veneration for science which amounted almost to a passion." It was, in other words, a coequal and formidable partnership.

Another clue that Savage was very much her own person, quite independent of her husband and as well a vigorous adviser in what became their life's work together: in *William Barton Rogers and the Idea of MIT*, Angulo conveys the startling intelligence that after her marriage, "archival documents suggest that Emma Rogers continued to use her maiden name," prompting him to the very pointed move of following suit: "I refer to her as Emma Savage in this study," he writes.

Convention in a rigidly conventional age seems to have compromised her attempt at independence, forcing her into compliance with conservative custom often enough—a problem that Lucy Stone, the well-known suffragist and abolitionist, and the first woman to retain her maiden name after marriage, contended with all her life. One decision in particular, reflected in my own research, seems to document Savage's preference: her gravestone. On it appears in bold capital letters "EMMA SAVAGE," and then under it, in upper- and lowercase letters, proudly but secondarily, "Wife of William Barton Rogers." Her name does not appear on the title page of her husband's *Life and Letters*. Instead, the title page reads, "edited by his wife."

Savage was actually a character more out of *Little Women* than *Carmen*. As Richard Francis points out in *Fruitlands: The Alcott Farm and the Search for Utopia*, at least one vignette in Louisa May Alcott's classic is known to have been drawn from Savage's own life experience. Alcott and Savage were girlhood friends and did not lose track of each other, as attested by letters from thirty years later, in Alcott collections both in Harvard's Houghton Library and at Brigham Young University. "Rather touchingly," Francis writes, *Little Women* has "Marmee bundling up used clothing…just as Mrs. Savage [that would be Emma's mother, Elizabeth Otis Savage] had for the Alcotts themselves" in a low time.

Madeleine B. Stern, in her *Life of Margaret Fuller*, opens with this telling window into Savage's youth at Bronson Alcott's Temple School, the radical educational experiment that was so formative in her life:

> Having contemplated spirit in the conscience of Infinite Being, the children [of the Temple School] trooped out toward [Boston] Common to contemplate spirit in external nature. Margaret [Fuller] and [Bronson] Alcott walked with them during their recreation. Sometimes five-year-old Louisa May Alcott could be seen dashing around the Frog Pond.…Though Louisa had once announced that she loved everybody in the whole world, she was more interested in fun than in her father's explanations of Eastern philosophy, which he intoned as he stood with little Emma Savage before the ginkgo tree.

The image is striking. It is *the* decisive image, I think, of Savage's life, and important, too, for the history of MIT. We have, furthermore, among the "rare and valuable sources" (in the words of Stephanie Kermes, BU professor of social science), Emma's own school journal, which reveals the "high level of education and freedom to develop their own opinions" that Emma and her fellow pupils were given.

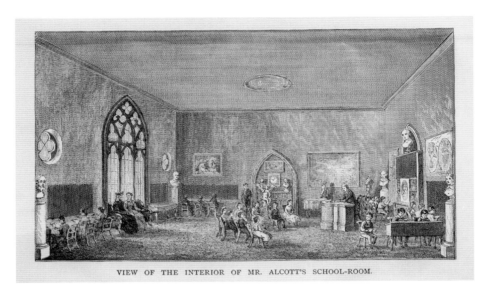

VIEW OF THE INTERIOR OF MR. ALCOTT'S SCHOOL-ROOM.

Emma Savage Rogers, arguably MIT's cofounder, was a star of Boston's Temple School, founded and operated by Bronson Allcot, Emerson's friend. The Temple School, which took its name from Temple Street in Boston, was perhaps the most radical educational experiment of its day in the Anglo-American world.

According to Kermes, it also shows how "Savage managed difficult declinations in Latin," for instance, how she "learned details about functions of human body parts"; how she "read broadly"; how, indeed, she was a star at Alcott's school, so much so that in later years "her teacher took this volume with him when he went to England in 1842, inscribing young Emma's book to a disciple there as a guide to founding an English version of Temple School."

Yet another clue that more was going on here than many have thought is that Rogers's future wife comes up at all in a biography of Margaret Fuller. Fuller wrote a pioneering feminist book that MIT's first woman president, Susan Hockfield, cited as one of the exciting elements of Boston life that attracted Rogers to the city in the first place. No wonder Savage all her life "had very positive opinions and expressed them freely and with vigor," according to James Munroe, another MIT observer whose take on Savage is more positive, in *Technology Review*.

Bronson Alcott's Temple School was revolutionary, its influence felt on both sides of the Atlantic Ocean. On Rogers's concept and establishment of so radically new a school as MIT, we can certainly surmise the effect of his wife and chief adviser having been a leading participant in Alcott's school. Certainly Rogers's theory at MIT—that education should be more laboratory based than lecture or recitation based—had much in common with Alcott's theory (which Savage took up so enthusiastically at Temple School) that education should be more conversation based than lecture or recitation based. It is likely that William Barton Rogers knew Bronson Alcott. In the Alcott papers in Houghton Library at least one letter has survived from

MIT's founder to the Temple School's founder. It was a very close and select circle in which both men moved. Consider this account by Thomas Glick in his book *What About Darwin?*:

> On January 1, 1860, Charles Loring Brace [who was visiting Asa Gray] borrowed Gray's copy [of Darwin's book] and took it to Concord where he dined with Franklin Sanborn, along with Henry David Thoreau and Bronson Alcott, and their conversation focused on Darwin and his book. Thoreau was so excited that he obtained a copy and took pages of notes. On January 2nd, 1860, William Barton Rogers told his brother he was looking into Darwin's argument.

Temple School was on the cutting edge so consistently that it reflects hugely on the Savage family that young Emma was enrolled there in the first place. Indeed, according to Bruce Ronda's biography of Elizabeth Palmer Peabody—she of America's first kindergarten, who also taught for Alcott before Fuller—the Savages were among the first to patronize the school, Emma being among the first eighteen students to open the school. The school was most notorious for Alcott's publication of his *Conversations with Children on the Gospel*, full as it is of discussions of Jesus's divinity—or not—and whether or not his miracles were literally true. Robert D. Richardson, in his Ralph Waldo Emerson biography, allows that this still-famous book of Alcott's "suggests something of the originality, courage, and brilliance of the man Emerson consistently admired." Emerson even wrote a public letter defending the controversial book.

So did Savage's father. Odell Shepard makes this clear in *Pedlar's Progress*, his 1937 biography of Bronson Alcott, where he writes: "Not all the comments upon Alcott's book, by any means, were adverse. There came comforting letters from the mother of Josiah Quincy and from the famous and influential fathers of Lemuel Shaw and Emma Savage." It is also significant that the Savage family's commitment to Alcott persisted even after his decision—which led to the school's closing—to admit an African American student. In *Fruitlands*, Richard Francis offers an anecdote that is also an example of "parents [who] still remained loyal," specifically Mrs. Savage.

Does all this mean Emma Savage Rogers was, possibly, a radical feminist? We will almost certainly never know. Little record remains of her opinions, as is so often the case with public figures involved in institution building, who are constrained by the sort of self-censorship that Savage visited—alas, from the scholar's point of view—on her and her husband's published correspondence. She was not Julia Ward Howe, a close friend of the couple who famously embarrassed them (which is not to say surprised or blindsided them) with her loud public protests about MIT's slowness to admit women. Did Savage disapprove? Suffice to say, as did Alice Howell in 1991 in her abridgment of Alcott's *Conversations*, that at Temple School already at the age of twelve, Savage was "revered by her peers for her virtue and wisdom."

Savage's prominent involvement in perhaps the most controversial episode in American educational history was by no means forgotten during her lifetime,

The letter from Ellen Swallow Richards to Emma Savage Rogers seeking her aid in a project to raise funds for women's toilet rooms at MIT. The letter was answered by William Barton Rogers on the reverse in the affirmative.

right up to and during her tenure as MIT's First Lady. So famously had Savage and one other—it is not clear who—extolled the Temple School that the two girls were apparently widely known as "talking pupils." In his *Recollections of Seventy Years*, published in Savage's lifetime, the journalist and philanthropist F. B. Sanborn makes mention of "the famous talking pupils of Mr. Alcott's at the Temple School, one of whom, Mrs. Rogers, survives as a leader of society in [Boston]."

Thus, while the silence of the wife of MIT's founder about virtually every great issue of the day, including all the women's issues, could conceivably be interpreted as suggesting that she was oblivious to them, her radical family background and education lead one to doubt that was the case. Consider this letter of April 24, 1882, from Ellen Swallow Richards, MIT's first woman graduate and the founder of its pioneering Women's Laboratory, to Savage, published here for the first time. In every walking tour in the second part of this book, whenever the visitor passes a women's restroom at MIT, he or she should remember perhaps the only time plumbing was ever expressly fund-raised for in Copley Square, a subject neither Richards nor Savage disdained in order to advance their cause:

The question of space in the new building for the suitable accommodation of women has been weighing on my mind....After consulting with General Walker—Miss Crocker, Miss Abby May, Miss Florence Cushing, and myself have undertaken to approach certain women with the plan of raising...perhaps eight or ten thousand dollars...that [the Corporation] may feel justified in including in the plans of the new building suitable toilet rooms in connection with each of the laboratories and...a reception room which shall be for the use of the women only.

   If this can be done the Institute may say that it is in a condition to receive women students and the three new courses General Walker has laid out will attract many good students. Several are now planning to come here from the Latin School instead of going to college....Miss Crocker mentioned the matter to Miss Quincy Shaw incidentally the other day and she received a check for five hundred dollars the next morning....We thus hope to have a good start before the May meeting of the Women's Education Association, and we should depend upon them a good deal. Now if Professor Rogers...will be willing to write to one of us stating his approval, in order that we may answer inquiries as to his opinion...

Richards, this letter's author, although celebrated today, didn't have an easy time of it at the Institute. Rogers, personally sympathetic to women's education, was constrained by MIT's financial dependence on a donor base that was by no means totally of a similar mind. As Philip Alexander points out:

From the moment she arrived, Swallow [Richards] was nudged aside...."I was shut up," she recalled, "in the Professor's private laboratory very much as a dangerous animal might have been....I was not allowed to attend classes." She steered clear of conflict, aware that any misstep might not only ruin her own chances but set back prospects for other women....She [kept] close at hand...needles and thread and scissors. The strategy worked for her. She graduated in 1873.

With how much of her dignity intact we may wonder, but her ability to keep her eyes on the prize compels admiration. Womanly attention to the men in her life was not Richards's only strategy. She went on to a distinguished professional career, which led to the first national water quality standards.

   Richards's letter to Savage above is a letter between confidantes, even conspirators. And it equally documents the strategy of MIT's first First Lady. Its subject, really, is women in science in the early 1880s. In the same decade, Harvard Medical School, the other scientific bastion of Copley Square, despite Dean Holmes's best efforts, rejected the idea of admitting women, a decision it did not reverse until the 1940s.

   The letter also says something about Savage's views of coeducation. The cast of characters is significant. If one never hears today of Savage's activities, one is forever hearing of her friends' activities. "Miss Crocker," twice mentioned, was

Lucretia Crocker, a graduate of the first American teachers' college, later to teach for Horace Mann at Antioch College, and who taught botany and mathematics at the Newbury Street School. Crocker also headed the science department of the Society to Encourage Study at Home, the "Silent University," as it was called. Founded by Anna Eliot Ticknor, a Harvard faculty daughter who was also a founder of the Boston Public Library, this "network of women teaching women by mail," according to the historian Harriet Bergman, was a "groundbreaking scheme" in which "correspondent-educators" included not only Crocker but also Elizabeth Cary Agassiz, later the founder of Radcliffe College. "Miss Quincy Shaw" was Pauline Quincy Shaw, Boston's foremost Brahmin woman philanthropist, who supported the first American kindergarten of Elizabeth Peabody as well as day nurseries for working mothers.

But nothing discloses more clearly the influence of the Brahmin/Unitarian "do-gooder" network at MIT, or the way Harvard and MIT at a deeper level were always more partners than rivals, than the way influential activists in this area at the two schools worked hand in glove. At the beginning of every annual report of the Women's Education Association of Boston mentioned in the letter—like most Brahmin groups it was a very hardheaded, issues-oriented organization—were two headings. The first heading read "Object," which was very clearly stated: "to promote the better education of women." Then there was the second heading, "Results," followed by a long list, always led off by the same first two items: the administration of the "Harvard Examinations" that were the vehicle whereby the Harvard Annex, before it became Radcliffe College, made it possible for women to receive a Harvard education, and second, the establishment at MIT of the Women's Laboratory by Richards.

Subsequent scholarship has confirmed the importance of the Women's Education Association. Barbara Miller Solomon wrote in her 1986 study *In the Company of Educated Women: A History of Women and Higher Education in America*, "In response to increasing pressure from women's groups like the Women's Education Association of Boston, the Harvard Corporation offered examinations to women graded by Harvard professors." We know from her memorial minute in the association's report of 1912 that Savage's "interest in it began in its very earliest years" (the group was founded in 1872).

"Mrs. Rogers's strong, well-trained mind and her native liberality of purpose" —notice how differently she is described in such contemporary reporting than in retrospect by so many MIT chroniclers—"were deepened by her participation in her husband's loving labor in the founding and development of the Massachusetts Institute of Technology," the minute affirms, adding (if anything more were needed to read insightfully between the lines) that "the power" Savage exercised in Boston was felt both "directly and through the wide influence she exerted." Four character traits seemed to her obituary writer to stand out: "kind and true" she certainly was, but also "strong" and "fearless."

Richards's letter to Savage also shows how things were done at the highest level at MIT in the earliest days. It is a letter not to the president of the Institute but to his wife, not only assuming her support in a highly controversial issue but also asking her to secure a note of approval from President Rogers. Which, by the way, was promptly forthcoming and very clear. Rogers himself responded by "wish[ing] to assure you that I most heartily favor the purpose of including in our new building the special accommodations for the use of women to which you refer, i.e., the toilet rooms." The reply is written on the back of Richards's letter.

Now, women at early MIT is a subject all its own, of course. One could speak of Marion Mahony Griffin (Frank Lloyd Wright's public face) or biologist Katharine Dexter McCormick (a 1904 MIT graduate who funded the long years of research needed to finally yield "the pill") or indeed Richards. ("The question is to be solved," Richards wrote boldly: "Have women the mental capacity for scientific work?") Nevertheless, one begins to understand the role of women at MIT.

President Richard Maclaurin commented at the unveiling of the portrait of MIT's first First Lady in 1912: "Those who know the inner history of the Institute's foundation realize that but for Mrs. Rogers it would probably never have been, and those who have followed its later development appreciate to what an extent its up-building was due to her inspiration."

In this as in so many of her convictions, Savage was very much her father's daughter. And if the daughter has been rather downplayed in most readings of MIT history, the father has been positively obscured, despite the fact that but for him too, MIT probably would never have been. Ask about James Savage today, and you will be told that he was an important Boston leader, but not an über–Boston Brahmin. Savage was the third person elected, for example, by the fourteen original members of the Anthology Society, which started the Boston Athenaeum, a foundational institution of the Brahmin Ascendancy in its earliest era. You might be told that James Savage was an eminent genealogist, but it somehow never registers that as such, he played a role in Brahmin Boston something like that of a vestal virgin of ancient Rome. His was a sacred office, one frequently referred to as a "pious craft" in a society that took very seriously indeed the descent and pedigree of its members.

You will also be told that James Savage was one of a group of capitalists who started the first chartered savings bank in the United States. But no mention will be made of the fact that while he did not found his bank to *lose* money, it was not primarily to *make* money, either; James Savage and his cofounders were all "do-gooder" Unitarian Brahmins who had studied the new banking idea in England and thought savings banks would enable the less fortunate classes of society to better themselves.

Finally, James Savage is usually identified as an important politician—a legislator, a member of the Governor's Council and of the Boston School Committee. That he was a leading progressive, however, and indeed a major reformer—an *educational* reformer, like Bronson Alcott—hardly comes up at all, despite the fact that once one knows this, its relevance to Rogers is evident. The Rogers-Savage marriage was as much an ideological alliance as a devoted partnership. When Angulo notes that "[Rogers] praised the quality of public education in the Boston area, claiming that many graduates of the public system would benefit from further study at the proposed MIT," he was referring exactly to James Savage's work as an educational reformer.

One must be careful here to avoid confusing our own attitudes and definitions with those of past generations. "The problem of anachronism," Bernard Bailyn has written, of "whether or not one's present views are read back into the past, and, therefore, whether the past is distorted, foreshortened," is ever with us. And his example is pertinent to James Savage. "Free education" in the eighteenth century meant something very different (that the school was open to members of all religions) from what it meant later (that there were no fees). Still, although history as progress is always a simplistic reading, it is possible to identify in the values of one generation earlier chapters, so to speak, of values that emerge more fully developed in later generations. Such is the case between James Savage, born in 1784, and Rogers, born a generation later in 1804.

The facts are that in 1818, "even in the face of a determined effort by a majority of the respectable people of Boston to prevent it, [a] Boston town meeting voted that primary schools should be established," according to B. A. Hinsdale's *Horace Mann and the Common School Revival in the United States.* James Savage's Massachusetts Historical Society biographer adds to the tale the fact that "in 1818 [James Savage] and Elisha Ticknor drew up a petition [favoring such schools] and to their efforts was due the large number of eminent and influential men who signed it.…[T]he report was adopted…and the Primary Schools were established."

James Savage was "for many years," his biographer adds, "secretary of the Board." More than a half century later in his *Boston Globe* obituary of 1873, he was hailed as "a founder of our primary school system." Similarly, he was recognized as chair of the Massachusetts legislators' Educational Committee, in which role he played a key part in creating the American state teachers' college. We know something of the beliefs that drove this "upright, single-hearted" man, whom Emerson praised so highly in his journal as "incapable of fear or favor," who "understood the need for such schools by pointing out that a constantly increasing foreign immigration…was swelling the size of this class of children," according to Stanley Schultz in *The Culture Factory.* MIT's diversities had, surely, another moving spirit in addition to Rogers. Schultz emphasizes those who "claimed the rights of the poor to an equal education with the rich," recounting that during those years, "egalitarian arguments became almost daily fare in the press. Most eloquent among these appeals was a statement signed 'Many' which appeared in the *Boston Daily Advertiser,* on April 21st, 1818." He continues:

> "Many" was the pseudonym of James Savage, a Boston lawyer. Savage had already demonstrated his sense of public responsibility in a variety of offices. After a visit to

The striking Arts and Crafts tile pavement of the William and Emma Rogers house on Marlborough Street.

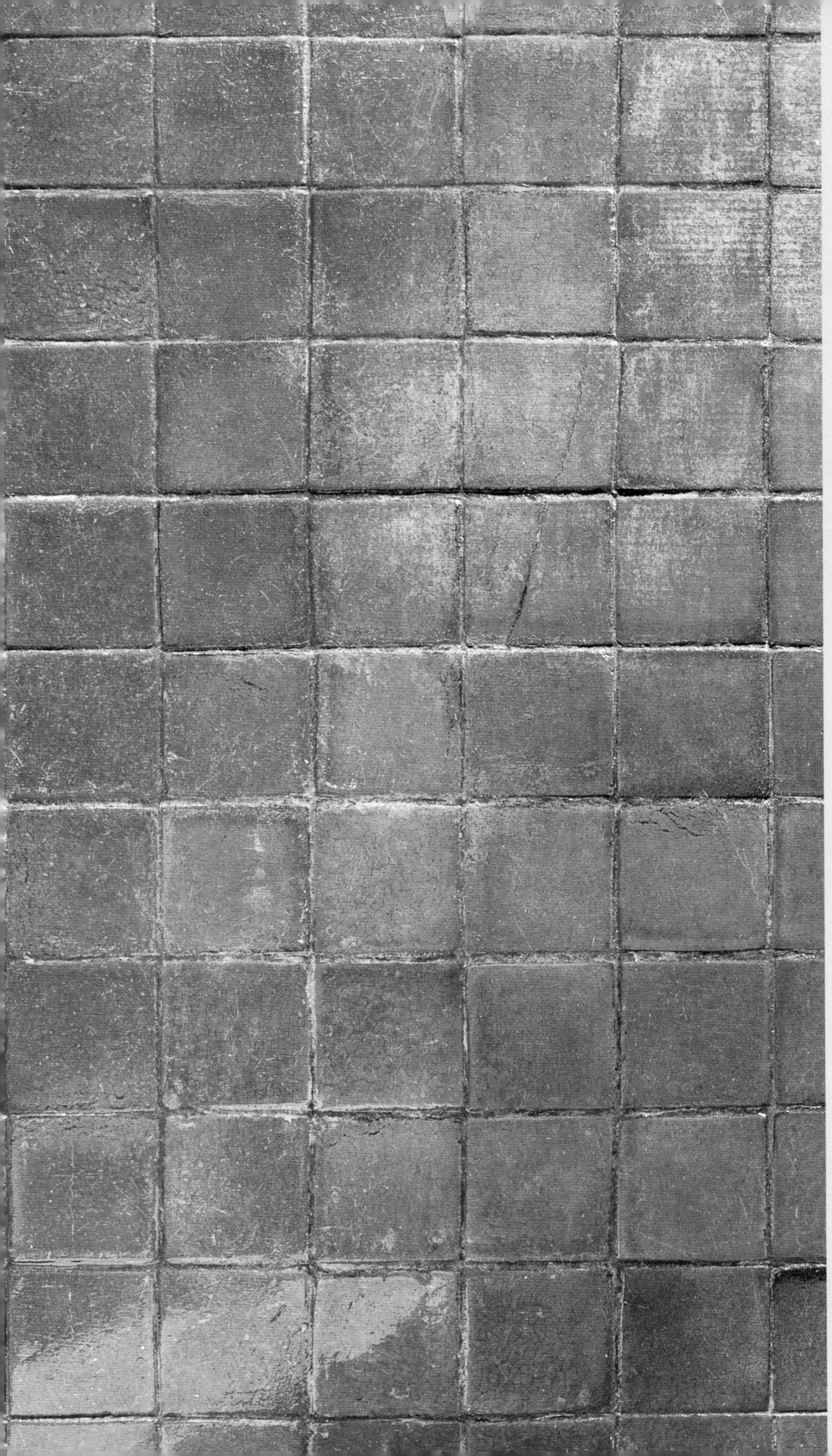

England where he had learned about a London savings bank, he had attempted to provide a similar institution for Boston....The institution was designed in part to encourage savings among the poor. As to education, Savage remarked in a discussion on the subject that the common schools were the children of religion and must serve their mother.

Interestingly, whereas many MIT observers over the years have dismissed James Savage, probably as a part of the general downplaying of Brahmins, he is by no means dismissed by present-day American conservatives, whose attacks on public education in the United States bring him up prominently and always in connection with MIT. For instance, in the works of the Southern conservative polemicist Samuel L. Blumenfeld, author of *Is Public Education Necessary?*, James Savage is the subject of virulent attack, along with many of his fellow Brahmins, including the antislavery leader John Quincy Adams and the educational reformer Horace Mann, and institutions such as Unitarianism, Harvard, and MIT. Noting that Rogers's brother Henry was a disciple of the British social reformer Robert Owen, in whose circle the word *socialism* was invented, and correctly believing that many Boston Brahmins—including textile magnate John Francis Lowell—were admirers of Owen, Blumenfeld concludes his attack on American public education with a considerable flourish, proclaiming that "[William Barton] Rogers married the daughter of [James] Savage, one of the leading Unitarian activists in the cause of public education." Indeed, quotes Blumenfeld, "It is not too much to say that America's leading scientific university" (that's MIT) "should have been founded by a socialist" (that's his view of Rogers) "working in common with Harvard Unitarians."

One reason James Savage is easy to lose sight of is that he doubtless took care not to be conspicuous in relation to MIT, unlike other educational achievements in which he played a leadership role. Rogers's father-in-law, like his wife, seems to have been careful to perform a distinctly supporting role in Rogers's grand plan. Yet a little digging can be rewarding. In 1883, for example, almost two decades after its founding, the Institute offered only eight named scholarships, and only two of those were established by individuals as opposed to institutions. Both of the latter, reports *Bacon's Dictionary of Boston*, were "scholarships founded by the late James Savage, LLD,...to benefit meritorious students on recommendation of the faculty."

As it turns out, Bronson Alcott's ginkgo tree, as described by Margaret Fuller's biographer, was replanted on Marlborough Street. By which I mean to suggest that the best place to catch hold of the man who so inspired not only the Savages but Rogers as well may be on that tree-shaded Back Bay street, between that liberal landmark, the Unitarian First Church in Boston (Emerson's father was

William Barton Rogers and Emma Savage Rogers's Back Bay town house on Marlborough Street near the corner of Berkeley Street. As befitted this über-Brahmin couple, it was elegant but not florid, and fashionable but sober in character.

the minister of this church, whose 1866 building on the corner of Marlborough and Berkeley Streets was designed, by the way, by William Robert Ware, the first head of MIT's architecture department) and number 117, Rogers and Savage's handsome brick town house, into which they moved in 1874. The house may have been Ware's design too. Savage lived there until her death in 1911. Today the three proud owners of this historic house make a point of calling it in their common master deed the Rogers House Condominium Trust.

It was likely in his Marlborough Street study that MIT's founder, in July 1879, addressed the matters of how he viewed the role of religion in education and the role of women in education and politics generally. He allowed that although he would be "glad to see educated and experienced women form a part of all our school commit-tees," he feared "that the interests of our schools would suffer from the passage of a law conferring upon all women the right to vote for members of school committees." For, he explained, "it seems to me that the great numerical force of the ignorant and superstitious class of women, wielded even more completely than that of the corresponding class of men, by influences which are known to be adverse to a true nonsectarian education…[would be] wholly unlike the liberal-minded and thoroughly trained who of late years have done such admirable work."

It was a progressive point of view, but also an aristocratic one, characteris-tically Brahmin. It was the sort of argument that founding father John Adams—a better choice, many think, than Emerson as the first Boston Brahmin—often urged on Virginian Thomas Jefferson, quite another kind of aristocrat. Unlike his Harvard counterpart, President Charles Eliot, or Eliot's father, Samuel, Rogers was not a "high priest in the Unitarian Sanhedrin that dominated Boston," as historian Richard Norton Smith so beautifully put it. Rogers's point of view emerges pretty clearly in his dealings with two of his Marlborough Street neighbors: the Reverend Rufus Ellis, minister of the First Church in Boston, in whose congregation William and Emma had been married in 1849, and his brother, the Reverend George Ellis, professor of systematic theology at that Unitarian citadel, Harvard Divinity School.

Rogers's interactions with Rufus Ellis come up in *Life and Letters of William Barton Rogers*, where he had accepted an invitation to appear at Ellis's church and discussed "some topic in physical science especially connected with human prog-ress," but added, "The religious aspect of scientific discovery would be beyond my province as a teacher of science," a rejoinder that is classically Unitarian. However, Ellis's brother George, who is described by Savage in *Life and Letters* as "an intimate friend," saw a more private side of Rogers. At his funeral, at which George Ellis presided, along with the leading Back Bay Unitarian divine of the day, S. K. Lothrop, George Ellis pointedly declared that "reverently and devoutly did that gifted and

The Rogers's first-floor dining room in their Marlborough Street town house. Rogers and his wife entertained the Thursday Club after lectures from time to time and vetted many a prospective MIT faculty member in this space.

The black marble front parlor mantelpiece of the Rogers house, the interior of which was stylish but not grand, as one would expect of William Barton Rogers and Emma Savage Rogers. Today this house is divided into three condominiums.

beloved man, sage, scientist, teacher, friend, whom we are now mourning, bow before that mystery with a serene and lofty Spirit."

In *Where Darwin Meets the Bible*, Larry Witham is probably right when he says that in terms of religion, Rogers "has been described [in Ronald L. Numbers's *Darwinism Comes to America*] as 'if anything, a Presbyterian, though he had close ties to Unitarians.'" (In Northern Ireland, from which the Rogers family came, Unitarian churches were known as "non subscribing" Presbyterian churches.) Rogers himself was very much the preacher—of science as progress. A very Unitarian gospel. His charisma as a teacher is clear in a thank-you note his wife reproduces in *Life and Letters* from someone who had attended a meeting of the Thursday Evening Club at their Marlborough Street town house:

> The thermometer was 85, the time was half-past nine, and the smell of the approaching supper already invaded the nostrils of an expectant audience of 60 cultivated persons. Then the Professor arose.... He proceeded to disclose the process by which gases might be converted into liquids. If I were a man of science I might tell you what he told the favored 60.... He demonstrated everything, so that some of the finest results of modern science were made plain, even to a capacity as limited as mine. But the vista he opened as to the progress of science, how shall I describe that? Nobody can describe it who did not hear it.

Pediment

Unitarians as the
First American Modernists

The First Church of Boston, diagonally opposite the Rogers's town house. William and Emma were married in this fashionable Brahmin Unitarian congregation and both were buried by the clergy of this church, which a later MIT president, James Killian, also attended.

Pediment
Unitarians as the First American Modernists

Nothing is more important to understand about early MIT than that it was intended to be a sister school to Harvard by Boston's Brahmin leadership, which through the Savage family not only welcomed but actively recruited William Barton Rogers so that he might implement his ideas. Similarly, essential to an understanding of the Boston Brahmins is that their liberalism was the result of, and expressed through, their Unitarianism.

    "Centered in Boston, the Unitarians dominated Harvard for much of the nineteenth century," Christopher L. Walton writes. "They were elites,...members of the merchant class, the leading figures in American literature....Daniel Walker Howe has described the Harvard Unitarians during this period as 'archetypal modern intellectuals.'...As moderns, the Unitarians identified themselves with the spirit of the times and celebrated the characteristic features of modernism...[which were] capitalism, theism, liberalism, and optimism." Samuel Eliot Morison put it this way: "Unitarianism of the Boston stamp...was receptive, searching, inquiring...a half-way house to the rationalistic and scientific point of view."

    William R. Hutchison, in *The Modernist Impulse in American Protestantism*, goes much further: It was through their "opening of religion...to scientific method," he writes, that "Unitarians made incalculable contributions....As pioneers of a modern synthesis, they had trafficked in complexity and doubt."

    "The Boston religion," as M. A. DeWolfe Howe, the leading historian of Boston at the turn of the twentieth century, characterized it, was the first American modernism. He also positioned early MIT properly in its contemporary context, announcing its parity with Harvard, but admitting the difficulties it had, given that it was by centuries the younger sibling. "It has been uphill work," Howe wrote in *Boston: The Place and the People*, "to carry through [its first] nearly forty years [as] an institution [that's MIT] so near to the oldest seat of learning in America [that's Harvard], making as it naturally does the first and strongest appeal to the affection and generosity of the community."

    Notice that Howe assumes MIT's "community" was the same community —Brahmin Unitarians—that supported Harvard. Boston's other new institutions of higher learning of the mid- and late nineteenth century—with the exception of Radcliffe and Wellesley Colleges, dedicated to women's education and also Brahmin oriented—were established by non–Brahmin Unitarian groups: Tufts College (founded by Universalists), Boston College (by Roman Catholics), and BU (by Methodists).

    From the start, MIT was a leading Boston Brahmin cause, providing as it did a much-needed aspect of education that Harvard was not supplying. The historian Philip Alexander, for example, pointed out that a lot of the Brahmins at

MIT—many of whom we've already met here: "Cabots, Appletons, Lowells, Conants, Bowditches, and Forbeses"—"hailed from generation upon generation of Harvard loyalists...[who] had grown concerned about [Harvard's] relevance in an age of rapid industrialization."

In this new role the Institute quickly achieved distinction, so much so that by 1886, Bacon's *Dictionary of Boston* would refer to MIT as a "noble educational institution." By the next generation, when Upton Sinclair was doing his research on his "documentary novel," as he called *Boston*, his Back Bay sources made very clear their strong feelings for "the great school [that's MIT] which next to Harvard itself was Boston's pride." That meant, of course, Back Bay Boston's pride.

Socially, the Institute must have sent mixed signals in providing—and bridging—elite and mass education. "A college education does not quite mean the same to a Tech man that it does to the average college man," a Class Day speaker in 1899 opined. "Men go to Tech not to have their Alma Mater seal them gentlemen, but to make them workers." This was, however, misleading. There were poor students at Harvard who were never likely to be so sealed. There were also rich students at MIT who wanted to "work."

Only seven years later, the *Boston Globe* reported on October 30, 1891, under the headline "Gilt-Edged Polo" that MIT students were in talks with Harvard students and several Brahmin clubs to create what the article described as "a league of swell amateurs" to compete in the most elite of all sports at the Irvington Armory just south of Copley Square. In its early years in Copley Square, MIT participated in the grand Brahmin social swirl quite as much as Harvard. On June 27, 1898, for example, a news report in the *Globe* notes that "the Harvard Seniors held their class dinner at the Vendome"; another on December 11 of the same year announces that "the dinner of the Class of 1898, MIT, was held at the Hotel Vendome last evening." Typical was the report of May 31, 1892:

> "Tech Class Day...Brilliant Was the Reception in the Evening"
> A reception and dance [was] given in the State Suite at the Vendome [last evening]. "From 8 o'clock until 10 o'clock" read the invitations which were so eagerly coveted, and for an hour previous carriages were depositing...fair women and gallant escorts at the end of the tented passage leading [from Commonwealth Avenue] to the private entrance to the hotel.

It was not the proletarian image lefty intellectuals always tried to project of "Tech" in Copley Square, and these mixed signals could be understood, and misunderstood, in many ways. In his book *The Forging of an Aristocracy: Harvard and the Boston Upper Class, 1800–1870*, the historian Ronald Story identified Tufts and BU as "two lower-class Protestant [institutions]," Holy Cross and Boston College as "two Catholic" institutions, and MIT as a "technical" institution, all of them "founded by groups who had been denied influence and access at Harvard and did not like it." Thus, a crisis in the first wave of Brahmin institution building—including the Boston Athenaeum, the Lowell Institute, and the Massachusetts General Hospital—was resolved by the second wave of Brahmin institution building, including the Museum of Fine Arts and the Boston Symphony.

But MIT, Unitarian in its attitude (like Harvard), was meant to be rigorously nonsectarian. Early MIT's Unitarian flavor—which persisted well into the twentieth century and reached a kind of culmination in the midcentury presidency of James R. Killian—is easily lost track of. Being so ardently nonsectarian, Unitarians tend to efface themselves, not only at MIT but also, for example, at Stanford, which was also founded by an active Unitarian. Additionally, the educational reformer Horace Mann was Unitarian and famously antisectarian. So was Rogers, who was married and buried according to Unitarian rites, and conspicuously silent on the subject in between.

George W. Cooke, in *Unitarianism in America*, writes, "Unitarians have not only been opposed to denominational colleges, but they have been leaders in pro-moting unsectarian education." Harvard's President Eliot himself—rather absurdly, really—stoutly maintained that the shrine of American Unitarianism, Harvard Divinity School, was *not* Unitarian, thank you! The closest Cooke gets to acknowl-edging MIT's place in all this is to admit that "the interest of Unitarians in popular education and the general diffusion of knowledge may be further illustrated by… the Lowell Institute in Boston… [which] has also included free lectures for advanced students given in connection with the Massachusetts Institute of Technology."

"Tech"—absolutely unlike Boston's new Catholic and Protestant institutions of higher learning—even developed a high-profile bohemian scene in the 1880s and 1890s. Its leading figure was Gelett Burgess, an engineering student at MIT who continued to be very active in alumni affairs. He was a denizen of the South Back Bay, the highly musical quarter along Huntington Avenue, which was sustained by a considerable bohemia on the square's southwestern periphery along St. Botolph Street on the Back Bay side of the railroad tracks that separated it from the South End. Burgess after graduation went on to become a high-profile national bohemian figure. He authored "Some Experiences of Haschisch," while at MIT, and "The Bohemians of Boston." The latter gives some of the flavor of the scene: "They talked of 'Art' and 'Philistine,' / They wore buff 'wescoats' and their hair / It used to make the waiters stare! / They were so shockingly behaved / And Boston thought them so depraved."

How depraved? Just around the corner from the heart of Copley Square on Dartmouth Street, the picturesque Moorish red brick and terra-cotta Hotel Victoria was where, in the 1880s and 1890s, area bohemians gathered regularly. As Ferris Greenslet, the legendary Houghton Mifflin editor, remembered it, "A gath-ering of literary lefties" regularly convened "at the Victoria in a basement so far below the street that one looking up could sometimes see even the scalloped tops of passing ladies' shoes." More of a titillation then than now. One can still have the experience, however, for there remains a restaurant there whose windows—the same ones—are level with the sidewalk. "Sometimes," Greenslet recalled, "Richard

Hovey would come in, black-coated, black-hatted, black-bearded, a revenant from the boulevards of Paris…to inquire whether [some new verse of his] was suitable for *Songs of Vagabondia*. I recall a particularly agreeable one, beginning 'Who is this I cannot see Tumbling over me?' and my regret when it was decided to be suitable but not possible."

What has this to do with MIT? By far the most popular offering of the *Songs of Vagabondia* was Hovey's "Stein Song," on which he collaborated with Fred Bullard, an MIT student who set Hovey's verse to music with such success that it became MIT's unofficial student anthem. Its "exuberance of the roistering spirit" moved Burgess to admiration time and time again, and even Institute president Henry Smith Pritchett, who had studied in Germany and thought he knew something about school spirit, sponsored MIT smokers where the steins were not empty by any means; the beer flowed freely.

Pritchett encouraged Bullard—who was, it should be noted, a serious musician and a teacher of the famous composer Edward Burlingame Hill—to publish in 1903 *Tech Songs: The MIT Kommers Book*, which was also full of beer, so to speak ("Here's to MIT. Drink it down, Drink it down"), and included, of course, the "Stein Song." Two decades later, in the face of Prohibition, *Technology Review* could hardly deal with the necessity of replacing it. Wrote its editors:

> Tech students no longer recognize the STEIN SONG…the "Fair Harvard" of Technology. It has been sung and honored wherever Tech men have got together. It is one thing which has never been missing at official functions or informal ones.…Tech does not have a large number of rules to be obeyed.…However, one rule that has always been promulgated. Whereas and wherever the STEIN SONG is played or sung, you are to rise and remove your hat. Tech is unique in many ways. It is the only undergraduate institution of its size that has no football team. The student cheer, "We are happy— Tech is hell" is probably unlike any other American college cheer.…To consider all possibilities: the STEIN SONG would be again in favor if the dry law were modified.

Somewhere between the workers and the swells and the bohemians, the Institute held its own. "MIT was no Harvard," the historian Russell B. Adams admitted, but continued: "MIT was no coarse parvenu either. In its minuscule maiden class [in 1865] were a Forbes and a Cabot, and its first professor of chemistry was the well-connected Charles W. Eliot" himself. "From the first," Adams added, "MIT had been generously supported by Boston's merchant and capitalist grandees."

There were, indeed, no Forbeses or Cabots at Boston College, those being very narrow-minded times in some respects. And even in better days, when the narrow ethnic and class and religious loyalties all schools depended upon broadened, these loyalties continued to matter, as they do even now. When Adams calls Eliot "well-connected," he means connected to that same establishment. And by "Boston's merchant and capitalist grandees" he means Boston's Brahmin ruling class, though he was certainly trying to avoid saying so.

Why? Because Adams was writing in the 1970s, by which time *Brahmin* had become a very loaded word. It was an era dominated by those for whom ethnic conflict is the best driver of narrative in nonfiction as well as in fiction, even when doing so perpetuates anti-Brahmin prejudice. Confusion between Brahmins and Yankees remains pervasive today, even after Harvard scholar Oscar Handlin's definitive 1941 book *Boston's Immigrants*. It is still widely overlooked that while the original Brahmins were all Yankees, not all Yankees were Brahmins, and certainly not all Unitarians, either.

The outstanding historical example of this distinction took place in 1834, when a notorious anti-Catholic riot shamed Boston before the nation. But it was not ruling-class Unitarian Boston Brahmins who notoriously burned down a Catholic convent school in Charlestown, north of the city. It was working-class fundamentalist Yankees. (Many Brahmins actually were sending their daughters to school at the convent, knowing what a good education they'd get there. In fact, only six of its forty-seven students were Roman Catholic.) It was not just in the Back Bay battles of wet docks versus palazzi, residential and institutional, that the Brahmin elite and lower- and middle-class Yankees were in opposition. The acquittal of the riot's ringleaders and the subsequent failure to reimburse the Catholic Diocese for the loss (despite support from the Brahmins) underlines the Brahmins' isolation (however lofty) in the Yankee community.

Paul DiMaggio, citing Ronald Story's 1980 study, offers yet another example of the Brahmins' ongoing conflict with Yankees of the lower classes, observing: "The political assault on Brahmin institutions by native populists proved even more frightening [than immigration]. The Know-Nothings attacked the social exclusivity of Harvard College.... Scalded by these attacks, Brahmin leadership retreated from the public sector to found a system of non-profit organizations that permitted them to maintain sure control over the community even as they lost their command of its political institutions." Here again is the claim that Brahmins turned from politics to cultural institutionalism while holding onto their social and economic authority, as a result of difficulties primarily not with immigrants but with the Yankee lower classes. Class trumps ethnicity. Class and religion. Between modernist Unitarians and fundamentalist Protestants there was no sympathy at all.

Hopefully by now it is clear that to think of Boston's Brahmins as the leaders of a united Yankee rejection of (at first largely Irish) immigrants in the nineteenth century profoundly distorts the history of America in general and Boston in particular. This misunderstanding also profoundly distorts the history of MIT, especially when the first misunderstanding is compounded by a second, ignoring the fact that Brahmin Unitarianism was actually the first American modernism.

Here is where MIT's founder comes into striking relief. The son of an Irish immigrant to the United States who had taken an active role in the Irish Rebellion of 1798, William Barton Rogers became not just a member of "that closest thing to an American aristocracy, the Brahmin class of Boston," in James Turner's words, "but a member of that ruling class's leadership cadre." Some may object that MIT's founder could not have been a Boston Brahmin, not even a Bostonian, because he was not a native-born citizen of the Boston city-state, nor from an old Boston family. This point of view has much in common with anti-immigrant sentiment then and now; to doubt that an immigrant can also be an American is hopelessly parochial. In fact, the classic definition of the Boston Brahmin caste (of which he was a leader) by Oliver Wendell Holmes Sr. was that while the Brahminate was hereditary in its scholarly vocation, it was otherwise more cosmopolitan than nativist.

Indeed, Boston "naturalized" at both ends of the spectrum. Arthur Mann, for instance, in *Yankee Reformers in the Urban Age*, describes many left-wing thinkers drawn to Copley Square (and some to MIT) by the same revolutionary, abolitionist, and Emersonian ideals that drew, for example, B. O. Flower, editor of *The Arena* magazine. Mann describes Flower as "a Midwesterner by birth, [who] felt compelled in his reminisces to write about Emerson and his generation as if they had been his immediate ancestors." With the steadfast zeal of converts, these new Bostonians, none Brahmins by birth or in waiting, "kept the faith...that America was not living up to its ideals" and that Boston was the place to address such issues.

Meanwhile, at the opposite (Brahmin) end of the spectrum, the same identification held, given the many adopted as well as native-born Brahmins. A comparable one to Rogers, for example, was the landscape architect Frederick Law Olmsted, famously the author of the Boston park plan. Writes Mona Domosh:

> The success of Olmsted's plan had as much to do with the social climate of Boston as with its aesthetic climate. Olmsted's record of achievement in Boston after his defeat in New York City...was owing to the social and political support he found there. Boston, unlike New York, still retained an effective intellectual and social elite.... Boston's Brahmins...always found effective means of shaping the city's built form.... Olmsted's original invitation to Boston came on behalf of the Lowell Institute, an institute completely controlled by Boston Brahmins.

In Rogers's case, the invitation was even stronger. Rogers was initiated— "taken into the sacred circle of the Back Bay" was how Upton Sinclair characterized the experience generally—twice over. There were the invitations to him and his brother Henry to lecture for the Lowell Institute ("Before the Civil War, in fact, a [Lowell] Institute lectureship sometimes helped to recruit a promising intellectual into the ranks of the elite," according to Story in *The Forging of an Aristocracy: Harvard and the Boston Upper Class*). There was also, even more importantly, Rogers's marriage into the über-Brahmin Savage family, whose values were so exemplary of what drew MIT's founder to New England in the first place.

The Savage connection is why I view Rogers as part of the officer corps. He was so keen, he could be described more as a convert than as a recruit or adoptee, at least intellectually, a certain gentility being taken for granted. In nearly every respect, Rogers reflected not necessarily the values of the caste as a whole—in which there were, of course, many reactionaries—but the values of the caste's leadership cadre, the über-Brahmins, as I like to call them. Sorting out the officer corps from the rest is not easy, and no one quite gets it anymore, but that's what the brilliant cultural and literary critic Van Wyck Brooks was trying to do when he wrote about the great age of immigration in America and its effect on the Boston city-state in *New England: Indian Summer* (1940):

> William James looked forward calmly....The Emersonian Charles W. Eliot believed in the future....The older and the bolder were the less inclined to think the world was going to the dogs. They were tough enough...like all true aristocrats, they believed in their country....Those who fought and bled in freedom's cause, like Justice [Oliver Wendell] Holmes [Jr.] and Colonel [Henry Lee] Higginson, were prepared to take the long view.... So was Edward Everett Hale, the grand old man of Boston, and Julia Ward Howe, the romantic old sibyl....They ignored the signs of the times and lived above them, as Emerson had all his life....It was easier for William James...and President Eliot to take the long view of the future. They were sufficiently realistic, but they were not New Englanders merely....Their ships were heavily ballasted and sailed on broad bottoms.

Not New Englanders merely! That's the key. Not localists, but globalists. I'd add Holmes Sr. to this circle of Emersonians, so to speak, who constituted the Brahmin leadership cadre. They were leaders sufficiently cosmopolitan to see not just from the inside out but from the outside in. All the better, Holmes Sr. once claimed, if they were "dual citizens" of some other city too.

Rogers was another such. His acceptance and election to the Brahmin social clubs was the third stage, we might say, of his initiation into the "sacred circle." Rogers was elected to the "venerable dining club...with a distinctly medical and scientific bent," the Thursday Evening Club, but also—and this spoke volumes about the esteem in which he came to be held—to the much more literary and artistic Saturday Club, which in his history of the subject Alexander Williams calls "the most famous of all the Boston dining clubs." Its legendary catalog of members included Emerson himself, Nathaniel Hawthorne, the artist John Singer Sargent, Holmes Sr., Harvard's President Eliot, and Trinity Church architect H. H. Richardson.

It was a seedbed of support for the idea of MIT. As later MIT president Henry Pritchett wrote in his Rogers biography in M. A. De Wolfe Howe's *Later Years of the Saturday Club*: "It is well nigh impossible to appreciate in our day how great a novelty this proposal [to establish MIT] appeared in the America of that time. It required many years, even in Boston, to awaken interest....Amongst the members in favor of the proposed institution who addressed the legislature was [the Harvard mathematician and astronomer] Benjamin Peirce, himself a distinguished member of the Saturday Club. Others of the Saturday Club...also lent Rogers their support."

Boston Brahmins have been famously painted as conservative in even the smallest things. But that is a misunderstanding. Walter Muir Whitehill, the leading historian of Boston studies in the second part of the last century, was never more penetrating than when he insisted in his 1966 book *Boston in the Age of John*

Fitzgerald Kennedy that the classic "Boston temperament"— meaning the Boston Brahmin temperament, though he avoided that sort of "divisive" usage—"more readily accepts change in large matters than in small ones, and in ideas rather than in the details of daily life." (Whitehill would have loved the story of how the Supreme Judicial Court of Massachusetts, having ruled that theirs would be the third jurisdiction in the world to legalize same-sex marriage, protested at lunch the same day a change in the recipe for their New England clam chowder. American founding father John Adams, whom more than a few would call retrospectively [even before Emerson] the first Boston Brahmin prototype, would have appreciated it as well).

Rogers's biographer A. J. Angulo agrees that it was supremely important that Peirce, widely regarded as the first American scientist to achieve world stature, addressed a meeting called by Rogers early in 1861 "heartily approving of the plan [for MIT,]...regarding it as a much needed institution." It was also very significant for MIT that Rogers was a leading figure in Boston clubland generally. That final seal of Brahmin approval arises in *Mind and Hand: The Birth of MIT*, though somewhat buried in the text, when the authors note that "when the Somerset and other clubs proved too solidly conservative for the more liberal [members,] other organizations were formed....In the fall of 1862 Rogers withdrew from the Friday Club....[By] 1863 he was active in the newly formed Union Club." The official invitations to prospective Union Club members, issued on February 28, 1863, by the founding members of what Cecelia Tichi in *Civic Passions* calls "the citadel of Brahmin nobility," were signed by only twenty-three members, including Holmes Sr., John Murray Forbes, John Amory Lowell, and Rogers, the best evidence imaginable of his acceptance into the leadership of Boston's ruling class.

Not only at his club did Rogers keep this company. He and his right-hand man, John Runkle (who was of a modest Yankee rural background; Rogers was not a snob), embedded many high-profile Boston Brahmins in leading positions at MIT. One of the best known was James Mason Crafts; the historian Philip Alexander pronounces Crafts "probably Tech's most distinguished scholar" in those early days. When in 1862 MIT's interim government was first set up, two of the four vice presidents—Lowell and Jacob Bigelow—were über-Brahmins. On the Institute's very first day of operation, February 20, 1865, the ancestor of all first-year MIT students ever since—one Eli Forbes—presented himself as "Rogers waited with the half dozen men he had pulled together" as potential students.

In 1866, the second year of the Institute's operation, Rogers's fellow Union Club founder John Murray Forbes (whom we already encountered in our clipper ship excursion in Portal Two) also appeared on the MIT scene, appointed to the new institution's crucial five-man finance committee (and recruited surely by Rogers). His son William Hathaway Forbes was an early example of the way MIT forged links between academia and industry. He risked his fortune to form the American Telephone and Telegraph Company to protect Alexander Graham Bell's patent of this MIT-related discovery, and he also married Emerson's daughter Edith. Their son, himself a life member of the MIT Corporation, was thus a grandson of Ralph Waldo Emerson.

Different portals, different perspectives, different voyages of the mind. And there was no wider portal than Emerson's eye, which he cast in the same direction as the widest portal perhaps thus far identified here: India Wharf. Was Emerson, after all, in the long Puritan-Patriot-Brahmin continuum, the first real-time Boston Brahmin? Most scholars would agree with Paul Brunton, who has already been cited once here as affirming in his *Indian Philosophy and Modern Culture* that "Emerson's Transcendentalism earned him the appellation 'the Boston Brahmin.'"

The importance of the way Emerson made a poet's lament (Wordsworth's) his own injunction—"plain living and high thinking"—may have been best acted out by Thoreau at Walden, but in our context here Emerson is not just the "American Plato." Even more often he was called "the Buddha of the West," something that would be ever more important to MIT as over time its contacts with Asia increased. "The Boston into which Emerson was born was a town of fewer than 25,000 people, proud of its revolutionary heritage, but a cultural backwater compared to London and Paris," Harvard scholar Lawrence Buell has written. "Yet within a mere half century…the Boston area…had become a center for literature, for avant-garde American thought in religion, philosophy, and education, and for a host of reform movements.…Emerson…was one of the primary reasons why." Rogers and MIT were part of the cutting edge of this new Boston. Boston was being transformed, wrote the historian Bainbridge Bunting, "into 'a great city' that might astonish visitors into thinking of St. Petersburg or Paris—comparisons hardly dreamed of, or even desired in the 1840s." Brahmin dreams.

There is, however, a footnote to all this that obscures somewhat the contributions of Boston Brahmin Unitarians who accepted—even gloried in—something many have deluded themselves over the years into thinking has no part in the American way: class distinctions. Boston Brahmin Unitarians were as elitist as they were intellectual. And while it is not hard to see what the French call "the weaknesses of their strengths," today the Unitarian tradition is in full retreat from that position. Consider an article in the *New York Times* on March 16, 2013, noting that "the American Unitarian Association, peopled and powered by the city's Brahmin elite, [which] announced its presence [at the turn of the twentieth century] with a stately headquarters at the very top of Beacon Hill, next door to the Statehouse," that had been sold for fashionable condominiums to raise money. What was now the Unitarian Universalist Association had retreated from a historically intellectual center to a new commercial section of the city. The UUA president explained, moreover, that the Beacon Hill headquarters "symbolized a kind of elitism that we are moving away from." Do they mean the elitism of President Rogers when he recruited Charles W. Eliot as one of MIT's first five professors? Or the elitism of President Eliot when he made Rogers's new educational philosophy his own at Harvard?

The entrance to the leading Boston Brahmin social club for those of more liberal or progressive beliefs, the Union Club, on Park Street in the shadow of the State House. Founded at the time of the Civil War in response to the perceived conservatism of the Somerset Club across the street, the Union Club's founders included William Barton Rogers.

Frieze

Artistic Engineers, Lefty Pundits

MIT was founded by Boston Brahmins who were concerned that Harvard was not keeping up in matters scientific and technological in the days before one of MIT's original professors, Charles W. Eliot, became Harvard's president and the founder of the modern university. The link between the great Brahmin institutions of higher learning is seen in the fact that icon Phillips Brooks frequently preached to both but to no other schools. Another link is that the John Harvard statue now in Harvard Yard is the work of MIT alumnus Daniel Chester French.

Frieze

Artistic Engineers, Lefty Pundits

The engineers surprised everyone. Not so much in their primary field, but outside it, in the role early MIT played in the art life of Copley Square. Even in literature, early MIT was a player. Arlo Bates, for example, senior professor of English in the 1890s, was the author of twenty-three best-selling novels. The literary "elite of New York and Boston all knew Arlo Bates," the critic Andrew Krivak writes. So much so that when William Carlos Williams, he of the first generation of modernist American poets, journeyed to Boston for mentoring in 1908, it was to Copley Square and to MIT. His "famous visit to see Bates at MIT" says much about the Institute's role in American literary history.

Beyond the fields of science and technology, MIT was chiefly known as an arts center. Few know that Boston's Museum of Fine Arts, already by the 1890s an institution of global stature—with the greatest Japanese collection outside of Japan, for example—was founded by MIT and two other institutions, Harvard and the Boston Athenaeum. Each had a very real need for such an institution: in MIT's case because there was not sufficient room in the first Rogers Building for the magnificent collection of plaster casts of sculptures that Ware, the founder of its architectural school, brought back from Europe for the students to study.

Further, when the Boston Art Commission was established in the 1890s, the first such commission in the United States, the Institute was accorded one of the four controlling votes on all decisions. (The other votes belonged to the Boston Public Library, the Museum of Fine Arts, and the Boston Society of Architects.) No statue in the Back Bay was put up after the 1890s that MIT did not approve. It helps in explaining the Institute's ongoing distinguished program of outdoor sculpture commissions for its Cambridgeport campus. Even today, by the way, a trustee appointed by MIT sits on the board of Boston's Museum of Fine Arts.

Not only did MIT play this important public role on the art commission, but also it was an MIT literary figure who created the context of that public role. Bates, Tech's senior professor of English, dedicated one of his best-selling novels, *The Philistines*, to this subject. The novel satirized the way corrupt politics made short shrift of artistic standards in public art. According to University of South Carolina historian Thomas J. Brown, it incited a lobbying campaign to establish the art commission, one of the country's first.

Nor is it startling that in such a context MIT developed its own internal artistic capacities, so to speak. Neither the great seated Abraham Lincoln in Washington, D.C.'s, Lincoln Memorial nor the *Concord Minuteman* outside Boston is popularly associated with MIT, but in fact both are the work of the Institute's most famous artist alumnus, Daniel Chester French.

It is a play in two acts, as Copley Square itself frequently was—acts that seem at first simply to show the mistakes young people can make, but in the end

MIT was one of three founders of Boston's Museum of Fine Arts, and students of the Museum School and at MIT's Architecture School could take courses for credit in either school. MIT was also a member of the Boston Art Commission and played a key role in approving public monuments. ABOVE: Many of MIT's casts were exhibited at the museum.

reveal what sort of community the New World Acropolis was. MIT was the corner-stone of that community in a very practical, everyday way for French, a student flailing about in his first year. Act one, scene one: French enrolls in the Institute in fall 1867. "Professor Brewster of the Institute of Technology who examined him in Algebra and Geometry," young Daniel's father reported in a letter to a friend, was sure "he would pass, without doubt." A year later, however, at the end of scene two, it became clear, in scholar Ann Lee Morgan's blunt words in the *Oxford Dictionary of American Art and Artists*, that French had "achieve[ed] only academic disgrace during a year at MIT." (According to Michael Richman, young French failed physics, chemistry, *and* algebra.)

But there was a second act. MIT's alliance with the Museum of Fine Arts made being a student at either one possible. So interlocking were their faculties and boards of trustees that Professor William Robert Ware of MIT on one side of the square became Secretary Ware (e.g., head) of the art museum's school on the other.

And what one side of the Acropolis couldn't do at all for young French, the other side did very well indeed. William Rimmer's message to the young sculptor-to-be—that "to make a clothed figure convincing, you had to first sculpt a nude figure and then add clothes"—resulted in the *Concord Minuteman*, French's first statue, modeled in 1873. French flunked Professor Brewster's course in the same MIT lecture hall where he triumphantly passed Professor Rimmer's. And lest moderns

assume that Rimmer's class was easier, note that the sculptor was "among the most original American artists of the nineteenth century," according to Morgan, producing "cosmopolitan, psychologically charged work in several media, including perhaps the first American male nude sculpture…[and] also reveal[ing] his lifelong preoccupation with themes of alienation and psychological suffering."

French went on to do a bronze bust for MIT of President Francis Walker in 1899. Nor did the third side of Copley Square escape his attention: he returned to the New World Acropolis in the early 1900s to execute the great bronze entrance doors of the Boston Public Library. Then, when it was decided to erect a statue of John Harvard in the center of Harvard Yard, that too was commissioned from MIT's most famous artistic alumnus, a commission all agreed French discharged extremely well, thereby underlining, as in the founding of the art museum, how often early MIT and modern Harvard have been not rivals but partners in matters great and small.

The close alliance early MIT forged with the new Museum of Fine Arts was based on more than the need to house the Ware Collection. As architectural historian Margaret Henderson Floyd points out in her *Architectural Education and Boston*, a study of the history of the Harvard and MIT schools of architecture and the Boston Architectural College, "[T]he curriculum at MIT,…as the only professional architectural school of the day, managed to blend the new French atelier system of instruction in the high arts with the English tradition of industrial arts." Although MIT's program was based on that of the École des Beaux-Arts in Paris, Floyd writes, "The Institute remained in close physical and spiritual contact with the Museum School [of Boston's new Museum of Fine Arts] where the program took its cues from the South Kensington Schools [in London]." According to the February 1881 MIT faculty minutes, "Voted that Professor Ware would be authorized to allow students at the Museum of Fine Arts [School] to attend lectures at the school [MIT] in exchange for the privileges of allowing the students of their school to attend lectures at the Museum of Fine Arts."

In fact, the link between the Institute and the museum could hardly have been closer. Nor in MIT's first-in-the-nation architecture program could the liberal arts have been more important. Because Ware concluded that "what the country needed," in J. A. Chewing's words, in "William Robert Ware at MIT," was "not so much well-educated architects, as well-educated men, in this profession," the original MIT architecture coursework constituted, as Chewing put it, "a professional curriculum itself analogous in its broadest outlines to a liberal arts curriculum."

There was, to be sure, a certain tension between the engineers and the architects. But the unpublished manuscript of Ware's biography in the MIT Archives demonstrates how the first Rogers Building, itself a work of art, mediated this

Daniel Chester French, an MIT man, was the sculptor of the statue of John Harvard in Harvard Yard, the *Concord Minuteman* (OPPOSITE), and the great seated Lincoln in Washington, D.C. Although he failed at MIT, he crossed the square to find great success studying art.

dispute, as it were, as well as the daily talk. Both engineering and architecture were intimately engaged in creating the Back Bay, an engineering feat often compared to the Suez Canal before it became architecturally a work of art.

MIT architecture also had ramifications that rebounded back. "Ware's approach to education helped to define MIT and advance professional standards not only for architecture," Merritt Roe Smith writes,

> but for the emerging professional disciplines of engineering and science as well. The more that sciences-based education advanced, the more that professionalism advanced, and the more that professionalism advanced the more...American business and industry turned to modern methods. MIT consequently stood at the center of a fundamental educational shift from craft to professional training in America. Though apparent to only the most astute observers, this shift played a pivotal role in the emergence of the United States as a leading industrial nation and world power.

What is so fascinating about the New World Acropolis is how all this sparked a wide-reaching and long-range exchange, as seen both then and from today's perspective. Consider, for instance, Bernard Berenson's somewhat mystical experiences in art and architecture at the Museum of Fine Arts. Confronted with its Japanese art collection for the first time, he wrote: "I was prostrate. Fenolossa [a curator] shivered as he looked. I thought I should die. Even Denman Ross [a collector] was jumping up and down. We had to poke and pinch each other to let off some sense of the tension and almost we fell on each other's necks and wept. No, decidedly, I had never had such an art experience." Added Berenson's biographer Ernest Samuels, who recounts the event, "[Berenson] walked through rooms [in the Copley Square museum] with glowing excitement, moved to ecstasy."

Some say there were many worlds in the square and they did not touch closely. But the reverse is true; time and again, incident and anecdote illustrate its fructifying quality. Even Berenson's experiences were shared, and long into the future. Generations later, MIT presidents would remain involved with the Museum of Fine Arts. Perhaps the greatest, James Killian, would in one of his speeches in the 1960s quote extensively from Berenson about a fifteenth-century Romanesque door frame:

> One morning, as I was gazing at the leafy scrolls carved on the doorjambs of S. Pietro outside Spoleto, suddenly stem, tendril, and foliage became alive and, in becoming alive, made me feel as if I had emerged into the light after long groping in the darkness. I felt as one illumined, and beheld a world where every outline, every edge, and every surface was in a living relation to me.... Since that morning, nothing visible has been indifferent or even dull.... As is the case in all mystical experience, I acquired faith in my vision and in its revelation of values. This faith has never abandoned me, although often enough one has moments of dryness when, as to the religious mystic, God is out of reach.

"It is the function of education," Killian concluded after quoting this passage, "to help us achieve this illumination with respect to conceptual and cognitive matters." Suggesting that Berenson's sudden "aesthetic" illumination was entirely "analogous" to the "inventor's flash of genius, the new concept of the scientist, the creative act of the poet," Killian declared: "This aesthetic experience of Berenson's, coming after a sustained effort to seek out the meaning of a subject, illustrates the quantum jump that sometimes can occur on our sensitivity, our perception, or our understanding. Suddenly we achieve what Berenson calls a 'life-enhancing' revelation of values that gives us a new insight or a new vision."

Aesthetics is thus seen as an ongoing theme of importance at MIT, and a key aspect of the Institute's contribution to Copley Square from the start. Myron Pierce argued in 1903 in *MIT Technology Review*, "The institute erected at much greater cost than they could afford, but which subsequent developments have fully justi-fied, a beautiful building, *the incentive for other beautiful buildings in Copley Square* [emphasis added]."

Elsewhere too. Ogden Codman Jr. studied architecture at MIT before launch-ing his career. He was the coauthor with Edith Wharton of *The Decoration of Houses*, a seminal book that essentially created the field of interior design in this country. They also designed The Mount, the famous Berkshires retreat where Wharton enter-tained her friend Henry James. Thus, we see that setting the pace for the work of art that Copley Square itself became was by no means the extent of MIT's accom-plishment. Even as far away as California, Stanford University's chapel, the work of MIT architects in H. H. Richardson's successor firm, is more or less Trinity Church all over again, with colorful exterior mosaics.

At home, in the square, the gift of Constant-Désiré Despradelle stands out. He was MIT's head of design from 1893 to 1913, and his spectacular Art Nouveau design at the corner of Boylston and Berkeley Streets, diagonally across from the MIT block, was an astonishing gift to the city. And, in the early 1900s, a very contro-versial one. One reason, the critic Frederick Coburn explained at the time, was its "frosty front of white terra cotta…its Gallic airiness…[and] touch of frivolity." "This structure at first excited both twitters and indignation," he reported, but concluded that it is "architectural champagne." The facades "have sparkle and snap."

They still do. Whether or not "the lace-like modeling on the thin strips encas-ing the steel framework, the décolleté appearance" is the best way to characterize its ornamentation, one begins to feel the more Parisian than Bostonian resonances Despradelle's design suggested in the early 1900s. "Naturally, some people were scandalized," Coburn wrote, adding, apparently with a perfectly straight face, that the Berkeley Building, as it is still called today, "was actually designed with reference to the display of the necessary luxuries that tempt all the daughters of Eve—an intent revealed in the cleverly modeled serpents which have squirmed into the grille-work over the main doorway."

If the reader is feeling a little dizzy at this point from these examples of early MIT's artistic ferment, it will perhaps steady our course to come to rest on the

A second building in Copley Square remains to remind of MIT's once-dominant presence: the Berkeley Building on the corner of Boylston and Berkeley Streets, which was the design of MIT's head of design, Constant-Désiré Despradelle. An early skyscraper, it is a superbly Parisian building of its period, "architectural champagne," one critic called it.

The work of artists associated with MIT is always most interesting when the connection with engineering is discernible, as in Calder's sculpture and the painting of Charles Woodbury, *Blue Wave*. He exhibited at the Boston Art Club in the square while an engineering student at the Institute.

central trope of all artistic experience, as, for instance, when Charles Woodbury met Ross Turner, the former a student in his junior year at MIT in the mid-1880s, the latter a well-known Boston painter (he showed with John La Farge at the art museum) who taught at MIT and at what is now the Massachusetts College of Art and Design on the other side of the square. Soon Woodbury was exhibiting his paintings at the Boston Art Club on one side of the square at the same time that he was pursuing his studies in mechanical engineering on the other side—shades of Daniel Chester French—thereby enabling him to pay his MIT tuition.

Art critics were keen on Woodbury's work from the start, largely because it seemed as much engineering as art. The poet Amy Lowell noticed this, and, writing lately, so has Christopher Volpe in his study of the artist's work. Volpe notes that Woodbury was "trained as a mechanical engineer" and that consequently "he saw and painted the world in motion, in terms of the 'conditions of force and resistance.'" In a similar vein, the curator Laura Knott, in the catalog for the MIT Museum's 150th anniversary exhibition, remarks that Woodbury's "scientific understanding of wave motion can clearly be seen, for instance, in his *Blue Wave*. In this painting he creates movement and energy in the swelling wave and swirling sky, exemplifying his direction to students to 'paint in verbs, not in nouns.'"

Woodbury was no anomaly. Not even an exception. Early MIT's key role in the art life of the New World Acropolis was clear in the annual exhibitions at the art museum, and at the St. Botolph Club and the Boston Art Club, which marked the life of the square year in and year out and frequently sparked or consolidated art movements throughout the country. Consider, for example, one exhibition in 1897, the first Arts and Crafts exhibit held in the United States. It is of particular interest because the MIT tradition of not privileging "pure" science over "applied" science met in that artistic movement the parallel idea that the so-called fine arts should not be privileged over the so-called decorative arts—stained glass, for instance, over easel painting.

The "stars of the show," Nancy Finlay has written in *Artists of the Book in Boston*, were Will Bradley (whom she calls elsewhere "the American Beardsley," describing his work as "the first examples of Art Nouveau in America") and Elisha Brown Bird, a recent graduate of MIT. Finlay points out that "perhaps because of his training at MIT, Bird emphasized the new printing technology enthusiastically; he actually preferred to have his work reproduced by photochemical means. He believed that the individuality of the designer was compromised when he submitted his work to be hand-engraved by another artist, who in Bird's view inevitably infused something of his own arrangement into the engraved plate."

Finally, one might point to Charles and Henry Greene, the celebrated California architects who were the brilliant California exponents of the American bungalow, and before that MIT students. These splendid luminaries (as they would become) of the American Arts and Crafts movement absorbed not only all those influences in Copley Square but also, even more fundamentally, the undergirding influence of Japanese art, being frequent visitors to the Asian galleries of the Museum of Fine Arts. They are an especially complete example of the way everything rubbed up against everything else in the New World Acropolis to such very good effect.

But to really take the measure of MIT's role in sparking Boston one hundred and more years ago as a major arts center—and to understand the role of the arts in MIT's DNA—one must look to the more advanced art of the day. And if the visitor today can access this portal in the Kendall/MIT subway station, all the better. This station did not exist until 1912, when the Boston Elevated (and subway) Company was extended to Harvard Square. In 1986–88, what has since become MIT's subway station was endowed with a remarkable "sound sculpture"—predominantly aluminum tubular bells—between the inbound and outbound tracks, played from levers on the subway platforms on either side. Activate the sounds—best heard as the screeching trains leave the station—and imagine the bells of Copley Square as early MIT heard them in the 1890s and the first decade of the 1900s. This is the work of Paul Matisse, grandson of Henri Matisse, Picasso's rival as the driving force of twentieth-century modernist art. Henri Matisse was, albeit at one remove, a player in the story of how early MIT came to perform its artistic role in nineteenth- and early twentieth-century Copley Square. The master in whose work Henri Matisse chiefly found inspiration was Paul Cézanne. "In modern art," Matisse said, "it is indubitably to Cézanne that I owe the most." Cézanne was the artist not only that Matisse called master but also without whom, Anne d'Harnoncourt has written, developments such as "the analytical cubism of Picasso and Braque…are all impossible." And in Copley Square in those days, however incredible it may seem today, the place to see Cézanne's work, and in some sense the future of Western art—the only place in America, actually—was not the Museum of Fine Arts but MIT.

One of the Institute's leading professors, whose European Civilization and Art course was widely influential, was John Osborne Sumner. A contemporary *Pencil Points* tells us: "His office in the Rogers Building, its chairs and tables heaped with as yet unclassified magazines or photographs, was most hospitably at the disposal of interested students. A comfortable arm chair and a friendly cup of tea brought the amenities of his wide knowledge and strong social inclinations to his guests and revealed the kindly qualities and profound learning for which he was valued by so many of his students and fellow teachers." More than that, hanging on Sumner's study wall (or no farther away than his Marlborough Street town house) was *The Harvesters*. When it was bought from his estate after his death, it was labeled by the Phillips Collection in Washington, D.C. as the "first Cézanne in America."

Another kind of modern art polemic also thrived at MIT: the articles on the sculptor Auguste Rodin by Truman Bartlett, a sculptor who taught at the School of Architecture. He was an indifferent sculptor but so penetrating a critic that these articles are still read by scholars. Then there was the effusion of Gelett Burgess, who received an engineering degree at the Institute but pursued a career as a humorist and critic, in which capacity he wrote a historic article in 1910 for *Architectural Record*—"Wild Men of Paris"—that introduced Americans to Picasso and company.

The great MIT figure in this arena, head and shoulders above everyone else, was in fact decidedly a practicing engineer: Desmond Fitzgerald, a man almost totally forgotten today in MIT's history. A graduate of Phillips Academy in Andover, Massachusetts, Fitzgerald made his career apprenticing to a number of engineering firms and working himself up to become head of Boston's Water Department. He was one of the first hydraulic engineers to study water pollution and established in the city of Boston the first biological laboratory in the United States connected with waterworks. He became a much-sought-after consultant, from New York and Chicago to San Francisco and Manila.

Without benefit of any formal training, Fitzgerald rose to great eminence in his field. His stature was such that he became a great MIT luminary, lecturing for the Department of Civil Engineering and becoming so closely involved in the Institute's affairs at all levels that he was ultimately accorded the honor of appointment to MIT's governing Corporation. He was also elected by his peers nationally to be president of the American Society of Civil Engineers. His American Academy of Arts and Sciences obituary declared: "Fitzgerald's position was unique. He was a great engineer."

Also on his own account and mostly through self-study—although he did have a postgraduate year in France studying art—Fitzgerald achieved considerable repute as a pioneering art connoisseur and collector of the era, sharing with Isabella Stewart Gardner the distinction of being Boston's leading art collectors; he was celebrated particularly for his patronage of the impressionists. The same obituary that

The first Cézanne in America, later shown at the Armory Show, was not to be found at the Museum of Fine Arts but in the MIT study on Boylston Street or in the home library on Marlborough Street of MIT professor John Osborne Sumner. After his death, *The Harvesters* entered the Phillips Collection in Washington, D.C.

called him "a great engineer" pointed out that he was also a pioneer patron and supporter of Claude Monet, with whom Fitzgerald was friends. When he was not lecturing at MIT or presiding over the semipublic museum attached to his Brookline home, he was very likely Monet's houseguest at the artist's storied retreat in Giverny.

Fitzgerald bridged art and technology on all sides of Copley Square for three decades. A member of the St. Botolph Club and largely responsible for that elite art club's historic first American Monet exhibition in 1892, at some point Fitzgerald also became involved in the Copley Society, as the Art Student Association of the School of the Museum of Fine Arts renamed itself in 1901. The group had identified with MIT since it leased from the Institute in 1893 what became Grundmann Studios on Clarendon Street (where the Hancock Tower is now). They were so closely associated that when Grundmann Studios was torn down in the 1910s, the Copley Society moved into MIT's central Rogers Building, keeping company with the architecture school for years. Moreover, in the 1910s Fitzgerald became even more intensely involved in this arena, becoming in 1914 a member and then chair of the art museum's Visiting Committee of the Department of Painting, then in 1916 ascending to the position of member of the board of trustees of the Museum of Fine Arts, appointed thereto—of course—by MIT.

Fitzgerald, in his capacity as a member of the Copley Society's Exhibition Committee, took in the International Exhibition of Modern Art—the famous Armory Show—which opened in New York in February 1913. The Archives of American Art website (the Desmond Fitzgerald papers) may surprise many with the revelation that this MIT engineer in 1913 "arranged to have the Armory Show come to Boston." In *The Battle to Bring Modernism to New England*, Boston Public Library fine arts curator Theresa Dickason Cederholm details the matter: "An engineer…who collected and wrote about art, Fitzgerald was at the time serving as treasurer of the Copley Society, and persuaded its President Holker Abbott and its board, to sponsor the Armory Show in Boston."

Boston's engineer–art educator, as Fitzgerald became known, thus seemed to ally himself with his fellow Dodge MacKnight collector, Isabella Stewart Gardner, who was herself both focus and facilitator of a discreet but perceptible movement toward the introduction of postimpressionism, as modernism in art was then called, in the New England capital, particularly the successful debut of Henri Matisse. Its beginning was very low-key. From 1909 onward, four of Gardner's intimates, including her chief art adviser, Bernard Berenson, and three fellow connoisseurs— Matthew Prichard (formerly of the Museum of Fine Arts), Byzantinist Thomas Whittemore, and fellow Back Bay collector Sarah Choate Sears—began to bring Matisse's work repeatedly to Gardner's attention, going so far as to gift her collection at Fenway Court with several works by the French modernist master, without which, they all seemed to suggest, her collection would be somehow incomplete. Gardner discouraged none of this.

A more public phase of what was going on opened in 1910, an early example of which William Gerdts cites in *The Color of Modernism: The American Fauves*, in which he writes:

> The American art writer Ann Seaton Schmidt published an important interview with Matisse in the *Boston Evening Transcript*. No proponent of Modernism…Schmidt nevertheless attempted an objective consideration of the French master.…Schmidt confessed her initial judgment of the artist as "slightly insane," but likewise admitted that further awareness of the controversy surrounding him had led her to the realization that he was "a genius, though to be sure a very erratic one…blazing a new path."

Matisse himself was quoted as asserting, "What I seek above all else is expression…represented not only by every line of the figure, but by…the composition [and] the arrangement of color tones."

The very next year, in a 1911 show at the Boston Art Club, Copley Square saw Matisse's work for the first time: six works by the French artist lent by Sears. It was three years after the first of his only two American shows, in New York in 1908 and 1910. Matisse's drawings elicited from critics a "reasonably positive" response, according to Museum of Fine Arts curator Carol Troyen ("a distinction that is well worth studying": *Boston Herald*; "extraordinary cleverness": *Boston Globe*), who has documented fully what may have been a follow-up exhibition at the Museum of Fine Arts, to which the lenders were Sears, Whittemore, the pioneering New York Matisse collector George Of, and, for the first time, Gardner herself. A "corridor show" perhaps, to which possibility Patrick MacMahon alerted me when I was writing my biography of Gardner in the 1990s. It was held in the Trustees Room and was highlighted by a "voluptuous nude" by Matisse from Gardner's own collection.

The *Christian Science Monitor* article that Troyen reprinted in her chapter in *The Armory Show at 100* confirms that this exhibition did in fact take place. (The only previous documentation, somewhat ambiguous, was the list of donors of Matisse's work to the museum, as noted in the Museum of Fine Arts's annual report of 1912.) The article's headline, "Post-Impressionist Pictures Here / Few Are on Exhibition at Museum [of Fine Arts], but Trustees Are Not Committing Themselves and Meanwhile Discussion Rages," surely tells it all. It would appear that only Matisse's work was shown, and the critical response to it from the *Monitor* was positive.

As it turned out, the Museum of Fine Arts trustees had no need to "commit themselves" further. That's what an alter ego is for—and was that not for Boston in 1911 the only-eight-years-old Gardner Museum? When the exhibition closed after just a few weeks, Whittemore, one of the lenders, gave Gardner one of the exhibition's thirteen works, a painting by Matisse, *The Terrace, Saint-Tropez*, which thereby became the first painting by Matisse to enter an American museum collection. Matisse had truly "come out" in Boston.

There is also a curiously intimate footnote to all this, a footnote also linking the Museum of Fine Arts with the French modernist master. In November 1913 Matisse achieved one of his greatest portraits in his drawing of Mabel Warren, widow of Gardner's great friend Samuel Warren, the museum's past president. "I couldn't do that every day," Matisse said of a session that left him "thrilled and shaken," according to biographer Catherine Bock-Weiss. The painter described "a constant movement in her [Mrs. Warren's] will forwards and backwards, giving and withdrawing, opening and closing," all unknowingly describing as well Matisse's debut in the New England capital.

Why Matisse and not Picasso, today perhaps the more highly esteemed of the two modernist rivals of the modern French school? For the same reason perhaps that Gardner is linked to Matisse and not his rival. In Troyen's Boston Armory Show one-hundredth anniversary article, the first comprehensive article on the subject, she is the first scholar, to my knowledge, to associate herself with the conclusion in my biography of Gardner that Boston's foremost collector of that era was not at all a traditionalist, as so many presume. In fact she was "a modernist, but one most comfortable at the more conservative end of the modernist continuum, . . . not the Boston School or Picasso, but Matisse."

All the foregoing perhaps explains why Gardner was the first of twelve honorary vice presidents—the list was *not* alphabetical—of the Armory Show when it opened in February 1913 in New York. There, it was neither Matisse nor Picasso whose work seized the day but Marcel Duchamp's highly abstract *Nude Descending a Staircase*. That this was the show's signature work points to the fact that if Desmond Fitzgerald, so closely identified with MIT, was the principal player on the organizing side of the Boston Armory Show, the chief player on the receiving end—indeed, the collecting end—was Walter Arensberg, a figure equally closely associated with Harvard.

Arensberg's part in the history of modern art in America is better known today than Fitzgerald's. While the latter's role in launching the Boston Armory Show remains obscure a hundred years later, the Harvard poet's role in perpetuating the show, and its effect through the collection he and his wife began to form in Copley Square (now housed in the Philadelphia Museum of Art), is in no danger at all of being overlooked. (Both Boston's Museum of Fine Arts and Harvard also sought the collection, but Philadelphia's terms were better.) Curator Innis Howe Shoemaker calls the Arensberg Collection "one of the greatest and most seminal gatherings of early modern art in the world." *Nude Descending a Staircase* is its star.

Walter and Louise Arensberg lived in Copley Square, on the block adjoining the MIT block. They were apartment dwellers in the Hotel Victoria, the elegant red brick and terra-cotta Moorish-style apartment house that still stands on the corner of Dartmouth and Newbury Streets. The Boston Armory Show was held at Copley Hall in Grundmann Studios, across the square in the block adjoining Trinity Church. Copley Hall was used by MIT for a variety of purposes, including in 1913 the memorial architectural exhibition of the head of MIT's architecture department, Constant-Désiré Despradelle. Or, for another example, a student play put on in 1915 by the Chinese students of MIT, Harvard, Radcliffe, and Wellesley. But chiefly it was where for years the Copley Society was based.

The son of a Pittsburgh steel tycoon, Walter Arensberg was a Harvard graduate who in 1913 returned to the university to study for an advanced degree. A published poet—in Boston, at Houghton Mifflin—Arensberg was, like his wife, Louise, drawn to modern art. The couple went down to New York in February of that year to see the first version of the Armory Show, and in the months following they could not let go of the experience, it was so transformative.

Their struggle entered its critical stage when the show followed them home to Copley Square, where it opened on April 28 after some weeks in Chicago. How many times the couple crossed the square to visit the exhibition no one knows. But we know the result. In the first place, the Arensbergs returned their one New York purchase, a relatively conservative one, during their first visit to the Boston show. The historian Robert M. Crunden in *American Salons* takes it from there: "The precise chronology that would establish Arensberg's progress through the weeks of the Armory Show, as it traveled from New York to Chicago to Boston, remains obscure. The essential facts seem to be that Arensberg lacked purpose and taste in modernist art before the show opened in New York; that he encountered the exhibition there, but was so shocked by what he saw that he went around in an aesthetic daze for several weeks...and that by the time the show closed in Boston in May 1913, Arensberg was a convert." Adds Crunden: "It was not until the last day of the show in Boston, before it was dismantled for good, that he...bought the last and smallest of the Villons....With this began his...interest in Villon and his brother, Marcel Duchamp, whose close friend he later became."

Arensberg's choice was number 235 in the Boston catalog; it cost him $81. That Villon oil was, two lithographs aside, writes Innis Howe Shoemaker in *Jacques*

International Exhibition of Modern Art

Under the Auspices of the

ASSOCIATION OF AMERICAN PAINTERS AND SCULPTORS, Incorporated

COPLEY SOCIETY OF BOSTON
COPLEY HALL
April Twenty-eighth to May Nineteenth

1913

The Boston and Chicago versions of the Armory Show are less well known than the New York version, but at least one of the New York organizers thought the Boston show topped them all as an art exhibition, calling it "a wonder." MIT's Desmond Fitzgerald was the moving force in creating Boston's very influential show and the most radical of its kind to that date.

Villon and His Cubist Prints, "the only work that the fledgling collectors Louise and Walter Arensberg purchased directly from the Armory Show in 1913 [and] perfectly presaged their unparalleled collection of early modern painting."

What had happened? Many a Harvard-MIT meal at the elite St. Botolph Club, I would hazard. On the block adjoining MIT, on the other side of the street from where Arensberg lived, was the convivial clubhouse of that artistic group. Both Fitzgerald and Arensberg were members. The reason why the Arensbergs' struggle with modern art reached its climax in Copley Square, and why they finally plunged headlong into cubism in the New World Acropolis and not in New York, had, I suspect, a lot to do with Desmond Fitzgerald's concept of the Boston Armory Show. It was a case of the MIT engineer and the Harvard poet seeing eye to eye.

The New York version of the Armory Show Fitzgerald saw in Manhattan was an extravaganza—huge and spectacular, but also sprawling and (some thought) unfocused, even incoherent. The third and final version was sufficiently different. As one might expect, the Boston Brahmin version of the show was serious, earnest, sober, and dignified, more upscale—in fact, elitist—and intensely focused. (The second venue, Chicago, was something else again, resembling nothing so much as a circus.)

The arrangements were handled by the Copley Society's Exhibition Committee, which wrote on January 27 to Walt Kuhn, secretary of the American Association of Painters and Sculptors, the sponsors of the Armory Show, expressing keen interest in "the exhibition of Futurists." When New York in turn expressed interest in Boston's proposal, Copley Society president Abbott dispatched a delegation to Manhattan to seal the deal. The four-man group was as much an MIT delegation as a Copley Society one, according to Milton Brown's classic text on the Armory Show. One member of the delegation was Fitzgerald; another was his MIT colleague, he of the Cézanne (which he lent to the Armory Show), Professor John Osborne Sumner.

Brown takes up the story from there: "Late in March…Mechanics Hall [a huge facility as large as the New York Armory and just west of Copley Square]…was suggested by [New York organizer Walt] Kuhn. In a telegram from Chicago to [another New York organizer, Arthur Davies,] he proposed, 'Suggest they secure Mechanics Hall and do it rich.'" But the Copley Society—which is to say, President Abbott and his board, influenced by Fitzgerald—made plain from the beginning that no such course of action was being considered. Abbott, in a letter of February 19, did not mince words. As quoted by Marcia L. Vose and Nancy Allyn Jarzombek in the winter 1999 issue of *Vose ArtNotes*, the Copley Society president wrote, "Our hall, Copley Hall, is not large enough for the whole, or nearly the whole of your exhibition," reports about the size and content of which he clearly had received. Nor did he regret the fact (tipping his hand) that Boston didn't want the whole show, not really. Echoing Boston's first inquiry about wanting "the Futurists," as Holker insisted, "We are very anxious, if possible," Abbott wrote, "to have the French portion, especially the Post-Impressionists." The Copley Society had no desire to "do it rich" and from the beginning was clear that the only possible decision was the one Milton Brown reported: "The final decision was to send [to Boston only] the foreign contingent."

It was further decided that in Boston there would be none of the free admission days that had swelled attendance in New York and Chicago, days Kuhn had despaired of, writing to his wife of one such: "A free day and we had 15,000 visitors… disgusted." It would also be a more select audience in Boston, where the admission price during prime viewing hours was set at twice what it had been in New York. But the smaller hall and the focus on the "foreign contingent" were most different. The Boston catalog made a point of this, announcing that nearly one thousand works had been rejected by Boston, the decision having been made that "the most important thing of all was to display the European section"—the most radical part. Kuhn, still by no means convinced, did remark about the Copley Society, once he reached Boston, "It's such a relief to deal with people who are not after every dollar." Education, not profit, was the order of the day.

Some have been skeptical of this "educational" aspect to the Boston show. Troyen has written that the Boston show's sponsors, among them Fitzgerald and T. Jefferson Coolidge, "disclaimed responsibility for the content of the show, explaining defensively that they neither approved nor disapproved of the art, but presented it as an educational service." Identified as he was with MIT and increasingly seen as an art educator, Fitzgerald certainly was dedicated to such a stance time and again in his activities. In its annual report the Copley Society confirmed this "educational" purpose, referring to Boston's many "schools and colleges," effectively stating clearly what differentiated Boston from New York and Chicago at the turn of the twentieth century.

Boston's increasing role as the country's "college town," its intellectual capital, was itself an expression of what might be called the Brahmin balance, the way Boston Brahmins could be at one and the same time America's progressive urban aristocracy (as opposed to the equally historic but more conservative rural aristocracy of Virginia), though hardly less conservative culturally than liberal socially.

For example, the adherents of the first American modernism, Unitarianism, were by no means head over heels modern art lovers. In her preference for Matisse over Picasso, Gardner showed herself, in this respect at least, more Bostonian than New Yorker. One Brahmin, the Harvard art historian John Coolidge, himself a scion of a venerable Boston Brahmin family, put it very well in his contribution to *Modern Art at Harvard* when he described an academic of the Armory Show generation, Arthur Pope—"conservative, but with the sensitivity of a painter and a scholar of painting, Pope was especially sympathetic to Matisse's brilliant use of color"—as an example of the way Brahmins, "if they had little active interest in modern art, neither did they actively oppose it, nor generally did they fail to 'see something in it.'"

Fitzgerald's point of view exactly, notable as he was for championing Dodge MacKnight, a turn-of-the-twentieth-century Boston painter whose work the historian William Gerdts concluded "bespeaks an awareness of Modernist and perhaps specifically Fauve sensibilities" but was nonetheless "basically Impressionist." Gardner also collected MacKnight—there is a MacKnight Room at Fenway Court—and it is significant as well that Fitzgerald, while he himself bought nothing from the Armory

Show, according to his diary, did take a friend to see it and to lunch afterward, noting that his friend bought "a charming picture…by Jacques Villon." A cubist!

Fitzgerald's own writings bear out this balanced Brahmin attitude. In his 1916 book on MacKnight, Fitzgerald argued, "There has always been a crisis in art, and we may add, with the utmost assurance, there always will be." He added: "Now we have crises in art with almost every revolution of our planet.…Just now we have the Cubistes flaunting their banners." Always interested, he was not converted but he stayed alert.

That said, no one, least of all Fitzgerald, doubted what "educational" meant insofar as the Boston Armory Show was concerned. Why, after all, had the Copley Society from the beginning emphasized the work of the "Futurists" and the French postimpressionists? The special issue of *Arts and Decoration* dedicated to the New York show explains why. There is a reason Fitzgerald in his diary called the show day after day "the Cubist Show" or the "Modern Show." That's where there was something to learn.

Something? Everything, to hear the postimpressionists tell it. The journal painter William Glackens remarked that he was "afraid that the American section of this exhibition will seem very tame beside the foreign section," while F. J. Gregg worried that "the American work…represents no such vigor as the European work." Lloyd Goodrich would affirm, "It was the foreign section that contained the dynamite —especially the fauves and cubists." That's what Fitzgerald wanted. The dynamite. Not less of a show, but a more focused, more pointed, *more educational* show.

Kuhn, though he seemed to see Boston's point, remained skeptical right up to the last possible moment. When on April 23 he commented that Boston would be "especially hard considering the show has been cut," it does not sound as if he approved. Yet on that day or the eighteenth—the date is illegible—when Kuhn telegraphed from Chicago to Boston, "American section too large.…After careful consideration our judgment mistake to try to add same and spoil force and appear-ance of show," his comment indicated at least an understanding of, if not agreement with, Boston's point of view.

Kuhn and Fitzgerald got on very well, and they may have increasingly become allies. In a letter of April 5, Kuhn pronounced on Fitzgerald very clearly, "He's the real stuff." We know also from Fitzgerald's diary that he and Kuhn planned the hanging of the show ("to Copley Hall," Fitzgerald wrote on April 23, "and met Mr. Kuhn and began work on Ex[hibition]"). Then too there was Kuhn's remark of April 9 to his wife. "Oh what a difference from Chicago. I feel absolutely at home here [in Boston] compared to that awful town," wrote the New Yorker. "We have decided to take our time and have a careful consultation…considering the show has been cut. Now that I am here the situation is looming up quite interesting. The very gamble of it is fascinating."

By which he surely meant the whole new "educational" slant. And the gamble paid off handsomely. Archives of American Art curator Garnett McCoy described Fitzgerald as having "spent many hours…reading and taking notes on the literature of Post-Impressionism" before the show. Boston Public Library's fine arts curator

Theresa Dickason Cederholm, with her access through the Boston Society of Independent Artists to the all-important oral history, most clearly identified what was on Fitzgerald's mind: "The fanfare provoked by the Armory Show in New York… proved to be just the opportunity Desmond Fitzgerald had been seeking to create [and here Cederholm is quoting art historian Barbara Haskell] 'a crash course on modernism—[that might close] the gap between American and European standards of reference.'" A course! What could be more Bostonian?

The design of the Copley Hall show more than lived up to such expectations. The visitor first encountered Cézanne, then Gauguin and Van Gogh, then Seurat, Signac, Munch. Standing out overall, massed on the stage, were the gorgeous Matisses. One of the contributors to *The Armory Show at 100* noted, "In the show's Boston venue, Matisse's works were shown alone on the stage in the hall, looking outward and crowning the story of modernism told within." Picasso, Francis Picabia, Wassily Kandinsky, Fernand Léger, Robert Delaunay, and Duchamp were quite a coda. The cubists had the adjoining Allston Hall all to themselves, and John Rewald notes it was the busiest room in Boston. In between were such delights as sculptures by Constantin Brancusi. (One of them, number 8 in the Boston show, *Une Muse*, sold for more than $12 million at Christie's in New York in 2012.)

The result was stunning. Fitzgerald, discoverer of Marsden Hartley and champion of Dodge MacKnight, was by no means uninterested in American work. But for the Armory Show he wanted only the dynamite that would clarify European and American standards of reference. That was the course's content. But in its quiet and serious way, the Boston Armory Show offered surely the most distilled, concentrated, and powerful modern art exhibition imaginable. It was more than educational. It was revelatory. Copley Square mounted a show the likes of which Paris had never seen. Kuhn, for one, organizer of all three shows, saw once the show was hung what a triumph it was. He wrote to a colleague, Art Young, back in Manhattan, that "the New York show was a great demonstration, but the Boston one excels as an art exhibition; it is a wonder!"

It would have been surprising if Arensberg had *not* been finally bowled over, driven forward in his thinking, by the Boston show, conceived as it was to appeal to artistic intellectuals just like him. Evidence of a wider effect is also clear in the perhaps more prosaic but still significant fact that while, yes, Boston's show attracted only about twelve to fifteen thousand visitors—many fewer than the seventy thousand who had seen the New York show and an even smaller percentage of the more than a hundred thousand who had visited the Chicago venue, the sale of catalogs, betokening a more serious interest, was proportionately a great deal higher. McCoy pointed this out as long ago as in 1980. For example, one in three visitors bought a catalog in Boston (almost five thousand), while only one in eight (about twelve thousand) bought one in Chicago.

Press accounts in Boston largely disappointed the New Yorkers. And they have had a similar effect on many scholars since, who seem unable to cope without the much more interesting narrative of conflict the Armory Show offered in its other two cities. Negative reviews certainly predominated. The *Boston Evening Transcript*, predictably outraged, pronounced the show's massed Matisses "a deliberate reversion to Barbarism." The *Christian Science Monitor*, hardly a radical journal, had much more positive things to say; it found the same display of Matisses "gorgeous in massed screaming hues." The *Atlantic* was philosophical: "We are all conservative and progressive at such odd angles." The Armory Show exactly. And then there was critic Philip Hale's quickly notorious limerick, ending with "[if] you should see on the stair / a lady quite bare"—the reference, of course, was to Duchamp's descending nude—"Now wouldn't that rattle your slats."

The *Monitor* also stressed Picasso's work. Number 145 in Boston, *Vase, Two Bowls, Compote and Lemon* (which had been number 345 in New York; note how much smaller Boston's exhibition was, with only 244 of New York's more than 1,200 pictures) stands out as symbolizing how provoking, in a thoughtful way, the Boston Armory Show must have been. Picasso's still life is easily readable. But its "strange elisions of planes," its "contradictory light sources" and "nervous shifting of concave and convex surfaces that undermine the effects of traditional chiaroscuro and perspective"—these are Robert Rosenberg's words in our own time—make this picture exceptional. (It is also now in the collection of the Philadelphia Museum of Art.)

Kuhn wrote to his wife of his reaction to the press opening, which was characteristically Bostonian: "About 120 present. All intelligent *and not a single silk hat* [emphasis added]. Some I met were…Mrs. Jack Gardner…[and] Dr. Pinz [e.g., Morton Prince, the psychiatrist]. They all say he will surely write an important paper on modern art as the direct result of the show." The eminent Harvard psychologist Hugo Münsterberg also attended the press opening, Kuhn noted, concluding: "They are all prepared to think in this town. There was not any tea party about it; just a lot of earnest *people seeking* [emphasis added]."

Desmond Fitzgerald exactly! The Arensbergs exactly! And if a crash course for earnest people is a less exciting tale than hanging artists in effigy in Chicago, or storming the gates in New York, so be it. Walter Pach, the chief sales agent for all three venues of the Armory Show—as well as its chief polemicist—testified: "[Walter Arensberg] not only came to study the pictures at old Copley Hall but had me come repeatedly to his [home]…for long evenings of talk about them."

As for Dr. "Pinz," what was the headline of the *Herald* review? "Dreams of Psychopathy." Freudianism was a larger aspect of the Boston show than most realize. Kuhn, decades later, on the eve of the decade that would mark his own descent into mental illness and institutionalization, when he tried to account for the "failure," as many saw it, of the Boston show, suggested that "local psychiatrists were especially vehement in their disapproval." Not true at all. Kuhn was probably misremembering twenty-five years later the furor modern art aroused among Philadelphia alienists. In Boston the effect was just the opposite. Copley Square's preeminence as a Freudian center worked very much to the Boston show's advantage. Indeed, Pach also remembered explicitly that "[Arensberg's] approach to modernist art was not merely literary, but was based on his studies in psycho-analysis."

Among Arensberg's closest friends, for example, was Elmer Ernest Southard, a professor at Harvard Medical School (for so many years MIT's scientific sister in the square) and head of Boston Psychopathic Hospital. Southard was very supportive of the Boston show. It is true that he gave a speech titled "Are Cubists Insane?"—a title Kuhn may have remembered—but the question was only rhetorical and was answered in the negative. Southard is significant in another way too. Like Professor Sumner, the MIT professor who owned the Cézanne, Southard was a member of the St. Botolph Club, as were both Fitzgerald and Arensberg, and it would have been strange if Arensberg hadn't encouraged the same sort of long conversations at lunch about the show he persuaded Pach into having in the evenings.

The Boston Armory Show, like early MIT's role as Copley Square's arts provocateur, has receded so deep into unread history because of the widespread belief in the truth of what McCoy wrote in 1980. "The fact is," McCoy insisted, "there is no known documentation directly revealing an influence arising from the Boston Armory Show." It is an astonishing thing to say—astonishing in two ways. That Boston's show was indeed "a denser concentration of twentieth century European artists than [in] either New York or Chicago" and that some people consequently "considered the Boston version a more coherent exhibition" is a conclusion I am not alone in reaching. Nor am I alone in thinking that the matter needs to be further explored. The distinguished art historian Gail R. Scott, in her splendid book about the American modernist painter E. Ambrose Webster (2009), comes to a similar conclusion.

The second and more fundamental reason why McCoy's assertion is astonishing is that documentation of a huge influence has long been known among those scholars who do not limit themselves narrowly to their own field. Most art historians look for influence among artists and go no further. It never seems to occur to them that it might be worthwhile to explore a possible influence on, say, poets. Art alone doth not drive civilization. Literature has its part. Research readily discloses that the exhibition registered primarily on American *literature*, and in a way, moreover, that no American, however unknowing, was untouched by.

The poet Amy Lowell, for instance, came away from the show with a most interesting response. "I had a faint idea," her biographer Samuel Foster Damon reports her having said, "of what the idiom of Cubism might be, but I could get no clue to the other schools." Typically, Lowell grasped the *most* radical work more easily than the less radical. And it was just a year after her visit to Copley Hall that her *Sword Blades and Poppy Seed*, Louis Untermeyer suggested, "sounded some of the first notes in the controversy which raged about the New Poetry."

McCoy apparently never saw Charles Bernardin's "John Dos Passos' Harvard Years," either. Published in *New England Quarterly* in 1954, twenty-five years before McCoy's article, Bernardin observes that in the first place, however more reticently, something was to be expected of Brahmins after all: "In Boston the Armory Show created a stir as it had in New York." You just had to probe beneath the headlines, negative or positive. "What one thought of Brancusi or Duchamp not only decided invitations to dinner, but one's respectability and standing in the community,"

Bernardin wrote. "'Monstrous,' gasped the diehards. 'Superb,' cheered the avant garde....As a result of the Boston showing, everyone at Harvard began talking favorably or unfavorably about Cubism."

A passing frisson? Not really. Was not Harvard undergraduate John Dos Passos, seventeen when he first saw the Armory Show, just the audience that Fitzgerald had in mind? Dos Passos's biographer is clear: "Parades, riots, strikes, protests, woman's suffrage, a presidential election—all did relatively little to pipe Dos Passos and his classmates outside the gates of Harvard Yard, but avant garde art did....The International Loan Exhibition of Modern Art set off a flurry of excitement in Boston's Copley Hall in the spring of 1913....Harvard professors and students hastened to [Copley Square]." Moreover, it was specifically noted that "many paintings from the show had been dropped....What remained was the most startling."

If Dos Passos, soon to be the author of the *U.S.A.* trilogy, ranked by the Modern Library as number thirty-three on its list of the one hundred best English-language novels of the twentieth century, is an example of how forceful a jolt and at how high a level the Boston Armory Show in fact delivered, his Harvard classmate E. E. Cummings is an even greater example of the Boston show's extensive influence. Richard S. Kennedy's history tells of how a friend took the young Harvard student "to the Armory Show in 1913." Kennedy's account of how Cummings grew "ecstatic over Brancusi" is riveting.

So is Kennedy's overall thesis, with which few would argue: that Cummings was "one of the leading American poets who revolutionized literary expression in the twentieth century," the formative stages of which were strongly influenced by the Boston show. Its effect on his thought is evidenced by his Harvard term papers. It was not long before "the first display of sympathy with the modern sensibility that appears in his writings comes in [a] term paper [Cummings] submitted [in 1915]... entitled 'The New Art.'" In it Cummings emphasizes work he first saw at the Boston show, including Brancusi's *The Kiss* and Duchamp's forever-descending nude. He tried to show "the interconnections among the new tendencies." The following year he discussed the Boston show in another paper and referred to Ezra Pound and Amy Lowell as the "Picasso and the Picabia of the new poetry." In Cummings's own poetry, moreover, Kennedy offers examples of the art's effect, citing "the crossover of sense and associations in [phrases like] 'the screech of dissonant flowers.'"

It exerted more than a little influence in art as well. Only a generation later, in the face of the conservatism of Boston's art museum and Harvard's Fogg Museum, the Harvard Society for Contemporary Art was founded by Lincoln Kirstein and Edward M. M. Warburg, "to pick up the torch," in John Coolidge's words, "lit by the Armory Show."

Notice how all these impacts of the Boston show on wider American culture—from Arensberg to Cummings—have stayed sufficiently alive so as to surface when the matter is probed, whereas the MIT origins of the Boston Armory Show are much harder to dig up. Yet in a very real sense, the Boston show was not simply MIT's greatest artistic gift to Copley Square; it was another of MIT's gifts to Harvard. The latter was very far behind MIT in the area of modern art. Harvard Art Museum curator Caroline A. Jones says of the famous founding director of the Fogg Museum, Edward Forbes, in *Modern Art at Harvard*: "[His] concept of acceptable modern art did not include the work exhibited in the Armory Show, which had come to Boston in 1913....There is no evidence that Forbes was affected by the Armory Show." Whereas Desmond Fitzgerald made imaginative use through the Copley Society of the historic MIT–art museum alliance to achieve in the Boston Armory Show a most potent modernist cocktail.

My favorite result of Fitzgerald's great coup of bringing the Armory Show to Copley Square and completely reimagining it was distinctly technological. Hugo Münsterberg, whom Kuhn spoke of meeting at the press opening, wrote a historic paper three years later on the photoplay as modern art, the first scholarly treatment of the motion picture. The *Christian Science Monitor*, the one Boston paper that got behind the show's "educational" thesis, was also first to see the connection between the Armory Show and Münsterberg's seminal paper. In its review of the show, comment was made about the Duchamp nude forever descending: "M Duchamp appears to have been inspired by moving pictures to attempt a representation of complete action."

Clearly, early MIT had an exceptional role in American artistic life of the era. And not only art and architecture, but philosophy as well was everywhere part of early MIT. Politics too. When in 2005 MIT professor Noam Chomsky was dubbed in an internet poll—conducted by the British magazine *Prospect* and the American journal *Foreign Affairs*—"the world's greatest intellectual," many wondered if it was for Chomsky's seminal work in the field of linguistics or for his libertarian socialist thought and activism. It was a striking commentary on "the Pentagon on the Charles," as the Institute is often called, that Chomsky, famously leftist, held its highest faculty rank, Institute Professor. The incongruity was pronounced by many as very MIT.

Chomsky, in a fascinating interview given to the *Boston Globe*, explained that "the spirit of rebellion" he personified at MIT was "a natural by product of the MIT culture," in the context of which faculty and students are "constantly testing out their theories and a strong premium is put on the free flow of information." He was referring to the sort of "questioning subculture" that Benjamin Tucker experienced the first stirrings of in Copley Square almost a century and a half ago. Benjamin who? First, George Holmes Howison.

In his *Essays, Comments, and Reviews*, William James highlights "a little philosophical club that used to meet every fortnight in rooms in Temple Street, off Boston Common, a club of perhaps eight or so colleagues." One of its members was Howison, of whom Ralph Barton Perry writes: "Although George Holmes Howison was James's senior by eight years, they were philosophical contemporaries. In 1872, only a year before James began teaching at Harvard, Howison became professor of logic and the philosophy of science at the Massachusetts Institute of Technology....

[Seven years later he left MIT and] in 1884 he was appointed to the University of California [at Berkeley]....Despite their wide separation, James and Howison maintained a close friendship until the year of [James's] death."

Howison enjoyed a long and prominent career in his field thereafter, but it was during his years at MIT that "he began his earnest writing and lecturing," Randall Auxier writes in the *Dictionary of Modern American Philosophers*. "Most important among the activities of those years were the informal meetings in the Temple Street rooms [of the philosophical club]....American philosophical pluralism and American personalism," Auxier believes, were both "founded in those fortnightly meetings."

Linda Simon, one of James's biographers, agrees that Howison's influence was always very much present in Pragmatism, which he launched as a public movement at MIT at the Lowell Institute. Writing about his eight lectures there in 1908, James admitted: "I didn't know, until I came to prepare them, how full of power to found a 'school' and become a 'cause' the pragmatistic idea was. But now I am all aflame with it, as displacing all rationalistic systems...and I mean to turn the lectures into a solid little cube of a book." *Pragmatism* it was called, and it is now a very famous book indeed.

In this discourse as in art, it was not just by faculty but also by students that this chapter was written. Which is where Benjamin Tucker comes in. Tucker was an MIT student who after graduation went on to become, to quote the *New York Times*, "an icon of the intellectual [e.g., nonviolent] anarchist movement." His *Boston Globe* obituary explains him best: "This brilliant man, known throughout the world for his intellectual leadership, became convinced of the efficacy of anarchism after his hero, Horace Greeley, had been defeated for the Presidency in 1872. This was when [Tucker] was 18 years old, when he met the man he called his 'first great teacher,' Josiah Warren....At the Massachusetts Institute of Technology, which he entered in his sixteenth year, he had heard such men as [Unitarian] D. B. Frothingham of New York, [the abolitionist] William Lloyd Garrison, and such famous women as [the feminists] Julia Ward Howe and Lucy Stone." Tucker described himself already at age eighteen as "an atheist, a materialist, an evolutionist, a prohibitionist, a free trader, a champion of the eight-hour day, a woman suffragist, an enemy of marriage, and a believer in sexual freedom." The obituary concludes: "At 19 he left MIT and went abroad, returning...[to] a post at the *Globe*, remaining there in various capacities from a printer to an editorial writer for eleven years....Then he determined to devote his talents to editing *Liberty*, termed by contemporaries as 'the foremost journal of anarchism in the world.' Mr. Tucker gleaned his background for much of his anarchist beliefs from wide reading of...Proudhon, Bakonine, and Kropotkin." Prince Peter Kropotkin himself lectured in Copley Square for the Lowell Institute during Tucker's time there. Tucker recalled in his old age, in his autobiography, his rejection of his parents' desire that he go to Harvard, and how Tech—which he described in 1869 as "comparatively young, but promising"—was the family compromise.

Tucker was just the sort of student who was likely to have been drawn to Howison, and the MIT Registrar's Office confirms that young Benjamin did indeed complete at least one course "in the first semester of the 1872–73 academic year" in his degree major of "Science and Literature," a course "our documentation does seem to indicate…was taught by Professor of Logic and the Philosophy of Science George H. Howison." Most today might find it surprising that MIT even *had* a professor of philosophy in anything in the 1870s, in only its seventh year of operation. Just as its having an instructor who gave watercolor classes would surprise, never mind a student like Benjamin Tucker.

One might assume that Tucker, as well as Howison and Turner, were eccentrics at early MIT. They were exceptional, to be sure. But that was true of many in the New World Acropolis. The truth is, although it would be too much to assert it was always part and parcel of the Brahmin playbook, no intellectual center of the stature of Copley Square could fail to attract a counterculture (as we would call it today) of important left-wing figures. Arthur Mann's *Yankee Reformers in the Urban Age* (1974) confirms how many there were, not least at MIT. The intellectual ferment of the Acropolis was sustained by that counterculture of Boston's two bohemias, the older one not very far away on Beacon Hill's North Slope, and the younger Copley Square's bohemia in the South Back Bay along Huntington Avenue and St. Botolph Street. And by the raucous and ribald life of the South End red-light district and the ghetto beyond, across the railroad tracks—a slum haunted, for instance, by T. S. Eliot as a Harvard student in the early 1900s.

To grasp the overall scene that was so formative in the creation of MIT culture, witness the chance encounter in September 1891 of two Yale alumni who bumped into each other at the start of term in Copley Square, their inevitable topic of conversation nearby Beacon Hill or South End lodging houses. One was a first-year student at Harvard Medical School on Boylston Street behind the public library, the other a returning student at MIT on Boylston Street behind Trinity Church.

We know a lot about the first student, Harvey Cushing, who would go on to become, as Sherwin B. Nuland wrote, "one of the greatest medical innovators ever produced by the United States—or any other country." The father of neurosurgery must have been the bane of guests at the Lenox Hotel across Exeter Street from the medical school, where Cushing was so brilliant at dissecting human heads that his instructors always placed him near a window, "which in the old gas-lighted room was important," if perhaps too public. We know as well that, confronted with the "splendid new Public Library," Cushing, in his biographer's words, "had a hard time dragging himself away."

About the MIT student we know nothing. But chances are that he also lived in the same sort of lodging house and also haunted the new library, and that he too went on to become a "radical innovator" in his field. MIT, Harvard Med—Copley Square—was like that. Take, for instance, Roger Babson, today honored as the father of one of the best business schools in the country, Babson College, which he founded in 1919. Babson in the 1890s was an MIT undergraduate at the same time Cushing was a medical student across the square. Certainly like Cushing, as Babson's biographer recalls, Babson "walked across the square and over the Dartmouth Street [railroad] trestle [bridge] in the South End to a very cheap restaurant—Priests by name—at the corner of Dartmouth and Columbus Avenue. It was a ten-minute walk from the heart of the Acropolis, and there one was." Columbus Avenue, Babson's biographer notes, "was a red-light district." In his South End essays, Paul M. Wright quotes from Siegel Fleisher's *The Lion and the Honeycomb* of a black pencil seller always peddling on the trestle in front of Back Bay Station, positioned midway between "culture" and "squalor." So were Copley Square's "lefties."

Besides MIT's Tucker, probably the best known of Copley Square's left-wing intellectuals in the early MIT days was BU professor Frank Parsons, whose engineering degree from Cornell perhaps accounted for his popularity at the Institute. Parsons was a Socialist but not a Marxist, and a humanitarian and a reformer. In 1905 he organized Breadwinner's College in Boston's North End "in imitation of Toynbee Hall's Workingmen's Institute" in London, according to Arthur Mann. "Together with…an ardent coterie of Harvard and Massachusetts Institute of Technology students as aides…the professor brought enlightenment and culture to the dwellers in the slums."

Better-known members of this circle include Laurence Gronlund, whose *The Co-operative Commonwealth* (1884), a foundational document of American socialism (the British edition was edited by George Bernard Shaw), was published in Boston, and Hamlin Garland, who, according to Van Wyck Brooks, "lived on forty cents a day," and as Arthur Mann tells it, spent "most of his time in the [Copley Square] Public Library reading Darwin and Spencer, Howells, Zola and Ibsen." Actually, he had come east from Wisconsin to Boston in search of an education but could win acceptance to neither Harvard nor BU and ended up deciding to get his own education at the Boston Public Library. When he began to write, he emerged as a champion of the Midwest farming frontier and of the Native American. His 1922 breakthrough biography *A Daughter of the Middle Border* earned a Pulitzer Prize.

All these lefties tended to gather around the square's great liberal standard bearer, the *Arena* magazine, founded in 1889 by B. O. Flower. "An energetic and idealistic young man," in Allen Matuson's words, Flower arrived in Boston from rural Illinois in the 1880s. He never envisaged the *Arena* as a profitable venture, but rather as "afford[ing] a field of combat"—Matuson's words again—for his causes on what he saw as "a nation on the eve of violent class warfare." He conducted the warfare in grand Copley Square style in the magnificent Pier Hall building between the art museum and the public library, above the fashionable S. S. Pierce grocery and wine shop, and underneath the hall where so many Boston debutantes came out.

Flower was not modest, asserting that the *Arena* was "the leading progressive journal of the world." It certainly was widely influential. "The Boston magazine became," Arthur Mann has written, "the champion of a new society, of a new art, a new religion, a new economy, a new government, a new education, [and] a new sexual ethic." Flower himself asserted, "After the appearance of *Looking Backward, The*

Arena became the recognized leader of the…Marxian Socialistic movement," and there is no doubt that that famous utopian novel by Edward Bellamy (whose base of operation was Boston) catapulted the *Arena* to the forefront and upped everybody's game. In the first issue of the *Literary Digest*, the lead article, friendly but not uncritical toward Bellamy's novel, was by no less than MIT president Francis A. Walker.

Not even best-selling fiction, however, survives to leave so indelible an impression as masterly architecture. Copley Square as a great cultural and intellectual Acropolis is still easily imaginable because of its surviving architecture of church and library. What does not survive is perhaps its greatest leftist image, because it is a cinematic rather than an architectural image—an image one must make an effort to recover, an image worthy of cinema legend Sergei Eisenstein but unseen by the great Soviet filmmaker or any American contemporary. It is an image of a protest march in 1908 led by another lefty often found in the square, the Socialist activist Morrison L. Swift: "Headed by Swift,…400 unemployed men yesterday morning… marched four abreast in a long line down Commonwealth avenue at the time when its residents were starting for church, and to the astonishment of all entered Trinity Church.…There was German, Polish, Greek, and Yiddish all within earshot.…An odor like unto garlic arose.…The congregation…stared in amazement, for a like spectacle was never before seen."

This is not the place to tell the story of that day, but it makes the point that, intellectually as well as artistically, the culture of MIT was formed in an atmosphere *both* aristocratic and radical. The Institute's very grand annual baccalaureate service always took place in Trinity Church, the sermon preached usually by MIT Corporation member Phillips Brooks, himself Socialist Frank Parsons's mentor.

The labor unrest of the 1890s and early 1900s in America had an equally dramatic if less cinematic effect on the life of Copley Square. President Francis Walker showed himself to be no hidebound conservative when he invited one of the leading American lawyers of the day—later to become the first Jew to sit on the US Supreme Court—to teach at MIT. Louis D. Brandeis, a Missouri native first seen in Boston when he entered Harvard Law School at the age of eighteen, was one of the city's leading lawyers by the early 1890s. With his Boston Brahmin partner Samuel Warren—who was president of the Museum of Fine Arts, by the way—he coauthored "The Right to Privacy," one of the most influential law review articles ever written. He was well on his way, furthermore, to becoming the public-interest advocate who would earn the title "the People's Lawyer." Some years later, in an interview with Livy Richards in the *Independent*, Brandeis had this to say about his years teaching at MIT, from 1892 to 1896:

> I had been asked to give a course on Business Law at the Massachusetts Institute of Technology, and had gone to some pains to prepare my lectures…when one morning the newspaper carried the story of the [July 6, 1892] pitched battle between the Pinkerton's [guards]…and the barricaded steel workers.…I saw at once that the common law, built up under simpler conditions of living, gave an inadequate basis for

the adjustment of the complex relations of the modern factory system. I threw away my notes and approached my theme from new angles. Those lectures at Tech marked an epoch in my career.

Even as he was moving leftward, he did not lose his balance. As David Roth, his biographer, notes, business law at the time "seemed perilously like the law of the jungle if one looked at the exploits of Goulds or Vanderbilts. But Brandeis offered a different ethic, one of public service"—the Brahmin ideal in an era when Brahmin businessmen themselves were not always upholding it. Brandeis's Yankee Brahmin alliances grew strained from the 1910s onward because of his leftward shift, exacerbated by the increasing anti-Semitism of the 1910s, 1920s, and 1930s in America.

Serving the public interest was an ideal that MIT's founder invested much in. William Barton Rogers was a progressive who had moved to Boston from the American South in no small measure because of the northern capital's liberal repute, a key aspect, as he saw it, of a "knowledge-seeking" community. In nurturing early MIT he had had to go much slower on many fronts—perhaps including women's education—than he would have liked. One of the chief aspects of his time at the University of Virginia that, by all accounts, deeply troubled him was the "frenzy of religious intolerance," in Philip Alexander's words, that greeted two faculty appointments there, one of a Catholic and one of a Jew. Rogers himself hired a Catholic— Gaetano Lanza—to teach at MIT in the 1870s. And his handpicked successor hired a Jew. The New World Acropolis did not shatter.

There was a still-larger dimension to Brandeis's teaching stint at MIT, as there would always be to his work at Harvard. The Boston Brahmin world was changing: Increasingly, Brahmins were not Yankees in the Puritan-Patriot-Brahmin continuum. The civilization of a "mother city," which Boston had become by the turn of the twentieth century, was growing even more powerful than in Rogers's day. Although Walter Muir Whitehill insisted on carrying the point even further into his own day in his seminally titled study of 1966, *Boston in the Age of John Fitzgerald Kennedy*, what the creators of the University of Oklahoma Press had in mind in their Centers of Civilization series was to follow *Athens in the Age of Pericles*, *Rome in the Age of Augustus*, and so on with *Boston in the Age of Ralph Waldo Emerson*. Brandeis's teaching stint at MIT sent a signal that the learned pool, so to speak, was distinctly expanding. Boston Brahmins could now be Jews.

Although some Brahmins clung to birth as a criterion for inclusion in the caste, according to Philippa Strum, by Brandeis's day Brahminism had become "almost entirely an intellectual creed. The path to that world lay through Harvard.... Such Brahmin thinkers as Emerson, Julia Ward Howe [a close friend of Rogers], Wendell Philips, [and] Edward Everett Hale"—headed, I must interject, by Charles W. Eliot and William James—"emphasized what one did rather than who one was and upheld the right of the newcomers to join.... Mark Twain summarized this attitude by commenting that, 'In Boston they ask, How much does he know? in New York, How much is he worth? in Philadelphia, Who were his parents?'"

Louis D. Brandeis, who has been called
the first Jewish Boston Brahmin, taught
at MIT years before his ascent to the
US Supreme Court, where he was the
first Jew to serve as a justice.

Strum continues, "By the 1870s the Puritan ethic had been transformed into Brahminism." While not denying that "the Brahmins were very aware of their colonial descent," she nevertheless adds that "the Puritan sense of God-imposed duty had become a secularized tradition of disinterested public service." I would go so far as to say that between Yankee Brahmin Unitarianism, for instance, and Reform Judaism, there was hardly any difference at all.

Strum again: "Brandeis got to Boston before the large-scale immigrations of Eastern European Jews and the threat of the combined political power of Jews, Irish, and Italians led to a xenophobia new to Boston." Furthermore, "The Brahmins who Brandeis began to meet in the mid-1870s were origin conscious but not exclusive." Indeed, "being a Jew was not a bar to intellectual Brahminism; on the contrary, being a Jew in the Boston of the late 1870s and 1880s was an advantage (as long as one was a Harvard-connected, intellectually gifted Jew)....Thus discrimination against the Jews was not acceptable to [Yankee] Brahmins."

As a Jew from a learned family, Strum explains, Brandeis "had no difficulty shifting from his family's world to that of Harvard and the Boston Brahmins; essentially the two credos were the same....Brandeis accepted both Boston and intellectual Brahminism as his own, and he would remain true to the Brahminism of Emerson and [Charles W.] Eliot for the rest of his life," even after his increasing leftist leanings ruptured many of his Yankee Brahmin relationships.

Of all of Boston's eminent nineteenth-century Yankee Brahmin institutions, it was MIT that would most dramatically and consistently demonstrate this expanding definition of *Brahminism*, rivaled only by the Boston Public Library and the Museum of Fine Arts. It is a definition that would finally in the twentieth century be seen to meet its Asian roots, preeminently at MIT, when Oliver Wendell Holmes, in naming the New England caste in 1861, had reached to Asia and specifically to India for his nomenclature.

Lest this all seem too long ago, the reader should know that *Louis D. Brandeis's MIT Lectures on Law* were republished as recently as 2012 in an authoritative new edition by the legal scholar Robert F. Cochran Jr. Meanwhile, Gerard Swope, one of Brandeis's MIT engineering students who also took Brandeis's MIT law course, went on to become president of General Electric *and* an important figure in Franklin Delano Roosevelt's New Deal. Swope, who saved his lecture notes from Brandeis's course and gave them to the MIT Archives, may have been the first Jew elected to MIT's governing Corporation. He served on it for nearly forty years.

The supreme "lefty" moment in Copley Square's history came in 1888, when, in surely one of the more dramatic events ever to occur at MIT, "Mark Twain rose from the audience at the Lowell Institute and [said] in a voice choked with tears: 'If such a government cannot be overthrown otherwise than by dynamite, then thank God for dynamite.'" The story is told by the literary historian Louis J. Budd in "Twain, Howells, and the Boston Nihilists" in the *New England Quarterly*.

Yes, there were not only anarchists at MIT, but nihilists too. Boston nihilists, their fury roused by a long-forgotten organization called the Society of American

Friends of Russian Freedom, headquartered in Boston in the 1890s. The society was founded by Russian exile activists who, Budd notes, realized "Boston was famous as the center of humanitarianism that encompassed not only domestic problems like slavery but also the struggles for liberty and freedom all over the globe."

Which is also to introduce the finale of "Part One: Global Portals," and insist on how wide open a global portal Copley Square itself was: first forced open by Rogers's defense of Darwin, and then on and on, finally demonstrated as well by two pairs of men and women.

How global? To have asked that of Alice Stone Blackwell or Vida Dutton Scudder would have yielded very different but entirely complementary and altogether global answers. Blackwell was the Unitarian editor of the *Woman's Journal*, the leading American women's rights publication, based in Copley Square (in the Chauncy Hall Building, a women's movement beehive). She was chiefly famous, however, as the founder of the Friends of Armenia, which Peter Balakian called "America's first international human rights movement," also run from her Copley Square office. It was not an honorary position. Blackwell herself translated a number of Armenian books into English in aid of this cause, while she extended her attention as well to Russia, editing also Catherine Breshkovsky's *The Little Grandmother of the Russian Revolution*. Blackwell was a graduate of BU, by the early 1900s also based in Copley Square. When her alma mater gave Blackwell an honorary degree, it hailed her for "her defense of the underprivileged and oppressed the world over."

Scudder was also a considerable intellect—the first woman to be admitted to Oxford's graduate program. She was, by contrast, a High Church Anglican, a Newbury Street resident devoted not only to St. Stephen's Mission in the South End slum but also to that neighborhood's most famous settlement house. Scudder founded Denison House, only the third in America, along with two fellow Wellesley College professors, Helena Dudley and Emily Greene Balch. With Balch she shared a family inheritance of ardent dedication to the devout but liberal religion of Phillips Brooks and Trinity Church.

First Balch's classmate at "her small private school for girls in Boston's elite Back Bay," then her Bryn Mawr roommate, Alice Gould did graduate work at MIT. Balch, according to Kristen Guinn, in 1896 planned to pursue her doctorate at MIT but was recruited instead to the Wellesley College faculty, where she met Scudder, with whom she not only founded Denison House but also organized a notable conference in the Back Bay, Socialism as a World Movement. One of the chief speakers was the British muckraker John Spargo, who spoke on the association between the world Socialist movement and American abolitionists.

Balch and Blackwell also made common if different cause in their efforts on the immigration front. These two women were among the most forceful members of the Brahmin leadership that kept the Yankee-dominated Immigration Restriction League, founded in 1894, in check. Effectively ridiculed by Charles W. Eliot, the IRL greatly increased in significance when Eliot's successor as Harvard's president, Abbott Lawrence Lowell, became an IRL officer. Balch's biographer named seven

The bronze bust of MIT president Amasa Walker, who guided the Institute to university stature in Copley Square, is the principal work of art on the west wall of the Boston Public Library courtyard. He faces the controversial nude of Bacchante that he had worked strenuously and successfully to banish, but which was restored to its central position long after his death.

of the Brahmin officer corps as in charge of countering the IRL, including former president Eliot; two Unitarian ministers, Thomas W. Higginson and Charles Fletcher Dole; two Harvard philosophers, William James and Josiah Royce; and the two women. Balch, for instance, authored *Our Slavic Fellow Citizens*, a book liberals rallied around, in which she argued that Slavic immigration would not only add "fresh vigorous blood to a rather sterile and inbred stock" but also compensate for "a rather puritanical, one sided culture."

Which is not to say that Balch, herself Brahmin, was not loyal to her own culture. When late in life, in 1946, she reaped her extraordinary reward, the Nobel Peace Prize, she wrote movingly of her fellow Brahmins and the "Boston aristocracy of goodness and public spirit," and how proud she was that "their ideas and reforms spread from Massachusetts throughout the whole country and the world." One cannot help being sorry that Balch opted for teaching at Wellesley over her doctorate at MIT, because she might very well have been MIT's first Nobel Prize winner. Balch—Boston reformer, Wellesley sociologist, and pacifist—was the ninth woman in the world, and the third American woman, to be awarded a Nobel Prize. Balch remained a divisive figure, however. According to her biographer, "When Balch was given the Nobel…she received no congratulations from the U.S. government.…

The official U.S. had long regarded her as a dangerous radical…[who] studied the living conditions of workers, immigrants, minorities, and women, and…declared herself a socialist as early as in 1906."

Where right and left could share ground in the New World Acropolis was in Huntington Hall, in the first Rogers Building, where for half a century and more the Lowell Institute, based at MIT, offered the Lowell Lectures. The series featured speakers the likes of which were Oliver Wendell Holmes Jr. and Franz Boas.

Holmes—the son and namesake of the man who first defined the New England Brahmin as more learned and hereditary than wealthy or even Yankee—is significantly on record, by the way, as fully accepting Brandeis as a fellow Brahmin. He gave his course not on business law, but on the larger subject of common law. Writer Louis Menand's description of the scene in MIT's Huntington Hall is full of the warmth and intensity of William Barton Rogers and John Amory Lowell's foundational and historic alliance, and Copley Square's spirit and its spiritual life: "*The Common Land* originated as a series of Lowell Lectures….[Holmes] spent almost a year composing the lectures. He delivered all twelve to a packed hall without notes….[They] formed the basis of all his later jurisprudence." Assented Edmund Fuller, "Here the genius of Holmes was first clearly revealed."

One more example of this almost sacramental expression of the New World Acropolis in the Lowell Lectures at MIT was the 1910 course by Franz Boas. A Columbia University anthropologist, Boas is sometimes called the father of American anthropology. He was a leading opponent of the then-widespread ideologies of "scientific racism," the sort of thing Louis Agassiz promoted and Rogers conspicuously did not. Boas did groundbreaking work in establishing culture, not biology, as the central analytical concept of anthropology. Thirty years before Alfred North Whitehead pronounced Boston the capital of Western learning, Boas arrived to pronounce that learning accounted for the cultural differences among all races. His key book *The Mind of Primitive Man* was based on his Lowell Lectures. It is such an important corpus of work that Thomas Gossett went so far as to say in *Race: The History of an Idea in America*, "It is possible that Boas did more to combat race prejudice than any other person in history."

If MIT was Copley Square's cornerstone, the Lowell Institute—MIT's partner since Rogers and Lowell first became allies in the 1850s—was the cornerstone's mortar, and the Lowell Lectures the real spiritual life of the New World Acropolis, right or left.

Court of Honor

Charles Eliot's Charles River Basin

Landscape architect Charles Eliot, the son of
Harvard's president Charles W. Eliot, designed
the Charles River Basin as the "court of honor"
of Boston's burgeoning metropolis. MIT was
involved in the basin's creation from the beginning, and so when MIT moved to Cambridge,
it was only fitting that the new design for the
campus brought the grandeur of the basin into
proper urban focus.

Court of Honor

Charles Eliot's Charles River Basin

The New World Acropolis lasted but a brief half century, from 1865 to 1915. The period coincided with the triumph and the eve of the decline of the Brahmin Ascendancy and the magnificent result of the Industrial Revolution. It was prophetic as well of what a later MIT president, Jerome Wiesner, would call "the second Industrial Revolution, the Information Revolution."

Wiesner's meaning was twofold. First, one legacy of the first Industrial Revolution was the textile fortune of Francis Lowell, the Boston Brahmin who launched the crucial American chapter of that revolution and, through John Amory Lowell and Augustus Lowell (note MIT's Lowell Court of 1916, off Killian Court) sparked MIT. Wiesner was also referring to MIT professor Vannevar Bush's differential analyzer—his analog computer of the 1920s—which "marked the begin[ning] of the second Industrial Revolution." Bush's doctorate of 1916 was the last one awarded in his department at Copley Square. Thus, the New World Acropolis bridged both revolutions.

Brief in duration, its influence has endured. The square was the modern seedbed—sprung from the ancient seedbed of Harvard centuries before—of Boston's modern galaxy of institutions, which outlasted (and in some sense perpetuated, and still do) the values of both the Acropolis and the Ascendancy, spreading over the Boston area in the twentieth century. In the ten years between 1906 and 1916 Harvard Medical School, the Museum of Fine Arts, and MIT all departed Copley Square. By the time Alfred North Whitehead in 1940 pronounced Boston the capital city of learning of the Western world, speaking in Copley Square at the American Academy of Arts and Sciences, the academy was the last academic institution within sight of the square. All that remained (and still does, stranded but magnificent) of the glories of Acropolis and Ascendancy were the architectural masterpieces of Trinity Church and the Boston Public Library, reminding us always of the glory that once was Copley Square. The Acropolis waned, but its legacy waxed.

The Institute's choice of locale for its second campus—the new home for what Russell B. Adams called "the spirit of Boston"—was as dramatic as its choice in 1861 of its first campus. MIT's bold culture was pretty fully formed after nearly half a century. And in that world of early MIT were not only artistic engineers and tech philosophers but ardent environmentalists too. Those "greenies," as we might call them today, played a large role in the matter of the Institute's relocation.

Copley Square was originally a very urban civic center; in its heart, not a tree in sight. Charles McKim's original design of the square was just like the great public piazzas of Rome: a civic square, not a park. It had a round basin with a soaring fountain in the center of an entirely paved area of the sort Americans seem to love so much more in Italy than in their own country. Today in Copley Square, small

An early plan for the development of MIT's "court of honor" that was the Charles River Basin.

forests of trees obscure so many once-prized architectural vistas. (Does Venice's Piazza San Marco have trees? St. Peter's Square in Rome? Trafalgar Square? Of course not.) The original design of Copley Square by McKim was content to proclaim the beauty of architecture.

Of course, magnificent parks have their place in the City Beautiful, and the Commonwealth Avenue Mall was only two short blocks from the square. And if the *conservation* of the natural landscape still visible in the hills and valleys around the core city was not an overt concern in the early 1890s, Copley Square certainly took the lead in studying it. Indeed, the square without a tree was in a very real sense the model, and MIT the facilitator, for the launch of a highly successful movement to preserve the natural environment on the city's outskirts, an attempt so revolutionary that it achieved worldwide repute almost at once. The significance of the event to MIT has yet to be thoroughly explored.

In 1891 the landscape architect Charles Eliot, son and namesake (without the middle initial) of Harvard's president, presided with Frederick Law Olmsted, the father of American landscape architecture, and MIT president Francis Walker over a conference at MIT in Copley Square. Out of it came the organizing committee of the Trustees of Reservations. This unique organization was composed of representatives of "all the Boston towns," as Eliot rather lyrically referred to the individual cities and towns (such as Brookline, Cambridge, Belmont) of the Boston metropolis, which would be empowered by the state "to hold small…parcels of land, free of taxes"—and here is the link to Copley Square as the model—"just as the Public Library holds books and the art museum pictures."

The art treasures of Copley Square and the countryside around Boston were more akin than anyone knew. And the news, heard first at MIT, traveled fast. Within a few years, the organization became the model for Britain's National Trust and, closer to home, the establishment at Eliot's behest of the Metropolitan Park Commission in 1893. The latter aroused Bostonians to the possibilities of the Charles River Basin, something today taken for granted but then a radical new idea.

"As early as [the] mid-[nineteenth century] the tidal estuary of the Charles was the focus of proposals," the historian Keith Morgan recounts. "Eliot began work on the problem in the early 1890s.…He joined a legislative commission to study the possibility of damming the Charles River near its junction with Boston Harbor to allow its development as a freshwater park.… Among the sources to which Eliot turned for inspiration [in preparing his designs] was the Alster Basin in Hamburg, which he had visited and photographed in his 1886 [European] tour.…It was not until 1910, more than a decade after his [Eliot's] death, that the damming of the Charles was completed," Morgan reports, and the water park "he had envisaged and fought for came into being."

Eliot's vision for the basin was exceptional. It was to be the culmination of his overall aspiration to make "Boston the best parked city in the world." Its centerpiece, "the broad basin, surrounded as it will be," he wrote in 1896, "by handsome promenades…is destined to become the central 'court of honor' of the metropolitan district [of Boston]," in every respect "a central water-park of surpassing beauty and usefulness."

That unusual duality was an expression of Eliot's own abiding philosophy. Olmsted had always seen "parks, parkways, and pastoral retreats as places in which modern city dwellers could find spiritual replenishment through passive contemplation of nature," Morgan explains. But "Eliot, on the other hand, discussed… provid[ing] settings for active enjoyment of nature," an enlargement rather than a repudiation of Olmsted's mission. "Eliot had been attracted early to the Transcendentalist belief in nature as an allegory for the divinity," but the younger man "practiced an *applied Transcendentalism* [emphasis added], actively securing the advantages of nature for the general public."

Eliot was "an environmentalist, long before the term had been coined"—Morgan's words—and his beliefs echoed in an almost uncanny way the great maxim of MIT's architect alumnus of the same era. Writing in his introduction to the 1999 reprint of President Eliot's biography of his son, Morgan reports that "a persistent theme in Eliot's public writings is the principle 'what would be fair must be fit.'… Eliot's philosophy resembles a landscape theory variation on the theme of 'Form follows function'—the battle cry of the Chicago architect Louis Sullivan."

Powerful allies crowded to Eliot's side and carried his work forward against many conservative forces for inertia after his premature death at age thirty-eight, forces not so much opposed to, as uninterested in, his vision of the basin. One such ally was the über-Brahmin civic leader James Jackson Storrow, who—invoking Charles Eliot's father, Harvard president Eliot—in testimony before the Committee on the Charles River Dam detailed at some length the recreational possibilities, not all of which have yet been realized even today. Paraphrasing Eliot, Storrow declared in 1903:

> The Charles River Basin ought to be the court of honor of Boston.… As President Eliot said, to appreciate the force of that argument requires imagination, as everything in the world that is worth doing, whether an engineering problem or anything else, requires imagination.…The basin is the center of the whole metropolitan [Boston] population.… How many people during a winter holiday or Saturday or Sunday afternoon would use the Charles River Basin for skating?…Who has seen a solitary person skating on that basin this entire winter? Yet how we see people crowd on to that pretty, perhaps, but stupid little Public Garden pond.…Then, take boating. It is absolutely impossible, with the present tides, to use the Charles River Basin as a general water park.

The committee Storrow testified before was an outgrowth of the 1891 MIT conference, the one that sparked the formation of the Trustees of Reservations, led by Eliot, Olmsted, and MIT president Walker. Moreover, the existence of the committee in the first place documents how the Institute's role in the conservation and improvement of the natural environment escalated after the conference. In fact, when the Charles River Basin cause engaged technology—the whole question of if and how to dam the river—as well as City Beautiful aesthetics happening only four blocks north of Copley Square, MIT took a decisive stand. The chairman of the committee Storrow testified before was Henry Pritchett, MIT's fifth president, after Walker's death in 1897 and the brief interim presidency of James Crafts.

The architect of the buildings associated with the dam would also be an MIT figure, an architecture alumnus who taught there as well, Guy Lowell. The year after Pritchett's appointment, he appointed to oversee the key engineering study of the project a third MIT figure, an eminent engineer, John Ripley Freeman. Then there was William O. Crosby, the country's top expert on dams, who was also an MIT professor and natural history museum curator. Crosby concluded that the Charles River Dam would not fundamentally alter Boston Harbor. The new dam that created the Charles River Basin was the creation of this foursome, all MIT connected.

Two apparently uncorrected reports of 1902 were crucial. First, Freeman's on the dam itself, which was so positive as it tipped the scales in favor of what had been a highly controversial proposal. And second, Pritchett's MIT annual report of that year, in which he endorsed the eventual move of MIT from Copley Square, following the already announced decisions of Harvard Medical School and the Museum of Fine Arts. Both had opted—well before Freeman's report—to move to the neighborhood westward of Back Bay, the Fenway. It is probable that MIT ended up choosing the neighborhood northward of the square instead because of its deep investment in creating the spectacular new Charles River Basin.

When the basin was completed in 1909 and stood resplendent and waiting, so to speak—in that year, at a huge "Boston 1915" exposition in Copley Square, the basin occupied an entire room of its own, according to Karl Haglund in *Inventing the Charles River*—MIT's new president, Richard Maclaurin, made it clear that the Charles River Basin was his choice as the place for MIT's relocation. The new president and his wife, writes Maclaurin's biographer, Henry Greenleaf Pearson, "stayed with the Charles A. Stones on the water side of Back Bay Beacon Street: upon their arrival their hosts had received them in the library at the rear of the house and had immediately led them to the window for a view of the newly created Charles River Basin....Maclaurin gave it one look and asked, 'Why isn't that a good site for Technology?'" A Cambridge graduate and a rower, Maclaurin had an eye, as Eliot had, for recreational as well as aesthetic possibilities. That eye had been drawn at once to the Cambridgeport riverbank opposite, "his choice," his biographer affirms, for the site of the new campus "the moment he saw it out the window of the Stones' library."

Thereafter at some point the new president agreed that Freeman, the engineer whose study had made the basin possible, should examine the load-bearing capacity of the Cambridgeport site he had so fallen in love with. There were many twists and turns along the way, as the issue was entangled with yet another Harvard-MIT merger proposal of the time, and there were other sites it was only prudent to consider (one in Allston, for instance, was actually favored by Freeman). But in the end, MIT decided upon the Charles River Basin.

Another clue that this was always in the back of the mind of Tech's collective leadership was the otherwise somewhat amazing series of proposals for an island in the middle of the basin. If one imagines Copley Square's principal cross-street projected across a bridge, this island could be seen as virtually a resumption of the filling in of the Back Bay. It was most prominently the idea of Ralph Adams Cram, an architect whose campuses at West Point and Princeton commanded respect, and whom Maclaurin ended up appointing head of MIT's Department of Architecture.

Several of these proposals provided explicitly for a New Tech campus, in one case "an expandable island [onto which] the Institute could make new land in the river as its departments grew."

Amid all the public discussion involved, there was a somewhat underground but most persistent force showing Maclaurin the way, so to speak. Charles Eliot was twelve years dead in 1909, but his vision of the Charles River Basin continued to capture minds. His answer to what was the big question all along: Where do you go from the Acropolis of the New World, of which you have been the cornerstone? To "a central water-park of surpassing beauty," of course, in "the best parked city in the world." To Eliot's vision of the Charles River Basin, a water park that he declared would become the "central court of honor of the metropolitan district [of Boston]."

Maclaurin demonstrated time and time again that he shared Eliot's vision, as in an interview in the *Boston Globe* in October 1911: "The Charles River Basin [is] a feature of Boston which has wonderful possibilities, artistically and otherwise, which seem hardly to be recognized.... Scarcely another city in the world has such opportunities," he told the *Globe*, which went on to report: "The feeling that *the institute should be kept a Boston institution and located within the limits of Greater Boston* [emphasis added], even if not in Boston proper, it is explained, was one of the main reasons [for the committee's choice of the Cambridgeport site]."

Maclaurin's description of MIT's new site to George Eastman, the Eastman Kodak tycoon whose millions would build what is still the nucleus of today's riverfront campus, included not a word about moving from the Back Bay. Not one word. Nor is there a word about moving to Cambridgeport. Instead, it's all about moving to the Charles River Basin, which Maclaurin feels is Boston's greatest site. On February 29, 1912, MIT's president solicited Eastman's support on the basis of this description: "A site of forty acres has been purchased in the very center of Greater Boston—a tract of land with a frontage of a third of a mile on the Charles River Basin. This site is ideal for the Institute's purposes,—near to the heart of things, wonderfully accessible from all parts of the city and surrounding country, and occupying a position that commands the public view and must command it for all time."

If it was a bold move, it was quite in the Bostonian tradition. John Coolidge, a Brahmin Harvard professor and lifelong Cantabrigian, pointed out in his introductions to Donald Freeman's *Boston Architecture* and to the Old Cambridge volume of the Cambridge Historical Commission's distinguished series of historical writings what has long been a peculiarity of New England's capital: "From the founding of Cambridge in 1630 to the establishment of the industrial parks along Route 128 in our own day, Boston has created these out-of-town communities as specialized complements to the central city. The peculiar relationship is expressed politically by the fact that there has never been any strong or sustained urge to amalgamate. Today, the mayor of Boston is responsible for a smaller portion of 'his' metropolis than any comparable executive except that ceremonial personage the lord mayor of London."

The municipality of Cambridge, like that of Brookline, would become virtually a part of core Boston in the twentieth century. But in the early 1900s Cambridgeport was a wasteland with a nearby factory district. Still, if the centerpiece of Old Cambridge was created by Boston's Puritans in the early seventeenth century for Harvard, the present-day nucleus of modern Cambridgeport, a very different neighborhood indeed, was effectively founded by their Boston Brahmin descendants in the early twentieth century for MIT, just as in the nineteenth century Concord had become "philosophical Boston," Brookline "horticultural Boston," and Lowell "industrial Boston."

Still, it was a very bold move. Cambridgeport, not to put too fine a point on it, was "a dump," as Maclaurin's biographer described it. People then as now throw around the name *Cambridge* with little knowledge of history. *Cambridge* then meant the area around Harvard Square, the venerable and beautiful "academic suburb," as Henry James called it, that surrounded and sustained Harvard College. The authors of the Cambridge Historical Commission's volume *Cambridgeport* describe MIT's new locale as mostly industrial, a scattered and secondary neighborhood that had sprung up in the shadow of the West Boston Bridge (where the Longfellow Bridge now stands) in the early nineteenth century and never really amounted to anything.

Maclaurin, however, was not the only person who had bought into Eliot's vision. Important elements were supportive in the Back Bay, which was at one and the same time deeply proud of and often annoyed by MIT. Student behavior, for example, could be a problem. "Guests in the Hotel Brunswick across [Boylston Street]," according to Philip Alexander, "would rush to adjacent windows to watch … a barrage of water-filled paper missiles, say, dropped from inside [the] Rogers [Building] thirty feet up, sending [passersby] scampering for cover, a towel, or, perhaps, a change of clothes." Even the "aristocratic rectangle" was not safe. It all sounds very cheerful and exuberant to learn that the night of one MIT president's inauguration "a thousand or more students … marched with torch-lights to [his] residence at 337 Marlborough Street," where a band played outside, but one doubts many other residents of Marlborough Street emerged from their homes "beaming" like the president did. More likely they pulled the draperies tighter.

The Cambridgeport site solved many problems. The Back Bay hardly "lost" MIT; its new splendors would enhance Beacon Street's view, while at the same time improving the Back Bay lifestyle considerably, ending student hijinks (mostly, that is; a century later, MIT's fraternities are still housed in the Back Bay, which remains the residential neighborhood of the Institute) and making a lot of Back Bay residents quite a bit richer. Two members of the three-man site selection committee were Brahmins—George Wigglesworth and Everett Morss—and the third, Edwin Webster, would soon rise sufficiently in the world to buy the Back Bay's grandest palazzo, at Commonwealth and Dartmouth. Finally, Dr. Henry Marcy, who lived across Commonwealth Avenue from Webster, was a major owner of the Cambridgeport site. According to Maclaurin's biographer, Marcy "believed that he could accomplish a consolidation that would give Technology about thirty acres of land extending from the [river] rather more than half way back to the railroad tracks."

In Cambridge, too, there was support. As early as 1898 the *Cambridge Tribune* editorialized, "In this basin there is a priceless opportunity for the creation in the very heart of Greater Boston of an unrivaled 'Court of Honor,'" distinctly echoing Eliot's language. "This in the course of time would be bordered by stately architecture...and the basin would naturally become the scene of grand civic festivities and celebrations whose beauty may be imagined in the recollection of the enchanting scenes at the Chicago World's Fair; fireworks, illuminations, and all the diversified order of pleasures which such a place suggests."

The "fireworks" would come with the Boston Pops Esplanade Orchestra's Fourth of July concerts, begun in the 1920s, and the "civic festivities" would crest with the establishment of the Head of the Charles Regatta in the post–World War II era. The skating, because the large area does not freeze consistently enough, has never materialized, but the boating has. In 1909, when the dam was new, the first of the "celebrations" was not that many years away, as it turned out, from that visionary *Tribune* editorial: they would mark the dedication of the new MIT campus, exactly the "stately architecture" Eliot had envisioned. The Gods of Copley Square found a worthy home for the New Tech on the grand new stage of the Charles River Basin, where MIT still presides over what Keith Morgan has called, with brilliant insight, "Boston's Central Park."

PART TWO

Inventing the Future on Boston's Left Bank

1

Neoclassical Reflections
William Welles Bosworth's New Tech

> The kind of human being we are trying to educate [at MIT is a person]
> with one eye on the facts, and the other on the stars.
> —The Reverend Theodore Ferris, Trinity Church, Copley Square,
>   eulogy for President Compton in Killian Court, 1954

To describe MIT's move in 1916 as from the Back Bay to Cambridgeport, as many unthinkingly do, is misleading, even distorting. In fact, MIT moved from Copley Square to the Charles River Basin, "a feature of Boston which has wonderful possibilities," MIT's then president Richard Maclaurin wrote, adding that "scarcely another city in the world has such opportunities."

Imagined by Charles Eliot as a water park of "surpassing beauty," as discussed at the end of "Part One," Eliot's vision and William Welles Bosworth's design for MIT's architecture, now before us at the start of "Part Two," came together in 1916 to create Boston's grandest new stage. Neoclassical reflections indeed: first seen rising in Copley Square in the Boston Public Library of 1888, and at the Chicago World's Fair in the Great White City in 1893, mirrored in the Charles River Basin, gave spectacular answer to Maclaurin's charge to Bosworth that the architecture of New Tech must represent "as noble an ideal as any that can be expressed by man."

1   The View from Harvard Bridge

When MIT transferred its campus from Copley Square to the Charles River Basin, the fact that the campus was relocated in Cambridgeport in no way changed the fact that the Back Bay was the Institute's residential neighborhood. Cambridgeport, an entirely industrial area, was hardly the Back Bay's equal as a place to live. Thus today most MIT fraternity houses are still in the Back Bay, including one where in 1958 brother Oliver Smoot was pressed into service in one of the most famous and enduring MIT hacks ever, as the unit of measurement of the bridge most members traversed from frat house to classroom or lab. He repeatedly lay down—all five feet seven inches of him—the full length of the bridge, whose length is officially "264.4 Smoots and an ear."

The best view of the Great White City today is from the bridge of Smoots, whose real name is the Harvard Bridge. The name of this span sometimes provokes comment among newcomers or visitors to MIT, but a short history lesson always calms the protests. When the bridge was built, in 1899, MIT was still based in Copley Square, and the Harvard Bridge connected MIT's Back Bay neighborhood with Harvard's Old Cambridge neighborhood. Its name, honoring Harvard's eponym John Harvard, was recognition of Harvard's stature among American institutions of higher learning; as the first college established in America, Harvard always takes precedence whenever academics convene on ceremonial occasions. I often wonder if the Harvard Bridge was designed to play a central role in what was for Brahmin Boston *the* ceremonial occasion of year: down Beacon Street from the State House and across a predecessor bridge, the governors of Massachusetts were driven for centuries—in the state carriage, escorted by mounted lancers—to preside over Harvard's commencement, the most ancient such ceremony in the country. (The custom was abandoned only recently, when a populist governor preferred to take the subway to Harvard Yard.)

In 2014 it was announced that a $5 million gift from an anonymous MIT alumnus—who, rumor has it, still lives in an apartment building overlooking the river—would fund a redesign of Harvard Bridge's lighting by the Boston design firm of Rosales and Partners, whose principal, Miguel Rosales, also an MIT alumnus, took the lead in the design of the spectacular new Zakim Bridge in Boston. The description of the new design by sponsor Charles River Conservancy includes this evocative passage:

> A series of blue globes will highlight the steel beams supporting the bridge sidewalks. Gentle, diffused LED lighting will illuminate the bridges arches and dramatic granite piers while reflecting on the water below. Linear, interactive lights will also be placed on all sidewalks to highlight the infamous smoot [sic] measuring system painted on the bridge by MIT students.

The magnificent Charles River Basin spreads out to either side of the bridge, dominated to the east by MIT and to the west by Boston University. It is very different from the view seen by those a century ago who looked out the windows of Back Bay Beacon Street. They saw the Cambridgeport riverbank as a wasteland with a cluster of grim factories around the West Boston Bridge. But Maclaurin was not one of them. MIT would pioneer the development of this Cambridgeport wasteland as boldly as it had the vast emptiness of the Back Bay when that was first built up a half century before. In a sense the Back Bay as Boston's great educational concentration had proved in its great success ultimately a failure; Cambridge, across the basin, would help solve the problem that the educational concentration in the Back Bay was by 1900 growing as fast as the whole metropolis.

Even the academic centerpiece of it all—Copley Square—had become too big for the Back Bay to contain it. Old Cambridge, Henry James's "academic suburb" of the 1870s and 1880s, would not be a suburb much longer: Harvard and MIT (in Cambridgeport) would make a newly urbanized quarter of Cambridge the premier neighborhood of Boston, and education would be its crowning glory. "Boston's Left Bank," as a present-day City of Cambridge tourist promotion puts it, is rivaled only by the downtown Financial District (which fuels everything) and a newly reconstituted Back Bay quarter. This last was rather challenged to find expansion room in the Back Bay Fens area just for Boston's museums, musical institutions, and medical facilities.

It was a measure of the huge new metropolitan scale that Stanley Abercrombie (in a review in the *Journal of the Society of Architectural Historians* of

Mark Jarzombek's *Bosworth's New Tech*) called the New Tech of 1916 "the largest educational facility ever built"—anywhere. Charged with conceiving and erecting a new campus of some distinction for MIT, the Gods of Copley Square as their last act, really, produced what the visitor today will encounter at the heart of the Institute: some of the most eloquent neoclassical architecture in the New World.

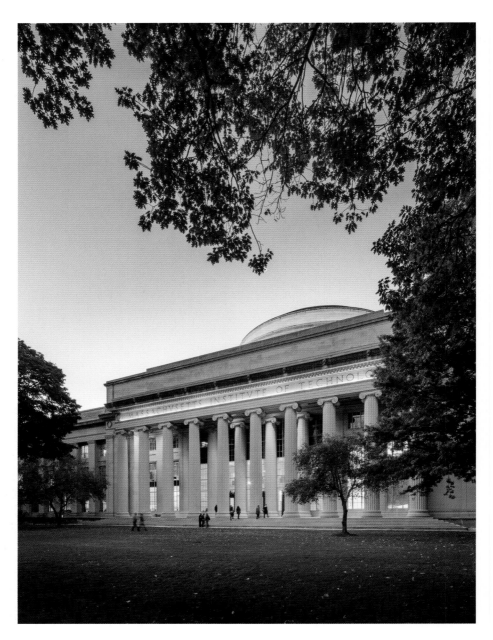

The grand Ionic portico of Building 10.

Neoclassicism, moreover, that brilliantly engages not only with Eliot's beautiful Charles River Basin water park, but also with the aesthetic of early twentieth-century modernism.

The visitor will need, however, to keep a critical and expectant eye cocked to see this, as well as an open mind. The lazy eye will assent to critiques of MIT's architecture such as this one: an art (though not architecture) critic opined that even on a good day, although it possesses "an amazing range of noteworthy architecture… this city within a city, its daunting architecture, its dearth of trees…can make you feel like you've wandered onto a futuristic film set or a painting by de Chirico. There is definitely no ivy about." Although the mention of Giorgio de Chirico suggests that the critic mostly had MIT's original neoclassical core in mind, he never makes clear what that artist's eerily classical squares, painted in his signature dry and desiccated manner, with their forlorn geometrical shadows, could have in common with the refined and serene neoclassicism of Bosworth's slender, attenuated proportions and sharp delicacy and elegance.

Nor is it easy to understand where our critic's standard of measure comes from. Are London's St. Paul's Cathedral, the Royal Hospital at Greenwich, or Sir Christopher Wren's other great works any less daunting? What about the Place de la Concorde in Paris? Or Edwin Lutyens's Rajpath and hilltop New Delhi Acropolis? Or, closer to home, the glorious Boston Public Library in Copley Square? To switch to modernism, one might ask the same question about Rockefeller Center in New York. Or of anything by Louis Kahn. Enough! The dictionary definition of the word *daunting* is "difficult to deal with, intimidating." If St. Peter's Square in Rome, a world religious mecca, is daunting, so may be the world's greatest scientific university (Cambridge University excepted?). Perhaps the fact that Bosworth modeled MIT's domed centerpiece on the Roman Pantheon gives the clue. Who complains, I wonder, that the Pantheon is daunting?

Not the Gods of Copley Square, certainly, whose aesthetic is the dominant one by any measure in the Bosworth complex. Even so broad a survey as R. Stephen Sennot's *Encyclopedia of 20th-Century Architecture* is very clear, parsing the matter in the words of historian Kerry Dean Carso. Carso explains it was not H. H. Richardson's robust modern medievalism that inspired MIT, but the serene classicism of Charles McKim's library in the square:

> The neoclassical architecture displayed at the Boston Public Library and the World's Columbian Exposition of 1893 at Chicago led to a renaissance of this style across the country. Boston enhanced the planning principles of the "White City" with its "Boston 1915" movement, a Progressive Era crusade….The most important legacy of this City Beautiful movement was…buildings such as [the new incarnations of the three institutions that moved from Copley Square in 1906–16:] Shepley, Rutan and Coolidge's Harvard Medical School (1907), Guy Lowell's Museum of Fine Arts (1909), and William Welles Bosworth's Massachusetts Institute of Technology (1916), called "the great white city" on the Charles River.

There it is again, a grandiose phrase, it might seem today. Yet it was a phrase used repeatedly by President Maclaurin, a proud architectural boast of the early twentieth century that reflected William Barton Rogers's equally bold institutional boast of the late nineteenth century that his new institute in Boston would "overtop all the universities of the land." In both cases, these are boasts MIT would hardly make today, institutionally or architecturally. Having in some sense achieved both goals, it has learned the more careful language of preeminence.

Maclaurin's architectural vision for the Great White City was very practical. As the historians Karl Wilde and Nilo Lindgren document in their history of electrical engineering and computer science at MIT, "For Maclaurin *the unobstructed view* [emphasis added]" of the "New Technology" on so prominent a site would show "the permanence, power, and prestige of scientific and technical education."

Today the architecture at MIT is more likely to be praised for its practicality and flexibility than for its beauty and nobility. That would have troubled Maclaurin, who agreed with one critic that it was a *compliment* that Bosworth was said to be a "designer with a special talent for cold, cerebral evocations of the drama of ancient Rome and Greece."

Although Louis Sullivan, the author of the iconic phrase "form ever follows function," was famously an alumnus of MIT's architecture school, that dictum, in its most widely understood meaning, is very arguable. No less than the eminent economist John Kenneth Galbraith, a close ally of the distinguished Catalan architect and city planner Josep Lluís Sert, argued with it in a now little-known but still arresting keynote address of 1968 to one of Sert's urban design conferences at Harvard's Graduate School of Design. Galbraith declared that he "regard[ed] the theory of function as an effort of an artist with a marked inferiority complex to crawl under the blanket of economic priority."

Asked if he thought of "aesthetics as a functional thing at all," Galbraith replied, "No, I don't," continuing: "I have suggested to Dean Sert many times that the architectural profession...should have a blacklist of architects who insist that they can work within a functional environment and assure their clients that beauty in the long run pays. Absolute nonsense. *It doesn't have to pay* [emphasis added]." Sullivan's dictum is rather like the argument that a college degree will enable a person to earn more money. True or not, that is not the primary reason for earning a college degree; a well-educated citizenry is.

What Bosworth *was* known for was his virtuosity. He was an admired landscape designer—the creator of the spectacular country estate gardens of John D. Rockefeller Jr., who recommended him to Maclaurin. An example of the enthusiasm Bosworth's work could arouse is Hugh McCauley's assertions in "Visions of Kykuit" that Bosworth had "created magic for the Rockefellers." He would try to do the same thing for MIT. Bosworth, a graduate of the Institute in architecture, had apprenticed in Boston to H. H. Richardson and gone on to enjoy a similar relationship with the legendary landscape designer Frederick Law Olmsted. In Olmsted's office he would certainly have become familiar with the work of Charles Eliot, Olmsted's partner.

Bosworth's and Maclaurin's visions coincided, both shaped by the Charles River Basin vision of Eliot, which was grand, boastful, based on a vision of a "court of honor" for the whole metropolis. Maclaurin walked a tightrope. "Some will look for gothic architecture and some for factory construction," he said in a New York speech to alumni, reported in the *New York Times* on January 18, 1913. But he was also candid, if careful: "We want beautiful buildings.... At the same time we want buildings that are as efficient for educational purposes as are the best factories and mills for their purposes." What rings truest, however, with no verbal persiflage, is his injunction not just that the new MIT preside over the Charles River Basin in such a way that it "commands the public view" but also that—and the emphasis here is his, not mine—it "*must command it for all time.*" Talk about grandiosity.

Some in the MIT community were skeptical. But Maclaurin's vision—and Bosworth's architecture—converted a great many. The historian Bruce Sinclair noted, culling in 1986 reports from 1916 in *Technology Review*, "Those who saw the [riverfront MIT] buildings for the first time...in June of 1916 were astonished at their appearance: 'long and low, stately above the quiet waters of the Charles,' one said, and then added, 'you hadn't expected it was going to be quite so splendid.'" Notice the business about the buildings being "reflected in the Charles." Between water park and architecture there was nothing to inhibit the "unobstructed view" Wilde and Lindgren made so much of, a view that was of the essence in the visions of Eliot,

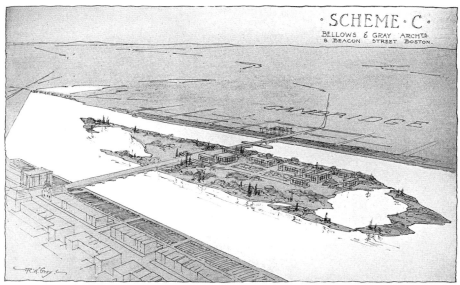

SCHEME C. — Larger Island, for Recreation and Other Purposes.

Early plans for the Institute's new Charles River Basin campus were to extend Copley Square's Dartmouth Street from Copley across the Charles to an island where the new MIT campus would be built. Ralph Adams Cram, head of architecture at the Institute, was a great champion of the idea of an island in the Charles.

Bosworth, and Maclaurin. Nobility is what Bosworth sought. And just as "cerebral" is very different from "picturesque," so is nobility very different from coziness; nobility more apparent perhaps because more easily seen.

Bosworth's majestic architecture worked both ways. The early inhabitants of the Great White City felt the drama of the Back Bay, now across the water, as they never had before: the towers, the domes, the steeples, the long, stately blocks of houses. In a catalog of the 1960s, the Museum of Fine Arts pointedly referred to the place as "Back Bay Boston: The City as a Work of Art," redolent of the "City Beautiful" ideal. It was enchanting, particularly at sunset, when "Beacon Hill glows in reds and violets behind the blue waters of the Back Bay, with the gold dome of the State House reflecting the sun like a burning ember, [making] an ever changing panorama of beauty, as fine as any town and water subject in the world, not even forgetting Whistler's impressions of Venice."

Similarly the other way. Back Bay residents had complained at first that the new Charles River Basin, for all its beauty, needed focus. Hence the many ideas for islands. "From an artistic standpoint," architect Ralph Adams Cram insisted, "the basin was empty, vague and uninteresting." Until MIT, that is. After MIT, the enchantment was felt even at night. The Danish architect Steen Eiler Rasmussen would later write that "MIT should be seen at night, when it lies bathed in floodlights and… looks like a fairy palace under its mighty Parthenon dome."

Human-made and natural beauty thus courted each other. The effect of the "surpassing beauty" of Eliot's water park, and of Bosworth's "noble" architecture reflected in it, must have been very Venetian, somewhat in the way Maria Alessandro Segart describes it in one of her MIT courses, as a "landscape [of] the suspended space of the Venetian lagoon… suspended between water and earth, hybrid, ambiguous, with hazy boundaries." Worthy of Whistler in Venice *or* Boston.

There would also be a decidedly less romantic and more robust American boast: a grandiloquence, even braggadocio, about "Bosworth's New Tech." In 1923, seven years after the complex's completion, although the baccalaureate service was still held in Copley Square at Trinity Church and the inauguration of the new president at Symphony Hall, the Institute would make a bold decision: for the first time, trumpeted the *Tech* on June 8, 1923, on page one, "Commencement to be held in Great Court"—"with no covering," either, and seating for five thousand. A further innovation was that seniors were now to wear caps and gowns, while "for the first time in years academic costume [would be] worn [by MIT's faculty]."

Furthermore, "members of the institute and residents of Boston who were within sight of the Institute" were in for quite an experience: "The dome over building 10 was lighted with a veritable spectrum… done by means of colored searchlights, replacing the customary plain searchlight that lights the dome, making it a familiar sight for Bostonians," all this under the heading "Dome Appears in Coat of Many Colors."

It got built, all of it, in the first place only because Maclaurin kept such careful watch. "We have a glorious site and a glorious opportunity," he boasted, "but our task

Bosworth's MIT turned its back on industrial Cambridgeport; "Bosworth's complex faces the world primarily in one direction," wrote List Visual Arts Center curator Katy Kline. "The orientation toward the Charles River and the Back Bay acknowledges the Institute's aspiration to command the public view [as President Maclaurin said] for all time."

of design is not made more easy by the great expectations of Boston." He might have illustrated his remarks by quoting the braggadocio of his own student newspaper, *The Tech*, in 1912. "There has never been selected in this country a site comparable to this for an educational institution," its editors opined, describing it in wonder: "In the midst of the great metropolis of Greater Boston there has been established a water park of hundreds of acres." Four years later, in 1914, when MIT's new buildings were sufficiently visible, the metropolitan press chimed in, the *Boston Herald* assuring Maclaurin that the new MIT was indeed "incomparably the most conspicuous architecture in New England."

Bosworth's program for carrying out Maclaurin's charge could not have been clearer. As originally designed, the architect's Great Court of stone and mortar engaged Eliot's watery "court of honor" so intimately that "the major point of arrival" at MIT, as List Visual Arts Center director Katy Kline detailed in her *Art and Architecture at MIT*, was via the basin through docks and "water landings [that] strengthen[ed]...the axial gesture toward [Back Bay] Boston."

Karl Haglund in *Inventing the Charles River* explains a critical part of why this design was so attractive: "The row of trees along [what is now Memorial Drive] and the uniform line of the seawall were broken and a pair of stairs framed a long

OVERLEAF: "A site of forty acres has been purchased in the very center of Greater Boston—a tract of land with a frontage of a third of a mile on the Charles River Basin. The site is ideal for the Institute's purposes," President Maclaurin wrote donor George Eastman in 1912: "near to the heart of things, wonderfully accessible from all parts of the city and surrounding country."

low platform on the water's edge, where almost unplanted terraces stepped down to a boat landing along the water." All of which was very strategic. As Kline noted, "Bosworth's complex faces the world primarily in one direction....The orientation toward the Charles River and the Back Bay acknowledges the Institute's aspiration to *command the public view for all time* [emphasis added]."

There is Maclaurin's charge again, always at the heart of Bosworth's design. And by commanding the public view he meant not only the hub of America's fifth-largest city, as Boston was in 1910—not to mention a metropolis of well over a million and a famous city-state larger still—but also, above all, its global portals. Boston is a city manned historically by the Brahmin ruling class whose "knowledge-seeking" values were what drew Rogers to New England in the first place.

When MIT's founder first saw Boston, and when the Institute was founded in 1861, the controlling portal was easily grasped. Very physical as well as very global, through it came books and ideas—and people—as well as goods. It was Boston Harbor, the same portal that was controlling when Harvard was founded more than two centuries earlier. There is perhaps no better explanation of the importance of the presence or absence of such a portal than Samuel Eliot Morison's analysis of what made Harvard and Yale such different kinds of schools then—and, some might say, because such experiences can be formative, forever after. The difference, wrote Morison, "between the two colleges was determined very largely by their respective communities: New Haven was a small place and Connecticut a rural colony, curiously isolated from the outside world, at a time when Massachusetts was a royal province with a miniature vice-regal court, and Boston a trading metropolis that aped the manners and reflected the fashions of England."

The fact of Boston Harbor as controlling is surely the explanation, which seems to elude some modern-day MIT chroniclers, for the spectacular and extravagant river pageant that marked the dedication of MIT's present campus in 1916. The dedicatory event challenged even Maclaurin's imagination. It was, perhaps, too telling. It was the Venetian connection again. People actually sailed to Boston in 1916 through its harbor to participate in MIT's river pageant, centered on Cram's one-hundred-foot-long Venetian state barge, the *Bucentaur*, which conveyed the Institute's charter from the first to the second campus.

Just like the fabled Grand Canal and Venice's lagoon off the Adriatic, the Charles River, dammed or not, leads into Boston Harbor and thence to ocean routes that encircle the globe. The river caught everyone's attention as New Tech was being built in 1914–16. The May 1915 *Technology Review* article was not the first time Venice had arisen in connection with the Charles River Basin. As far back as in 1897, *New England Magazine* had used an illustration of St. Mark's Square where it meets the Venetian lagoon in an article about the proposed basin design.

With the passing of the Brahmin Ascendancy in the 1920s and 1930s, there was great danger that more small-minded and less globally inclined locals and nativists would let those portals "silt up," as it were. But as it turned out, even as Brahmin influence waned, the institutions the Brahmins had founded—Harvard, Massachusetts General Hospital, the Museum of Fine Arts, the Boston Symphony, and above all the Massachusetts Institute of Technology—would play the largest role in keeping those portals from contracting, as core Boston generally did in the Depression and corruption-ridden interwar years.

When Boston's revival came in the 1960s and 1970s, the significance of those portals having been kept open by those institutions was very clear. So much so that today, the most authoritative definition of the global city, derived from Saskia Sassen's *The Global City: New York, London, Tokyo* (as updated in 2010 with Sassen's help in the journal *Foreign Affairs*), states that of all cities worldwide, only six that are American "set global agendas." They are New York, Chicago, Los Angeles, Washington, San Francisco—and Boston.

Eliot's water park was not only a harbor gateway; it was also in and of itself an important global portal. The Charles River Basin, modeled after the Alster Basin in Hamburg, a freshwater basin lined with magnificent architecture and promenades, could be classified, indeed, as a portal of many kinds, being an enhancement of the natural landscape and proceeding from Eliot's deep investment in Emersonian and Transcendental perceptions, and also a product of Eliot's own creativity.

When Eliot wrote of it as a "broad Basin...destined to become the central 'court of honor' of the metropolitan district," he referred to the Boston metropolitan park system, the creation of which he was presiding over. It was one of the first such systems in the world, celebrated, for instance, at the Paris World's Fair in 1900. It was a system that prompted Olmsted to write as far back as 1893 to his partners: "Nothing else compares in importance to us with the Boston work, meaning the Metropolitan equally with the city work. The two together will be the most important work in the profession now in hand anywhere in the world."

MIT's part in all this, beyond its creation of the Charles River Basin in the first place, has not really been acknowledged. Consider this from "The Listener" in the *Boston Evening Transcript*, reprinted proudly in May 1915 in *Technology Review*:

> The new Tech as [it has] risen into view across the waters of the Charles—a new feature, hereafter ever to be the great feature, of Boston's Back Bay Venetian aspects. Now that the roofs are on the great wings and one gets the shadows under the cornices and in the long low window embrasures in a colonnade effect, and in the mass and skyline, the reserve and refinement of the Renaissance architecture show even across the river....The beauty is in the harmony of proportions, the ornament is strictly and solely in the lines and elements of the structures.
>
> The greatest factor of all is the size, the imposing scale, and with such masses and weight much mere ornament would be impertinence....These masses and the combined extent of them along the waterfront...have also narrowed the river, notwithstanding that it is here at its broadest—so broad, indeed, that it has been a favorite idea [to] build an artificial island like that in the Seine in the heart of Paris....[But] the river is now not a whit too wide to carry the magnificent proportions of the new Institute.

The enchantment, however, took no account of what would become the spoiler: the noisy and visually distracting traffic that would soon make Memorial

"The Charles River Basin is a feature of Boston which has wonderful possibilities, artistically and other-wise....Scarcely another city in the world has such opportunities," President Maclaurin declared. The *Tech* echoed him: "There has never been selected in this country a site comparable to this for an educational institution. In the midst of the metropolis of Greater Boston there has been established a water park of hundreds of acres."

Drive, created in 1922 out of quiet Charles River Road, a barrier between the campus and the water park and between MIT and the Back Bay, to which the chief architecture had been addressed. Thus emerged a problem that would bedevil all of MIT's prized riverfront architecture forever after: how to counteract this visual and aural unpleasantness at its doorstep. All along the riverbank, one gifted architect after another in the twentieth century—the Architects Collaborative, Anderson & Beckwith, Hugh Stubbins, Pietro Belluschi—has had to address this problem. A good example is the striking New West Campus Houses of 1973 by Josep Lluís Sert, Le Corbusier's protégé, whose work at both Harvard and Boston University so brilliantly reordered the campuses' most problematic passages.

Meanwhile, it did not help that the Institute encouraged virtual forests to grow up after World War II all along Memorial Drive and even in Killian Court, where the formal terraces and pools and fountains of Bosworth's design were never implemented. Nor did the Institute make any effort to realize at the court's center the huge statue of Minerva, goddess of wisdom, which MIT's architect had argued for. How did MIT lose by failing to rise to Bosworth's imaginative idea? The architect had wanted the Minerva of MIT's Great Court to be modeled by his friend, the sculptor Paul Manship, whose huge gilded *Prometheus* dominates the plaza at Rockefeller Center in New York with now-legendary elegance and distinction. MIT's self-inflicted wound reminds us of Harvard's when the glass pyramid of I. M. Pei's proposed Kennedy Library in Harvard Square, which Margaret Henderson Floyd felt would be "the crown of Harvard's *arch l'diadem*," was rejected, only to end up as an ornament at the Louvre in Paris, an ornament now world renowned for its style.

It did not help that Bosworth's projected landscaping within the Great Court never really happened, either. O. Robert Simha notes that Bosworth was hired in large part for "his reputation for developing projects...in attractive landscape settings," but Maclaurin hired instead an MIT graduate, Mabel Keyes Babcock, to design the landscape of what is now Killian Court. Simha is the best source for what happened next: "The original plan envisioned a gravel-covered court in the French style. An English green court flanked by two rows of trees with smaller plantings aligning the base of the new buildings later replaced this plan. The Court was designed to be the front entrance to the Institute, but the trolley car stops at the corner of Memorial Drive and Massachusetts Avenue ultimately determined how people entered MIT. Thus the Great Court became a green oasis."

An urban plaza on a spacious water park overlooking the city of which it was a proud boast, the Great Court of MIT soon became a hidden oasis with a river view between the trees. Babcock took the principles of her President's House garden, which was charming at that small, private, domestic scale, and applied them to the Great Court. The anti-Bosworth classicism of her design is hard to miss. The *Boston Sunday Herald* observed, "Under Miss Babcock's supervision [there has been] the setting out in opposite corners...of six nearly full grown maple trees....These trees which will normally grow a few feet higher, serve a decorative purpose in relieving the severe lines of the architecture"—a severity, it will be recalled, that was insisted on by Maclaurin and hailed by so many critics.

"They will at the same time," the *Herald* continued of Babcock's trees, "form a scale up to now somewhat lacking, by which to eliminate the vastness of the structure behind and will serve as an agreeable screen"—thereby also overthrowing the majestic scale and proportions the *Transcript* writer so admired from the river, and screening the stately mass the *Technology Review* writers loved. "To command the public view," so desirable at first, seemed increasingly less desirable as time passed.

The Great White City more or less disappeared. Not entirely, though. Looked at head-on, some of the portico's columns are still to be seen, and even from the side, something of the dome still emerges. But for how long even that?

More serious issues engaged the Institute, to be sure. MIT's first years in Cambridgeport were unsettled. The culture shock of relocating to an industrial wasteland, however magnificent the site looked from the Back Bay, had to be considerable. There was a reason why, when expansion dictated a move, so many of Copley Square's institutions relocated to the Fenway, almost within sight of one another. One example of how isolated MIT was: When Albert Einstein came to Boston in 1921, the world's most famous scientist was feted in Copley Square at the American Academy of Arts and Sciences, which had built its clubhouse next to MIT's original complex. He was also wined and dined at Harvard. But, in Philip Alexander's words, "Einstein showed up just about everywhere, except MIT."

He adds that "more than twice as many National Research Council fellows in chemistry chose the University of California, Harvard, or Caltech over MIT in the 1920s." Einstein must have driven past MIT to get from Copley Square to Harvard Square. Why didn't he stop? The uprooting of the Institute from intimate, day-in, day-out contact with other institutions of world stature certainly had its effect. So too did the unexpected and abrupt changes in presidential leadership during its first years in Cambridgeport.

There are other reasons not to forget the original riverfront orientation of MIT, detailed now on the Division of Student Life website:

> When MIT was built in 1916, the central group of buildings on campus was oriented toward the Charles River [Basin]. The Dome Building which is Building 10 with a large foyer (Lobby 10) was meant to be the main entrance. All other buildings were arranged around Building 10, with the odd numbered buildings to the right as you face the river and the even numbered on the left [, which is to say, Buildings 1 through 8]. Buildings beyond the central area of the campus have numbers that are preceded by letters corresponding to compass points: W to the west, across Massachusetts Avenue,... N to the north, across the railroad tracks,...E to the east across Ames Street,...and NW to the northwest across Massachusetts Avenue beyond the railroad tracks.

That's not the whole story, however. One rather more picturesque link does survive between Institute and water park, dating back to President Maclaurin's first delighted recognition of where he wanted Tech to be. According to the online history of MIT rowing, in 1909 the new president's first reaction to seeing the Charles River

"'The great white city' on the Charles," in K. D. Karso's words, was resplendent in 1916 and equally dazzling by night, presiding over landscape architect Charles Eliot's Charles River Basin.

The water park Eliot designed now thrives, but today, "the great white city on the Charles" is no more, a forest having grown up in front of it, obscuring Bosworth's splendid architecture except the dome. Yet elsewhere on campus, where the architect wanted trees—defining Kresge Plaza as a setting for MIT Chapel and the Auditorium—none have been planted.

Basin was to exclaim, "All this water and no crew." Maclaurin was a graduate of Cambridge, and that storied British university is almost as famous for rowing as for learning. Maclaurin at once began to dream of a boathouse at the new campus.

MIT rowing went on to great success, but a different water sport was given the coveted spot for what turned out to be a sailing pavilion. Sailing—"part technology, part math," as one MIT official put it to me—seized the day. Francis Wylie explains: "MIT practically invented sailing as an intercollegiate sport and has won

more championships than any other school. It had the first dinghy facility in the country, introducing the 12 ½-foot boat designed by George Owen, '94, professor of naval architecture, in 1935. The Tech dinghy set the standard for college racing." The sailing pavilion, designed by Coolidge and Carlson in 1936, is a gem.

Against all odds, a century later, the original connection between water park and Institute persists, not so much in MIT's culture as in its imagination. Perhaps surprisingly, perhaps not, when the Institute celebrated its sesquicentennial in 2011, it turned out that all the romantics had not died out. Two of the most gifted contributors to the 150th-anniversary festivities were Americans born, respectively, in Iran and Lithuania: Nader Tehrani, the Boston architect who today is head of MIT's Department of Architecture, and his colleague in the Art, Culture, and Technology program, Associate Professor Gediminas Urbonas. For the river pageant—itself a reminder of the 1916 dedicatory pageant—the two professors collaborated on the design of Liquid Archive at MIT. This "giant inflatable screen shaped like the letters MIT written as a starburst, will float in the Charles," the *Boston Globe* reported, "sporting projections of plans for the [basin] proposed in years past by MIT faculty." And so this floating interactive work of art did, magically as it seemed, bridge past and present in order to "imaginatively extend MIT's Killian Court beyond Memorial Drive into the Charles River [Basin]." Charles Eliot and William Welles Bosworth could have imagined no more Venetian a dream.

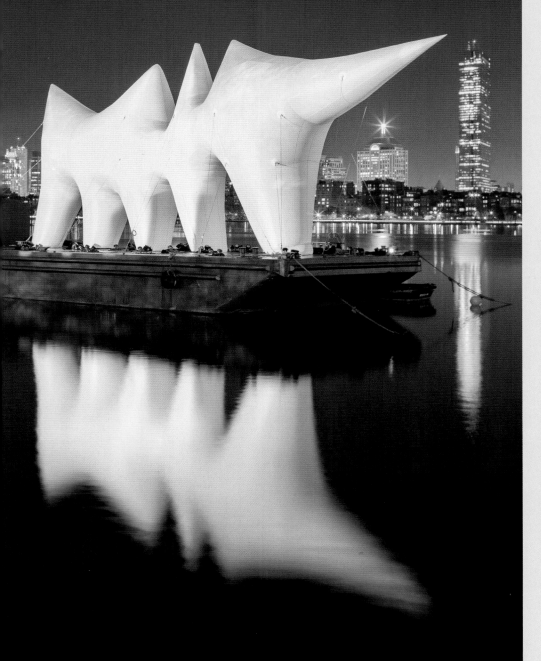

OPPOSITE: The new campus was inaugurated in 1916 with a water pageant. This picture shows the ceremonial barge that transported the charter of MIT to the Cambridge campus. THIS PAGE: Another pageant marked MIT's sesquicentennial in 2011. Shown here is the spectacular inflatable screen shaped like the letters *MIT* "written as a starburst," a float designed by two professors, Nader Tehrani and Gediminas Urbonas.

"Marble Index"
The Outward Sign of the Inward Force

"Marble Index"
The Outward Sign of the Inward Force

**2   Second Rogers Building
Building 7**
William Welles Bosworth, Henry J. Carlson consulting, 1937

Here is where MIT begins every day for virtually everyone. Ask "any taxi driver in Boston," insisted Katy Kline as far back as in 1982 in *Art and Architecture at MIT*, "and the address is always 77 Massachusetts Avenue."

This was not a part of President Maclaurin's vision. Nor of William Welles Bosworth's either, originally. To both, the Charles River Basin facades, the Great Court, and the grand entrance were everything. In a letter of nearly a thousand words to his principal donor, Eastman Kodak tycoon George Eastman, neither Massachusetts Avenue nor the Harvard Bridge nor even Cambridge is mentioned once. Only Boston and the Charles River Basin. Why, then, a quarter century later, this second frontispiece? Why this second front door apparently facing not global portals but local trolleys? (The 77 Massachusetts Avenue entrance is certainly not a back door nor even a side door, although because it is oriented toward a street and not a river, its boast of dome and colonnade is proportionately less.) Why in 1937–38, twenty years after building the first frontispiece, did MIT spend more than a million dollars in the heart of the Great Depression to commission Bosworth to design this second monumental entrance? It is the first of several aspects of the campus that can be disorienting.

Remember Robert Simha's observation (in Walk One) about trolley cars on Massachusetts Avenue? The key factor in creating MIT's Massachusetts Avenue entrance was that, although the avenue certainly would never possess the grandeur of the Charles River Basin, it would become a sort of inner metropolitan Main Street, a thoroughfare so important that in Mark Jarzombek's definitive book on MIT's original campus, the concept of Massachusetts Avenue—along with its feeder, Huntington Avenue—as Boston's iconic corridor is an important vitalizing principle.

In *Designing MIT: Bosworth's New Tech*, Jarzombek recounts how on and just off this avenue "the monumental Ionic style…was certainly the favored style, and [in the design of MIT] Bosworth no doubt wanted to continue the Ionian theme that had already been established by such public buildings as Symphony Hall (1900), Horticultural Hall (1901), Harvard Medical School (1906), the [second] Museum of Fine Arts (1909), Langdell Hall of Harvard University (1906), the Boston Opera House (1909), and the monumental colonnade of the [Fenway facade] of the Museum of Fine Arts (1915)."

Along with all this went the magnificent sequence of architectural murals beginning with the Boston Public Library in Copley Square, continuing at the

The portico of the second Rogers Building—the Architecture School—was erected on the Charles River Basin campus after the first Rogers Building in Copley Square was torn down in 1938-39.

new Museum of Fine Arts on Huntington Avenue near Massachusetts Avenue in Boston, and concluding at Harvard's Widener Library on Massachusetts Avenue in Cambridge, all by John Singer Sargent. With these murals Sargent endowed Boston at the end of the nineteenth century and the beginning of the twentieth with a splendor that recalled Renaissance Rome. Sargent's friend Edwin Blashfield, as great a muralist (the painter, for instance, of the Library of Congress dome), would perform the same function at MIT (see Walk Four).

Along with these buildings, Jarzombek also notices two other great classical temples: the huge Christian Science basilica at the Back Bay end of Massachusetts Avenue and Widener Library. Both were Corinthian rather than Ionic temples—perhaps because of the traditional womanly associations of that order, the respective founders of Christian Science and the library being Mary Baker Eddy and Eleanor Elkins Widener—showing that MIT was part of what Jarzombek calls "Boston's emerging neoclassical silhouette" of the day and a key "link in a chain of great neoclassical buildings." Certainly Bosworth's younger collaborator on the Rogers Building, Henry J. Carlson, suggested all this when he described MIT's second front door as a "noble entrance to a noble group."

Another difference between MIT's two front doors is more spiritual. When the Institute's first riverfront frontispiece was erected in 1913–16, the original Rogers Building honoring MIT's founder still stood, as it would for another two decades (as the home of the School of Architecture until 1938) in Copley Square. When the Massachusetts Avenue frontispiece to the new Cambridgeport campus was built two decades later, in 1937–38, it was to replace the iconic old Rogers Building, which was being torn down as the new building in Cambridgeport was rising. The iconography of the Massachusetts Avenue entrance is much more personal than that of the riverfront: "William Barton Rogers Founder" is the only name blazoned on this second and later frontispiece.

How any institution thinks of its founder is always interesting; no less how the outside world reacts. One of America's notable poets of the middle of the last century was moved to say a great deal indeed. David McCord, the *New Yorker's* favorite poet, as it sometimes seemed, was as much a historian as a poet in his time. Witness his *About Boston*, wherein, looking at this grand portal of past as well as present times, McCord nailed both founder and portal in fourteen telling words: It was, he wrote, "the marble index of a mind forever / Voyaging through strange lands of thought, alone."

It is an arresting image—famously William Wordsworth's of Sir Isaac Newton—and what a huge compliment to apply it as well to MIT's founder. McCord explained himself this way: "More than any building I have ever gazed upon," he declared of the second Rogers Building, "this one comes nearer to satisfying Wordsworth's equation for Isaac Newton," adding, "It is, after all, something worthy of remark for an institution to suggest so vividly in its architecture the functional quality of its being."

McCord clearly knew (and went on to quote) William Barton Rogers's well-known words in MIT's charter about "the advancement, development, and practical application of science." He also knew (and again quoted) lesser-known words by Rogers that followed in the same charter. "He further stipulated," McCord recounted, "that the Institute should serve 'in some respects a higher purpose by leading the thoughts of the student into those wide and elevated regions of reflection to which the study of Nature's laws never fails to conduct the mind.'" McCord, Oregon born and Harvard educated, responded in his very Western way, "Those were mighty original words in 1861." And MIT still struggles to live up to its founder's charge to be more than just a seat of scientific learning.

Less original, it may appear, was Bosworth's classical style in 1937, which was no longer the predominant architectural language. Bosworth was a dedicated lifelong classicist. For his original plans of 1913–16, for instance, according to Maclaurin's biographer, Henry Greenleaf Pearson, Bosworth "cited as precedent Jefferson's plan for the University of Virginia, with its pantheon, dome, portico, and buildings integrated as one structure by colonnades—a suggestion which led to a trip to Charlottesville where Bosworth had no difficulty in convincing Maclaurin…of the chance for beauty and impressiveness in such an arrangement as he proposed."

The University of Virginia was by no means Bosworth's only, or even his primary, source. The Bosworth complex's domed centerpiece probably owes more to McKim, Mead and White's Low Memorial Library at Columbia University in New York. McKim scholar Leland Roth has pointed out that "in using a domed library based indirectly on the Roman Pantheon, McKim may well have had in mind the library Rotunda by Jefferson for the University of Virginia." The results of this back and forth between Rome and Virginia, New York and Boston, each marked by the differing modes of the architects involved in their several generations and locales, offer more than a few architectural surprises. At MIT, some of Bosworth's most interesting ventures occur at 77 Massachusetts Avenue.

The Rogers Building lobby, for example, as Jarzombek explains, "has a rather unusual plan consisting of two spatial structures: a portico and a lobby linked by a common set of columns….Normally, neoclassical protocols would have demanded a reduction in scale from outside to inside, much as, for example, in the somewhat similarly shaped octagon room in [Boston's] Museum of Fine Arts. Designed by MIT alumnus Guy Lowell in 1909, that room has pairs of Ionic columns that coordinate and emphasize the intersection of axes at the center of the building."

He continues, "The 77 Massachusetts Avenue building defies this Beaux-Arts tradition by fusing two monumentally scaled structures," adding, "The Pantheon in Rome is of a higher order than the MIT lobby, but the combination of porch and grand domed space with interstitial vestibule is relatively rare among the neoclassicists." Among the very few examples of two equally monumentally scaled spaces in the classical tradition, I wonder if anywhere outside Rome is there another to match MIT's entrance in both grandeur and intimacy. The reason, perhaps, why it is so lively a center of campus life.

A problem for some is that this can be seen as "fake grandeur," as one critic, Robert Taylor, put it in 1970 in the *Boston Globe*. This reflects the view, urged so often by modernists, that columns like these—not solid stone, but made of stone

The lobby of the second Rogers Building responded more to Massachusetts Avenue than the river and virtually became MIT's main entrance when it was completed. Along with the Barker Library's domed reading room, it is Bosworth's most spectacular interior.

surrounding steel—are dishonest. This sort of thing is a long-standing issue; the nineteenth-century French theorist Eugène Viollet-le-Duc "condemned the Romans for cladding vaulted construction" while he "praised the Greeks for making the orders and the structure one," according to Edward R. Ford's excellent study of the matter in *The Details of Modern Architecture*. And it can get very complicated, never mind moralistic.

Of steel columns surrounded by ornamental plaster in imitation of stone, for example, Ford writes, "Each column…is expressive in the sense of being a plaster casing around a real column." The columns of the Rogers Building are *not* plaster (although the interior of the dome is). But they are not "real" stone, either, as David Fixler, a local architect, pointed out in 2008 in an article in the *Bulletin/Journal of Preservation Technology*, where he described the cast stone of "Bosworth's monumental 1938 Beaux-Arts lobby for Building 7," as "virtually indistinguishable from natural limestone." Why then does it matter? Or that, as Fixler also notes, "the balcony railings are filigreed metal panels in cast aluminum that are detailed and painted to imitate bronze"?

There is more than one philosophy and many more than one system of building—the literal and the analogous systems, for example. In the era in which Bosworth was trained, such issues had not yet been resolved as they eventually would be when a new aesthetic more intimately and exactly expressive of steel construction evolved. Until that resolution, early attempts to wrestle with the question ought to be respected. Meanwhile, the real reason the classical style continued to hold its own is that as the great British architectural historian Sir John Summerson explained in *The Classical Language of Architecture*, "the orders are, in many Roman buildings, quite useless structurally, but they conduct the building, with sense and ceremony and often with great elegance, into the mind of the beholder."

A more serious criticism of this monumental entrance lobby is its muddled message, expressed now only by "sound-bite" banners. The four empty pedestals at each chamfered corner disclose that content equal to the form was initially intended: namely, four huge standing statues of the great figures of Western history in the arts and sciences. That the pedestals are empty is evidence of an ongoing issue at MIT for more than a century and a half now. Philip Alexander in *A Widening Sphere* recounts how Karl Compton, the Institute's president when the question of the identities of the statues first arose, vetoed the suggestion that between Sophocles and Socrates, for example, "Sophocles would be a better choice than Socrates to represent the humanities. Nor did Compton much like the all too many options floated with respect to science. Without consensus, and with money in short supply, the plan was abandoned."

It is telling that MIT's founder himself hardly registers now inside what is after all the Institute's second Rogers Building, the chief memorial to its founder and cofounder. The dedicatory plaque brought from the first Back Bay Rogers Building is well hidden and ill lit, over to the side of the lobby. It is the work of Truman Howe Bartlett, a well-known American sculptor in his day who studied in New York, Paris, and Rome, and was for twenty-one years MIT's instructor in modeling. Its image of Rogers is striking and could hold its own in the limelight it deserves. The entire Rogers lobby, in fact, demands considerable rethinking as to the message conveyed, so to speak, in between the columns. First, the Bartlett relief of Rogers should be moved to the east wall, balancing the bronze MIT seal. And the splendid Jacob H. Lazarus portrait of the founder, in a protective glass enframement, should be hung,

Dramatic perspectives are available from three levels of the lobby of the second Rogers Building. Located in the lobby on the ground floor is the principal memorial at MIT to William Barton Rogers, a relief in bronze (not pictured) by the well-known sculptor Truman Bartlett, transferred from the first Rogers Building in Copley Square. Important aspects of the lobby's detail, however, were never finished.

well lit, on the south wall in its place, where early photographs document that a portrait, probably of Rogers, originally hung.

Then MIT's first First Lady—being Rogers's cocreator in the Institute's making—deserves her due. The fine portrait of Savage of 1906 by the American painter Ernest Ludwig Ipsen should be rescued from its forlorn location in the third-floor corridor above (as forlorn as the nearby Emma Rogers Room it announces), brought down to the lobby, and hung in its own protective, well-lit glass enframe-ment on the north wall opposite her husband, replacing Under the Dome, the video machine, which belongs somewhere else.

Then, in lieu of the huge sound-bite banners, on the four chamfered walls above the plinths, where Bosworth planned inscriptions as well as statues, there should be carved into the stone wall inscriptions with gilded letters (of the same sort as occur in the Memorial Lobby of Building 10, which we will visit farther along in this walk) relating to Rogers and Savage. Two should certainly relate to Rogers, and one could do no better than to repeat these words from his *Boston Evening Transcript* obituary:

> Those who know what an intellectual turning point in modern civilization [the scientific] spirit illustrates are as profoundly moved by the example of a man like President Rogers as by the memory of Emerson or Darwin.

and

> By the scientific spirit he understood the openness to conviction and the sincerity and intellectual receptiveness which made men dread false evidence and false reasoning as they dread sin.

In equally gilded lettering on the two other chamfers should occur two more inscriptions, the first drawn from President Maclaurin's words at the 1912 unveiling in the first Rogers Building in Copley Square of Savage's portrait:

> Those who know the inner history of the Institute's foundation realize that but for Mrs. Rogers it would probably never have been. Those who have followed its later development appreciate to what extent its up-building was due to her inspiration.

and the equally splendid tribute by MIT biologist William T. Sedgwick to Savage at the time of her death in the *Boston Evening Transcript*:

> In a sense [Emma Savage Rogers] was herself the maker of the Institute. From her father she inherited a strong and original mind and a profound love of accurate scholarship, while with her distinguished husband she shared a veneration for science which amounted almost to a passion.

Ernest Ludwig Ipsen, a Danish American, was a Boston- and later New York-based painter trained at the School of Boston's Museum of Fine Arts and at Copenhagen. His Back Bay studio was part of Copley Square's musical and artistic Bohemia along Huntington Avenue and Saint Botolph Street. ABOVE: MIT's cofounder, Emma Savage Rogers, from a portrait by Ipsen

Jacob Hart Lazarus, a noted New York–based Jewish portraitist, had exhibited at the Boston Athenaeum. ABOVE: MIT's founder, William Barton Rogers, from a portrait by Lazarus

A startling change? Yes and no. Certainly this lobby is a teachable moment now squandered, and it will startle those unaware of Savage's role as "Co-Laborer… in creating the Institute," in the words of James P. Munroe in his 1911 *Technology Review* obituary of MIT's first First Lady. But it would also fulfill something Munroe himself hoped for in that obituary more than a century ago: "When the Massachusetts Institute of Technology erects upon its new [Cambridgeport] site a memorial to its eminent founder"—which the second Rogers Building of 1937 is— "it will do well to make it a memorial also to Emma (Savage) Rogers, his wife…. Seldom have man and wife so completely supplemented one another in the carrying forward of a work of great public consequence."

3   The "Infinite Corridor"
First Leg Building 3
William Welles Bosworth, 1916

As you pass through the small central doorway on axis with the portico, prepare yourself: The ceiling drops from nearly a hundred feet high in the lobby to just about sixteen feet high in the corridor. The psychological shock is even greater, for it is the narrow corridor, not the lofty lobby, that often provokes the most thought. Certainly that was true of William J. Mitchell, a recent dean of the Institute's School of Architecture, whose drafting rooms and classrooms make up most of the upper floors of the second Rogers Building. In his *Imagining MIT*, Mitchell insists that "this dim, crowded passageway, flanked by doors of brown woodwork and frosted glass," as he describes it, is "the most unforgettable architectural feature of the campus— MIT's equivalent of Harvard Yard." "In its grim way," he asserts, the "Infinite Corridor," for that is what it is called, "may even be more memorable."

Grim, maybe. Fascinating, certainly. Ask even a classical scholar, one who cherishes the Greco-Roman architectural splendors of Bosworth's New Tech—as writer Elizabeth Durant of *Technology Review* did when in 2006 she asked Mark Jarzombek, the building's chronicler. The reply may startle, as it praises quite a different aspect of Bosworth's design than one might expect of a classicist. Jarzombek described it as "a building with a reinforced concrete frame and supporting columns at its center creating a corridor [with] walls perpendicular to the corridor [that] could then be dropped into place to create classrooms or offices and moved later to accommodate the Institute's changing needs." Even a classicist, then, unhesitatingly declares the Infinite Corridor to be "an icon without equal in the American architectural context" of the time.

In his "Corridor Spaces," Jarzombek traces the history of the corridor as "a public space" that "rose to become the spatial element par excellence of civic modernity" over many centuries, up to the nineteenth, culminating in the 1860s *Korridoren* of German academe, and he takes careful yet striking measure of the Institute's own legendary corridor. He writes:

McKim, Mead and White did use the corridor in some of the university buildings that they designed, but because these buildings were basically conceived as "pavilions" —which was the popular form of university building in the United States at the time— they cannot compare to the grand German Korridoren. The notable exception among the U.S. universities was the design in 1913 of the Massachusetts Institute of Technology, which—modeled specifically on the German university—featured a wide corridor that soon became nicknamed "the infinite corridor," that ran through the entire building. For decades, until the construction of the Pentagon (begun, 1941) [the Bosworth complex] was the largest corridic building in the world.

This is, so to speak, a corridor with a mission, serious enough that there arises in its wake not only serious architecture but also serious music. At the Boston Convention Center at the Institute's 150th anniversary celebration, the MIT Wind Ensemble—all in black tie—performed "Infinite Corridor," by Keeril Makan, "an arrestingly gifted young American composer," according to the New York Times. Not a lot of architecture inspires musical composition at this level.

Apart from music, the Infinite Corridor has also its own liturgy, which may intrigue those who feel my use in this book of the concept of the portal as a means of access, material and immaterial, to parallel universes, real or imagined, verges on the mystical or even the religious. It is a festival liturgy, detailed in Up the Infinite Corridor by Fred Hapgood, a distinguished science writer. While he never quite argues for corridor or event as a transformative life experience, he is quick to recount what can only be called a sort of religious ritual that has over the years waxed rather than waned in MIT lore and, unlike some other Tech student customs, seems to disclose deeper meanings. He directly relates the ritual to the design of the Bosworth complex and to the MIT matrix Bosworth's storied corridor initiates:

> The real campus, the heart, is [MIT's] matrix. Twice a year the sun sets such that for a few moments its rays run parallel to the walls of the corridor: these days have become the subject of a low-key semi-annual celebration. A few minutes before the instant of perfectly parallel alignment, students and staffers gather along the walls, sighting up the broad strip of gold being poured by the sun from which the floors of the corridors were built. It must be calculated, but of course, it is, and at exactly the right moment the conversations die out as if a command had been given. I have seen some participants, celebrants [emphasis added], reach into the corridor as if to shake hands with the rays as they fly by....What seems to touch the spirit is the thought of the sun penetrating the matrix, plunging down the corridors.

Hapgood also relates, "The first act of citizenship of a new member of the community...is to find a map and internalize—'memorize' is too weak a term—the matrix." He calls it "Freeman's matrix," which requires some explanation. We first encountered John Ripley Freeman in "Part One" as the man who, more than anyone else, made Charles Eliot's idea of the Charles River Basin possible. He also, with

MIT's famous Infinite Corridor has been called the Harvard Yard of MIT. Until the erection of the Pentagon in Washington, D.C., the original Bosworth complex at the heart of the Charles River Basin campus was the largest corridored building in the world.

Over the years the narrow confines of the Infinite Corridor have at strategic places been opened up to dramatically disclose the inner workings of the various departments located along it. These openings have proved very effective, but care has been taken to not multiply them or destroy the original historic character of the 150-year-old corridor.

respect to the Bosworth complex's overall design, played the role of what I can only call "Bosworth's ghost." Certainly he was a critical design muse of Bosworth's, and may indeed be well and truly accounted the grandfather of MIT's matrix—the Infinite Corridor and its interconnecting multifloor system of corridors and stairwells. Yet the credit must be shared, for Bosworth had his own reasons for wanting connecting buildings. Sixty-five years after graduating from MIT in 1889, he still remembered (as described in a letter of April 19, 1954, to a Miss Schillabes) that in Boston winters, "just going from the old Walker Building to the old main building for different classes without an overcoat was cruel."

As Jarzombek points out, Bosworth's plan, "with its wide corridors, high ceilings, concrete frame, light-weight interior walls, and generous staircase light wells [, took on] the unmistakable imprint of Freeman's layout." For good reason, then, he calls it the "Bosworth-Freeman synthesis," and, overall, the Bosworth (not the Freeman) campus. Freeman's view, a very simplistic one, never got beyond the efficiency of the interior "factory," which was surely the reason why nothing more was heard of him after Bosworth was chosen by President Maclaurin as architect. Bosworth was more flexible. "With his ear to the ground," in Jarzombek's words, he "accepted with dignity many of the novel engineering features" that Freeman had urged, but never lost sight of the need for a larger conception that would respond to the fact that more than factory-floor efficiency was needed. "Although the president felt that [the] engineering aspect of the task was very properly the first to be dealt with, Maclaurin was far from subscribing to Freeman's dictum that the problem was ninety percent engineering and ten percent architecture." Maclaurin was "determined that Tech students should receive the education of beautiful surroundings, as he had done at Cambridge, and that the appearance of the [MIT] buildings should be in every way adequate to the magnificent site and to an institution of learning which was to be first in its field."

If it would be too much to say the exterior design concept of this campus's original buildings is Bosworth's and the interior design concept Freeman's, to traverse the Infinite Corridor is nevertheless to experience one side of a real duality, to experience one of two parallel universes, to participate in a kind of dialectic of design. The interior comes off as all factory efficiency, the exterior as classical splendor. It is a case of daily life inside and public purpose outside, each rubbing up against the other, and each marching in tandem, side by side. Each, indeed, intimately related to and reinforcing the other.

The depth with which Bosworth felt and detailed this duality is such that even Jarzombek only recently, reading the manuscript of this book, fully realized how far Bosworth took it, putting into words for the first time this fascinating speculation based on an easily missed fact:

> When one moves through any of the doors into the second Rogers Building Lobby one
> hardly notices Bosworth's clever sleight of hand. The fluted columns become unfluted.
> The part of the columns outdoors are fluted; the part of the columns inside the lobby

are not fluted, but plain. What is the meaning of this? It can only be a message about an Ionic order on the exterior that addresses the public and is more formally attired in its fluting and an Ionic of the inside that is meant to reflect the purpose-oriented nature of MIT. Nor does the sobriety of the interior columns detract from their nobility. Rising three stories, they produce one of the most majestic interior spaces anywhere in the Boston area. Both the public announcement of MIT's mission and the private mandate to accomplish it are seen as noble.

This duality has elicited from subsequent observers a wide variety of responses. The most interesting may be F. S. Conway's in his study of the life and work of the great MIT mathematician Norbert Wiener, of whom we will learn more in Walk Three. In *Dark Hero of the Information Age*, Conway notices that as early as 1919, when Wiener joined the faculty, "behind its soaring entrance," by which he meant the Great Court entrance, "MIT's interior was startlingly plain. A single, labyrinthine corridor cut through it like a cubist alimentary canal."

More smart than penetrating is Robert Venturi's view, quoted by William J. Mitchell, that MIT's Bosworth complex is "a transvestite kind of building, wearing clothes that are different from the body inside." More perceptive is Michelangelo Sabatino's view of the matter, perhaps because it is more strictly historical. He believes that MIT's "quirky mix of utilitarian and monumental...reveals the double identity of the [Bosworth] building [as] somewhere between historicism and modernism."

The Infinite Corridor signifies much, historically, about how the role of architecture is understood in MIT's culture—Institute-wide, that is, aside from within the School of Architecture. That Institute-wide understanding of the role of MIT architecture must be understood if the visitor is to grasp either end of the stick, so to speak—MIT *or* its architecture—despite that it involves acknowledging that this book, for instance, is somewhat of an uphill bike ride against the wind. MIT's culture generally, you will be told by many, insofar as it addresses architecture at all, has come to do so more negatively than positively.

The only place in the literature of the subject where this surfaces definitively as a coherent discourse—those who hold the antiarchitecture view tend to be taciturn—is in the 1985 work of Robert Campbell and Jeffrey Cruikshank, in which the supreme architectural good is held to be "a neutral grid of architectural space in which lines of communication can be kept open even while the grid accommodates with almost infinite flexibility, radical changes of functions as departments of knowledge grow, shrink, are born, and die." The premise is that "[w]hat [is] special about MIT is the work the teachers and students do in its spaces, not the spaces themselves. It suggests that perhaps the work may be more special if the environment is less special."

The idea that the work done in a space is quite apart from the space itself—indeed, that the work may well be *better* insofar as the space is *worse*—is actually not at all observable in the life and work of any of the three outstanding and formative shapers of the Massachusetts Institute of Technology before our own era: Rogers the founder, and Presidents Maclaurin—who built the present Bosworth campus—and Killian. They taught something a good deal more subtle. Each of the three seemed to strive for a very distinctive architectural balance: a bare-bones utilitarianism that on the one hand got the job done, and on the other sustained an elegance and grandeur that underlined not only the importance of getting it done but also the nobility of the work. It was a balance, so to speak, of two equal messages, each deployed quite functionally. One inside, where the utilitarianism—because so malleable, so plastic, so immediately shapeable and conformable to need by both scholar and worker (*mens et manus*?)—far from being uninfluential, was a potent aspect in facilitating the job in the first place. And on the outside, a nobility of form that compelled attention not just to the form itself but also to the function it announced to the world. Maclaurin put it rather eloquently in a speech to the alumni association (quoted by Henry Greenleaf Pearson):

> I am thinking particularly of the advantage to the engineer and architect of the future to have spent some of the formative years of his life on a magnificent site, looking out as he will on a majestic river…surrounded, as he will be, by noble buildings…. Do not think, gentlemen, that this is mere sentiment…. I think you will find many a hard-headed Oxford or Cambridge man doing great things in the world and not much given to sentiment, who will tell you seriously that one of the great formative influences of his life was what he derived from the silent effect of college halls….These things mean much in building, as President Rogers said we ought to build on the basis of a broad, general cultivation.

This Oxbridge influence on both Rogers and Maclaurin, and on both the Back Bay and Cambridgeport MIT buildings, has been largely ignored, even by scholars of the stature of Paul V. Turner. In *Campus: An American Planning Tradition*, Turner noticed that "in 1875 the English biologist Thomas Huxley visited Baltimore while on a lecture tour, and surprised his audience by praising the utilitarian buildings of Johns Hopkins…. Daniel Gilman, president of Johns Hopkins, had been impressed with the practical laboratories of German universities and frequently argued that American schools had no need for 'splendid architecture.'" Turner connected this utilitarianism with 'the spirit of science and rationalism.'"

In Boston at the height of the Brahmin Ascendancy, however, where art and culture held their own even though science was increasingly the Unitarian gospel, Rogers made no such argument. Far from it. And naturally this confused Turner. So does the fact that MIT's first building—the first Rogers Building in Copley Square—was "an elegant classical structure," but that "the Institute's catalogues…juxtaposed engravings of this building with views of the forthrightly inelegant metallurgy and mining laboratories in it." The only way Turner could explain this duality was by suggesting that it resulted from "an ambivalence about whether grandeur or stark utilitarianism was the proper image for a technical school."

It is a view rejected, I am glad to say, by the latest scholarship, and not only mine here. In his *William Barton Rogers and the Idea of MIT*, A. J. Angulo observes that "rather than the result of ambivalence," MIT's earliest architectural expression—which, I will add, Rogers had a decisive hand in, as we know through Building Committee records of the Copley Square MIT block—"presents a reflection of Rogers's useful arts plan." A later MIT president, Susan Hockfield, explained the background of this plan very well in one of her welcoming speeches to first-year students:

> [Before the Civil War] America's scientific elite had little interest in practical affairs. So…engineers and architects, mechanics and farmers, chemists and manufacturers were held back by their meager grasp of the science of the materials and forces they worked with. In effect, Rogers saw a double opportunity: to make scientific knowledge useful, and make the "useful arts" scientific—and thus to advance them both. The MIT motto, mens et manus, Mind and Hand, reflects that symbolic idea…[a] powerfully productive symbiosis.

Angulo might have been talking about the Bosworth complex in Cambridgeport of the 1910s when he described the first Rogers Building in Copley Square of the 1860s:

> Characteristic of Rogers's useful arts ideal, the kind of spaces created for MIT reflected a dualism between theory and practice. The exterior of the building, elegant and classical, alluded to the theoretical aims of the Institute. Its facade, with…classical columns…drew on the imagery of antiquity and would have called to mind knowledge and scholarship of transcendent value. The interior…was radically stark by contrast… [with] an array of pipes, tools, vents, and furnaces that resembled the floor of an industrial factory.

There is an even deeper layer. Writing in *Vitae Scholasticae* in 2009, Angulo adds: "The useful arts also stand for [Rogers's] belief that the exploration of the practical and theoretical scientific knowledge as separate fields of inquiry would naturally yield insights into the inter-relationships between the two. Theory would inform practice and practice could inform theory."

Speaking of the architectural form of the intersection of theory and practice, of exterior concept and interior concept, what is that bright light in the darkness ahead? It is surely every visitor's query about three hundred feet down this infinite but also long, narrow, dim, and windowless corridor. Like the light at the end of an automobile tunnel, it signals that a dramatic change is at hand. The two parallel universes are about to intersect. The idea factory inside is about to engage the Great White City outside. The light ahead is another lofty Ionian lobby.

The design concept of the Bosworth complex reflects that of the original Copley Square buildings. ABOVE: The exterior of Lowell Court, off Killian Court, shows the world the classical pomp of a great scientific university. BELOW: The very plain, practical workaday world interior. The original MIT aesthetic is to show on the outside the grandeur of science and technology education while on the inside cultivating very practical, flexible interior spaces.

In Copley Square (ABOVE), for instance, the splendor of the exterior of the first Rogers Building, designed by leading Boston architect William Gibbons Preston, insists on the importance of the task, while the interior spaces of the Laboratory of Mining, Engineering, and Metallurgy (BELOW) were very basic and practical.

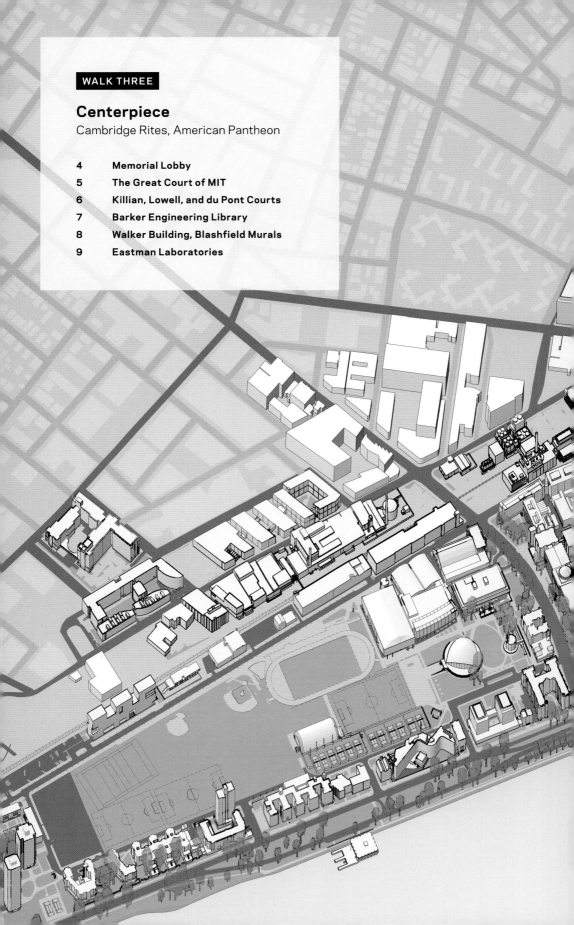

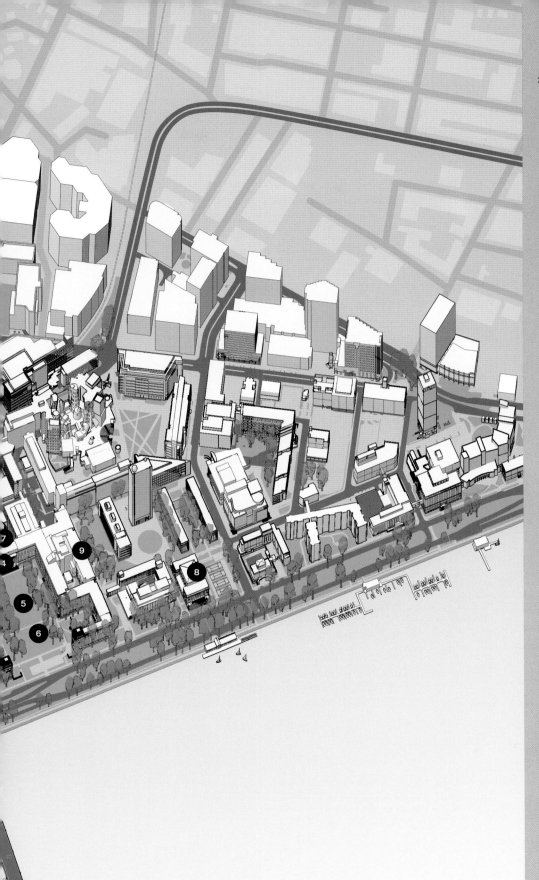

Centerpiece
Cambridge Rites, American Pantheon

4 Memorial Lobby of Maclaurin Buildings
Building 10
William Welles Bosworth, 1916

The Memorial Lobby, the original entrance to MIT as conceived by William Welles Bosworth in 1916, is more regal in its proportions and more elegant in its detail than the Rogers lobby we visited in Walk One. It is churchlike in its stateliness and solemnity, its walls inscribed with the names, filled with gold, of MIT's war dead. Today, however, the effect of the Memorial Lobby is felt rather differently, approached as it always is now from the famously long, narrow, low main corridor of the Institute, the so-called Infinite Corridor.

Light floods in from what is virtually a glass wall to the south overlooking the Back Bay skyline, through an immense colonnade of stone columns. Instantly the workaday practical side is left behind, and even though the lobby is no longer the grand entrance, Boston's global portals are immediately front and center. All the more so today, when there are not only steeples and domes and stately blocks of town houses but also the skyscraper towers of our own era. The Back Bay skyline is not so dense and magisterial as that of the downtown Financial District with its massed towers, but it is actually rather more artistic, culminating in the spectacular Hancock Tower, one of the world's great skyscrapers of its time, the work of the office of MIT's most illustrious graduate in architecture, I. M. Pei.

5 The Great Court of MIT
William Welles Bosworth, 1916

Although the message of the lobby's wall-to-wall glassiness could hardly be more intense, stepping outside into MIT's Great Court at once widens and focuses the perspective. When this view was first framed in 1916, the core city of Boston (population, according to the 1910 census, 670,585) was the fifth largest in the United States, after New York, Chicago, Philadelphia, and Saint Louis. Today the core city is a small part of the Greater Boston metropolis. MIT's view now frames the skyline of the sixth-largest "combined statistical area" in the nation, with a population (according to the 2010 census) of 8,041,303.

The detail of the Bosworth buildings always rewards study and is always felicitous. This was designed to be MIT's front door, the central entrance from Killian Court into Memorial Lobby. Notice that it is on axis with the Prudential Center on Copley Square's western boundary.

From the loggia on the second floor, where the offices of MIT's president, treasurer, and other officials are located, the grandeur of the Memorial Lobby, intended originally as the Institute's main entrance, is very evident. The dedication of these first buildings to President Maclaurin is proclaimed in the carved inscription to the right of the main entrance (not pictured).

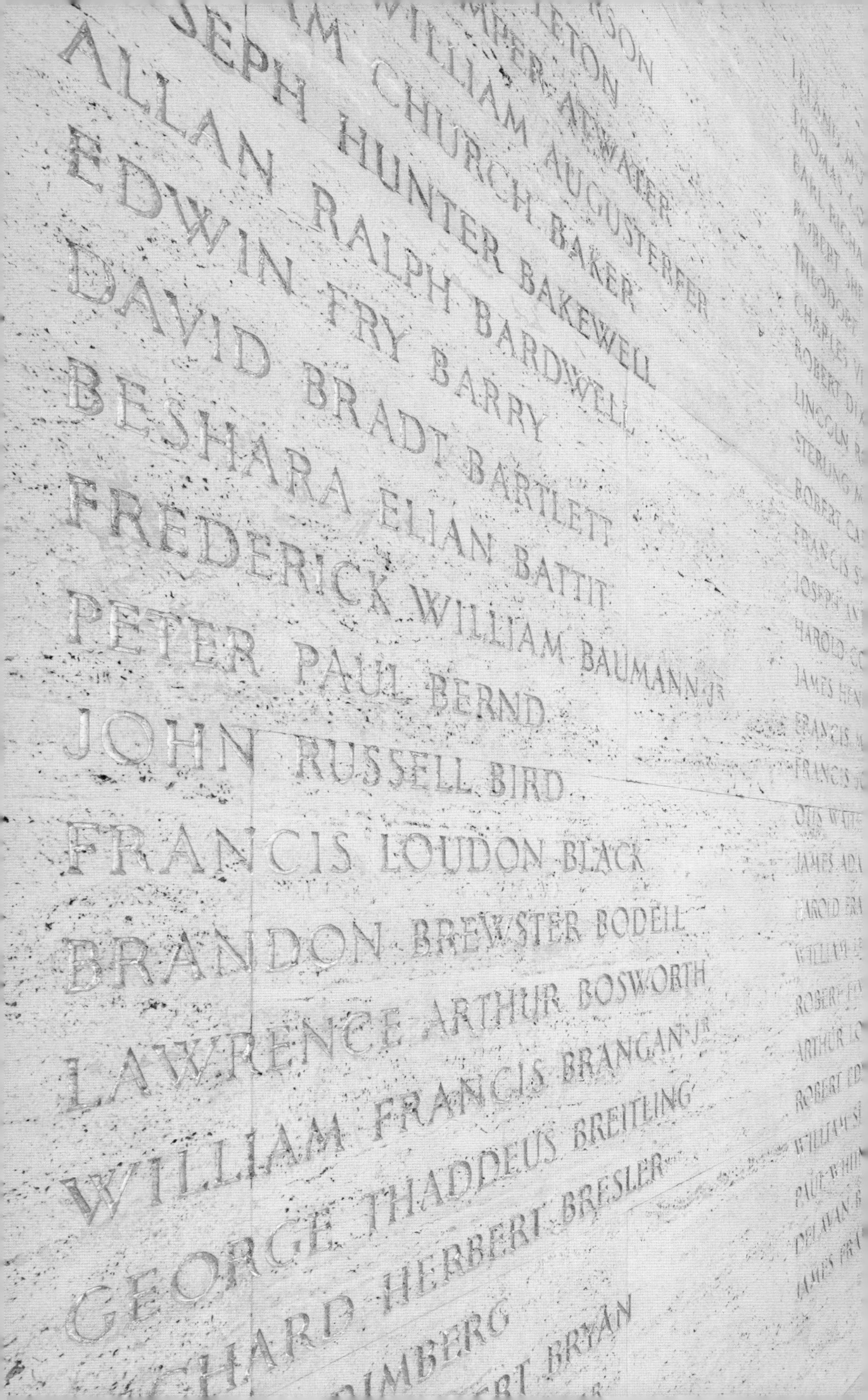

...SON
...IM ...PER ATWATER
...WILLIAM AUGUSTERFER
...SEPH CHURCH BAKER
ALLAN HUNTER BAKEWELL
EDWIN RALPH BARDWELL
DAVID FRY BARRY
BESHARA BRADT BARTLETT
FREDERICK ELIAN BATTIT
PETER WILLIAM BAUMANN JR
JOHN PAUL BERND
FRANCIS RUSSELL BIRD
BRANDON LOUDON BLACK
LAWRENCE BREWSTER BODELL
WILLIAM ARTHUR BOSWORTH
GEORGE FRANCIS BRANGAN JR
...HARD THADDEUS BREITLING
...IMBERG HERBERT BRESLER
...RT BRYAN

When President Maclaurin decided to move the Institute to the Charles River Basin site, even though it was in another municipality, the *Boston Globe* opined, "[The city of] Boston is sorry to lose the Institute, but since it will be in Greater Boston it will still be in the family." Politics was not the main consideration in choosing the site. What mattered was centrality and symbolic openness to Boston's global portals. From MIT's perspective, what may matter most today is the new concept of the "global city" pioneered by the sociologist Saskia Sassen in *The Global City: New York, London, Tokyo*. Translated into numbers by the *Wall Street Journal* in an article titled "U.S. Cities with Bigger Economies Than Entire Countries," Boston's economy ranked seventh among US cities, and with a gross metropolitan product of $311.3 billion was the fortieth-largest economy in the world that year. In a celebrated 2005 article in the *Atlantic Monthly*, Richard Florida of the University of Toronto explained the implications: "The continuing dominance of the world's most productive urban areas is astounding. When it comes to actual economic output, the two largest US metropolitan areas combined are behind only the United States as a whole and Japan. New York's economy alone is almost the size of Russia's or Brazil's, and Chicago is on par with Sweden. Together, New York, Los Angeles, Chicago and Boston have a bigger economy than all of China. If U.S. metropolitan areas were countries, they would make up 47 of the largest 100 economies in the world."

How intensely such things have always mattered to the Institute is essential to understand. For instance, the erection of the vast new Charles River Basin campus in 1916 was so great a strain on the Institute that its first years on the basin were characterized by flagging finances. In response, Maclaurin forged a policy described thus by James O'Connell in *The Hub's Metropolis*:

> MIT developed the Technology Plan (1918) to encourage large corporations like General Electric, Eastman Kodak, and Du Pont to provide financial support for university research. During the 1920s, MIT established the Division of Industrial Cooperation and Research to promote corporate research contracts. One of the first was with Raytheon [cofounded by MIT's Vannevar Bush]....Raytheon became the [Boston] region's premier electronics and defense contractor....Another MIT defense industry spinoff was the Lincoln Laboratory [see Walk Five]....The formidable cluster of defense industry research entities...attracted and spun off many for-profit companies....[For many years after World War II] MIT, together with the firms located near the junction of Route 128 and Route 2, formed the nation's leading electronics center.

By the end of the 1980s Boston's Route 128 would cede its dominant position to Silicon Valley in California, and by the early 2000s Cambridge had replaced Route 128 as the East Coast locus of innovation. In 2009 O'Connell wrote, "Microsoft CEO

The old main entrance lobby has through the years taken on a very sacred role, commemorating and honoring all the Institute alumni who have died in military service, with their names carved into the walls in richly gilded lettering.

The exterior detail of the Bosworth complex at the heart of the Charles River Basin campus is worth perusing, as these drawings by Professor Mark Jarzombek show. Although deliberately spare, the detail is telling.

Steve Ballmer said of the Greater Boston tech sector: 'Cambridge is a great brand. Route 128 I don't think is a tech brand anymore.'" Meanwhile, Boston has become the world leader in the life sciences, and "the cutting edge," in O'Connell's words, "has moved back to the city," mainly to Kendall Square in East Cambridge and the Seaport District in South Boston.

The Technology Plan was hugely controversial, seen by many as compromising MIT's teaching and research mission by too-close contact with the commercial sector. Philip Alexander says the plan involved quid pro quos that some found objectionable but others saw as examples of exactly the educational and industrial exchange MIT was founded to encourage. Writes Alexander, "In return for an annual fee paid up front, a company was entitled to technical advice from faculty and staff," quoting a contemporary who recalled that "a good deal of hell broke loose" over the repercussions of the program. Whichever side appeals, what is not in dispute is that the economy of the surrounding area as well as the global portals to other economies have always been key to MIT, from the age of the telephone to that of the spaceship.

One who strongly opposed the Technology Plan was Arthur Noyes, one of the stars of the chemistry department and a former MIT acting president, who as a result of his unhappiness was lured away to the California Institute of Technology in 1919. Caltech's success in attracting Noyes, though perfectly aboveboard—all schools try to lure away faculty of other schools—is perhaps what first aroused the Institute to its most storied intercollegiate rivalry. It is a "Rivalry Between the Best," as *Time* magazine put it, because Caltech has always had the reputation of being the other prestigious American university of the type MIT pioneered. The MIT-Caltech rivalry made the top ten list of such in the United States in *Newsweek* in 2008, where it was paired with the most venerable rivalry of them all, that between Harvard and Yale.

The Caltech-MIT relationship has thrived in part because it played a role in sparking MIT's "hacking" tradition, which certainly meets its equal in Caltech's "pranking" tradition. (MIT's attempts to "hack" schools without a pranking tradition invariably fall flat because, of course, there is no response.) Perhaps Caltech's best effort occurred at the 1984 Rose Bowl game between UCLA and Illinois, where the scoreboard was rewired to show Caltech defeating MIT. The Institute's outstanding hack was to manage to transport a landmark Caltech cannon across the continent to MIT, where it was set up in McDermott Court.

6   The Divisions of the Great Court
Killian, Lowell, and du Pont Courts
William Welles Bosworth, 1916

If the Great Court—Killian Court and its flanking du Pont Court and Lowell Court—intensifies the lesson of Memorial Lobby's wall-to-wall glass windows and thus underlines the outward-looking aspect of MIT, these courts also disclose in detail the face of MIT that Maclaurin and Bosworth put forward for Boston and the world. It was always a two-way street, and one that has retained its importance a century later. Though no longer the main entrance to MIT, the Great Court is still its iconic centerpiece—portico and dome—and as such, the backdrop every year for commencement.

For the visitor, this is the best place to consider in detail Bosworth's original riverfront architecture. Bosworth's facades were well received at first and are without question masterpieces, but within a generation, as the different tastes of modernism came to the fore, they were considered problematic. Eero Saarinen, for instance, thought that Bosworth's MIT facades were an example of what "we all disliked in the '30s and '40s because of their pseudo-classical sterility," as that generation was apt to see it. Yet the modernist master was quick to counsel, "Let us not dismiss [these buildings]....One can see that they form a unity; they create an environment." As Bosworth's architecture here marks its one-hundredth birthday in 2013–16, the question increasingly is: What accounts, finally, for the success of this environment?

We can only speculate on exactly how the disparagement of Bosworth's classicism in the 1930s and 1940s figured into the way the once-proud Great White City

was allowed to disappear behind a forest. Suffice to say that misguided attempts to turn a great urban classical court into a tree-shaded park have had a bad effect. Trees and foliage can play a valuable part in a certain kind of picturesque architecture—from the way the Mogul water garden integrates with architecture to the proverbial rose-covered cottage or tree-shaded suburban street or ivy-covered country church. But Bosworth's MIT is not that sort of architecture. Towering, spreading oak trees no more belong in this great classical court and urban plaza than in St. Peter's Square in Rome or St. Mark's Square in Venice.

In order "to study the visual effect of the dome from various angles," Mark Jarzombek notes, chiefly as it would appear from the Back Bay, "Bosworth used a clay model that allowed him to move the dome up [and down]." He chose the ancient Athenian Erechtheion theme of the portico cornice but detailed it by adding the motif of lions' heads, probably modeled on the fourth-century-BCE Temple of Athena Polias in Priene. It was all painstaking. Furthermore, if one studies closely the ten majestic columns of the portico, they do not stand in a straight line. There is a slight outward curvature; the columns at the center are some nine inches forward of those toward each end, all this the result of Bosworth's study of William Henry Goodyear's *Greek Refinements: Studies in Temperamental Architecture*, published in 1910. In the same vein, he varied the distances between the columns. The central bay is almost a foot wider than those at the ends. "Bosworth took great care to avoid that automated over-perfection that is often the death knell of perfunctory classicism," according to *Designing MIT*. "He preferred to arrive at a sort of vibrating, living organism, an organic classicism, so to say."

Organic and more than just skin deep, something Jarzombek hints at more than once as he grapples in his book on Bosworth's New Tech with the central issue—mystery, almost—raised by these riverfront and court facades. On the one hand, "Few if any academic buildings of that era could, in their construction, be considered as advanced as MIT." But on the other hand, "in the United States in 1916, such modernity had not yet been identified and appeared in public buildings only in the form of largely invisible construction elements. Steel and concrete construction were very slow in being allowed to surface."

But as a matter of fact, "a pioneering example of the use of reinforced concrete," what was then "the largest structure of that material in the world"—I am quoting from the National Historic Landmark designation of Harvard Stadium, built in 1903—stood brand new and resplendent farther up the Charles River from the site soon to be selected for New Tech. It was built by the Aberthaw Concrete Company of Boston, whose engineers in 1902 submitted reinforced concrete beams for testing to the Massachusetts Institute of Technology in Copley Square (according to Amy

MIT's innovative steel and concrete construction is expressed at various places throughout the interior. This 1916 photograph of a corridor running off the Infinite Corridor clearly shows the outline of the steel beams supporting the floor above.

Slaton's *Reinforced Concrete and the Modernization of American Building*). The stadium, with its classical facade, was the design of none other than Charles McKim.

Margaret Henderson Floyd in her Harvard architectural history asserts that "the elegance and power of [the stadium]...proved conclusively the aesthetic visibility of massive ferroconcrete—the material Frank Lloyd Wright would use two years later at Unity Temple in Chicago," noting the success as well of the concrete Weld Boathouse of 1906. Even so, as gifted a classicist as the senior partner of McKim, Mead and White did not quite pull it off. It is an engineering marvel, to be sure, but the concrete surfaces of McKim's facades still seem today curiously dead. Ralph Adams Cram, head of MIT's architecture department in the 1920s, had a similar problem with his Central Congregational Church in Honolulu, whose poured-in-place concrete steeple is somewhat dead in appearance. One understands why Bosworth chose to clad the Great White City on the Charles in brilliant Indiana limestone. Jarzombek said in an interview for this book: "MIT was the first building erected in the United States for academic purposes, the structural system of which was reinforced concrete. Although it was clad in limestone on the exterior, Boswell did allow glimpses of the bones of the building on the interior in the extraordinarily high (about sixteen feet) first-floor public corridors, where the exposed ceiling beams of concrete—painted but not plastered over—give the corridors their distinctive rhythm."

Consider the old photograph of the corridor of Building 4 (p. 228), running from near Memorial Lobby to Lowell Court. It shows the same concrete beams in 1916 that are evident in the 2014 photograph of the Infinite Corridor. Note, too, the corridor's height in proportion to its width—a small thing, it may seem, but this verse of long ago finds inspiration in exactly that: "I often wonder," wrote a student of 1956 in MIT's humor magazine, *Voo Doo*, "what race of men / Supreme intellectuals, mighty giants, / Once strode these halls and corridors of Tech / That they should be so high and lofty."

In the 1910s *American Architect*, a leading journal, was typical in that it intermingled articles that featured Beaux-Arts designs with those about the latest advances in concrete and steel construction with little discussion of how these two disciplinary environments might be coordinated. The truth seems to lie between the lines, so to speak, an impression I find conclusive when one encounters the work of a critic who seemed, indeed, to *feel* the concrete of MIT right through the limestone, Werner Hegemann.

An early twentieth-century Berlin-based international urbanist, active as much in the United States as in Germany, Hegemann lived in Boston. He worked on that characteristic achievement of the Progressive Era, the Boston 1915 exposition, just when New Tech was being broached. He was attracted to the New England metropolis, according to the historian Christiane Crasemann Collins, in large part because of his admiration for Edward A. Filene, the department store magnate who had such enthusiasm for Boston 1915, on which Hegemann labored throughout 1909. Hegemann responded to Filene as he did because he saw him, so to speak, in his native habitat, Filene being a twentieth-century Jewish Boston Brahmin.

Hegemann's "reactions to the ambiance cultivated by the Bostonian elite... dispelled [his] European misconceptions of an American lack of sophistication," wrote Collins. "Upon returning to Europe in 1922...he interwove many Boston rec-ollections in his fiction. In his 1924 novel, *Deutsche Schrefton*, he fashioned a com-posite portrait of one Manifred Marie Ellis, a member of the Boston Brahmin class. Occasionally he referred to the fictional Ellis as a character based on the socially prominent [and eventual Harvard Business School professor] Philip Cabot, a member of the 'Boston 1915' committee." Writing in his *Werner Hegemann and the Search for Universal Urbanism*, Collins details how Hegemann used his experience in 1909 in Boston to mount the First International City Planning Exhibition in Berlin in 1910, and how acute his perceptions were.

It seems to me no coincidence that it was Hegemann who saw deepest into Bosworth's MIT architecture, uniquely intellectually positioned as he was between very avant-garde architectural circles in Europe. As Collins relates, "among those affected by [the Berlin 1910 exhibition] was an individual whose reactions contrib-uted in consequential ways to architecture and planning. In the coming decades, Le Corbusier, [who] considered the Greater Berlin projects [of Hegemann's exhibition]... to be 'impressive'"—and progressive Boston Brahmin circles in America.

Writing in *American Vitruvius* in 1924, only nine years after New Tech's ded-ication (which he probably attended), Hegemann insisted not only that Bosworth had conceived what he called "a forum of great strength," but also—making one remarkable assertion the explanation of another—that "no traditional American detail has been used, but the design...shows *an Americanization of its own* by using classic forms with an austerity that *suggests steel and concrete*." The emphasis in both cases is my own, but the insight is Hegemann's—a double insight and powerful, especially when one recalls Jarzombek's assertion of "Bosworth's conviction that the Graeco-Roman style represented American architecture at its best."

The best subsequent commentary, occasioned exactly by Hegemann's critique, is Turner's in *Campus*, his history of American academic architecture. Bosworth's MIT facades, Turner thought, illustrated the fact that "sometimes a par-ticular style was considered appropriate to a school's orientation or curriculum [, such] as...Bosworth's stark interpretation of classicism at MIT," which, as we saw in previous chapters, arose out of William Barton Rogers's curriculum and orientation with the Yankee Boston Brahmin Unitarian reformers of the nineteenth century. Bosworth, who spent formative years in Boston, and specifically among Boston Brahmin Yankees in the last years of the nineteenth century, was drawn to and well reflected the Brahmin code. He saw "himself as both a gentleman architect *and* a gentleman," in Jarzombek's words, something "particularly attractive to the likes of [John D.] Rockefeller," one of the clients who recommended him as MIT's architect, "who shunned the gaudy display and social pretensions of some members of their class. Bosworth's neoclassical aesthetic also appealed to [the Brahmins], as it spoke of control, restraint, and timeless validity."

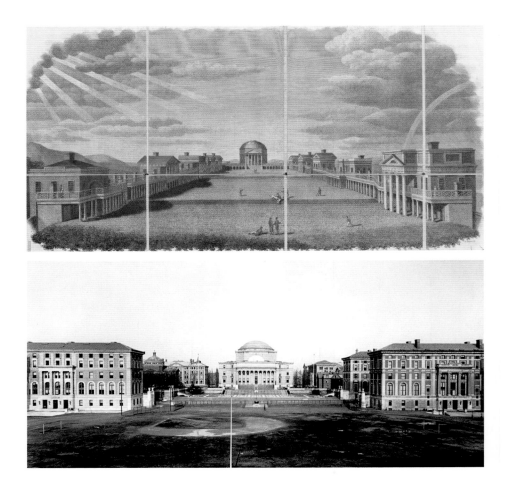

The overt inspiration of Bosworth in designing the central complex comes from Jefferson's eighteenth-century University of Virginia (ABOVE) and Charles McKim's nineteenth-century Columbia University in New York (BELOW)

Brahmin aesthetic? The Brahmin influence at MIT is not exhausted by the Rogers-Savage alliance, nor by Hegemann's engagement with the Cabots and Filenes. A continuing institutional influence is forcefully proclaimed in one of the two courts that open so grandly off Killian Court, MIT's Great Court. Each honors a great family whose devotion to the Institute brought it to the place where all the splendors of Bosworth's New Tech were possible and, indeed, required.

The left-hand court as you face the entrance portico in the Great Court is du Pont Court. It speaks to how quickly MIT became a truly national institution, seminal in its forging of alliances countrywide between academia and industry, not least with this Delaware-based American family whose firm was the country's leading supplier of gunpowder at one time and went on to develop nylon. Many du Ponts have attended MIT, the best known being the American engineer and Republican US senator (from Delaware, in the 1920s) *COLEMAN DV PONT*, whose name is blazoned in Roman capitals in stone above this court as its principal honoree. It was to Coleman, a great-grandson of Eleuthère du Pont, the founder of the company in 1802, that President Maclaurin turned for the half-million pre–World War I dollars that made up two-thirds of the purchase price for the land on which all these buildings by Bosworth stand. Without Coleman du Pont, no Great Court, no New Tech.

The court that opens off the Great Court to the right honors a debt of even longer standing, one reaching back to the prehistory of the Massachusetts Institute of Technology. This is Lowell Court, where at MIT's first commencement here in 1917, according to the *Tech* of May 16, a dais was "erected…below the inscription of the name of the family that has been represented on the Corporation of the Institute since its founding." An honor, but one fully justified, for without this family, which ranks with the Adamses, the Eliots, the Lees, and the Forbeses as what I call über- or great Brahmins, there would be no MIT.

In the earliest period, two Lowells particularly stand out in this respect. Francis Lowell, the textile magnate who made Boston the New World capital of the Industrial Revolution, had an equally remarkable son, John Lowell Jr., a notable philanthropist who undertook a legendary global odyssey that is still widely celebrated. While at Luxor on the banks of the Nile, he conceived the now-famous Lowell Institute, which sparked in nineteenth-century Copley Square at MIT so many breakthroughs, including becoming virtually the prototype of university extension in the United States.

A quintessentially Boston Brahmin institution, its governance in the hands of a hereditary trustee (always a Lowell), the Lowell Institute thrived under its first such trustee, John Amory Lowell. He was a cousin of the founder and, going back to the 1840s, a mentor and ally of Rogers. He did not, as Rogers wanted him to do, fund MIT's founding as a Lowell Institute project, but when MIT *was* founded, he was so strong a backer that he was named first vice president of MIT.

MIT historians tend nonetheless to downplay Lowell's role, because he also sat on Harvard's Corporation and seems an example of divided loyalties. But it has always been more partnership than rivalry, and Lowell was not the last person by any means to serve on the governing boards of both institutions. Lowell Institute historian Edward Weeks, though he does not scant Lowell's loyalty to Harvard, stresses his intense commitment to MIT, emphasizing how "exceedingly fond" Lowell was of Rogers and noting that Lowell was not "slow to take the initiative…when the time was ripe to found MIT." Weeks suggests that Lowell privately made significant financial contributions, as well as endowing an evening school and lecture series that would ensure the Institute's financial security.

But the most famous Lowell of them all, as MIT saw it, whose name is thus the one grandly blazoned in bold Latin capitals above the court, is *AVGVSTVS LOWELL*. He was the senior member of the executive committee that, according to the founder's wish, ran MIT after Rogers's death. Augustus Lowell served for more than two decades, through thick and thin. Weeks described him as "not cautious; indeed, as

MCMXVI

MASSACHVSETTS INSTITVTE OF TE

Killian Court soon after
construction in 1916.

7   **Barker Engineering Library**
     Building 10 (Fifth Floor)
     William Welles Bosworth, 1916

However difficult it became in the post–World War II period to see the Great White City outside, the great dome remained—and remains—visible and dominant. It is more than could be said for the inside, where a complete disdain for Bosworth's classicism led eventually to its being completely obscured—not by a forest, of course, but by a suspended ceiling. Finally in 2011–12 the vandalism was undone and the dome's interior gloriously restored, making the Barker Engineering Library again an absolutely vital stop on any tour of Bosworth's New Tech.

All here is not as Bosworth intended. "Had the central dome been built with the vast interior space initially planned, it would have been," Jarzombek assures us, "the largest indoor space in Boston." There was a grand staircase that led to an assembly hall, which became a library, whose rotunda because of financial constraints was finally confined to the fifth floor and above, just under the inner dome's vault, and shorn of any grand staircase. Instead, there are elevators to the domed library in a small hallway off the Memorial Lobby.

Once found, the rotunda—when you emerge from the elevator, just follow the twists and turns of the library's entry—is undeniably magnificent. It does not establish any connection with the Great Court, which it "overlooks," alas, from behind the dome's windowless drum. But the interior dome, nestled within the larger exterior dome and sharing with it what has been called "a capacious oculus" (twenty-seven feet in diameter and recently reopened to allow natural light again into the rotunda), recalls the Roman Pantheon and is coffered in the same manner as that ancient landmark.

The dome's color scheme now faithfully respects again its original seven shades of off-white and oxidized bronze green, and the encircling Corinthian columns create a zone both serene and grand—the rotunda's diameter, at seventy-two feet, is the same as its height—and such classical grandeur has its effect. So the mind turns again to those larger thoughts we first took up outside. Like the Great Court, MIT's rotunda stakes a claim, and each claim is closely related to the other.

The interior claim, however, does not involve architecture as such, not as the exterior claim does. The same issues do not arise. There is nothing of the Boston Brahmin aesthetic inside. Indeed, the rotunda is more elegant than one might expect, distinctly baroque in feeling: "an inside-out quotation," Jarzombek calls it, "from St. Paul's Cathedral [in London]." Here Bosworth seems to have loosened up somewhat.

The reading room of the Barker Engineering Library is directly underneath MIT's center dome, which was modeled by Bosworth after that of the Parthenon in Rome. It has recently been carefully restored.

8   Walker Building
Blashfield Murals
William Welles Bosworth, 1920–23

Down the elevator again, the route of this walk suggests the visitor retrace his or her steps back into the Great Court on the way now to Memorial Drive, the street that runs along the river in front of the Institute. Now walk a few blocks eastward to Bosworth's Walker Memorial, the second of the freestanding buildings that lie eastward of the main Bosworth group, easily recognizable by the majestic Doric colonnade that fronts the building. Once inside, go through the entrance hall into the large room straight ahead, where in the center of the far wall you can finally see the Great White City along the Charles as originally conceived by Maclaurin. Eliot's "court of honor" and Bosworth's Great Court are joined in a dream sufficient to embarrass the Chicago World's Fair itself.

How so? On this north wall is a spectacular painting of 1920–23, *Alma Mater*, by America's greatest muralist of the era, Edwin Howland Blashfield. This mural, Mina Weiner notes in her book on the artist, shows an "almost unparalleled mastery and brevity of touch, executed by Blashfield when he was well into his nineties, and bears witness to an artistic reputation ripe for revival." *Alma mater* is the traditional appellation for one's college, a personification of which presides over the composition. To the right and left Blashfield depicts various personifications of the arts and sciences, and of book learning and laboratory learning—William Barton Rogers's mind and hand. In the center at the bottom under *Alma Mater* and between the choirs of figures is the beautiful, misty water park of Eliot's "court of honor" of the Boston metropolis. Reflected in it is the Great White City, serenely presiding with truly Venetian splendor and grace. Blashfield, an MIT alumnus from the days of Rogers himself in the 1860s, captured brilliantly the long-obscured vision of Bosworth's New Tech.

9   George Eastman Laboratories
Coolidge and Carlson, 1930–32

If the Blashfield murals of the Walker Building, to which we will return in Walk Four, celebrate the vision of Maclaurin and Bosworth (and, indeed, of Charles Eliot) of the shining white city on the Charles River Basin, the Eastman Laboratories building near the Walker Building, itself a memorial to the donor who made the Cambridgeport campus possible, was meant to be the solution to a variety of problems that beset MIT in its splendid new isolation in the 1920s.

Samuel Wesley Stratton was named president in 1923 after Maclaurin's death in 1920 and the illness of his successor, Ernest Fox Nichols (who was appointed in June and resigned in November of 1921). As MIT took possession of its magnificent new campus, evidence was accumulating, in Philip Alexander's words, that "the Institute's reputation as a center for both pure and applied research had waned." (Recall the anecdote in Walk One of how Einstein on his 1921 visit to Boston drove right past MIT.) As an example, Alexander notes that the 1910 edition of *American Men of Science*, issued during MIT's last years in Copley Square, ranked it first in the nation in chemistry and seventh in physics. Seventeen years later, at the end of MIT's first decade and a half in Cambridgeport, the 1927 edition dropped MIT to third in chemistry, and in physics it had fallen entirely out of the competition. Stratton's response was to try and shift Tech's emphasis more toward basic science, a policy that culminated in a very real sense in his 1927 *President's Report*, in which he called in the most urgent terms for a new building for "research work in the fields of biology and chemistry." He insisted, moreover, that this building "must be provided at the earliest possible moment."

But the Eastman labs were far from the president's chief concerns in the late 1920s, given the gathering social unrest of those years. It was an era in which racism, ethnic bigotry, and anti-immigrant prejudice were notoriously gaining ground in America, even at Harvard, where the über-Brahmin progressive Charles W. Eliot had resigned in 1909 and been succeeded by an equally über-Brahmin bigot, Abbott Lawrence Lowell. Stratton's situation was complicated as well by the fact that his sexual orientation was the subject of widespread speculation. He thus found himself not only weakened politically but also, only four years into his presidency, at the center of what William Grimes in the *New York Times* would later call "one of the blackest pages in the American national story," the international cause célèbre of the Sacco and Vanzetti case.

MIT's president was tapped by Massachusetts governor Alvan T. Fuller to be one of three members of the Governor's Advisory Committee whose final approval of the verdict cleared the way for the execution of two anarchists, Nicola Sacco and Bartolomeo Vanzetti. Many believed these Italian Americans were unjustly convicted of murder primarily because of their ethnicity and immigrant status. It was an appointment Stratton only "very reluctantly accepted," according to the *Tech*, as it turned out with very good reason. The repercussions reverberate to this day. The committee's unanimous support of the death penalty provoked riots all over the world. The furor subsided, but still today, at New York's Whitney Museum of American Art, visitors will see an extraordinary triple portrait by Ben Shahn, the culmination of his series *The Passion of Sacco and Vanzetti*. It depicts the presidents of Harvard and MIT and Judge Robert Grant all gloating over the open coffins of the two executed immigrants. It is not the sort of presidential portrait any university would want, meant as it is to haunt all concerned more or less forever.

In this fatal situation, MIT's alliance with Boston's historic ruling class did not serve it well. Upton Sinclair proclaimed in *Boston*, his best-selling novel of 1928, that all three of the men the governor asked to make this judgment were Brahmins: "three elderly Brahmins," Sinclair calls them again and again, singling Stratton out especially. "Two of the three members of the committee were registered blue-bloods," the novelist wrote, "the third [Stratton], though he came from the west, had been adopted and placed in charge of the great school which next to Harvard was [Brahmin] Boston's pride."

The Great White City on the Charles is now obscured by the forest in front of it in Killian Court and on Memorial Drive. It can still be seen in all its glory in the Walker Memorial's resplendent central mural by Edwin Howland Blashfield, Sargent's rival as the greatest muralist of the era.

The committee, dominated by Lowell, conspicuously failed to hold the high moral ground, which was seen as evidence that Boston's ruling class had lost its nerve, and with it what old China traders called "the mandate of Heaven." Stratton, the adopted Brahmin from whom more might have been expected in terms of bringing a fresh eye to the proceedings, sat virtually silent during every meeting of the committee. Although, as Sinclair admitted, "[Stratton] would have needed tremendous moral courage to have opposed a domineering person like President Lowell." He surely knew how vulnerable he himself was to Lowell, who would have heard the rumors about Stratton's homosexuality, widespread by 1927. Lowell was notoriously the persecutor of not only Jews and blacks but also immigrants (he was vice president of the infamous Immigrant Restriction League) and homosexuals. Lowell once advised a faculty member in danger of being exposed for his sexual orientation that the best solution would be to get a gun and kill himself.

What this may have cost Stratton, normally a rather assertive person, is suggested in Philip Alexander's *A Widening Sphere*, which documents the fact that, unlike Lowell at Harvard, "Stratton, by contrast, favored a more inclusive environment. When Charles Richards, president of Lehigh University, asked [MIT's president] to divulge the methods used by MIT to limit the number of Jewish students, Stratton's response was unequivocal: 'The Institute of Technology has never to my knowledge taken any steps to control its attendance as to nationalities….I have never looked into the question of the proportion of Jewish students.'"

Stratton's MIT was very different from Lowell's Harvard and unilaterally asserted with some success what in Eliot's day had been Harvard's liberal leadership role in such matters. This is evident in the case of faculty member Norbert Wiener. The son of one of Harvard's first tenured Jewish professors, appointed in 1895 by President Eliot, Wiener in 1919 felt he was the victim of President Lowell's frankly anti-Semitic policy, and in President Maclaurin's last year he was be recruited by MIT. Thus did MIT gain—and Harvard lose—"one of the great minds of the Twentieth Century," as the *New York Times* would later pronounce Wiener, who went on to thrive at MIT. Many hail him as the father of the information age and the inventor of cybernetics.

Wiener, in turn, recruited Dirk Struik, a Dutch scholar, who became one of his greatest allies. Recalled Struik (who was not Jewish) in a 1999 interview in the *Harvard Educational Review*, "In the 1930s I do not think Harvard had more than three Jews," whereas by contrast, "MIT was never very anti-Semitic. [In the mathematics department] we had several Jews on the faculty." And politics, of the most activist kind, was encouraged. "We published manifestos," Struik remembered, "and organized to fight Hitlerism." Stratton pulled a vigorous oar in this arena, conspicuously inviting to MIT Max Born, a German Jew whose work in quantum mechanics in the 1920s was so important that he eventually won the Nobel Prize in physics, but whose career in Germany was ended by the Nazis. Born turned down Stratton's offer of a permanent appointment, preferring the University of Edinburgh, but he agreed to an ongoing nonresident affiliation with MIT. His best-known lectures there were published in 1927 as *Problems of Atomic Dynamics*. Born also coauthored a major article on quantum mechanics with Wiener.

The historical ground in the 1930s was shifting under everyone; had been, perhaps, since the 1890s. The Sacco-Vanzetti trial in Boston, like the earlier Dreyfus trial in Paris (the issue there was anti-Semitism) and the Oscar Wilde trial in London (there the issue was sexual orientation), sparked a sea change, not least in the Boston Brahminate. "In New York," always alert to any perceived weakness in the New England capital's intellectual leadership, "men could read the [*Lowell-Stratton-Grant Report*] and judge it for what it was," wrote Upton Sinclair, "a revelation of the mental breakdown of a once great civilization; but in Boston hardly anyone could judge it. Mr. Lowell did the thinking for half the city." By the 1930s Jewish Boston Brahmins were there—shades of Werner Hegemann and Edward Filene and certainly Harvard law professor Felix Frankfurter—to put up a magnificent fight, smiting the descendants of the Yankee Brahmins now passing from the scene. But it was not enough.

When Albert Einstein himself protested the Sacco-Vanzetti affair, it must have seemed to many at MIT the last straw. Stratton's complicated reign was brought to an end, and he was eased into a power-sharing arrangement with his successor. Stratton became chairman of the MIT Corporation, and Karl Taylor Compton assumed the presidency in 1930. And with Compton's drive now behind Stratton's plan for the urgently needed new building—according to Philip Alexander it was Compton who persuaded the Corporation to set aside $1 million to launch the project—the Eastman Laboratories finally began to rise in 1930-32. Stratton and Compton were both involved in the planning of the facility, which at its dedication Compton called "the finest in the world."

A final example of the shift Stratton engineered toward more pure science at MIT is the founding of a new unit in the physics department, the Laboratory of Theoretical Physics, with the president's full backing. It is also significant as illustrating his inclusive policy. Among the new unit's first staffers was Manuel Vallarta, a Mexican physicist who discovered that the intensity of cosmic rays varies from one latitude to another because of variations in the earth's magnetic field. Vallarta had earned both his undergraduate and his doctoral degrees from MIT in the 1920s, and was a full professor by 1927. Likely he was also the first of his ethnic group to be considered as a possible department head. Alexander has uncovered a striking example of what Vallarta was up against in the testimony of one of his colleagues, "I felt uncertain about him...and did not trust my impressions as to his personality and character, until I learned that his mother was English-American."

Vallarta's character was made clear when he remained loyal to Stratton even as the president's power waned, pointedly praising him for his "splendid services to the cause of pure science" and saluting him for "the rebirth of pure science at the Institute." Today MIT president L. Rafael Reif, born in Venezuela of émigré Jews who fled Europe in the 1930s, is the first MIT president born and raised in Latin America, a tenure that promotes the legacy of Stratton's vision for a global MIT.

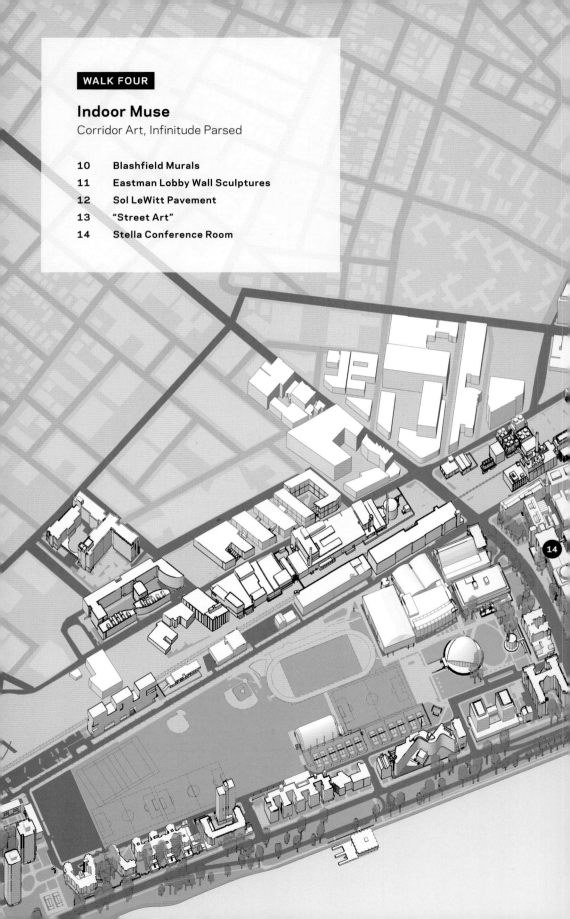

Indoor Muse
Corridor Art, Infinitude Parsed

**10 Walker Memorial
Blashfield Murals**
William Welles Bosworth, 1923–30

President Francis Amasa Walker was a key figure in the development of both the Back Bay and Cambridgeport campuses of MIT. Walker, who turned down the opportunity to be the founding president of Stanford University in order to succeed William Barton Rogers in the MIT presidency (he later became an adviser to Stanford), stands second only to Rogers in shaping the formative years of the Institute. At a crucial point when events were bearing down heavily on the twenty-plus-year-old school in the mid-1880s, including Rogers's frequent illnesses, Walker seized the shaky Institute at Rogers's own behest and guided MIT through one crisis after another, finally sparking a tremendous growth in faculty, students, and facilities to the point where, as noted in "Part One," what had begun as a technical school emerged as a scientific university.

Thomas Edison, who like Alexander Graham Bell had early links to the Institute (in his Boston years in the late 1860s, Edison lived in a Beacon Hill rooming house with MIT students), was asked by a reporter where he would send his son to college during Walker's reign in the 1890s. "To the Massachusetts Institute of Technology," the great inventor replied. Edison thought so highly of Walker's MIT that he gave the Institute a dynamo and 150 lamps in the 1880s, remarking that "the best school in the country is the Massachusetts Institute of Technology. The men they turn out there are the best in the world and practically run our up-to-date businesses."

Edison's opinion was shared by the donor of the millions that built the Cambridgeport campus, George Eastman. Elizabeth Brayer documents in her study of the Eastman-Kodak tycoon that he went on record as being "impressed with the stock of material recruited from MIT to run his company, [including]...Darragh de Lancey, a graduate of the Institute in Walker's day." Note the woman. Walker was distinctly rightist, verging on racist, which was unusual among MIT's early leaders, but he was relatively open to women enrolling at the Institute as regular students.

Eastman lived to see the new Bosworth complex and is on record as greatly liking its lack of artistic flourishes. Writing to a friend (without disclosing that he was the donor; "Mr. Smith," as he was long known, was very secretive), he exulted in the

The oldest of MIT's wall art, still to be seen in the architecture studios, are the plaster casts of ancient Greek sculpture from the Parthenon brought from Europe by Professor William Ware and originally shared with Boston's new Museum of Fine Arts, which MIT founded with Harvard and the Boston Athenaeum in Copley Square in 1876.

fact that the buildings were "perfectly splendid in every way, monumental in charac-
ter, magnificent in size…not a bit of carving anywhere except in the fluted pillars."
Nor was he above enjoying scoring over rival donors, such as J. P. Morgan, who
largely funded the new Harvard Medical School campus in the Fenway: MIT's Great
Court, called Eastman Court for many years, was "big enough to contain the Harvard
Medical Buildings," he wrote proudly. Edison, too, lived to see Bosworth's New Tech.
He was among the guests at MIT's first Commencement in the Great Court in 1923,
when his son Theodore graduated.

 The Walker Memorial is most immediately of interest to the twenty-first
century for its interior wall paintings, the significance of which I noted at the end of
Walk One when focusing on their triumphant record of Maclaurin and Bosworth's
design concept for the Great White City. This walk is less about architecture and
more about what the arts of painting and sculpture bring to architecture. The study
of this at MIT particularly demands separate treatment, even if it requires of the
visitor a certain retracing of steps.

 These murals are not, as is sometimes suggested, MIT's first architectural art.
The Institute's earliest and most important interior artworks are the plaster casts
(by whom we do not know) of the great reliefs of the Parthenon in Athens that were
brought to Boston from Europe by William Ware in the 1860s. These reliefs continue
to function at MIT just as they did 150 and more years ago, adorning the walls of
the architecture school's working studios. But they are also important documents
of early MIT's artistic claim to being one of the three institutional founders of the art
museum that remains among the world's greatest today, Boston's Museum of Fine
Arts, on the board of which MIT still has voice and vote. Six hundred of these casts,
for which there was no room at MIT, were exhibited at the museum for many years.
Barely a half dozen survive, but they are precious links to the origins of MIT's School
of Architecture, the first in America, a role that was never an easy one.

 How uneasy is clear in the history of MIT's first-ever interior architectural
art commission: in 1870, the result of the fact that, according to William G. Preston,
the Rogers Building's Hall was designed by Ware, who also "deserved to produce an
example of mural decoration appropriate to the objects of the Institute."

 A twentieth-century president of the Institute, James R. Killian, in a 1935
pamphlet on the Walker Memorial murals, recounted how—in order to understand
them—one needed to look back on the old Huntington Hall murals and take account
of the fact that "in 1870 President Rogers appointed Paul Herman Nefflen, to make
a decorative frieze in Huntington Hall." In 1898 the editors of *American Architect
and Building News*—architects all—launched a furious public attack against MIT on
behalf of its architecture school, "always at a disadvantage because of [the] antago-
nism between architectural and engineering science." They continued and escalated:
"One can hardy dwell among barbarians without adopting some of their manners and
habits of thought," they assert, "but we never expected…such an act of vandalism
as implied in the painting-out of the broad frieze that decorated Huntington Hall…
[which was] wholly worthy of preservation, not only because of its intrinsic worth,

The first murals in America by contemporary report, the work of Paul Herman Nefflen in 1871, adorned MIT's Huntington Hall in the first Rogers Building in Copley Square. Their significance is all the greater when it is remembered that parishioners worshipped in this hall while building Trinity Church in the mid-1870s, famously featuring vastly more ambitious murals by John La Farge that for the first time in American architecture brilliantly fleshed out and empowered the architect's work.

but because its appearance in Boston, as practically the first piece of mural decoration in the country, was epoch-making." Barbarians? In Copley Square? Among the most riled up was William Preston, the architect of the first Rogers Building. He rose to the murals' defense on the grounds that their subject was "the trades and professions allied to science and the arts."

What had happened? In an article seven years later in *Technology Review*, Frank Bourne stepped gingerly through the debris, noting that the murals were "in watercolor, directly on the plaster, and were not permanently fixed, so that during the summer of 1898, as they had become badly damaged, painters were requested to put the hall in presentable shape; and a few pails of water, with a scrubbing brush, was the quickest and easiest solution of the problem....But what a disagreeable surprise it was to returning students and alumni to no longer find the frieze." The evasions are obvious; so is the criticism of Nefflen's work.

Nefflen, a German American artist born and trained in Stuttgart who came to America in 1851, spent considerable time on these murals in terms of both execution and research. According to Frank Bourne, he painted them in "the bitterest winter weather, with no windows in the hall, as it was in an unfinished condition, the only fire being a tiny stove with just enough heat to keep his colors warm." And prior to that he had spent many months traveling around the country, watching the workers, for example, at their looms in the great factories. The result was a kind of heroic frieze of Rogers's maxim of mind and hand in the context of the Industrial Revolution in America. Whatever Nefflen's shortcomings as a muralist—no one ever suggested he was Michelangelo or Sargent—he achieved a considerable artistic breakthrough. When the fracas over his work's removal grew so insistent that nothing would do but to restore it seven years later, the art critic Frederick Coburn in *Brush and Pencil* asserted in June 1906 that "the restoration of [Nefflen's] paintings for the Massachusetts Institute of Technology [could be] held an event of considerable national importance." Nefflen, declared Coburn, and not the better-known William Morris Hunt, was "the first mural painter in America, the painter chosen by Professor William Ware as the artist most competent among the men then painting in America to do the frieze." Nefflen's panels, he continued, were "put in place in 1871, five years before John La Farge finished his monumental works for Trinity Church, Boston," those being, of course, still the most famous early murals in American history.

All this adds up to yet another example of MIT's extraordinary but overlooked role in the history of American art. Bowdoin College Chapel in Maine has what are usually thought of as America's earliest murals—from 1852. But those are anonymous works, and not original, but copies of old masters. Subsequently in the 1860s two New York churches, Pilgrim and St. George's, boasted elaborate painted interiors, but in both cases the work was almost entirely ornamental. Thus it seems clear, as they were acclaimed by *American Architect* in 1898, that Nefflen's extensive cycle of seventeen original works of art, constituting the frieze of Huntington Hall in MIT's first Rogers Building in Copley Square, was indeed the first original mural cycle in any American building. Moreover, it is inescapable, given the fact that Trinity Church's congregation worshipped in Huntington Hall until the church was opened in 1877, that these MIT murals, although never mentioned in the scholarship on Trinity, stand in the most immediate relation to Trinity's decoration of 1876–77 by La Farge.

Given the importance of this mural cycle, the subjects of Nefflen's murals, one of which is illustrated here, are herewith fully enumerated:

Modeling	Ropewalk	Freehand Drawing
Carpentry	Weaving	Mechanical Drawing
Pottery	Physics/Astronomy	Navigation
Glass Painting	Printing	Textile Printing
Chemistry	Glassblowing	Brick Making
Mining	Iron Casting	

All of this President Killian did well to bring up when he hymned, in a 1935 pamphlet, the Edwin Blashfield murals of 1923–30 that the visitor sees today at the Walker Memorial. Killian not only saw the connection; he specifically celebrated the fact that Nefflen's very MIT-specific iconography of the arts and crafts of science and technology in 1871 was paralleled more than a half century later in the Blashfield murals—paralleled and also considerably deepened by one mural that is particularly probing and edgy, *Good and Bad Uses of Science*.

According to Weiner's *Edwin Howland Blashfield: Master American Muralist*, this unusually "dramatic" mural, undertaken in 1930, when the artist was in his nineties, "was a departure for Blashfield." Like most murals of the period, it is both highly moralistic and allegorical, and thus unfashionable today on two counts, but it was brave of MIT to sponsor *Good and Bad Uses of Science*, in which, Weiner notes, not just the usual positive but "the negative alternative to inspirational aspirations is made visible." Anna Vallye points out in her Columbia University doctoral dissertation *Design and the Politics of Knowledge* that Blashfield's mural conveys "with catechistic solemnity the promise of *scientia* commanding the labors of the Institute," in this case specifically a scientist, "white haired, clad in a lab coat, releasing with an impartial gesture symmetrical spirits of beneficent and maleficent nature from two identical jars. The dogs of war, the cherubim of peace, counter align," while Hygeia, the personification in Greek and Roman mythology of good health, crowns the scientist for—presumably—preferring the beneficent spirits.

The mural sustains not only more than one doctoral thesis, but blogs both learned and popular. One such—Real Physics—presided over by a Columbia PhD in the field, Lawrence Gage, offers in many ways the most thoughtful critique of Blashfield's mural. Citing rumors that at MIT "a building on campus featured the empty promise of the serpent in the Garden of Eden, 'You shall be as Gods,' inscribed on a wall," Gage paid his own visit to the Walker Memorial. He reported to his readers along the lines already outlined here, but added, after seeing the mural as well as reading the inscription: "But then you have to ask yourself: why reproduce a lie [the serpent's promise] without clearly demarking it as such? The mural itself seems to be rather more ambiguous than the description. Is the emphasis on the dangers of technology to men and creation, or on the crowning of man as god?"

If Blashfield's mural is "a warning against technological hubris," why is the scientist whose releasing gesture, as Vallye notes, is seemingly "impartial" being crowned? And who or what does the crowner—metaphorical Hygeia—represent? Why would MIT make itself so vulnerable to these questions? One hopes it was because the hall the murals adorn was then used as a student dining hall, and these were just the sorts of questions students need to be confronted with. Also important, perhaps, was the fact that the murals were the gift of MIT's treasurer at the time, a position one of the rewards of which was surely a certain independence of thought and action. The treasurer in question was Everett Morss, a Back Bay grandee. Morss had previously commissioned Blashfield to do murals for his own Back Bay palazzo. Like MIT's treasurer and his wife, other Bostonians were keen to endow the American-Athens-become-the-American-Rome with suitable civic art, a tradition Sargent—who has been called by the art historian Jane Dini "Boston's Michelangelo"—had started at the Public Library in Copley Square and continued at the Museum of Fine Arts and Harvard's Widener Library.

The MIT work was at once seen to be comparable to Sargent's work at the Copley Square library. In a January 1924 review of the MIT murals, the art critic A. J. Philpott lauded Blashfield's *Alma Mater* as "the largest mural decoration in America"

THE PHYSICAL WORLD

HUYGENS · NEWTON · RUMFORD · AMPÈRE · FRESNEL

GALILEO · FARADAY

AL HAZEN · HELMHOLTZ

ARCHIMEDES · MAXWELL

ORBIT OF MERCURY
ORBIT OF VENUS
ORBIT OF THE EARTH
ORBIT OF MARS

MATTER · ENERGY · RADIATION

》》》》》 GROSS GRAVITATING MATTER 《《《《《 RESPONSIVE TO
ENERGY CONSISTING ITSELF OF AGGREGATES OF ENERGY,
· REVEALED IN ITS INNERMOST STRUCTURE BY THE STUDY
OF RADIATION FROM WHICH BOTH MATTER AND ENERGY
AT LAST SEEM WHOLLY INDISTINGUISHABLE 《《《《《《《《《《

in what he judged to be "one of the finest halls in a decorative way in this country." Blashfield is not Sargent, of course, but the *New York Times* hailed him as the "dean of American muralists," and he was certainly, as a muralist, Sargent's greatest rival. These gorgeously luminous wall paintings of Blashfield's are worthy of comparison with his best work, the great dome of the reading room of the Library of Congress in Washington, D.C.

11 Eastman Lobby and Laboratories
Building 6
Coolidge and Carlson, 1931
Lobby art: Greenough Thayer Richards, architect, 1934;
A. Lukeman, Eastman plaque sculptor, 1931

By now, the truth of the *Boston Globe* Pulitzer Prize–winning architecture critic Robert Campbell's assertion should be clear: "MIT is an institution that does not have, conceptually, any outdoors. There are handsome quads and plazas, of course, but they always feel extraneous. They're not part of the DNA of MIT. The true public space at MIT is the famous 'Infinite Corridor' grid that ties everything together." Of course, this is too simplistic. "Extraneous" is not the word I'd use to describe the Great Court, or the view of Kresge Auditorium past the Chapel. But Campbell's point is well taken. As much as MIT's iconic dome, this is Bosworth's legacy. Nor does it seem outrageous to claim a central place for it as shaping MIT's culture. Like it or not, the Infinite Corridor is unique.

The last two stops of this walk are both artistic responses to this legacy. The first response in the 1930s, just after the departure from Copley Square, tried to adjust the new aesthetic and redirect it. The second response, which dates from just a few years ago in the early 2000s, was more accepting of what had, in fact, become part of MIT's quirky culture.

Just short of the exterior door at the end of this second leg of the original Infinite Corridor, if the visitor turns right down the last cross-corridor, he or she will soon find him- or herself walking down a few steps into a sunken lobby, where he or she will be engaged by some unusual art: two sequences of bronze sculptural wall reliefs set in marble—"bronze murals" they were called when new in 1934. They are part of a truly exceptional overall setting designed by Greenough Thayer Richards, a Boston architect and educator (the son of a Nobel Prize–winning Harvard scientist and the brother-in-law of Harvard president James Conant) who was the editor of *New England Architect and Builder* and taught for many years at Virginia Polytechnic Institute and State University.

One of the two bronze wall sculptures (1934) of the Eastman Laboratories lobby shows in outline form the periodic table. Another more modern variation can be found in the lobby of the Dreyfus Building. It was designed by Felice Frankel (2005) and is illustrated in Portal Three, page 73.

GEORGE EASTMAN

>>>>>> ·OF·RARE·MOULD
FINE·GRAINED ‹‹‹‹‹‹‹
>>>>>> SENSITIVE·TO
BEAUTY·RESPONSIVE
TO·TRUTH·CONSERVER
OF·HUMAN·VALUES
>>>>>> PIONEER·IN·THE
SUSTAINED·APPLICATION
OF·SCIENTIFIC·RESEARCH
TO·INDUSTRY ‹‹‹‹‹‹‹‹‹‹‹

>>>>>>>>>>>>>> FRIEND·OF
THE·MASSACHUSETTS
INSTITUTE·OF·TECH-
NOLOGY ‹‹‹‹‹‹‹‹‹‹

These unusual works of art, according to an article of 1934 in *Technology Review*, were part of a campaign to "relieve the sterile reaches of corridors and entrance ways and to give such utilitarian spaces a part to play in stimulating the mind and delighting the eye," a campaign that did, however, cede this much to the pace of MIT: "These murals [are]...presented," the article opines, "so that even those who run may read." MIT may not have invented "corridor art," if there is such a genre, but here a masterpiece of the genre was achieved. The subject of these wall sculptures is the development of physics and chemistry. To the left as one descends into the lobby, the "study of the chemical elements throughout history" is interpreted. Portrayed here are both alchemists and chemists, the most modern of the latter being Dmitri Mendeleev, who devised the periodic table that coordinated extant knowledge of the chemical elements. His periodic table is then actually illustrated by the large bronze outline relief in the center of the wall. "The physical world and [the] discovery of its laws" is the subject of the wall sculptures opposite, on the right. Phenomena relating to matter, energy, and radiation, studied by investigators from Galileo onward by computing the forces at work in pendulums and in heavenly bodies, is suggested by bronzework in the center. There is a pendulum and the planetary system, where also "the micro-cosmos is represented...by an atomic lattice arrangement of a simple crystal."

It is a cavalcade of heroes. There is only one American—Benjamin Thompson, Count Rumford—and particularly noteworthy, from today's perspective, is the presence of three non-Westerners, two Muslims, and one Chinese figure. Bearing in mind Rogers's intimate involvement with the defense of Darwin's theory at the very moment of its being put forth in 1859–60, Maclaurin's determination not to lose sight of core Boston and its global portals in the 1910s, and the Boston Brahmins' and MIT's long history with India from the 1880s onward, these figures are yet another example of MIT's global perspective. The two Muslims are Abu 'Ali al-Hasan (ca. 965–1039 CE) an Arab astronomer, mathematician, and physicist, whose "work on optics exerted a great influence on Western science," and Jabir ibn Hayyan (721–815 CE), "whose writings were an important source of the chemical knowledge of Latin Europe." The Chinese figure, Ko Hung (ca. 283–343 CE), was a noteworthy early chemist, who may have been "the first man to manufacture tin foil."

Richards's work in the design of this exquisite vestibule, a sort of Art Deco aesthete's paradise, is remarkable, painstakingly executed and having at least as much flair as the best of Copley's famous history painting. Everything is considered in relation to everything else to create a complete artistic unity. "The display cases placed against the wall are an essential part of the composition [and] bear the same relation to the murals aesthetically as do flowerpots to the plants they hold," explained the article describing the installation, the cases built of "extruded bronze

The much shinier bits of the Lukeman bronze reflect the generations-old custom at MIT of students about to take exams touching the Eastman relief for good luck. This is now the chief memorial to Eastman, for whom Killian Court, the Great Court of MIT, was originally named.

with gray harewood panels." Meanwhile, "benches, not too comfortable," were also carefully designed, "built of stone to harmonize with the walls," and even the "new ceiling" was designed with specially built-in electrical fixtures so arranged that "emphasis is placed on lighting the walls rather than the ceiling or floor." Also "nine large luminous panels," the article continues, "of low intensity, glazed with flashed opal glass set in extruded bronze frames, provide mild general illumination without glare. In addition, floodlights built into the ceiling over the end walls emphasize the bronze murals."

What an attack on the "factory aesthetic." It was made in connection with the chief memorial created by MIT to the great benefactor whose vision made the whole Bosworth complex possible, George Eastman. A bronze sculptural relief of Eastman, by Augustus Lukeman, is observed as you ascend the stairs to leave the lobby and dominates the entire scene at the head of the stairs.

The *Boston Globe* put it baldly in a headline on October 23, 1934: "Memorial to Eastman Placed at Technology: Bronze Bas Relief in Foyer Named for Him to Commemorate His Gift of Nearly $20,000,000." The words of the memorial, by contrast, are very understated:

> George Eastman of Rare Mould Fine Grained Sensitive to Beauty Responsive to Truth Conserver of Human Values Pioneer in the Sustained Application of Scientific Research to Industry Friend of the Massachusetts Institute of Technology.

Six small bronzes surrounding the central relief, its nose rubbed shiny by generations of Tech students for good luck during finals, illustrate Eastman's chief interests: photography (he was the father of popular photography as the founder of the Eastman Kodak Company), big game hunting, music, chemistry, drama, and medicine.

Why did it take MIT two decades to honor and memorialize its greatest donor? "Mr. Smith," the pseudonym by which he was universally known at MIT until a gift of his own stock forced him, so to speak, out of the closet because of tax reporting laws, seems to have wanted it that way. Certainly his biographer, Elizabeth Brayer, offers more anecdotes than answers, for example: "When the MIT buildings were first opened in June 1916, throngs descended upon Boston for a week-long celebration. The public announcement at a banquet of 'Mr. Smith's' latest gift was linked by telephone with similar celebrations in 36 other cities. Because of his $300,000 gift as Mr. Eastman, Mr. Smith was invited to attended the Rochester [New York] Banquet." Mr. Eastman, of course, cheered Mr. Smith to the rafters. Another example is the time Eastman came to inspect the brand-new campus in person. As a later MIT president, Susan Hockfield, would write, New Tech had come into being as the result of "George Eastman's insistent vision, spectacular generosity, and well-informed faith in the promise of MIT." But his report on this occasion of what his millions had paid for, in a letter to a friend, never let his friend in on the secret.

Particularly interesting of Building 6 are the contents of a time capsule within the cornerstone: not only construction photos and copies of current Boston newspapers and of the *Tech*, but also "two glass tubes filled with carbon dioxide gas, with sheepskin scrolls on which are the names of faculty of the department of physics and chemistry."

12   The Sol LeWitt Floor
Sol LeWitt, 2007

Bronze "murals" on the walls in the 1930s did not launch, as it turned out, reform of "the unsatisfying aesthetic" of Bosworth's corridors, although at some time in the 1970s various ideas for color-coded decor and the introduction of painted murals enjoyed a brief vogue. The next time a serious work of art arose in this connection, the murals were on the floor—magnificent terrazzo works executed by DePaoli Mosaic of Boston after the design of the conceptual artist Sol LeWitt. And this time the Infinite Corridor, as it had meanwhile come to be called, was not disdained but celebrated.

That was not, perhaps, LeWitt's original point. But the terrazzo floor in a U-shaped glass-covered atrium formed by three Bosworth buildings—4, 6, and 8—and a new building by Payette Associates of Boston, all of which are connected above by bridges that span the atrium and are highly suggestive as a sort of commentary on MIT's corridor grid. Indeed, finding the atrium requires careful attention. Retrace your steps back down the Infinite Corridor for just a bit, and a short vestibule on the left will disclose a small notice of LeWitt's work, reached through the vestibule. It is titled *Bars of Color Within Squares (MIT)*.

Because the atrium is a cul-de-sac, a corridor that connects with nothing and goes nowhere, as opposed to the usual MIT through-corridor, it is something of a secret garden. *Boston Globe* critic Robert Campbell wrote in his rave review: "One of the remarkable works of art in Boston is hidden away like a secret...surrounded on all sides by other buildings. Finding the work of art, therefore, is like opening a Chinese puzzle: a box inside a box inside a box." In this box, furthermore, are concentrated all the mechanicals now necessary to support the Bosworth complex, sparing the Infinite Corridor from becoming less an "indoor street"—the term is Campbell's—"and more like a utilities tunnel." He continues:

> Ecstatic and jazzy the MIT mural is, but it is also vigorously ordered....It consists of 25 squares...line[d] up to cross the floor of a corridor that runs around three sides of the ground level of a new building. The squares are divided geometrically and unpredictably into six or seven colors, and the colors are bright and intense...electrifying.... But it's more than that. MIT is an institution that does not have, conceptually, any outdoors....The true public space at MIT is the famous "Infinite Corridor" grid that ties everything together. MIT, in other words, is organized as a systems of (more or less)

OPPOSITE: "One of the remarkable works of art in Boston is hidden away like a secret . . . surrounded on all sides by other buildings." Thus architecture critic Robert Campbell described the Sol LeWitt pavement, reached by an inconspicuous side door off of the Infinite Corridor. ABOVE: The LeWitt pavement fills the gap between a part of the old Bosworth complex and a new building for mechanicals erected in a service yard of the complex. New work so located is preferable to the legacy of sprawl on campus and here has occasioned a wonderful example of corridic art.

rigorous squares, inside which all kinds of crazy stuff goes on...[and] LeWitt's mural, whether intentionally or not, reads as a depiction of the essence of this way of ordering the world.

In this brilliant review, Campbell goes on to note that turning what was a dreary service yard into this bright new experience is part of a master plan study by Payette Associates, which aims to inhibit what I call academic sprawl, nudging MIT instead to, yes, build new buildings, but to densify in the gaps between the old buildings. "The mural turns out to be a metaphor for MIT," Campbell concludes, and the new building "a metaphor for the future city. It is the kind of double shot of logic you associate with MIT."

13 Infinite Corridor Murals
1970s

The subsequent history of MIT's long preoccupation with enlivening supposedly dull corridors is worth exploring further after the Eastman Lobby by retracing your steps back down the Infinite Corridor just beyond Memorial Lobby.

A 1970 *Boston Globe Magazine* story by the critic Robert Taylor describes the circumstances under which a whole series of "wild murals," as one contemporary calls them, were allowed. "The administration permitted murals on the walls of the corridors...and expected, not illogically, that whatever the murals might depict, no matter how controversial, artists would strive for a standard of aesthetic excellence," Taylor writes. But those being the obstreperous 1970s, a faculty member in charge had other ideas. "The point was not to do good murals," Taylor quotes him saying. "Distinctions between beautiful and ugly, the criteria of taste, usually result in an elite trying to manipulate art to suit elite purposes." He did not apparently recognize himself, and Taylor was not the man to enlighten him. Instead, the *Globe* critic describes with a perfectly straight face a whole series of murals of which two stand out. Both survive in differing ways. There is what he describes as "a crowdscape of diverse student and street types" (actually "executed with considerable finesse"), which seems to be the wall mural now surviving on the north side of the Infinite Corridor just before Memorial Lobby. It is signed "Andrew Pritchard," and as Taylor recounts that only one mural was signed (the one he thought showed "finesse"), this would seem to be as close to an identification as is now possible. For signing it, by the way, the faculty member in charge apologized to Taylor for such "elite behavior," doing so "with a shrug."

Informal, amateur wall murals along the Infinite Corridor have appeared over the years, like a dollar bill drawn by a philosophy major and an electrical engineer with a magic marker, intended to call attention to the offices of the bursar and the cashier. When those offices were moved an etched dollar bill in new glasswork memorialized the old mural.

A second mural, a twelve-by-twenty-five-foot depiction of a dollar bill, "done by a philosophy major and an electrical engineer using a Magic Marker pen," is also described. Taylor calls it "perhaps the most finished of the walls…wrapped around the offices of the Cashier and Bursar, and demonstrat[ing] an impressive visual wit." That mural, long since destroyed, is memorialized by the etched image of a dollar bill on the glass wall that now separates the corridor from a lounge area that at some point replaced the bursar's and cashier's offices.

Continuing to retrace your steps—to return to the Rogers lobby at 77 Massachusetts Avenue, where Walk Two begins—will give access eventually off that lobby to the truly glorious finale of nearly a hundred years of MIT interior wall art, whether in bronze, paint, or whatever. From the Rogers lobby, take the elevator to the third floor, to the domain of the School of Architecture and Planning, wherein— you will have to ask someone which doorway of the labyrinth to go through—is one of the great artistic treasures of MIT.

14 The Stella Conference Room
Frank Stella, 1994

Frank Stella's *Loohooloo* wraps around the entire circumference of a departmental conference room, creating what has been called "a total environment of wildly shifting colors and shapes" based in part "on computer-rendered smoke rings and four-color printing dots." The work takes its name from a night scene in Herman Melville's 1847 novel *Omoo, A Narrative Adventure in the South Seas.* To quote from the contemporary press release of the MIT news office, which can hardly be bettered:

> The fantastic imagery in *Loohooloo* got started in a still, hot room in Cambridge when Stella found himself blowing smoke rings and found they did some interesting things. They hovered. They held. Then they dropped slowly into other smoke rings. Returning to his studio, [the artist] photographed smoke rings in a black box, then fed those images into a computer to create computer renderings of them. For *Loohooloo*, that imagery was then painted in acrylic on sprayed urethane foam, creating one continuous curve ten feet high, 97 feet long, and projecting [unevenly, in great "billows"] 34 inches into the room all around [it].

This four-wall sculpture blurs the boundaries that usually separate painting from sculpture and both from architecture. The conference room was specially constructed in 1995 to fit the artwork's circumference. The fantastical images on the continuously curving and undulating surface, itself wavelike, in turn create sensations of waves. It is an altogether remarkable work, a worthy finale to three-quarters of a century of MIT wall art that makes Bosworth's "New Tech" of 1913–37 seemingly newer and newer. One hopes the one-hundredth anniversary of the Bosworth complex will be commemorated by another such effort in 2016.

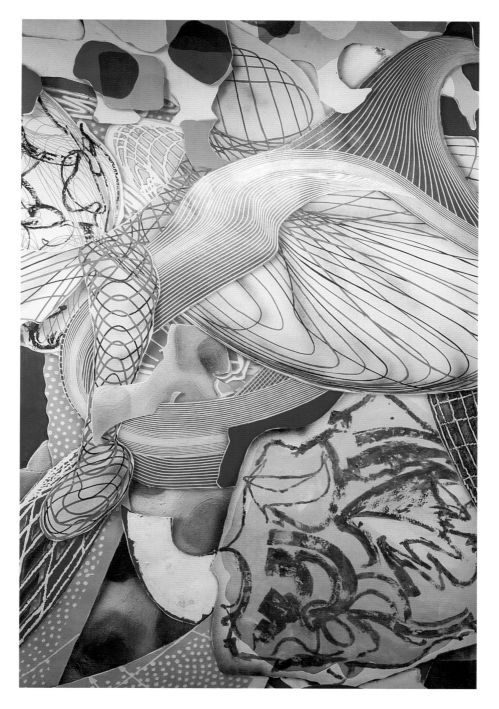

Detail of *Loohooloo* (1994) by Frank Stella, in the Stella Conference Room, located in Building 7A across from the headquarters of the Department of Architecture

MIT's corridic art achieves its apotheosis in the Stella Conference Room, which takes its name from Frank Stella's mural in acrylic on sprayed urethane foam, *Loohooloo* (1994), which in turn derives from Herman Melville's novel *Omoo*. The mural is wrapped all around the room so as to envelop the conferees, raising the question: is this the most spectacular conference room in the world?

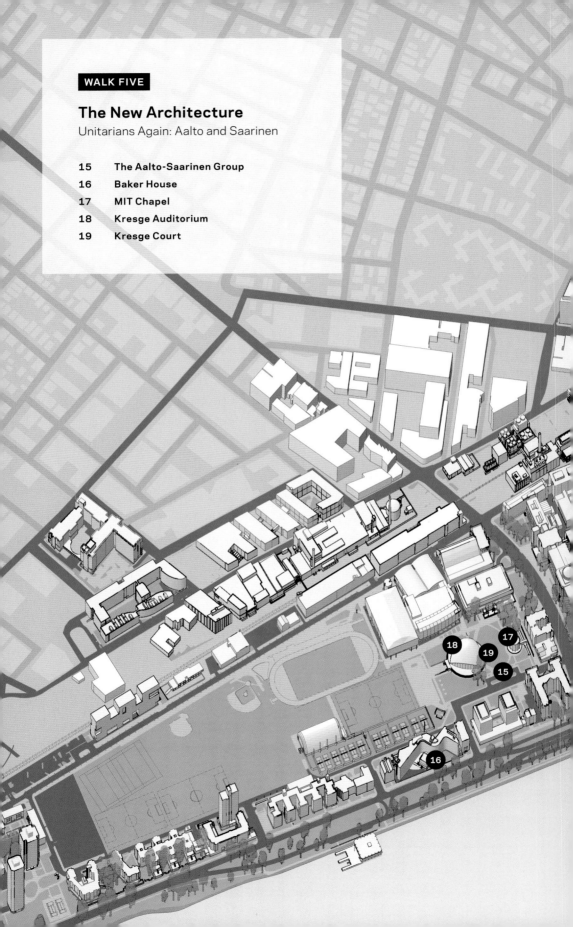

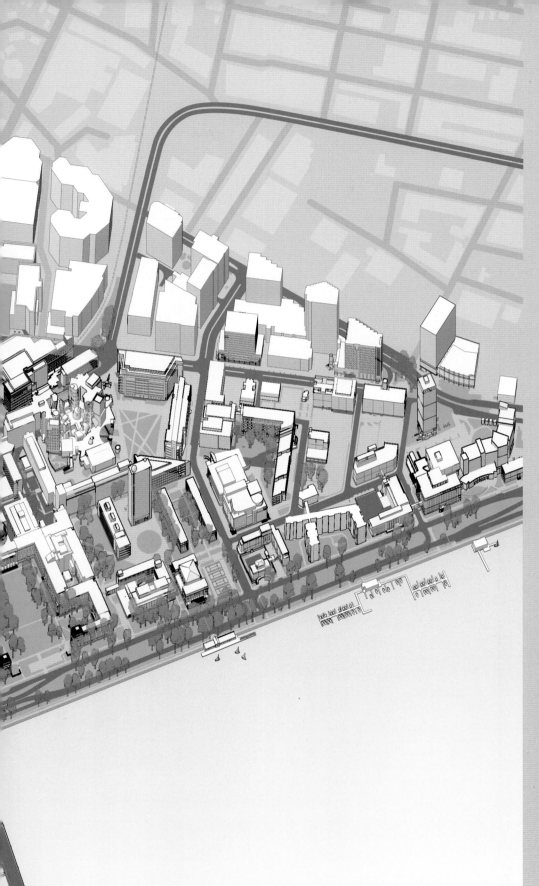

The New Architecture

Unitarians Again: Aalto and Saarinen

The tidal wave of the Second World War transformed MIT—so much so that MIT Museum historian and curator Deborah Douglas could write of "a new type of laboratory, a new type of student, a new type of professor, and a new life of the mind." She might have added a new type of architecture, though here it was a case of accelerating ideas already in motion. And as always, it is the architecture, the outward and visible sign, that catches the eye first, rather than the inner institutional transformation, the founding of a whole new school of learning and of new research laboratory of national importance.

Douglas's exuberance reflects the fact that by the war's end, MIT was, in David Kaiser's words, "the largest beneficiary of federal research dollars of any institution in U.S. history." Moreover, "The end of World War II brought no real demobilization to campus." Kaiser continues: "The Cold War sustained the Institute's wartime pattern of operation. . . . A fire-hose of federal funding, most of it from the Department of Defense and related agencies, helped launch new laboratories on campus and expand old ones."

These laboratories, however technically sophisticated, were to be found for the most part in rather ramshackle temporary structures that have subsequently been torn down—a story told in Walk Eight. Meanwhile, under its now legendary new leader of those days, President James R. Killian, three campus landmarks were born in the 1940s and 1950s that are so spectacular, each compels a unique deference:

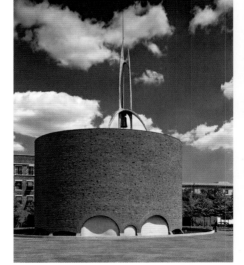

New York Times architecture critic Ada Louise Huxtable wrote, "Boston's great educational institutions, Harvard and MIT, were the real crucible in which American modern architecture was formed." She listed Baker House as the third of eight key buildings that launched modernism in America in the late 1940s.

MIT Chapel by Eero Saarinen (OPPOSITE), Baker House by Alvar Aalto (ABOVE), Kresge Auditorium by Eero Saarinen (BELOW)

Baker House, MIT Chapel, and Kresge Auditorium. By near-universal consent today, the first two in particular rank among the greatest monuments of twentieth-century architecture anywhere.

It was an architectural critic, not a historian, who first fixed these MIT buildings on the world stage: Ada Louise Huxtable. As cosmopolitan as she was brilliant, Huxtable was one of a small, elite group of New Yorkers who in many respects—perhaps because educated in Boston or married to a Bostonian or in the habit of summering nearby—understood the New England capital's place in the world far better than many twentieth-century native Bostonians. (Other such New Yorkers who come to mind are the composer Aaron Copeland and the architects Charles McKim and I. M. Pei.)

From that unique pulpit of the American intelligentsia, the *New York Times*, Huxtable was plainspoken: "Boston espoused modernism early and with characteristic intellectual conviction.…Boston played a leading role in the practice and dissemination of a movement that changed the face of the twentieth century.…What happened in Boston was the architectural shot heard round the world."

She made clear, moreover, MIT's crucial role in all this. Her roster of landmarks in architectural modernism's rise began with "the familiar icons of the first generation…the tradition-shattering houses of the 1930s by Walter Gropius [after his appointment at Harvard] and Marcel Breuer," but then fixed on "Alvar Aalto's Baker House dormitory at MIT [and] Eero Saarinen's MIT Chapel" of the late 1940s and 1950s before moving on to Le Corbusier's 1960–63 Carpenter Center at Harvard. She paid equal attention to the "second generation of the 1960s that includes Kallmann McKinnell and Knowles's Boston City Hall, Philip Johnson and John Burgee's Boston Public Library…and the design of I. M. Pei and Henry Cobb's John Hancock Building." She concludes: "These buildings were brought to Boston by something else that the city's intellectual leadership has specialized in—enlightened patronage.…Boston's great educational institutions, Harvard and MIT, were the real crucible in which American modern architecture was formed."

To this we can add the observation by the Harvard art historian John Coolidge that it was a very Bostonian trait—inherited from Brahmins of old—to seek the best in everything to such an extent that nativist sentiment never mattered very much. For centuries, the city has not hesitated to "import [architects] or their designs, with the result," Coolidge wrote in 1977, that "in one day" one could see in and around Boston "a collection of Modernist architecture by great masters hard to rival anywhere else in the world."

Killian was not just amassing architectural trophies. These three landmarks were part of his postwar vision for MIT. In keeping with his role as President Eisenhower's chief science adviser—establishing NASA, for instance, in the wake of the Soviet launching of Sputnik—Killian turned his mind first to the urgent need to consolidate the Institute's new postwar role as the premier scientific research university of the world. His commitment to this brave new architecture was meant to spark and to stand for new ways of thinking in the most startling public way in every field.

Not least at Lincoln Laboratory, which Killian founded at MIT in 1951. Located for security reasons far from campus in the Boston suburb of Lexington, this complex is thus beyond the reach of these walks. Originally designed by the Boston firm of Cram & Ferguson, this federally funded research and development center of MIT was tasked with applying advanced technology to the most critical problems of American national security. It was charged first of all, as Paul Gray pointed out in his memorial tribute to Killian years later for the National Academy of Engineering, to "develop an electronic continental [air] defense system so vast and sophisticated that it could not have been imagined even a few years earlier. During the same period," Gray added, "the MIT Instrumentation Laboratory was developing inertial guidance systems for intercontinental ballistic missiles—and the space vehicles and nuclear powered submarines that were yet to come. There were other projects too, of course, but these two large developments were especially notable among those for which Killian had a major initiating role and ultimate oversight."

There were also much broader aspects to the work at Lincoln Lab, as Stephen Segaller points out in *Nerds: A Brief History of the Internet*: "The seeds of the Internet were planted by the U.S. government....But the soil had already been tilled, fertilized, and watered by a prior succession of federal government and military research that [was] based at the engineering powerhouse of the Massachusetts Institute of Technology and its rural outpost, Lincoln Laboratory."

Killian summoned more than architectural genius to his task. The figure he selected as his champion, so to speak, in forging his postwar vision for MIT was as conspicuous as Lincoln Laboratory was not: Winston Churchill. The British wartime leader agreed to be the keynote speaker at MIT's Mid-Century Convocation in 1949, a weeklong series of events that culminated with Killian's inauguration as president. Certainly the visit to Boston just to speak at MIT by the Institute's nominee for man of the century (an honor that nearly three-quarters of a century later most would still award Churchill) underlined the Institute's new stature.

The significance of Churchill's speech was captured in an NBC *Special Report* on Churchill's life by Merrill Mueller, which aired on the occasion of the British leader's death in 1965. In the relevant portion of the transcript, Mueller explained the meaning of Churchill's coming to America for what he called "two decisive speeches": "What Sir Winston really foresaw was the need for a constantly alert ring of safety. In the first speech of 1946 he announced famously the descent of the iron curtain across Europe and spawning both the Marshall Plan and the NATO Alliance." Of the second, the MIT speech, Mueller continued, "But only three years later, Russia's reach for nuclear power brought Sir Winston back to America to warn at MIT of a new kind of warfare," a warning delivered before fourteen thousand people crowded into the Boston Garden sports arena, where convocation was held. Churchill's message, as always, was Olympian and bracing. "If there is to be a war of nerves," the British leader declared, "let us be sure our nerves are strong."

Sitting behind Churchill on the platform, Killian, looking ahead, must have been shifting gears somewhat to the other aspect of his postwar vision for MIT. In

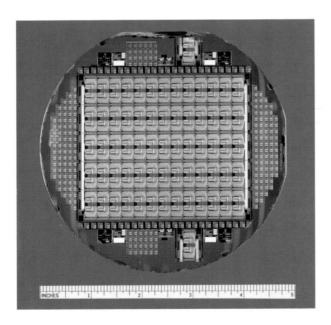

These two photographs courtesy of Lincoln Laboratory show a dramatic juxtaposition between early Killian-era computers (ABOVE) and today's lab-developed, special-purpose computer chip of far greater processing capacity and yet much smaller size (LEFT). First articulated by Intel founder Gordon Moore in 1965—that the performance of integrated circuits (microchips) regularly doubles about every two years—Moore's law reveals, as Michael Malone has written in the *Wall Street Journal*, "the heartbeat of the modern world."

addition to consolidating the Institute's research preeminence, equally important was the need to rejuvenate MIT's basic educational philosophy. Although Churchill paid the Institute the compliment of lamenting that Britain had nothing of "comparable stature," a lack he was trying to remedy, in a speech a week later MIT's president shared the fact that Churchill had spoken to him of the importance of the humanities. Killian shared with his audience his response: "I told him, as I tell you today, that we have not and we shall not [forget]."

What Churchill probably didn't know, but Killian did, was that "a [recent] blue-ribbon faculty panel [had] asserted that students in the nuclear age also required an appreciation of history, literature, and patterns of decision making in a democracy"—faculty backing, in other words, for Killian's determination to reassert a broadly humanist position at MIT. This had been somewhat lost after the move to the Charles River Basin and the separation from the architecture school, which stayed in Copley Square until 1938. The result was the founding in 1950—within a year of the establishment of Lincoln Laboratory—of MIT's new School of Humanities and Social Sciences on an equal footing with the schools of science, engineering, and architecture. Eventually the arts, too, would be added to the name and the mandate.

All this was the result of the still-cited *Lewis Report*, named after Warren Kendall Lewis, whose lifetime significantly linked the MIT of Copley Square with the post–World War II MIT of the Charles River Basin. A Delaware native raised in suburban Boston in the 1880s and 1890s, Lewis enrolled at MIT as a student, then joined the faculty. By 1920 he was the head of the Department of Chemical Engineering, established soon after the move to the Charles River Basin. A considerable scientist—a key player in the development of the atom bomb and a member of the senior advisory panel of the Manhattan Project—Lewis was also a man of broad humanistic values. Accordingly, he was tapped to chair the blue-ribbon committee.

In light of all this, Baker House particularly comes into focus. Consider what the historian Gail Fenske wrote: "[Alvar] Aalto's design for Baker [House]... visually crystallized and decisively established a particular modernist position within the American culture of architecture,... demonstrat[ing] the significance of modern architecture's many humanistic and, indeed, person-oriented variables." The timing, Michael Trencher notes in *Aalto and America*, was perfect: "The attitude among leadership at the Massachusetts Institute of Technology concerning the place of the individual in the postwar years was surprisingly very sympathetic to Aalto's ideas."

Killian, if he believed in the value of science and technology, also believed that the life of the mind needed to be sustained by what he called the life of the spirit, these being his own categories. First Aalto's and then Saarinen's work at MIT in the 1950s stood for pioneering new thinking but also for fundamental verities.

Before I deal with the three great landmarks of the Aalto-Saarinen group individually, they might be considered as a group. The somewhat bewildering-seeming brick cylinder, the MIT Chapel, is the group's heart and could well be considered by the visitor first, before Baker House, which was designed almost a decade earlier. The Chapel's design, hard to understand initially, ought to be studied, so to speak, inside out, though it is worth pausing first somewhere along the path that leads to the inconspicuous entrance to contemplate the trees. They are meant to suggest a sacred grove, to create a place apart where you can begin to detach your mind. If you can dwell on these trees as you approach the Chapel, you will find your mind better prepared for the experience of the interior.

I have written elsewhere of Harvard's Civil War Memorial Hall, which takes the form of a vast cruciform structure in which the nave, where the congregation would normally be, is a college dining hall, and the chancel, where the altar would normally be, is a theater. It is effectively a Victorian essay on the idea of a Boston Brahmin cathedral, displaying all the splendor of such but detached entirely from any supernatural religious content and rooted instead in learning and do-gooderism. That Boston Unitarian cathedral idea helps penetrate the design concept of the MIT Chapel. It is arguably a more sophisticated, twentieth-century version, this time more nuanced and more overtly spiritual, full of meditative power, a totally nonsectarian space that is nonetheless a deeply religious place. A fascinating comparative study might be made of the MIT Chapel with Frank Lloyd Wright's Unity Temple in Chicago's Oak Park, Illinois, more overtly Unitarian because Wright himself was, philosophically, of the Boston Unitarian persuasion; Killian was, and Saarinen was not.

The Unitarianism of the Boston Brahmin Ascendancy, which thrived throughout the nineteenth century and survived the Brahmin fall of the early twentieth, was a worldview rooted in rationalist philosophy. It was a supremely confident worldview. The Gods of Copley Square—which is to say, the Brahmin Unitarian leadership, men like Charles W. Eliot, a founding professor of MIT and later the founder of modern Harvard, and William Barton Rogers, who early on concluded that Boston was the only place for MIT—had no doubt of Boston's place in the world. It was what people today sometimes refer to as a "world-class" city. Unlike their heirs in its governance today, so nervous of being equal to such an opportunity, they had no doubts about the "hub of the universe." And the underlying belief system of that worldview, as sure as the Puritan vision of the city upon a hill, was Boston Unitarianism.

It is both a worldview and an underlying belief system, as deeply and persistently held as any religion on the planet. Among its adherents it has been rather a case of now you see it, now you don't—and mostly don't. For instance, in the case of the two-volume *Life and Letters of William Barton Rogers*, you will (despite her own distinct dedication to Unitarianism) never find it named, even in the index. Nor in Killian's *Education of a College President*. In fact, Killian was much influenced by the Brahmin legacy through his Unitarianism—or vice versa, if you prefer. He was a dedicated Unitarian, serving ultimately as moderator of the American Unitarian Association. In that capacity, Killian, the closest thing there was to what used to be called "the Unitarian pope" after Eliot's death, went on record saying, "I find in Unitarianism the freedom and stimulus to seek a lofty sense of the meaning of life."

It is true that MIT's tenth president found himself in rather a different position than MIT's first president, living as Killian did in the post-Brahmin era. Yet according to his papers in MIT's archives, all the time he was president, making no fanfare about it at all, probably unknown to most, Killian and his wife regularly attended Sunday services at the First Church of Boston on Marlborough Street in the Back Bay, the same congregation in which Rogers and Savage had been married one hundred years previously and whose minister had conducted the funeral of MIT's founder in 1882.

Without identifying these values as Unitarian or reform Jewish, Killian repeatedly insisted on exploring the Institute's values in this context, which may be the deepest level from which MIT's culture has evolved. He left no doubt in his memoirs about the importance of what he called "the spiritual values which are inherent in our institution." He detailed them plainly: "We should remember that MIT was founded by unselfish men for altruistic purposes and that it has always been an implicit expression of high moral purposes and standards. As a consequence we have a community held together by a humane and tolerant spirit of mediation, reconciliation, and reverence for the individual, a community governed by a passion for truth, freedom of inquiry, and a preoccupation with ideal aims."

If there seems to be a stark distinction here between science and the humanities, that is to take up the position Killian was trying to banish. On the eve of the Chapel's dedication, Killian was equally straightforward—and captured the urgency of his two polarities for MIT as only a contemporary and not a retrospective statement could—in an interview with the *New York Times*:

> We must demonstrate that science and engineering are great liberating humanizing forces.... Dr. Killian said MIT was considering a new course of study that would be made up of about half engineering and half courses in the humanities and social sciences.... In recognition of the need for attention to the scientist's spiritual life, MIT is constructing a small, devotional chapel, he added. "The chapel will stand," he continued, "as a symbol of the place of the spirit in the life of the mind and as a physical statement of the fact that MIT has a right and responsibility to deal with ideals as well as ideas and to be concerned with the search for virtue while we become proficient in the search for other things."

Whatever was happening to bring all this to the surface in the 1950s and 1960s, it wasn't just happening to Killian. How deep-seated these Unitarian associations are at MIT can be glimpsed in American literature as well as American architecture of the mid-twentieth century, in both cases in a manner widely accessible—so conspicuously so that one of the sources a visitor might consult is *Wikipedia*. The entry under "MIT in popular culture" is particularly interesting. There one learns that in the opinion of many, "MIT is a recurring motif in the works of Kurt Vonnegut," the American author of the countercultural 1960s still widely read today, who, though he completely rejected Christianity, describing himself variously as agnostic or humanist or atheist, self-identified as Unitarian-Universalist. (Those two traditions merged institutionally in 1961.) Witness this passage from Vonnegut's autobiographical *Palm Sunday*:

> We no longer believe that God causes earthquakes and crop failures and plagues when He gets mad at us. We no longer imagine He can be cooled off by sacrifices and festivals and gifts. I am so glad we don't have to think up presents for Him anymore. What is the perfect gift for someone who has everything? The perfect gift for someone who has everything, of course, is nothing. Any gifts we have should be given to creatures right on the surface of this planet, it seems to me. If God gets angry about that, we can call in the Massachusetts Institute of Technology. There's a good chance they can calm Him down.

The überliberal influence of Trinity Church on Copley Square—important at MIT as far back as the 1870s, when Phillips Brooks, Trinity's nineteenth-century rector, sat not only on the Corporation of MIT but also on its directing instructional subcommittee as well—also reasserts itself in the 1950s. Historically, Trinity was contested ground between "true believers" (Episcopalians) and "do-gooders" (Unitarians). Trinity's rector in Killian's day, Theodore Ferris, also served on the MIT Corporation. And Killian, according to his papers in the MIT Archives, relied on Ferris for advice about the Chapel particularly. Perhaps it was through Ferris that MIT's president was in touch with the relatively liberal Roman Catholic archbishop of Boston, Richard Cardinal Cushing, in whose diocese MIT Chapel was located, and who, according to Killian, overruled his advisers and agreed that Catholic chaplains could use the unconsecrated chapel for Mass—unconsecrated because "nonsectarian" Unitarians do not do such things. Cushing himself celebrated the first Roman Catholic Mass in the Chapel.

A jolt in the postwar period was the impact on the MIT campus of the arrival of the School of Architecture. Since the 1860s it had been the standard bearer of the liberal arts at MIT. During the 1920s and 1930s it had been physically isolated in Copley Square, and when it moved to the Cambridgeport campus, the architects were suddenly forced to take up relations again with the scientists and the engineers. Assimilation did not come quickly or easily on either side. Even fifteen years after the move, ten years after the war, in 1955, Frederick Stahl, a fourth-year architecture student, is quoted by Margaret Henderson Floyd in her *Architectural Education and Boston* as testifying that "the ethos of the MIT School of Architecture derived from its almost total independence from the Institute [as a whole]."

Killian seized on all this as aiding him in yet more ways in his forging of a new direction for postwar MIT, which, looked at from one point of view, really meant restoring MIT. In the 1950s MIT reasserted its presence in Copley Square, when Rapson-Inc. raised anew the MIT flag at 282 Dartmouth Street, in the square. (It is an idea that never dies; there is still a movement for MIT to buy the old Museum of Natural History Building, which Rogers built and where Sullivan took his classes, as a showcase gallery on Boston's main drag for the MIT Museum.) Rapson-Inc. was one of three American shops (the others in New York, Illinois, and California) that presaged Design Research (and today's Crate & Barrel) and pioneered the introduction of modernist design to the United States. (You can still visit Rapson-Inc.com.) The shop took its name from Ralph Rapson—a University of Michigan graduate who had studied under both Eliel Saarinen and his son Eero Saarinen. He was Aalto's rival and a young architect who gladly undertook what he called "my pilgrimage to Boston as a Midwesterner's educational dream" in response to Dean William Wurster's ardent recruitment.

Rapson took the lead in the design of the Eastgate apartment house at 100 Memorial Drive in 1951. This apartment complex proved to be quite a stellar new attraction in its day on the Charles River Basin. "Contemporaries considered [Eastgate's] siting…in relation to Baker House, when viewed from across the Charles, as appearing like bookends framing the MIT campus…a striking contrast with [the 1930s] neo-Georgian 'Harvard River Houses' upstream. As a consequence, they proudly announced to the city of Boston MIT's commitment to a particular type of modernism." As in architecture, so in education generally, Killian's postwar MIT sent very clear messages.

16 Baker House
Alvar Aalto, 1946–49

A second look at Baker House, this time purely architectural, a discussion it deserves, as it may be one of the half-dozen greatest works of American architecture. And this time the theme must be Alvar Aalto's own: "Nature, not the machine, is the most important model for architecture." So he wrote in 1938, and that is the idea the visitor should be prepared to consider—and perhaps to challenge, I would argue, for neither nature nor the machine have much to do with the architecture en route from the Rogers Building portico up Massachusetts Avenue to the river and to Baker House on Memorial Drive. Turn right at the river. Two blocks' walk will bring you to Baker House, if not to your own answer as between nature and machine.

To settle on nature and not the machine is to repudiate utterly the essence of the characteristic teachings of Le Corbusier, the preeminent architectural theorist and architect of the twentieth-century modernist movement. Yet Corbusier himself came to abandon the machinelike forms and sleek finishes of his early formula— white walls, cubic volumes, and flat roofs, which, as the critic Martin Filler points out in *Makers of Modern Architecture*, was always a more regional than international formula, certainly more Mediterranean than Nordic—for the "bio-morphic contours and rough materials" of his later work.

In his analysis of Aalto's maxim, the very next thing Filler cites is the Finnish architect's telegram to the founding dean of MIT's new School of the Humanities and Social Sciences, John Burchard, a telegram that might well have been the motto of MIT's new school: "The architecture the real thing is only where man stands in center." Or, more precisely, woman. Here is Filler's version of the well-worn but still riveting story of how one of the greatest architects of the twentieth century began most days at his drafting board:

> [Aalto] demonstrated his favored warm-up technique when he taught at MIT...during the design and construction of the Baker House dormitory of 1946–49, his most spectacularly curvaceous structure. Aalto would arrive in the studio at 9 AM, place a bottle of aquavit on his drafting table, and proceed to sketch the nude female model he had added to the curriculum. By noon the bottle would be empty, Aalto's drawing arm would be sufficiently loosened and the master—who, it seems fair to say, was a high-functioning alcoholic—felt ready to face the challenges of architecture.

In case anyone missed his point, Filler added the observation that "the human body, so palpable in the voluptuous contours of his designs," was what Aalto really meant by nature.

How much of this survives in the visitor's experience of Baker House itself is doubtful, however, for this is heart-stopping architecture that claims attention on larger grounds. There were other (perhaps more important) reasons for the form of Baker House. Even thirty years after MIT's arrival, Cambridgeport remained so nondescript a neighborhood that Aalto refused to design any rooms facing north overlooking Cambridgeport, and even for the south-facing or riverfront views, he insisted on rooms that looked upstream or downstream and avoided Memorial Drive traffic. Hence the curve. The public spaces of the interior were equally diverting. As one moves up the stairs "and along the passages, as they widen and narrow in response to the variable geometry," they seemed reminiscent to Michael Trencher of "the streets and squares of the Italian hill towns that Aalto so much admired."

"It resembled no other building in the United States," the critic Paul Goldberger wrote of Baker House when it was new, and he pronounced it the key building of the architect's career, in the wake of which Aalto was recognized "not only as his nation's preeminent architect but as an acknowledged world master." Baker House was more beginning than climax in Aalto's career. He had been in practice as an architect only seven years when he first came to MIT in 1940, and while he certainly endowed MIT with sufficient genius, he took away a good deal that shaped the architecture of his mature years. As notable MIT architectural historian Stanford Anderson remarked in *Aalto and America*, "Finland was with [Aalto] in America, so to speak; yet at the same time he was sounding the depths of New England culture."

What about New England inspired him? "Red brick is the standard of Boston," Anderson observed. True, William Welles Bosworth saw deeper, looking toward Charles Bulfinch's Massachusetts General Hospital and understanding that the

The rear facade of Baker House, though not as lyrical as the riverfront facade, is certainly a striking piece of architecture. Only the lack of a properly landscaped plaza between Baker, Kresge, and the Chapel deprives the observer of the chance to take in this eloquent trio of masterworks that was uniquely important in the dawn of the modern movement in American architecture.

Boston Granite style was in fact Boston's most characteristic architecture, an indigenous architecture of world rank. But Aalto did indeed respond to the more pervasive, warmer, and more appealing red brick face of the New England capital, and the effect on him can be judged by the fact that, as Nicholas Ray points out, "brickwork was to become a material theme in all his major buildings in the next decades."

I would also argue that one has only to look at Baker's disciplined picturesqueness, the robustness of its brickwork in contrast to its elegant, undulating form, to think at once of H. H. Richardson, Boston's premier late nineteenth-century stylist. As it happens, "Aalto was the heir of…a powerful strand of romantic theory," Ray observes, that was "not confined to Finland but was clearly observable in Richardson's work."

This is, so to speak, MIT's family history. Floyd eloquently affirmed it in *Architectural Education and Boston* when she noticed "the alternate Modernism," that is, to the conventional International Style of Le Corbusier, "of Scandinavia's Alvar Aalto and its alignment with the American tradition of architecture in the landscape, epitomized in the collaboration of H. H. Richardson and Frederick Law Olmsted, and leading to the design of Frank Lloyd Wright." Aalto's exposure to Richardson in Boston surely reinforced lessons absorbed early.

This aspect also bears on why Aalto ended up at MIT. Although it is perfectly true, as Ray has documented, that the Finnish architect was "wooed by Harvard… to be a full professor and potential rival to Gropius, "Gropius was Harvard's first choice and Aalto MIT's. It was not entirely a matter of Aalto's close friendship with William Wurster, the dean of MIT's School of Architecture. As Floyd says, the alliance between the MIT School of Architecture and the School of the Museum of Fine Arts, reaching back to the 1870s, remained very strong. Floyd again: "This deep affinity in American architecture had been carried from Boston to California by Greene and Greene [important Arts and Crafts architects of the 1890s] who attended MIT…. Now through Wurster it would return to Boston newly invigorated by the [San Francisco] Bay Style concept." Talk about global. Boston to California and back via Finland, and then back to Finland.

A mistake people make with respect to Baker House is to be content with its famous serpentine southern river facade. The visitor should make a point of retracing steps along Memorial Drive to Danforth Street and walking up it so as to inspect the northern facade. For Aalto did not entirely ignore industrial Cambridgeport. "The north stair wall,…a cascading constructivist element that plays masterfully off the serpentine dormitory block and the old industrial landscape of East Cambridge [and Cambridgeport] which it originally faced, was a subject of intense study by Aalto," David Fixler has written. It has since become a sort of memorial to that old cityscape, now largely disappearing.

17   MIT Chapel
Eero Saarinen, 1955–56

Considered strictly architecturally, MIT Chapel also owes a large debt to H. H. Richardson, a debt Aalto pointed to in an article in *Arkkitehti* in 1945, in which he remarked on the fact that the nineteenth-century Boston master had a strong influence on European designers in Richardson's own era: "Many turn-of-the-century Finnish architects (including…[Eliel] Saarinen)," the father of the architect of the MIT Chapel, "owe a significant debt to Richardson."

This mattered to President Killian very much. As important to him as an open-minded spirituality was an architecture equally bold and unfettered. This was especially the case in the age of Howard Roark, the hero of Ayn Rand's "blood-and-thunder novel of modern architecture in the making," *The Fountainhead*—I am quoting James Trilling from the *American Scholar* in 2012—which debuted as a movie starring Gary Cooper in 1949. At once it was identified with MIT, both in that Roark is expelled from the "Stanton Institute of Technology" (whose students party in Boston,

The MIT Chapel is one of the most beautiful churches in the world, a masterpiece by Eero Saarinen. Light enters the chapel through a rooftop oculus over the altar and shimmering screen, and through the low arcades in the moat, which reflects light from the waters bathing the undulating brick walls of the serene interior.

removing any doubt that MIT was Rand's model), and also in that the hero himself, modeled after Wright, is mentored by a character inspired by MIT's most illustrious alumnus in architecture, Louis Sullivan. In 1956, a year after the MIT Chapel was completed, its architect was on the front cover of *Time* magazine.

Three decades later, in 1984, the architecture critic Wolf von Eckardt, writing in the same magazine, pronounced Saarinen's MIT Chapel "one of twentieth-century architecture's greatest triumphs," validating Killian's vision. Killian explained himself in *Education of a College President*, and, not surprisingly, Ada Louise Huxtable's name came up:

> At the time the chapel and the Kresge Auditorium were dedicated, I made a brief statement about my attitude toward traditional or modern architectural designs. In the design of the Anderson and Beckwith swimming pool [see Walk Six] and of the Aalto

dormitory MIT had taken the lead in the Boston university community by introducing the contemporary style to its campus.... In an article in the *New York Times* Ada Louise Huxtable generously wrote: "Most of the [modern] buildings...were brought to Boston by something else that the city's intellectual leadership has specialized in—enlightened patronage. Strictly speaking, Boston's great educational institutions, Harvard and the Massachusetts Institute of Technology, were the real crucible in which American modern architecture was formed."

For Saarinen the MIT Chapel was a considerable opportunity, not least because, as Jane Merkel observes, the Charles River Basin overlooking core Boston was a much more conspicuous location than the hills of suburban Waltham, where Saarinen and Matthew Nowicki had designed a chapel for Brandeis University. That proposed design was ultimately rejected, but it was a source for much of the MIT Chapel's design.

Physically, the Chapel is beguiling. The purpose of the moat around the outside of its cylindrical form becomes wonderfully evident inside, where an inner brick wall, set off from the exterior cylindrical one but also set in the moat, undulates throughout the interior, and the light reflected from the moat from the exterior washes up the interior walls in a shimmering and changeful light. Furthermore, the deep red of the interior brick walls is transmuted by the gilded sculpture of the altar screen by Harry Bertoia, and by the starlike lights in the black ceiling and the travertine marble floor.

This extraordinary building would have been noticed wherever it was built. "An architect of the geometric sublime," William J. Mitchell called Saarinen. "His composition of straight lines and arcs has the simple yet awesome clarity of Euclid's great proof constructions. Fifty years after the construction of Kresge and the Chapel, architects still make pilgrimages with their sketchbooks and census, and try to figure out how this master of mid-century modernism did so much with seemingly so little." Mitchell wrote of "the soft glimmer of subtly shaded brick and the interplay of glitter and gloom." Saarinen's own explanation? As the architect saw it, his challenge was to create

an atmosphere which was not derived from a particular religion, but from basic spiritual feelings.... I have always remembered one night on my travels as a student when I sat in a mountain village in Sparta. There was bright moonlight over head and then there was a soft, hushed secondary light around the horizon. That sort of bilateral lighting seemed best to achieve this other-worldly sense. Thus, the central light would come from [an oculus] above the altar—dramatized by the shimmering golden screen by Henry Bertoia—and the secondary light through the arches [allowing into the interior light reflected through the water in the moat]. The interior wall was curved...[undulating] to give the space...an increased sense of turning inward.... I am happy with the interior of the chapel. I think we managed to make it a place where an individual can contemplate things larger than himself.

For all its radicality—and Killian did not exaggerate when he spoke of Saarinen's "dazzling designs," nor of their approval by MIT's "brave Corporation"—the MIT Chapel has evoked in scholars very historical and mostly Catholic resonances, and in so mysterious a way that most register the effect rather than the source, but recognize at once the source when pointed out. Leland Roth in *Understanding Architecture* compared the MIT Chapel to Santa Maria della Vittoria in Rome, the chapel built for Cardinal Federico Cornaro in 1647, a masterpiece of the high Roman baroque, where Bernini's *Ecstasy of Saint Teresa* above the altar is lit by a hidden window. At MIT, Roth explains, "there is no figure of heavenly rapture à la Bernini, yet the effect of focused light is much the same." Not least—and here Ada Louise Huxtable is the best witness to call—the way "the gilded floating leaves of Harry Bertoia's sculpture" above and behind the altar in MIT's Chapel "captures light in just the same theatrical way the gilded rays do above St. Teresa."

At the same time, the Chapel's symbolism was seen as expansive enough to extend to Eastern religions as well as Western, theistic or not. It was suggested that the Chapel's bell tower should contain a Korean temple bell, according to papers in the MIT Archives. It was an idea Pietro Belluschi, then dean of architecture at MIT, advanced in a letter to Saarinen in January 1955, and which Killian himself enthusiastically endorsed ("the Korean bell. The idea is a good one.") in a letter to E. L. Brooks now in his papers at the archives.

People are often surprised how small the MIT Chapel is, seemingly geared more to the individual than to the community, as Boston University architectural historian Keith Morgan seems to sense when he describes the Chapel's interior as "spell-binding…a small space with immense power."

Not, of course, for everybody. Even today there are those who find Saarinen's masterly chapel "a bit embarrassing"; see Stanley Abercrombie's much-ballyhooed article in *Architecture Plus* cited on the Baker House website. The *New York Times* baldly and matter-of-factly reported that the MIT Chapel was "absolutely unlike anything else" and that "the chapel resembles a gas storage tank." In *Education as Transformation*, Victor Kazan and Peter Laurence reiterate the oft-made observation around campus when it was new that MIT's Chapel was "the Gas Can on the Charles."

18 Kresge Auditorium
Eero Saarinen, 1953–55

Far more lyrical was the response of *Atlantic Monthly* editor Edward Weeks to the Chapel's companion: "The opal on the Charles" was what Weeks called Kresge Auditorium, and no one disagreed. During an interview he gave in 1956 to the *Tech*, Boston Symphony Orchestra conductor Charles Munch dropped something of a bombshell: "In fact, it was I who suggested the idea to [MIT's] president of inaugurating [the orchestra's] new season with a concert of the Boston Symphony Orchestra in the [Kresge] auditorium." Munch was not only signaling the importance of the new concert hall but extending his hand in just the way that had characterized early MIT's relations with the rest of Copley Square. The *Tech* responded in kind, reporting on the symphony's season opener in Kresge that "the dedication ceremonies for Kresge auditorium were held last May. Yet they were not completed until Monday night when the BSO under Charles Munch gave its first concert in the new hall....It was the first real 'test' of the auditorium." It was also the first full-length television broadcast from the new auditorium.

The acoustics actually received a mixed reception from musicians. But no architects withheld their praise from the building. Its form proceeded from Saarinen's own belief that, as he put it, "A domed structure seemed right....There was the large dome of Welles Bosworth," adding that "as an auditorium requires a triangular shape, we tried spanning this one-room building with a dome supported at three points—the shape of one-eighth of an orange." A bold move. "At first it seemed strange," Saarinen felt, "but gradually it became the loved one."

Like the architectural historian William Jordy, who was beguiled by Kresge's "curvilinear drama of reinforced concrete," most thought its form was just as memorable as the Chapel. But few notice how Kresge compensates for the small size of the Chapel. As President Killian saw it, the auditorium was as much a larger chapel as the Chapel was a very small auditorium. In other words, distinctly companion facilities. Notice how MIT used the New England term for a church—*meetinghouse*—in what Killian had inscribed above the Kresge stairwell. It proclaims that Kresge is "the meeting house of the Massachusetts Institute of Technology." When Coretta Scott King spoke on Martin Luther King Day at MIT, she spoke in Kresge, not in the Chapel. Similarly with the Dalai Lama.

Nor was there any disconnect in the fact that Kresge was built to be the principal performance venue at MIT for music and drama, very much a part of Killian's mandate for a more humanistic MIT. How seriously all this has been taken is certainly clear in the support given through the years to the work of the prolific American composer John Harbison, who has found a home at MIT that even a most eminent composer such as he must cherish. A student of Walter Piston and Roger Sessions, Harbison, a Harvard graduate, made the voyage from Old Cambridge to the Charles River Basin in 1969, joining the MIT faculty and ultimately being named Institute Professor (the highest faculty rank bestowed by the Institute) just a little over a decade after Kresge's dedication. Within the next decade Harbison's *Diotima*, premiered with the Boston Symphony, attracted wide attention, and he has gone on to win the Pulitzer in music (in 1987 for *The Flight Into Egypt*) and a MacArthur Fellowship in 1989. He has been commissioned to compose for the Boston Symphony his Symphonies nos. 1 and 5, and for the Metropolitan Opera his *The Great Gatsby*.

The erection of Kresge was not only an architectural event, but of great consequence to Boston's overall arts life. The Boston Symphony Orchestra inaugurated its 1956 season in Kresge, and the auditorium was very important to the early activities of the Lowell Institute Broadcasting Council and Boston's pioneering PBS station, WGBH.

Kresge's role is important not just to Harbison's work. For example, "Harbisons Host Mozart Marathon at MIT Featuring Boston Premieres of Mozart Completions" was the headline of a news report in 2012 of performances in which Harbison played the viola, Robert Levin the piano, and Harbison's wife, Rose Mary Harbison, the violin. The event was free and open not only to the MIT community but also to the general public.

Kresge Auditorium was also the spearhead of MIT's leadership in the matter of the genesis of Boston's flagship PBS station, WGBH (producer of *Masterpiece Theatre*, *Nova*, and much more), illuminating the whole sweep of the Institute's history in a way that illustrates a side of MIT's culture few understand. This association shows how the Institute repaid a century later the debt it will always owe in some sense to that foundational Brahmin institution, the Lowell Institute, for its promise that the Lowell Lectures would be based at MIT in Copley Square. In the Institute's earliest years, that promise was vital to MIT's continued existence. A century later, the repayment, furthermore, showed how constant and ever fructifying this link was in MIT's relationship to the entire Boston city-state. The Institute's role in the founding of WGBH proved key to the establishment not just of Boston's station but also of PBS as a whole. The *New York Times* in its obituary of Killian hailed MIT's president as the "father of public broadcasting" in America.

Edward Weeks explained the significance of all this to Killian's vision for the Institute in his *Architectural Record* article, writing that "the MIT of the latest word in science has just unveiled the latest novelty in the field of humanities.... [Kresge Auditorium] will call forth a yearly program of drama, music, speaking (and television)"—this in 1955—and that "television cameras will be installed with a direct line to station WGBH."

Notwithstanding wits who insist that *GBH* stands for God Bless Harvard, MIT actually shared with the older university the initiative in this project. *GBH* actually stands for Great Blue Hill—the site of the transmitter in suburban Milton. *Time* magazine described the content as "learned lectures as a typically Bostonian bluestocking scheme of adult education." Sniffed *Time*, "The venerable Lowell Institute refuses to admit its age." In fact, "MIT laid the groundwork," according to Mark Gelfand, biographer of station champion Ralph Lowell, by donating the FM transmitter for WGBH's radio station by way of the engineering school. MIT was one of the four original incorporators—with Harvard, the Lowell Institute, and the Boston Symphony—of the Lowell Institute Broadcasting Council.

Then in 1955 came WGBH-TV. Its first shows from Tufts University and Boston's Museum of Fine Arts aired that year via MIT, where the soon-to-be-famous television station's first studio was established, at 84 Massachusetts Avenue, where the Stratton Student Center now is, between Kresge and the Rogers Building. Opined *Time* magazine: "Through WGBH the Lowells now speak not only to the Cabots but to some thousands of Bostonians a day." Nothing better illustrates Killian's close rapport with the idealism and sense of civic pride that remained in the first generation of Brahmin descendants after Boston's ruling class fell from power so conspicuously in the early twentieth century than this tale of MIT and WGBH. Among those descendants, none was more respected than Ralph Lowell, the university's Lowell Institute trustee in the 1950s and a member of MIT's board a hundred years after John Amory Lowell joined it upon MIT's incorporation in 1861.

Writing of these beginnings, Jack W. Mitchell in *Listener Supported: The Culture and History of Public Radio* notes that "WGBH in Boston was the pioneer and model [in public broadcasting]....Created by money from old Boston families like the Lowells, WGBH combined the leadership of the premier educational institutions in the Boston Area like Harvard and MIT....In structure, governance, and funding it resembled the museums, symphony orchestras, the BBC...representing something of noblesse oblige." Focusing on MIT's role, Mitchell observes that the Carnegie Corporation "had connections and influence in the Kennedy-Johnson administration, as did the Boston educational establishment, the source of the vision and energy that had taken educational television so far." He adds that it was Carnegie that funded the report that was "the basis for the Public Broadcasting Act of 1967, which provided federal funding for the Corporation for Public Broadcasting." Ralph Lowell turned to Killian for leadership as the chairman of the Carnegie Foundation on Educational Television in 1965–67. Notice that what Mitchell said of public television was what Huxtable said of modern architecture: not simply that Boston had taken the national lead in each field (to be expected, perhaps, of the intellectual capital) but that the spearhead in both fields had been Harvard and MIT, as partners more than rivals.

Kresge was the first large-scale concrete building in the United States. Complications abounded, not just that during its construction Saarinen's father and mentor died and his marriage of more than a decade ended in divorce. No wonder Kresge seems finally to have depressed its architect. This at least is the impression he left when in *Eero Saarinen in His Own Words*, he remarked in connection with his TWA terminal at Idlewild (subsequently JFK) Airport in New York that "we wanted to counteract the earthbound feeling and heaviness that prevails too much in the MIT auditorium."

Earthbound? Not everyone agreed. Saarinen's worthy praise singer, MIT Architecture dean William J. Mitchell wrote of Kresge as "a gorgeously romantic example of spatial poetry." But that was when its dome was "the great white billowing roof" of Mark Tarsombelk's memory—like a sail almost—before today's overweight and clunky copper, ironically the material Saarinen had first wanted but deemed too heavy. If architecturally Kresge was not the enduring success the Chapel was, the structural experimentation initiated at MIT was continued at Yale, in Saarinen's famous TWA terminal, and finally in Sydney, where, as a judge for the architectural competition for the Opera House, he would urge the young Jørn Utzon toward what would become the greatest curved concrete structure in the world.

Trees played a crucial role in Saarinen's design for Kresge Plaza, yet these landscaping elements have not been incorporated, as opposed to Killian Court, where trees have been planted where Bosworth called for none, now obscuring the Great White City.

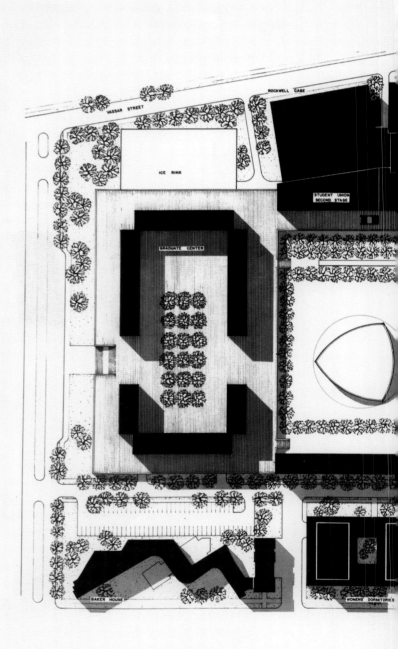

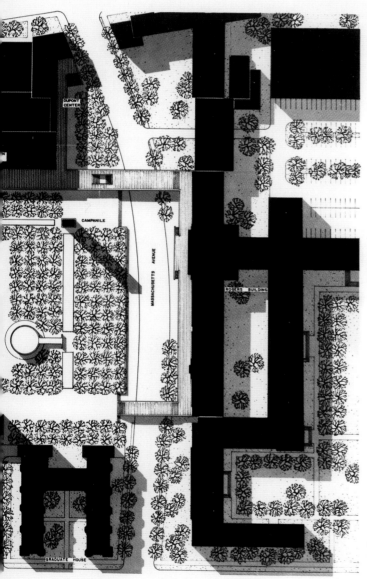

DUPONT CENTER

CAMPANILE

MASSACHUSETTS AVENUE

ROGERS BUILDING

GRADUATE HOUSE

SITE   PLAN
10 0 10 20   40   60   80

19   Kresge Court
Eero Saarinen, 1959

Kresge Court—Saarinen's final projected setting for his two masterpieces—is still a work in progress, stalled for many years now in a sort of compromise called Kresge Oval. The idea of Kresge Court was to evoke a continuity with Bosworth's original complex of 1916–37, of which Saarinen thought highly as a unifying aspect of the campus and upon which he was determined that his modernist architecture, however radical, should not turn its back. Bosworth's great dome, as we have already seen, inspired Kresge Auditorium. Similarly, Saarinen also "designed an enclosed court for Kresge Auditorium and Chapel" that, in Mitchell's words, the architect "intended to reflect the spirit and character of Bosworth's original Great Court" while at the same time proposing to "daringly…bridge Massachusetts Avenue"—that was the Infinite Corridor—"so that Bosworth's facade would become the [new court's] Eastern edge." Yet none of it happened.

Saarinen himself bears some responsibility. "From the beginning, we con-ceived of [chapel and auditorium] as on a great public square," he is quoted as saying in *Eero Saarinen and His Work*, where he admitted that he had originally "neglected to define and crystallize exactly how it would be achieved. This," he concluded, "we should have done," adding, however, that finally he had achieved a design that satisfied him, and in his words, "My hopes are that we will be able to create a large court." Alas, not even the "triangles of grass and paving" of Kresge Court have proved possible, just a lawn.

Even Saarinen's simplest wish—"The buildings immediately around [chapel and auditorium]…are no damned good and may come down. I hope so."—has never been fulfilled. Robert Simha explains why in his *MIT Campus Planning, 1960–2000*, in which he records that it was not until 1959 that Saarinen accepted the Institute's invitation to provide a master plan for the area, along with a design for a student center. At about the same time, the idea for McCormick Hall arose, built eventually between Kresge Auditorium and the river. Kresge had, in fact, been originally intended for the McCormick Hall site, right on the riverfront, but Saarinen "argued persuasively against the Memorial Drive location…convinced that [his] plastic shapes would be out of keeping with the other staid buildings fronting Memorial Drive." Instead, he hoped to design a whole new court, and a whole new architec-tural world, really, directly opposite the grand entrance of the Rogers Building at 77 Massachusetts Avenue.

That court (pp. 292–93) was defined by a rigorously orthogonal grid of trees laid out to create allées to the north and east, the eastern allée parallel with Massachusetts Avenue and leading to the Chapel, its beginning marked by a tall freestanding campanile. A campanile for Massachusetts Avenue! How has MIT been able to resist building so glorious a landmark—never mind the bell tower by Theodore Roszak on the Chapel roof that presumably was preferred.

Truth to tell, however, despite all the pride the Institute justifiably took—and takes—in Saarinen's work there, that work was always difficult to assimilate and unsettling in effect. Then architecture school dean Pietro Belluschi, himself a notable architect, "face[d] opposition from the administration" over Saarinen's proposals. According to Belluschi's biographer, Meredith Clausen, the dean wrote to President Killian in June 1952 urging support of Saarinen: "Creative masterpieces do not come easily or by timid approach." Yet that timidity is evident still in the pedestrian 1920s brick apartment house that blocks any view of the MIT Chapel across Massachusetts Avenue from the Rogers Building's grand entrance.

Simha details the original fiasco on all sides, noting particularly that Saarinen's design for the student center was found to be "inhospitable" (not enough windows) and too expensive. What had changed, however, was presidents: Killian's successor, Julius Stratton (no relation to previous president Samuel Wesley Stratton), had very different views and commissioned Eduardo Catalano to design the much more aggressive student center of today—an aircraft carrier of a building —which won the new president's "enthusiastic support." In fairness to MIT, Saarinen himself was increasingly out of touch, crippled by illness. He died in 1961 from a brain tumor at age fifty-one. Kresge Court remained unrealized.

The ideal action plan? Above all to plant the allées of trees that would now have the additional benefit of obscuring some subsequent architecture and bringing more focus to Saarinen's pair of masterpieces. About which trees, by the way, Saarinen was as specific as about the buildings: two allées on the north provided for three parallel rows of trees in front of the student center; to the west and south only a single row; and then to the east on Massachusetts Avenue, a dense mass of eight rows of trees to set off the Chapel.

Whereas too many trees have been allowed to obscure Bosworth's Great Court (where he provided for very few and only ornamental trees in the corner) destroying the sweeping views of his facades that so impress in old photographs, in Saarinen's court, where trees are an integral part of the architect's design, MIT seems reluctant to plant any trees at all. Any planting today, while certainly completing the west wall of the court, should allow the opening out to the southwest of an allée that would annex Baker House, bringing it into harmonious relationship with chapel and auditorium. To do so would transform the architectural experience of the entire West Campus, incorporating Alvar Aalto's masterpiece into the picture. By bringing dormitory, chapel, and auditorium into visual relationship, MIT could create a modernist American acropolis reminiscent of both the ancient classical Acropolis at Athens and the nineteenth-century New World Acropolis of Copley Square, of which MIT was the cornerstone.

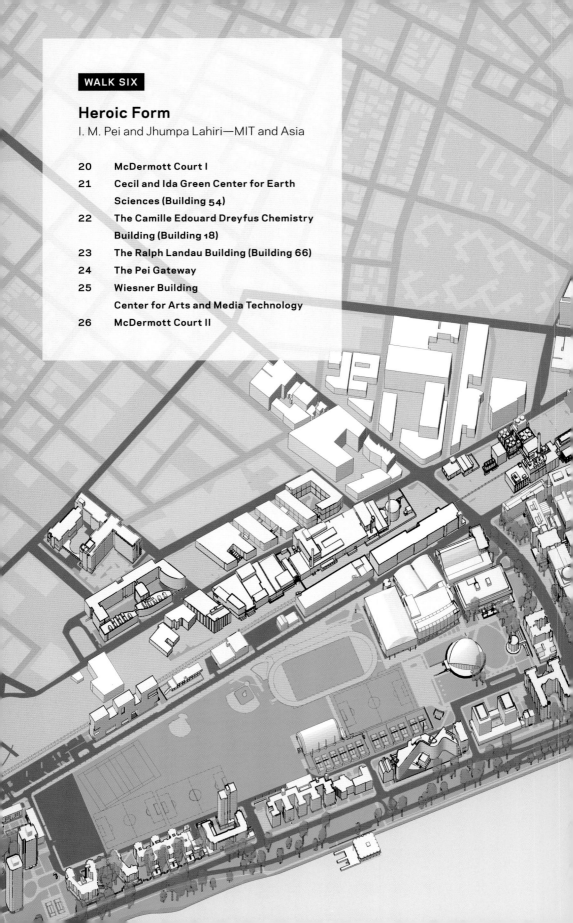

Heroic Form

I. M. Pei and Jhumpa Lahiri—MIT and Asia

A 1940 graduate of MIT Architecture, I. M. Pei was of the generation that first seri-ously confronted architectural modernism in its most radical form—the International Style—as clearly the wave of the future.

The situation Pei found at the Institute's architecture school in Copley Square in the 1930s was considerably more interesting than most now realize. Despite the fact that the skyscraper was the Boston-born idea of MIT's most illustrious architec-ture graduate of the nineteenth century, Louis Sullivan, MIT remained in the 1930s committed to the very traditional architectural worldview of its inspiration, the École des Beaux-Arts in Paris. Yet the Beaux-Arts–trained head of design, Jacques Carlu, professor of architecture at MIT from 1924 to 1933, was also a star architect of the *Art Moderne*, or *Art Deco*, style. This was not *modern* in the sense in which the most radical intellectual leader of modernist architecture, Le Corbusier, understood the word. But the history of modernism is now seen as not only the cubistic International Style but also a highway of several parallel lanes—and several parallel "modern-isms"—not least Carlu's Art Moderne.

International Style pioneer Edward Durell Stone relates in his *Evolution of an Architect*, "Jacques Carlu at MIT was beginning to experiment with modern design, so I decided to change schools," which meant for Stone transferring from Harvard to MIT, which he promptly did. There he found another disciple of Carlu, Robert Dean, who would go on to become a helpmate of Alvar Aalto in the erection of Baker House. Carlu, whose best-known work is the Palais de Chaillot in Paris of 1937, came up in the MIT Museum's Boston Grads Go to Chicago exhibition because he too in his era preached the virtues of the skyscraper. Other ardent advocates included several prominent MIT alumni of the period, such as Raymond Hood and Cass Gilbert.

What made Carlu a Moderne star, and a very glamorous one, were his interi-ors, full of Lalique glass and emerald-green and silver-gray murals mostly painted by his wife, Natacha. They appeared in the Ritz-Carlton (now Taj) Hotel in Boston and in Eaton's department stores in Montreal and Toronto. All were inspired by Carlu's work on the interiors of the S.S. *Île de France* and the S.S. *Normandie*, perhaps the most spectacular of 1930s transatlantic ocean liners. The fact that MIT's head of design was responsible as well for the gorgeous interior of the Rainbow Room on the sixty-fifth floor of the new Rockefeller Center in New York—MIT graduate Raymond Hood was the center's principal designer—underlines that in a real sense, MIT Architecture in the 1930s, while not from everyone's point of view on the cutting edge, was hardly staid or old-fashioned.

When Lawrence Anderson succeeded Carlu as head of design in 1934, things began to move toward the more radical modernism of the International Style. Five years later, Anderson and Herbert Beckwith, MIT grads of 1926 and 1930, respectively, would design for MIT the Alumni Swimming Pool, which has been described by Robert Bell Rettig as notable for its "sharp-edged cubistic masses." Another architectural historian, Gail Fenske, in her chapter in *Aalto and America*, remarks on the fact that in New York, "Curator [Elizabeth Bauer] Mock's Built in U.S.A. [exhibition of 1944 at the Museum of Modern Art]...featured Anderson's MIT Alumni Swimming Pool as the first modern building built in any [American] university campus."

It was sure evidence that MIT was in the modernist vanguard, very derivative of the work of the Swiss-born French architect Le Corbusier, the great modernist master whom Anderson and Beckwith, as well as Pei and his fellow freshmen in 1935, were eagerly hero-worshipping from afar. When suddenly in 1935 there appeared in Copley Square Le Corbusier himself—"a cadaverous figure dressed in his usual black suit and thick owl-eyed glasses," in the words of Pei's biographer Michael Cannell—Pei and his cohort crowded around the intellectual leader, Frank Lloyd Wright's only rival as world's greatest architect. Mardges Bacon in *Le Corbusier in America* details the scene: "On the afternoon of his second day in Boston, Le Corbusier met with journalists and then lectured on 'Modern Architecture' at MIT's Rogers Building....[The] *Christian Science Monitor* emphasized the architect's appearance...brown shirt of geometric design, black bow tie with red spots." Le Corbusier emphasized "what he considered to be the toxic effects of a moribund Beaux-Arts program" in drawings hanging on walls everywhere, which he condemned as "'boring,' 'shameful.'...[He] confronted the teachers and students, questioning why they had not done away with such 'horrors.'"

Back at his hotel, Le Corbusier calmed down, and when his book about America was published, he pronounced more sagely on his Copley Square experiences: "Boston, city of thought and meditation," as he pronounced it in *Quand les cathédrales étaient blanches*. He reported having indulged in a fascinating meditation while "dining alone at the Copley Plaza"—let's hope the dean at least gave him lunch—a meditation that might well have been titled "Three MIT Engineers":

> I am bored and have time to observe. In the dining room of this excellent hotel there is a religious silence. Opposite me are three men who are certainly engineers. Every five minutes one of them speaks. Silence and mastication. The three men have handsome heads, characteristic of their country: balanced, strong, energetic. One is old, one young, one middle aged. The meal is finished. Coffee. Silence. Then after a long time conversation begins. Unquestionably they are talking about their discoveries, but without passion or excitement. They masticate their words, speak quietly and reflectively. I should even say that they seem as if they were under the influence of a religious event. Those men won me with their handsome faces. I think: what a grave and serious country! When such men take hold of an idea or begin to act, they do not let go.

This was nothing new for him. He had already famously written in *Towards a New Architecture*, "Let us beware of American architects," but only after "Let us

MIT's Alumni Swimming Pool made history in 1939
as the first example of International Style architecture on any American campus. Its "sharp-edged
cubistic masses," to quote architectural historian
Robert Bell Rettig, show that MIT was receptive
to modernism before Gropius's first building
at Harvard, in 1946, or Aalto's arrival at MIT in
the same decade. The architects were Lawrence
Anderson and Herbert L. Beckwith, both MIT
Architecture graduates between the wars and
then faculty members.

thinking, an idea well made by the cover of the book, which shows an ancient statue of the Chinese sage against a background of the modern Boston skyline. It is a provocative contrast, the power of which, even in the face of the more modest 1930s skyline, young Pei must have felt keenly upon his arrival in America.

How America received Pei is another matter, especially at the level of some-one Mandarin born and at an elite institution such as MIT. Throughout his career as it unfolded, extremes on both right and left presented themselves, ranging from the terrors of the "yellow peril" to the more subtle fears put very well by critic Henrik Bering when he lamented, "One of the most striking traits of American and European academics is a kind of masochism that manifests itself in books celebrating the superior claims of cultures not their own."

As an alternative, Bering recommends a survey of the subject of our own day, *How the West Won* by the sociologist Rodney Stark. Above all because of the "unique Christian conviction that 'progress was a God-given obligation entailed in the gift of reason,'" writes Stark, "reason and therefore Christianity [are the] pass-port to modernity." He cites in support of his thesis facts as various as that "China is credited with inventing the blast furnace [but] in the 11th century the Chinese court killed a private budding iron industry as a threat to its rule; that in 1485 the Ottoman Empire banned the printing press; and that both the Chinese and Ottoman Empires forbade the mechanical clock." All this is contrasted with how keen medieval Europeans were to adopt windmills and gunpowder.

It is more than masochism—a sign instead of fair-mindedness and self-confidence?—that so many American scholars study with an open mind the "superior claims" of those that fail. Still, to rejoin Stark's thesis at arguably its crucial point, "invention per se is not the most critical factor," he writes, "to consider with tech-nologies. More critical is the extent to which a culture values inventions and puts them to work." He finds an aversion to doing so specifically in Confucianism, but just the reverse in Christianity, its link to a dynamic economy famously acknowledged by the "frugal entrepreneur" of Max Weber's *The Protestant Ethic and the Spirit of Capitalism* (1904), even though many scholars see capitalism as first surging in the Catholic Dark Ages. (So called by anti-Christian eighteenth-century intellectuals not prepared to admit that it was then that Europe took the great technological and intellectual leap forward, its most brilliant minds dedicated to the pursuit of knowl-edge—"not only about God," Bering notes, "but about the whole creation.")

In this connection, the vibrant capitalism of mid-twelfth-century Venice is often cited. Works such as Mark Peterson's *The City-State of Boston: Ebb and Flow in the Atlantic World, 1630–1865* (forthcoming) compare MIT's birthplace to the Serene Republic, and the point has been made repeatedly by scholars as eminent as Perry Miller about Puritan Harvard, where, not incidentally, America's first printing

Pei's first building at McDermott Court was the Cecil and Ida Green Building, as historian Keith Morgan pointed out, "directly on axis with the Prudential Center" on the western border of Copley Square, where Pei had experienced Le Corbusier's revelatory lecture.

press was set up in 1638. Behold the finale of Pei's era: Britain and then the United States, one after the other the spearhead of the Industrial Revolution, possessing what Bering calls "the right mix of freedom, property rights, and an educated population." Recall Steven Shapin's assertion in "Part One" that MIT was the world's first entrepreneurial university.

Pei was a refugee from a then increasingly deteriorating China. Although he had not originally planned to stay in the United States, he eventually became a citizen. He arrived in this country on the eve of its rise to world power, a development that does not usually lead in national life to a greater openness to other cultures. But the Boston Pei arrived in, in the 1930s (having transferred to MIT from the University of Pennsylvania in Philadelphia, which he did not like at all), offered him something new: if not the supremely confident Boston Brahmin Ascendancy of the nineteenth century, then a city whose upper classes were still imbued with Brahmin values and included Brahmin descendants who not only emulated an Asian caste model but also were knowledgeable about—and very admiring of—things Chinese.

A good deal of this attitude survived in the 1930s in Copley Square. It had admittedly ceased by then to be any sort of acropolis, or even much of an academic center, but it still preserved something of its once-considerable Asian heritage. The art museum with its great Asian collections had moved, but Yamanaka, the legendary import house through which many of Isabella Stewart Gardner's treasures had passed, was still there in Despradelle's flamboyant Berkeley Building. And as long as MIT was there, there was still its own considerable Asian legacy, for already in the 1870s, in its first decade of operation, Philip Alexander documents half a dozen Chinese and Japanese students. By Pei's day he was able to join a branch of a national Chinese fraternity with a chapter at MIT. All things considered, he was made welcome. "I was able to enter Boston society very early on, long before I managed to speak English," Pei remembered. "I had rather a comfortable experience as a foreign student."

His biographer is quick to pick up on the significant word: "Pei felt more comfortable in Boston," he wrote, because "[Boston's] banks had commercial ties to China dating back to the…nineteenth century, when Yankee clippers had plied the Far East trade routes." Pei's father was an important Chinese banker, so "Pei had consequently arrived with introductions to his father's business acquaintances." And that only begins to explain why the young Chinese architectural student found himself very much at home in the old China trade capital. Of course, the China trade can be seen with good reason as exploitative and disrespectful of China on the part of the West. But from Boston's perspective, historically, the legacy was much more positive and very pro-Chinese. Consider, for instance, this aspect of Chinese-Bostonian relations evident in Copley Square and the Back Bay in 1935, the year Pei arrived at MIT. There was at that time what was called a Chinese Parlor in the Commonwealth Avenue town house (hardly three blocks from the Rogers Building) of the grandfather of Henry Ashton Crosby Forbes, who until 1964 taught history at MIT (and to whom, with Rawson Lyman Wood, this book is dedicated). Crosby

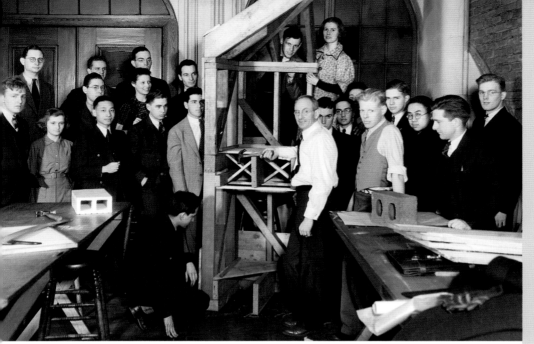

Pei in class at the MIT Architecture School in the old Rogers Building in Copley Square, standing third from the right.

Forbes was the great-grandson of Robert Bennet Forbes, the famous China trade entrepreneur and sea captain, the first speaker at the first meeting in 1862 of MIT as a Society of Arts, and the brother of John Murray Forbes, a member of MIT's first Finance Committee in the same decade (see Portal Two in "Part One").

　　Three-quarters of a century later, Crosby told an interviewer from *The Oklahoman* that when he was a boy, he and his parents used to go to his grand-parents' home for Sunday lunch. And although the Chinese Parlor's "door was always closed," Crosby recalled, "twice I did get to see it, and I was transported. It was an elegant room, full of silk embroideries, silver, furniture, porcelain, screens, and paintings," all centered on an ensemble surmounted by a portrait (now in the Forbes House Museum in the Boston suburb of Milton) of the legendary early nineteenth-century Chinese merchant of Canton, Houqua, leader of a group to whom the Chinese emperor entrusted China's foreign commercial relations. Still a figure spoken of with reverence among Boston's old China trade families, Houqua was the principal subject of what amounted, Crosby told me, to a Chinese family shrine.

　　It was about 1935, the year Pei arrived at MIT, when young Crosby first saw the Chinese Parlor with his grandfather. The more intimate backstory of this visit, as Crosby recounted it decades later in 2008 at the first meeting of Back Bay Historical at Boston's Chilton Club (diagonally across Commonwealth Avenue from the site of the old Chinese Parlor), was his grandfather's insistence that Houqua was to be revered always for his wisdom, honesty, and generosity, and as virtually the founder of the Forbes family fortune (and of course some of MIT's). Confucius in the shadow of Copley Square? Houqua was born in Canton. So was Pei. And the portrait in the

Forbes Chinese Parlor might well have been of Pei's own grandfather. "Young Ieoh Ming Pei often visited his grandfather as a boy," biographer Cannell writes, "and years later in America spoke of him as 'the very symbol of Confucian values.'"

While Crosby Forbes was first encountering Houqua, Pei was first encountering MIT's dean of architecture, William Emerson, a Boston Brahmin, and in fact Ralph Waldo Emerson's grandnephew. MIT's architecture dean at once "took a benevolent interest, . . . walked Pei all over Boston, and even," according to Cannell, "invited him to Thanksgiving dinner at his Brattle Street home." Louise Slavicek takes up the tale: "Convinced that he would never be able to draw well enough to be a successful designer, . . . Pei entered MIT with every expectation of specializing in architectural engineering. To his surprise, however, the school's dean of architecture, William Emerson, immediately decided that his new transfer student had a gift for design. When Pei tried to tell Emerson that he had no talent for art, the dean replied that such thinking was nonsense. It was a well-known fact that all Chinese could draw."

"Pei later recalled Dean Emerson's wild generalization," Cannell wrote, "with amusement. 'Of course, it's not true, but it was his way of saying, Don't be discouraged, . . . study architecture.' . . . Buoyed by Emerson's faith in him, Pei decided to recommit himself to architectural design. From that point he never turned back."

The dean's assertion to Pei—incredible in a different way from, but rooted in, the same attitude as the Forbeses' Chinese Parlor—reflected the fact that while Bostonians responded ardently to Indian philosophy and religion (think Transcendentalism), they responded *artistically* not to Indian but to Chinese decorative arts. It was only the first act of an evolution in the Brahmin response to Asian art that would be ultimately dominated by Japanese art and eventually encompass Indian art, the collections in Copley Square's art museum being how these stages registered. But first and foremost artistically came Chinese art.

Neville and Weiming were told at a conference at the University of California, Berkeley, that "Bostonians might be Brahmins, but only East Asians could be Confucianists." The assertion dramatically raises the question of why Oliver Wendell Holmes, who must have known more than one Chinese Parlor, likened Boston's elite not to Mandarins but to Brahmins? Ignorantly, many assume today that he hardly bothered about the difference. But that would be disrespectful to both Chinese and Indian history, never mind Holmes. Boston's China trade families certainly did know the difference.

The answer seems obvious when one considers Reinhard Bendix's discourse on the differences between Mandarins and Brahmins in his study of Max Weber. "The Chinese intelligentsia," he wrote, "was a status group of men who were officials or who aspired to office, while the Brahmins were a somewhat motley group of royal

Critical to Pei's great success at MIT was the welcome he received by the old China trade Brahmin families. That deep-seated ethos is clear in this photograph, in the Forbes town house on Commonwealth Avenue only a block or two from MIT, of what was virtually a family altar to the famous Chinese merchant Houqua, with whom the Forbes family formed a close alliance in the nineteenth century.

chaplains, family priests, theologians, and jurists who functioned as spiritual advisers and administrators, teachers, consultants, and authorities in ritual propriety.... The mandarin considered the career of an official the only one worthy of a cultivated man.... For a Brahmin such a career would appear a matter of expedience and without merit," for the Brahmin was not at all a bureaucrat, not even of the highest rank. He was a priest-teacher. Which Trevor Boddy also understood, perhaps the reason why he contended that it was the Boston Brahmin part that was crucial in Pei's career, the part that would separate the "sometimes Brahmin Pei" with his somewhat academic air from "the alphabet soup of his peer firms—SOM and the rest." Being, in fact, what most historians would agree differentiated Boston Brahmins from bureaucrats, and also from what many Americans think of in connection with Brahmins and Mandarins: great wealth.

Holmes specifically disdains that connection, pointing out that while there was indeed a moneyed aristocracy in America—in Boston, too—it was a distinctly different group. And while they often coincided (many Brahmins were rich), what was definitive for a *caste* descended from seventeenth-century Puritan clerics and professors and eighteenth-century Patriots was not to be rich but to be erudite. You did not have to be rich to be a Boston Brahmin. Some of the most influential Brahmins were not wealthy. Everyone knew the high priest himself, so to speak, Charles W. Eliot, was more famous than well-off, yet he was positively revered. McGill University literary historian Peter Gibian put it this way in his *Oliver Wendell Holmes and the Culture of Conversation*: "If in the past New England's secular priesthood had combined intellectual, political, and social leadership, by the time Holmes named the caste [in the early 1860s]...the 'Brahmin caste' is purely an academic class, a community of scholars.... Holmes's writings can be seen as primary signs of a shift in the ideal of 'the life of the mind'...to that of an alienated avant-garde, from a model of end-oriented intellect in the service of power to disinterested intelligence with a goal of free speculation and criticism, from living off ideas to living for them." It was an essential stage in the evolution of the intellectual capital. At the same time, New York was emerging as the economic and media capital and Washington, D.C., as the political capital, to be joined in the early twentieth century by Los Angeles as the nation's entertainment capital.

Whether "living off ideas" or "living for them," ideas were what mattered most to the Brahmin leadership by Holmes's day. To be sure, "the Boston religion," like the China trade, had its dark side. In the case of the China trade, that would be the opium trade, which more or less sustained it. In the case of Boston Unitarianism, it would be what some today would call elitism or classism. But opium, though illegal in China then, was entirely legal in the United States, often prescribed by physicians and thought to be no more problematic than alcohol is thought to be today. And as to elitism and classism, they are essential to the whole concept of the Brahmin, Indian or Bostonian.

By Pei's day in the 1960s—a century after Holmes's day—the field that was most prestigious and could with most authority sustain all this was no longer theology or philosophy, but science. Consider a book by Spencer Klaw, a Harvard graduate who taught at Columbia, titled *The New Brahmins: Scientific Life in America*, published in 1968. If for a Boston Unitarian there was no higher calling than professor, by the mid-nineteenth century there was for such a person no more hopeful or promising field than science, as William Barton Rogers repeatedly declared. If the Puritan / Patriot / Brahmin continuum through Harvard nurtured and empowered Boston as the American intellectual capital, MIT or something very like it was almost bound to have become its most characteristic expression in that era—"the spirit of Boston," in Russell B. Adams's words. By Pei's time that spirit had evolved to such an extent that, as in the case of Rogers, it was hardly surprising that scientists were called Brahmins *because they were scientists*. Do you recognize "the Boston religion"? It is but a later chapter. And one of its sacred precincts, where Pei's magnificent architectural ensemble is more than worthy of the New Scientific Brahmins, is the Green Center for Earth Sciences building, the Dreyfus Chemistry Department building, and the Landau chemical engineering building.

20 McDermott Court I
The Pei Ensemble
I. M. Pei & Associates, 1959–76

Here one encounters both the New Scientific Brahmins and Pei's acknowledgment of Chinese traditional thinking. When in the early 1940s Pei went on to do his graduate work at Harvard under Gropius, he once erupted in that master's class to insist that the International Style could no more than any other style ignore, for example, climate. Then he added: "What about history? What about tradition?" To which Gropius responded as any good teacher would: "Prove it to me." Pei took up the challenge and created a memorable design for a museum in a tea park, explaining that the space between the buildings was as important as the buildings themselves in this tradition. In the Western tradition, art was public. In the Chinese tradition, it was private, behind garden walls. Very modern in style, Pei's project was very traditional in concept.

One cannot but notice the parallel with all this in the fact, according to Philip Jodidio and Janet Adams in *I. M. Pei: Compete Works*, that at MIT the goal was to create an ensemble that would "eventually enclose and organize space." They add: "The primary concern was not the solids but the voids around and between the build-ings." One thinks of the vast atrium of the Kennedy Library in Boston, the essence of which Pei has always asserted was its "emptiness."

21   Cecil and Ida Green Center for Earth Sciences (Building 54)
I. M. Pei & Associates, 1959–64

The entrance to the Pei group of buildings in McDermott Court from either the east or the southwest is marked by a classical motif Bosworth knew well: the triumphal arch. From the southwest, the Green Center rises from a ground-floor story in the form of that motif—lifting as the tower does from its double-height, triple-arched foundational story. The overall effect is, suddenly, serenity. Not what one expects in the face of such a formidable weight of history as can be felt in McDermott Court. But Pei's buildings here are stylistically, to use University of Oregon historian Leland Roth's term, "Heroic Expressionism."

Detractors of this style prefer to call it "brutalism." The best American architectural critic of the modern era, Ada Louise Huxtable, disparaged the term, observing that whatever its more neutral origins, "Brutalism" had become "a term of opprobrium." It is a term favored by those who, however highly educated in their own fields, are uneducated in architecture. Its use is most widespread, I find, among those with what I like to call "lazy eyes," able to appreciate only the most conventional designs.

Sarah Williams Goldhagen defined what I mean quite well when she wrote of the circle of Louis Kahn—whose Phillips Exeter Library in Exeter, New Hampshire, is the great global masterpiece of this style in Boston's orbit—that very few of those around Kahn were "interested in beauty, a classical concept that was understood to rely on eye-soothing formulas and familiar motifs." The same be may be said of Pei's and Paul Rudolph's circles—those two architects being respectively the most rational and the most flamboyant of Kahn's rivals in the Heroic Concrete style.

It does not help this much-abused style, either, that whatever one calls it, it is sometimes confused at first glance with the neo-Fascist style of the 1930s and 1940s, a dilemma the legendary architectural historian William J. R. Curtis addresses when he writes that the essence of the Heroic Concrete style was to "handle public buildings with appropriate degrees of presence and accessibility, to establish the terms of democratic monumentality…for the liberal minded." He adds, "Monumentality is a quality in architecture which does not necessarily have to do with size but with intensity of expression."

Intensity is something not everyone is comfortable with. Not everyone likes Beethoven. Consider, for example, Boston's famous City Hall by Kallmann, McKinnell and Knowles. Those who do not admire this building, Boston's greatest masterpiece of the twentieth century, are much quicker to see in its design Le Corbusier above than Alvar Aalto below. Yet the minute it is pointed out, the important role MIT's Baker House plays in City Hall's design is clear.

The profiles of Pei's MIT look westward toward the original Bosworth complex and the great dome of Barker Library.

Still, a concrete *skyscraper* was something else when Pei proposed it to MIT in 1959. Even when it was completed in 1964, it turned many heads, winning the J. Harleston Parker Gold Medal of the Boston Society of Architects for the most beautiful building erected that year in Greater Boston. Pei's most brilliant Boston disciple, Frederick A. "Tad" Stahl, an MIT alumnus, explained it all when—insisting on the tradition that stone and steel were noble materials, as brick and wood were not—Pei extended it to the modern era by accepting concrete as noble. Pei, Stahl wrote, "had undertaken a mission to prove that cast-in-place concrete could be a truly noble material, equal or superior to the best natural stone."

How controversial was the award of the Parker Gold Medal to MIT's Green Center? Just two years previously, in 1963, when the same medal was awarded to Le Corbusier's Carpenter Center at Harvard, one of the first exposed-concrete structures in the United States, the Boston Society of Architects "balked at the committee's choice," refusing to approve the award. One member explained to the *Boston Globe* that he found the building too "loathsome" to consider. It took two years to reverse the embarrassing decision. In the same year Pei won his Parker Gold Medal, turning the tide, it would seem, Le Corbusier was given his, in Paris.

It was all very courageous of Pei in view of the fact that the Green Center—the first time MIT abandoned its tradition of horizontality on its central campus—was his first big job in his own name. The building is signed "I. M. Pei Associates." Cannell confides, "Banking on this commission, Pei, at age 43, formally broke with Webb and Knapp," the real estate developers he had previously worked for since graduation. He had been, Pei told *Technology Review*, "a hired hand" before the Green Center; "I became an independent practitioner at MIT." And in the same place he had lived in an undergraduate dormitory.

The task was not an easy one. Not the least difficulty was the mistake made in connection with the ground-floor bays, left open to encourage pedestrian flow in McDermott Court. Quoth *The Harvard Crimson* cheerfully: "The doors...were difficult to open because of the strong winds coming from Boston Harbor." Pei was embarrassed. "Here I was from MIT, and I didn't know about wind tunnel effects."

It was more important, as Richard Guy Wilson, the University of Virginia architectural historian, has pointed out, that Pei had before Green been "submerged under the economics of redevelopment" and lacked "artistry and nobility." At MIT, "once freed from these constraints, the shift in attitude was notable. He rediscovered architecture as art." For which Boston, on which Pei left an imprint comparable to Charles McKim's in another century, was the gainer. He was able to do this because of the support of his close ally, Boston's legendary historian Walter Muir Whitehill. "Pei, who had trained at MIT," Whitehill wrote, "was sensitive to Boston's historic atmosphere."

22 The Camille Edouard Dreyfus Chemistry Building (Building 18)
I. M. Pei & Associates, 1964–70

The star of the McDermott Court Pei ensemble is not the Green Building, but the Dreyfus Chemistry Building, the second of Pei's three Heroic Concrete buildings here. It also won a Parker Gold Medal. This second clear public endorsement of Pei's work in concrete powerfully illustrates the architect's uncanny knack for knowing how to design in concrete. Mark Pasnik, a Boston-based architect and associate professor at Wentworth Institute, who with Chris Grimley and Michael Kubo is the presiding intelligence behind the forthcoming *Heroic: Concrete Architecture and the New Boston* (based on their groundbreaking exhibition at Boston's Pinkcomma Gallery), puts it this way: "Nobility comes from the way the architect's design brings into play the physical strength of concrete, and how that strength is expressed visually." Pei knew how to do both.

That is perhaps what *Boston Globe* critic Robert Campbell meant when he wrote of "the muscularity of concrete." The great historian of modernism, William J. R. Curtis, is also worth reading on this. "Concrete," he writes, "of all materials, is one of the most flexible, one of the least determining of form," relying on "the shape of the mould and the shaping intelligence of the designer." He cites Frank Lloyd Wright's particular affinity for this material, so easily "moulded to his spatial ideas."

This was equally true in the case of Pei concrete. Bernard Spring and Donald Canty in *Architectural Forum* in September 1962 noted that "the design of the [Green] Earth Science Building at MIT…reflects the lessons of Pei's research and experience." The authors recount how "the architects began their search for the proper concrete mix by prospecting for raw materials in the Boston area. Samples of all available sand, gravel, and crushed stone were collected along with samples of all cements produced by plants within shipping range.…All were evaluated for color, texture, strength." Then there was also the matter that the concrete was "dependent for its impact on a few beautifully crafted plastic forms (the final choice of the plastic was made from the contractor from three alternatives specified by Pei)." The final step was "a light sandblasting, which skims off the pasty hard skin of surface cement."

The Dreyfus Chemistry Building stands out as exemplifying all this superbly. The Green Center, for all its stature, is not the equal, for instance, of the skyscraper in Pei's Christian Science Center in the Back Bay. And because of its knife-edge profile, the most distinctive feature of the Landau Building inevitably invites comparison with the National Gallery in Washington, a comparison bound to be at the expense of the Landau, as the National Gallery may be Pei's masterpiece of all time. With all the qualities that most appealed to Pei—it is "geometrically pure, minimal, and sculptural"—the Dreyfus Building is an outstanding example of something the *New York Times* critic Paul Goldberger remarked upon amazedly many years ago: "Pei's ability to bring rhythm and texture to a facade that is just a grid of concrete is absolutely superb." By putting the corridors along the exterior walls, Pei made the moving people at night the building's ornament. By day it is the grid's deep shadows.

Pei's masterwork at MIT is the Dreyfus Building, which kept open the southern end of the building to perpetuate a well-traveled campus pathway, the direction of which is indicated by the diagonal slab that establishes the design motif for the entire facade grid. "Pei's ability to bring rhythm and texture to a facade that is just a grid of concrete," former *New York Times* critic Paul Goldberger has written, "is absolutely superb."

Finally, there is the inspiration that qualifies Dreyfus as a modest masterwork: the way the architect tweaked the design of the whole building to reflect the striking support he gave to its cantilevered southern end, left open (again) to encourage pedestrian flow through the court and supported by two diagonal slab uprights whose slant carries up and everywhere else in the window grid of the entire facade, formed throughout of diagonal columns and spandrels. Wrote Robert Simha: "The windows on the elevation reflected the angular pattern of the diagonal walkway. When Professor Wiesner asked Mr. Pei why he had chosen this architectural device, he replied that the building plan had been developed with a certain discipline presented by the Chemistry Department and this was an opportunity for him to express the poetic license usually granted to an architect in these matters." Very droll. Very Brahmin.

23 The Ralph Landau Building (Building 66)
I. M. Pei & Partners, 1976

A familiar aesthetic is evident in the expansive facades of the Landau Building, first seen in Bosworth's facades. The Brahmin aesthetic—"Beethoven in Granite"—is clearly emergent in the slablike facades of this third of Pei's ensemble. The continuity is not only between Bosworth's MIT and Pei's, but also between the early and mid-nineteenth-century Boston Granite style and mid-twentieth-century Heroic Boston Concrete. Donald Lyndon points out in Pei's work elsewhere, "The masses of concrete that serve as attics, cornices, or endpieces…[are] cast in sections carefully stacked upon each other in a manner reminiscent of the severe granite slab buildings of Boston's [nineteenth-century] waterfront."

Curtis, ruminating in *Boston: Forty Years of Modern Architecture*, wrote, "The historian who is determined to define a 'Boston School' of architecture will have the most luck if he looks at the work…[of] the sixties [that shows] a preponderant tendency to plain geometrical forms, to…simple rectangular concrete frames and skeletons, to detail [of] a no-nonsense, no frills manner, and to…bare concrete finishes."

Notice how concrete dominates that era in Boston so dominated by Gropius and Josep Lluís Sert and by the Architects Collaborative, Arrowstreet, Cambridge Seven, Benjamin Thompson Associates, Hugh Stubbins, and Stahl Associates. And the Argentine-born American architect Eduardo Catalano, who taught at MIT from 1956 to 1977 and whose Student Center is a major work.

24 The Pei Gateway
I. M. Pei & Partners, 1984

The Landau Building is best seen, and the Dreyfus and Green buildings well seen, from the northeast, through the most surprising feature of this Heroic Concrete ensemble of Pei's: the monumental triumphal arch or gateway, all but freestanding. It is a flourish quite unusual in Pei's work, and it stands beside, and indeed is attached to, the Wiesner Building, of which more soon. This arch or gateway has not been universally admired, and Pei, who was much invested in it, has made an ardent defense of it, as Simha explains in his campus planning book: "Mr. Pei defended the arch and even proposed to forgo the fee for its design. Jean de Monchaux, the new Dean of the School of Architecture, supported the arch. In the end the arch was built. Yet there were mysterious forces at work. After the concrete was poured for the arch's foundation, it appeared that the concrete had not hardened.…Though the circumstance was corrected, I had the fanciful thought that there might have been another hand at work, telling MIT that this arch, perhaps, was a mistake."

It wasn't a mistake. And speaking of mysterious forces, the front cover of Simha's book is adorned with a striking photograph of the Pei buildings framed by what Jodidio and Adams hail as this "monumental concrete arch cantilever[ed] over the main pedestrian axis between the two campus precincts." Just as Pei's first axis

View along the south flank of the Landau Building (1976), by I. M. Pei & Partners.

Pei's four works in the heroic concrete style (or as its detractors call it, brutalism) at MIT are all visible in this perspective: through his splendid Wiesner Building concrete gateway, the Green Building to the left, the Landau Building to the right, and the Dreyfus Building in between.

from Copley Square to McDermott Court is important, so is his second axis, pointing as it does from the original Cambridgeport campus toward future development in and around Kendall Square in East Cambridge.

25 Wiesner Building
Center for Arts and Media Technology
I. M. Pei & Partners, 1984

The great concrete arch or gateway to Pei's architecture in McDermott Court—the Green, Dreyfus, and Landau buildings, all in the Heroic Concrete style—protrudes from the north facade of a fourth building by Pei in a very different style: the Wiesner Building, named after the president of MIT at that time and completed in 1984. The goal in this project was to design a building to house exhibit galleries, media laboratories, and performance spaces of MIT's Media Lab and List Visual Arts Center, both established that year, which would bring together traditional art forms and emerging media. (The Media Lab will be dealt with more fully in Walk Eight and the List Visual Art Center in Walk Seven.)

What such a building was supposed to look like was a sufficiently open question. An ambitious continuation of MIT's tradition of advanced research, "the building itself," Mark Jarzombek has written, "was an experiment, consolidating nine disparate arts programs from curricula grounded in science [and] combin[ing] traditional and vanguard media to create a world center of art and emerging technology." Which is why the great concrete arch is as important looking westward as eastward. It is Pei's own contribution, his own independent "work of art" in a building "radically conceived," in Morgan's words, "as a collaboration undertaken between Pei and a trio of artists—Richard Fleischer, who designed the plaza landscape, Scott Burton, whose balustrades and benches animate the sky-lit atrium lobby, and Kenneth Noland, whose five-story mural dominates the interior at first glance. Three color squares on the street facade are bisected by a blue band that circuits the building before surging through the interior like colored electrical impulses between the wall panels." This too is Noland's work.

Within, the effect is even more striking with light filtering all the way through the building from a skylight, brushing against the steel-paneled surface. The black rubber floors soften sound, and indeed there is something both elegant and grand in the overall effect.

The visitor must make a choice: which way to look through the Pei arch—eastward, toward Pei's bravura concrete architectural sculpture in McDermott Court, or westward, toward more than one rumor of the future.

26 McDermott Court II

Look eastward first; there is more to say in McDermott Court of MIT and Asia. Launching the career of the first-ever non-Western architect to achieve global stature takes on more meaning, perhaps, in the long trajectory of MIT's history in light of this headline of 2000 from the cover of *India Today*: "Boston Brahmin Jhumpa Lahiri: First Asian to Bag Pulitzer Award."

A Bengali Boston Brahmin? We have come full circle, have we not? Call it *Brahmin Global*, an interesting use of the term, odd-sounding at first, until one remembers that many great figures of modern India, "Tagore, Nehru, Gandhi," as Kumar Gupta points out in his *The Great Encounter*, "were among [Ralph Waldo] Emerson's admirers." Gandhi himself "published an extract from [Emerson's] *Over-Soul*, writing to his son in March 1909 ... that [Emerson] was 'a Western guru.'"

Evidence suggests that Holmes Sr. was in some sense Emerson's spokesman in the matter of the Boston Brahmin, which endows the concept with a whole different dimension. Emerson, whose "timelessness is persistent and striking," in Edward Hirsch's words, because of the "volcanic power, ... emotional depth, and searing intellectual intensity." Emerson, who has been called the first Boston Brahmin. The historian Peter Gibian, in his volume of the Cambridge Studies of American Literature and Culture series, stands behind that statement. Gibian notes that "a long March 1856 letter from Emerson to Holmes ... suggests that ... Emerson's notions about the 'American Scholar' ... may have had a significant impact on Holmes's later published description [four years afterward] of the Boston 'Brahmin.'" Indeed, two years before Holmes's famous *Atlantic Monthly* article, Emerson made a claim on his own behalf,

though slantwise, as it were, the significance of which many miss: "They know not well the subtle ways / I keep, and pass, and turn again....They reckon ill who leave me out; / when me they fly / I am the wings; / I am the doubter and the doubt; / And I the hymn the Brahmin sings."

The "Buddha of the West," as Holmes called Emerson, has today in this vein attracted the attention of Pico Iyer, an Oxford-born Englishman of Indian descent, because of just these resonances. "I would like to call myself a Transcendentalist," Iyer writes. "The higher form of globalism, I've always thought, is Emerson." It works both ways. If Iyer can be a Transcendentalist, Lahiri can be a Boston Brahmin.

Unlike the Chinese American Pei, the Indian American Jhumpa Lahiri was never a student at the Institute; her several graduate degrees are from Boston University. But the London-born Lahiri, who came to the United States at two years of age, is the daughter of Indian immigrants from West Bengal, and her subject has always been the Indian American experience, in which she was quick to observe (her father was an MIT librarian) that MIT played a central role. Her first novel, *The Namesake*, explored the life of a Bengali couple who immigrate to the United States so that the husband might study engineering at MIT, and MIT has figured in some way in every work of Lahiri's ever since. As much as Kurt Vonnegut in the 1960s, Lahiri in the American literature of the 2000s is firmly identified with MIT.

Does all that make her a Boston Brahmin? Of course, the backstory here can never be stressed enough. The star of the early twentieth-century Bengal Renaissance, the literary and artistic polymath Rabindranath Tagore, the first non-European to win a Nobel Prize, was himself influenced by Emerson, who comes up several times in his writings, according to University of Toronto PhD student in curriculum, teaching, and learning Sardar Anwarruddin. That scholar quotes other scholars as attesting to the fact that Emerson's presence became clearly visible during the period of the Bengal Renaissance; that "Rabindranath Tagore acknowledged that he was influenced by Emerson."

"Where are you from? Lahiri has never known how to answer this question satisfactorily," *India Today* reported. Pronouncing her a "Boston Brahmin" was its answer. Few American critics would have answered in a similar vein. Significantly, two critics who have are Siddhartha Deb in the *New York Times* ("Her fictional realm [is] that small, claustrophobic milieu of Bengali Hindus working research and academic jobs in New England, Boston Brahmins twice over") and Urmila Seshagiri in the *Los Angeles Review of Books* ("Lahiri's magisterial canvases portray the elusive, vexed promises that comprise the myths of the United States....Critics continue to overlook Lahiri's most significant literary achievement: a New England regionalism that contains the consciousness of a nation").

Pei's great gateway next to the Wiesner Building shows how inappropriate the *brutalist* label is for a concrete work that in this case is so lyrical and eloquent. Pei insisted on the arch, which not everyone liked, and designed it himself, foregoing his fee.

Most American scholars—for instance, Robert K. Miller Jr. and Stephen J. McNamee (*Inheritance and Wealth in America*), Betty Farrell (*Elite Families*), and Frederic C. Jaher (*The Urban Establishment*)—treat the Boston Brahmin as a historical figure primarily driven by the pursuit of wealth, social position, and political power. Far fewer (such as E. Digby Baltzell, author of *Puritan Boston and Quaker Philadelphia*) take seriously Holmes's view that the Brahmin leadership kept those ambitions in careful check.

Few Americans, in fact, use the term *Boston Brahmin* in any historically correct way anymore. When in 2004 John Kerry, a Yankee Brahmin descendant on his mother's side (his middle name is Forbes), ran for president, *Slate* senior editor Andy Bowers on March 1 wrote an article in which, while he acknowledged the emphasis originally put on their educational role by Holmes, seemed to confuse Brahmins with Yankees—all Boston Brahmins in the nineteenth century were Yankee, but all Yankees were by no means Brahmins—emphasizing not only Brahmin wealth but also Brahmin conservatism and narrowness, claiming that Brahmins were, for example, "well known for their hostility to the Irish and other immigrants." That was true of many prominent Yankees, but conspicuously not true of most leading Brahmins.

By contrast, in 2009 Chidanand Rajghatta in the *Times of India*—in an article entitled "America's 'Tech Brahmins'"—touched much more lightly on matters such as prejudice and wealth. Neither, any more than conservatism, was true of the high priest of the Boston Brahminate, Harvard president Charles W. Eliot. In doing so, and in ranging much more widely, Rajghatta offered Americans (Bostonians?) a much better history lesson:

> Indians who study or teach at Harvard or MIT (both in Boston) are often kidded about being Boston Brahmins....The expression is of much older vintage through. It was first used by...Oliver Wendell Holmes [Sr.] in 1860....Holmes...borrowed the idea of the pedagogic Brahmin from India, and saw [the New England tradition] as a "race of scholars" whose aptitude for learning was "congenital and hereditary." There was quite a bit of traffic in those days between Massachusetts and south and east India, so New Englanders must have been quite au courant with the term *Brahmin*....Holmes used the expression in the *Atlantic Monthly*, among its founders, besides Holmes, Ralph Waldo Emerson....Over time, Boston Brahmins produced generation after generation of scholars at Harvard, Yale, and other Ivy League schools, and dominated America's cultural and financial landscape.

There is no attempt to deny that many Brahmins became wealthy, but no suggestion that wealth was primary in defining the caste.

Holmes, dean of Harvard Medical School and thus one of the greater Gods of Copley Square and champion of the scientific spirit, is worth reading in the original in this matter. Dismissing the merely rich in America as rising and falling unedifyingly, he wrote in a piece significantly titled "The Professor's Story" in the *Atlantic Monthly* that there was indeed "in New England an aristocracy, if you choose to call it so, which has a far greater character of permanence [than the moneyed one]—It has grown to be a caste,—not in any odious sense,—but, by the reputation of the same influences, generation after generation....'The Brahmin Caste of New England' [is an] untitled aristocracy...which I am sure you will at once acknowledge in which aptitude of learning...[is] congenital and hereditary."

Holmes continued: "It is not fair to pit a few chosen families against the great multitude of those who are continually working their way up into the intellectual classes. The results which are habitually reached by hereditary training are occasionally brought about without it....So there are families which refine themselves into intellectual aptitude without having had much opportunity for intellectual acquirements....That is Nature's republicanism; thank God for it, but do not let it make you illogical....Our scholars come chiefly from a privileged order."

Holmes's New World definition of Boston Brahmins makes for an interesting comparison with India's Old World definition of Indian Brahmins. Recently, for example, trying to explain why so many of India's Nobel Prizes are won by Bengali and Tamil Nadu scientists, a distinguished Indian sociologist observed of Indian Brahmins that "cultural capital gets transmitted from generation to generation.... Brahmins have cultural capital....A poor Brahmin cannot be compared to a poor untouchable for the simple reason that the poverty of a Brahmin is only economic; but the poverty of an untouchable is both economic and cultural." Which is to say, the New England Brahmin exactly. Allowing for a certain Western elasticity. Rogers is a case not only of recruitment to the Boston Brahmin class by its leaders, but also of an almost Proustian act of self-invention. That sort of Holmesian Brahmin survives still, and the New England capital, needless to say, is the intellectual capital it is because of that sort. Boston has no monopoly on it, but it is so characteristic, historically, of the place that intellectuals from everywhere are drawn to it, as they are to all "centers of civilization," as Boston is described through its inclusion in the University of Oklahoma Press's celebrated series of volumes so titled.

Holmes went on to explain rich New England Brahmins by the fact that so great was the allure of the pulpit and the academy in Boston that successful merchants of Puritan and Patriot background tended to seek matrimonial alliances with intellectuals. Witness Fanny Appleton, the daughter of a textile magnate, marrying the poet Henry Wadsworth Longfellow, or businessman William Hathaway Forbes (a member of the MIT Corporation) marrying Emerson's daughter Edith. Thus the rich ruling class took on so pervasive a Brahmin character as to be properly called predominantly Brahmin.

Pertinent here is data from Paul Goodman's "Ethics and Enterprise": "The Boston elite formulated a set of beliefs that constituted a personal ethic and also defined its role in society as a republican aristocracy which stabilized as it transformed." He adds: "The highest prize was character. Trade was honorable because it sharpened one's faculties and trained one's character."

Consolidated by such alliances, the Brahmin ruling class, many compromises later, did not prove long-enduring. The founding of the Boston Symphony, for example, is certainly prefigured in the diaries of founder Henry Lee Higginson, in which the very wealthy banker detailed dismayingly his struggles with becoming a "money lover." The alliance between the academy and the pulpit on the one hand and the countinghouse on the other *was* fructifying and, so to speak, briefly brilliant. But for only a few generations before it began to flag and decline.

The Brahmin Ascendancy at its height must have been a grand thing to see. Its apogee was probably when "America's Headmaster," Eliot, a founding professor of MIT and the founding president of modern Harvard, publicly lectured the astounded brother of the German Kaiser, Prince Henry of Prussia, at a state dinner in Boston in 1902. His message was straightforward: if it wished to thrive, the German imperial family would do well to study the great families of Massachusetts. Arrogant? To be sure. But, as it turned out, the Hohenzollerns were dethroned and banished within two decades.

No such fate awaited Boston's great Brahmin families. Although the ruling class of pulpit and academy and countinghouse it had cooperated enthusiastically in contriving waned after a few generations, Holmes's learned and increasingly academic aristocracy not only survived but also waxed triumphant in the intellectual arena, much diversified and the stronger for it. When Oliver Wendell Holmes Jr., the son of the Brahmin namer, referred to Louis Brandeis as a Jewish Boston Brahmin, certainly by the time Whitehill implied that President Kennedy was an Irish Boston Brahmin (*Boston in the Age of John Fitzgerald Kennedy*, he titled his volume in the University of Oklahoma's Center of Civilization series), Brahmin had become a Holmesian honorific, as in its highest state it always had been.

Thus Pei and Lahiri, and people like lawyer Elliot Richardson and educator-philanthropist Ralph Lowell, continued to play their part for individual Yankees too. And of course Klaw's New Scientific Brahmins, of which Rogers and Louis Agassiz were a striking foreshadowing in the 1850s.

MIT's role in this discourse is especially significant, because of the great nineteenth-century Brahmin galaxy of Boston institutions, only the Museum of Fine Arts rivals MIT in the way the institutions cultivated a relationship with Asia, India particularly. In 1890, for example, the *Boston Daily Advertiser* noted how good was the effect when "Mr. Keshaw Malbar-Bhat of India, a student at MIT, [spoke] in Tremont Temple on Wednesday."

There was implicit in the Holmesian Brahminate a very real-world power comparable to that of the ruling class during the Brahmin Ascendancy. This has always been the case among the shapers of what I can only call MIT's foreign policy. Witness North Carolina State University historian Ross Bassett's "MIT-trained Swadeshi: MIT and Indian Nationalism, 1880–1947" in *Osiris*, in which Bassett explores this theme in Asian-American relations through a discussion of the establishment in India of institutes of technology. Evidence, as Bassett sees it, of "what an MIT education was and what it might mean for India," it was a key theme in Indian history just after independence from the British.

In "Exporting MIT," Stuart W. Leslie and Robert Kargon of Johns Hopkins wrote, "MIT redefined engineering education in the 1950s, then became a model and mentor to the rest of the world in the 1960s and 1970s....While acknowledging that the 'MIT Idea' might be difficult to define precisely, and even more difficult to emulate, its proponents agreed that they could identify 'the major characteristics.'... Predictably the 'MIT Idea' could be interpreted any number of ways....Whatever else the 'MIT Idea' may have implied...it meant national, indeed, international leadership." Therefore, "in planning for independence, Indian and British officials alike looked to MIT as the appropriate model."

The present-day exchange is just as mutual. Amar Gopal Bose, an Indian American entrepreneur and chairman of Bose Corporation (all music lovers know his name), in 2011 donated a majority of the company's nonvoting shares to MIT. He was the son of a Bengali revolutionary who fled from British-ruled Bengal in the 1920s, much as Rogers's father fled from British-ruled Ireland in the 1790s. One is also reminded of a 1977 graduate of the Indian Institute of Technology in Madras (now Chennai), Subra Suresh, who took his doctorate at MIT in 1981. Or indeed another Indian alumnus of MIT, Har Gobind Khorana, who shared the Nobel Prize for Medicine/Physiology in 1968.

The largest percentage (8.15 percent) of MIT's foreign-born faculty—who constitute about 40 percent of the total faculty—were born in India. Particularly in the School of Architecture and Planning and the School of Engineering, Indian-born faculty are the largest percentage of the foreign-born, almost 15 percent in the former and 10 percent in the latter, not to mention whatever number (for which there are no statistics) of faculty born in the United States who are of Indian descent. Consider, moreover, that in 1963, when Charles Correa, MIT MArch, designed the Gandhi Museum in Ahmedabad, MIT awarded a master's degree in engineering to Kanu Ramdas Gandhi, Mahatma Gandhi's grandson.

Finally, when in 2007 President Susan Hockfield led an MIT delegation to India, accompanying press releases stressed that "perhaps the most distinctive features of MIT as a research university" were its commitment to innovation and its "willingness to transcend disciplinary and national boundaries." It is an assertion Ross Bassett details significantly when he points out that the Institute's first foreign graduate, in 1874, was Asian, and that "over the long term Asia would be MIT's most important hinterland for foreign students."

The architectural reflection of MIT's early twentieth-century link with Asia is more Chinese than Indian, the literary reflection in the twenty-first century more Indian than Chinese. Taken together, both disclose not only what a global institution MIT has become, but also how global it has been from the beginning. If the Institute's international stature today reflects the rise of the United States to world power in the twentieth century, its long-standing culture as early as in the nineteenth century encompassed, unusually, a then all but completely subjected continent. It would empower MIT's further evolution in the twenty-first century, as America is said to pivot now toward Asia.

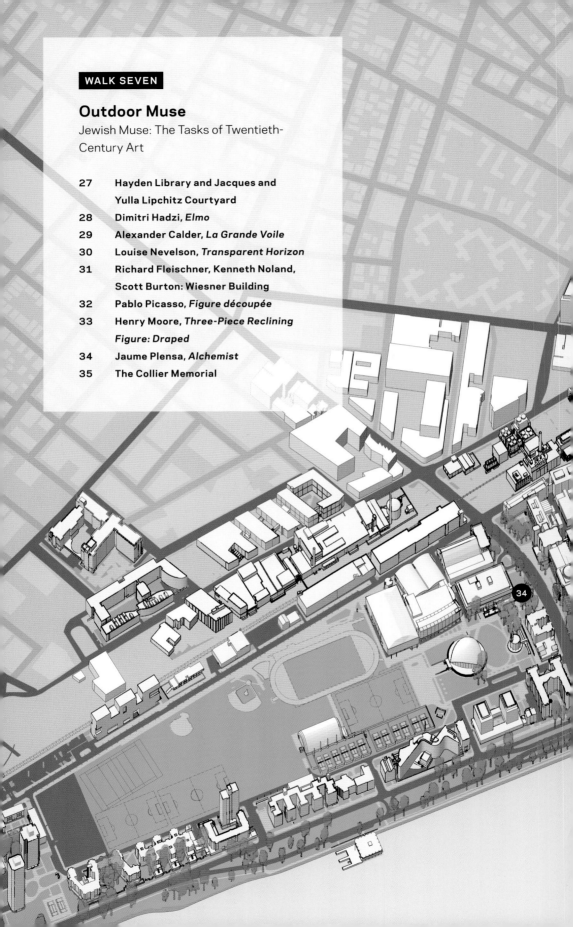

Outdoor Muse
Jewish Muse: The Tasks of Twentieth-Century Art

We saw in the last walk how McDermott Court's architecture discloses the Institute's long-standing links to Asia, and particularly to Chinese and Indian culture. The outdoor modern sculpture of the court, the nucleus from which the Institute's great collection spread throughout the campus, signals another aspect of MIT's historically cosmopolitan identity.

There are, in the first place, the Institute's important links with Jewish culture. "Edward H. Levi became the first Jewish president of a major university when he was inaugurated at the University of Chicago in 1968," according to *In the Golden Land* by Rita Simon. "Over the next three years Martin Myerson became president of the University of Pennsylvania; John Kemeny president of Dartmouth; and Jerome Wiesner president of MIT."

At the same time, MIT's modern art illustrates powerfully the artistic repercussions of the scientific advances of the twentieth century. The big dates most would fix on are the years 1905, when Einstein published his special theory of relativity, and 1919, when it was famously demonstrated.

Wiesner was a scientist—President Kennedy's science adviser—and, like Einstein, Jewish. Einstein was not uninterested in art either. The book to read is Arthur J. Miller's of 2002, *Einstein, Picasso: Space, Time, and the Beauty That Causes Havoc*. Or perhaps some poetry. One of the more striking verses by William Carlos Williams, the young modernist poet we encountered in "Part One" of this book in Portal Seven, who journeyed to Copley Square to find in MIT's Arlo Bates a worthy mentor, is "St. Francis Einstein of the Daffodils":

> April Einstein
> has come among the daffodils
> shouting that flowers and men
> were created
> relatively equal

It is fascinating in the light of that to explore McDermott Court, where the very American buildings—including a skyscraper, MIT's first and last in its central campus—are grouped in carefully organized spaces that reflect (as we saw in the last walk) ancient Chinese traditions. They are spaces made even more eloquent by outdoor sculpture, the most dramatic expression at MIT of its first Jewish president's most consistent cause, the humanities, and his most high-profile crusade, for modern art. "I happen to believe," Wiesner declared, according to Katy Kline, "that the arts are, in fact, useful knowledge, and that the imagination, the mental muscle of man's spirit, atrophies if not used."

Wiesner's rise at MIT occurred despite the fact that the Jewish experience in Boston grew increasingly troubled in the twentieth century. It had been triumphant in the late nineteenth-century era of Yankee Boston Brahmin *Hebrewphiles*—too strong a word, but there is none other—such as Harvard president Charles W. Eliot, symphony founder Henry Lee Higginson, and Trinity Church rector Phillips Brooks. At MIT, William Barton Rogers was known to have been conspicuously dismayed by prejudice against Jews, and so the fact that his hand-picked successor, Francis Walker, was a flagrant anti-Semite perhaps reflected less the Institute than the rest of Boston.

President Walker may have been "the most respected American economist at the beginning of the Progressive Era," as Princeton economist Thomas C. Leonard pronounced him, but he was also, so Leonard attests, "among the first to provide scientific respectability for race-based immigration restriction." Yet even Walker hired Louis Brandeis to teach business law at MIT, praising the work of the man who would go on to become the first Jew appointed to the US Supreme Court.

Furthermore, as we saw in my discussion of the Sacco-Vanzetti case in Walk Three, although anti-Jewish bigotry increased in America between the two world wars, MIT's president in the 1920s, Samuel Stratton, conspicuously did not emulate Harvard president John A. Lowell Jr.'s anti-Semitic program. It is true that Brandeis University historian Jonathan Sarna, writing in *The Jews of Boston*, recounts well-documented scholarly studies about how "MIT mathematicians worried about 'the tactical danger of having too large a proportion of the mathematical staff from the Jewish race.'" But other scholars at MIT felt able to organize actively in opposition to Nazi policies. Certainly no anti-Jewish sentiment interrupted Wiesner's rise at MIT. For almost thirty years before being offered the presidency, Wiesner was a leading figure in the Institute: professor of electrical engineering, director of the Research Laboratory of Electronics, then dean of the School of Science, then provost.

His close friend Elma Lewis, the African American artist, is quoted in *Jerry Wiesner: Scientist, Statesman, Humanist* as saying, "When Jerry was chosen to be president, he actually cried as he said to me, 'I never thought that a poor Jewish boy would get this opportunity.'" It says much about America then, and about their friendship, that Lewis replied, "The difference, Jerry, is that I *know* no black poor kid would ever get this opportunity, so you're ahead of the game."

That MIT was ahead of the game on several fronts is especially evident in and around McDermott Court, where stands the Hayden Memorial Library, with its magnificent sculpture court. A monument of the late 1940s to President Killian's partnership with Dean of Humanities and Social Sciences John E. Burchard, the library is a central landmark of Killian's postwar vision of MIT. It is the design of Ralph Walker, an MIT alumnus in architecture (1911) who designed a number of iconic New York office buildings, including what has been called the first set-back skyscraper and the first Art Deco skyscraper. The leading Walker scholar, the architectural historian Kathryn E. Holliday, finds that the "library lack[s] the spark of his earlier career," but some prefer this later manner. In its chaste, retiring way, this may be the most elegant building at MIT.

The burden of modern art in the twentieth century has never been expressed more movingly than in the evocative works of Jacques Lipchitz, an engineer and the leading Jewish sculptor of the period of the Holocaust and its aftermath. Hayden Library displays quite a number of works by the sculptor, whose wife was a close friend of former MIT president Jerome Wiesner.

27 The Hayden Memorial Library and Jacques and Yulla Lipchitz Sculpture Courtyard
Voorhees, Walker, Foley and Smith, 1946–51

Yulla Lipchitz was the widow of arguably the leading Jewish sculptor of his era, Jacques Lipchitz. He was a Lithuanian-born French and later American artist (Jacques was originally Jacob) who has also been called the greatest cubist sculptor. Yulla Lipchitz was a friend of President Wiesner, a well-known photographer, and a member of the Council for the Arts at MIT, which Wiesner founded as the artistic spearhead of his crusade. After Wiesner's death, Yulla Lipchitz gave the Institute the three sculptures by her husband in this courtyard in the late president's memory.

Jacques Lipchitz was no stranger to technology, having trained as an engineer before turning to sculpture. His work here seems to bridge so many cultural aspects, not least the fact that this youthful friend of Pablo Picasso and Constantin Brancusi brings to MIT more than a whiff of early twentieth-century Paris; Lipchitz was in the audience that famous night of the world premiere of Igor Stravinsky's *Rite of Spring* in 1913. But the sculptor was also witness to the horrors of history that followed. In an *MIT News* report of List Visual Arts Center, curator William Arning's commentary on Lipchitz's Hayden Library sculptures makes plain that visitors to the library are not spared the brutal details of the Jewish experience of the last century. To quote from the report, "Of the three sculptures by Lipchitz sited in the courtyard at the Hayden Memorial Library, Arning noted their evolving response to the Holocaust. 'In the 1920s, Lipchitz did pure, classic, good-as-it-gets cubism, studying form over time and space. After the Second World War, in *Hagar in the Desert*, he sought a shape and a voice for the horror wrought by Hitler. Later, in *Sacrifice III*, he found a way to express hope.'"

The story of how he did so is extraordinary. Since the destruction of the Jerusalem Temple in the year 70 CE, priestly sacrifice—either actual (with animals usually) or purely ritual (as in the Catholic Eucharist)—has been unknown to Judaism. Confronted by the Holocaust, Lipchitz felt bound to conceive *Sacrifice III* in such a context, as he recounted in an interview in 1961 with UCLA educator and director of its art gallery, Frederick S. Wight. Kline recounted it in her discussion of the work in her chapter titled "The Visual Arts at MIT: A History":

> After his escape from France in 1941, Lipchitz frequently turned to images of ancient Jewish sacrificial ceremonies, rooted in his history. *Sacrifice III*, modeled in 1949 and cast in bronze in 1957, was the final work of the series....The theme of ritual sacrifice was catalyzed by the fate of the Jews during World War II. Lipchitz remarked in an interview with Frederick S. Wight in 1961 that he depicted "a certain kind of ritual which we perform as a certain occasion. We are charging some kind of cock with all our sins, and we are offering the animal full of our sins for expiation." The 1943 image of this ritual was made "during the darkest moment of Hitler....I charged the animal...with all our sins and I prayed, it is like a real prayer, and afterward," Lipchitz affirmed, "I had to sacrifice the cock." The final sculpture is solemn, laden with the tragedy of the Holocaust.

The sculptor's widow probably felt that the Hayden Library courtyard was the right setting for these three important bronzes because the architecture has about it an astringent Art Moderne austerity, a very severe elegance. The building has absolutely no detail whatsoever. Moreover, although the new School of Humanities and Social Sciences, of which the library was the center, was not yet equally dedicated to the arts—which were added to its mandate and name in future years—from the very beginning the library housed an art gallery, the Hayden Gallery. Its director was one of the architects of the cubistic Alumni Swimming Pool, Herbert Beckwith. That gallery was described in the historical section of a 2011 arts report to the MIT faculty as "open[ing] in 1950 with a specific mandate to exhibit contemporary art, highly unusual in Boston at the time.... [Its] permanent collection was established in 1951.... Since there was no museum to house the works...the art was exhibited around campus. Thus began MIT's unique tradition of 'distributed art'...a distinctive aspect of MIT's creative landscape."

Many decades later, as *Boston Globe* critic Sebastian Smee has opined, "a Sunday stroll across MIT is actually a wonderful option for anyone interested in large-scale, boldly conceived modern and contemporary art," and while I can touch on only a few highlights of this collection here—the MIT art collection numbers more than a thousand objects—they include the ones that launched the program, beginning with Dimitri Hadzi's *Elmo (MIT)* (1961).

28 *Elmo (MIT)*
Dimitri Hadzi, 1961

"The first independent outdoor sculpture at the institute," Kline recounted, was "commissioned...from Dimitri Hadzi, his bronze *Elmo MIT*, installed on the Hayden Library plaza in 1961." Fourteen years a studio professor of visual and environmental studies at Harvard, Hadzi in the early 1960s scored great successes in New York and Rome and had three bronzes in the 1962 Venice Biennale. A version of *Elmo*, already in the collection of the Museum of Modern Art in New York, bigger than the one exhibited in Venice was made for a new building on the MIT campus.

Hadzi, a New York City–born Greek American, observed in an interview for the Archives of American Art years later, "This sculpture is...based on the helmet motif,...originated during the winter of 1957–58, when I spent several months preparing studies and models for an international competition for a memorial at the concentration camp at Auschwitz." This was a turning point in his life as an artist, Hadzi remembered in another interview for *Burlington Magazine* in 1965, "[when] I took up the war motifs that have predominated in my work [ever since].... In these sculptures I intend to evoke a complicated and often paradoxical range of meanings...protective as well as threatening."

These are somber thoughts, and the critic Peter Selz in his chapter of *Dimitri Hadzi* does not lighten the load much by insisting that *Elmo* invokes, yes, "the domes of Rome," where Hadzi was working then, but also "the cloud of the Atom bomb."

The most interesting art at MIT is the work of artists trained also as engineers. Alexander Calder, whose magnificent stabile, *La Grande Voile (The Big Sail),* is an example of such "aesthetic engineering," brilliantly sited in front of one of Pei's most eloquent concrete grids, that of the Green Building.

Nancy DuVergne Smith recounted in "MIT and the Atom Bomb" (for an MIT alumni tour to Los Alamos), the Manhattan Project was run and Presidents Roosevelt and Truman briefed by Vannevar Bush, MIT faculty member and founder of what would become Raytheon. Bush's influential essay on the aftermath of the project and emerging technologies appeared in the *Atlantic Monthly* in 1945.

Controversy about this will never cease, of course. When nine MIT faculty members who worked on the bomb shared their views in a 1985 Compton Lecture—"Forty Years After: MIT, Los Alamos, and the Bomb"—physicist Victor Weisskopf opened the lecture thus: "The scientists at Los Alamos believed that such powerful weapons would make war impossible. We were naive."

Hadzi was not, and his sculpture was well received. As Kline put it, *Elmo (MIT)* "immediately inspired" perhaps MIT's most iconic artwork of all time.

29   *La Grand Voile (The Big Sail)*
Alexander Calder, 1966

In his *Einstein, Picasso: Space, Time, and the Beauty That Causes Havoc*, Miller declares controversially that "Picasso's great breakthrough was to realize a connection between science, mathematics, technology, and art." At one point he brings up "the faceted breast on the right hand standing demoiselle" of Picasso's *Les Demoiselles d'Avignon*, asserting that this "'folded card' structure will be central to Picasso's subsequent experiments toward analytical cubism."

He identifies this structure as showing the influence of William James, via the ninety-odd sittings Gertrude Stein had with Picasso for her portrait. Stein had been James's student at Harvard from 1893 to 1897 (and something of a fixture at the art museum in Copley Square). Admitting that "the question is how much of James's visual experiments she actually discussed, and whether Picasso actually incorporated any of them into his art," Miller concludes that he certainly must have: "Picasso was undoubtedly struck by James's 'folded visual card' experiment."

James was a well-known presence in the 1890s and early 1900s in Copley Square, at the Boston end of the same modernist impulse that was sparking Picasso at the Paris end. James, in Miller's thesis, lifts somewhat the somberness of the artistic message in McDermott Court and its environs and points us toward the other aspect, the more scientific one. There is nothing here by Picasso—although MIT owns a later and rare work that will come up shortly—but there is an exceptional work by Alexander Calder, who was quite in Picasso's league, revolutionizing modern sculpture in the twentieth century. Vania Malloy explains in her article of 2013 on non-Euclidean space":

> [In the 1920s and 1930s] new concepts of modern physics fundamentally changed our understanding of time and space and had substantial philosophical implications which were absorbed by modern artists.... Seeking to internalize the developments of modern science within modern arts [were] prominent figures of the avant-garde

such as…Alexander Calder. Of particular interest…was the new concept of the fourth dimension, which in many ways revolutionized the arts. Importantly, its interpretation varied widely in the artistic community, ranging from a purely physical four-dimensional space, to a kinetic concept of space in which space and time are linked, to a metaphysical interest in a space that exists beyond the material realm.

Einstein was seen at the 1943 Calder exhibition at New York's Museum of Modern Art, transfixed, more than once by Calder's work. Years later, a senior curator at the Los Angeles County Modern Art Museum told the critic Hunter Drohojowska-Philp that Einstein reportedly "spent 45 minutes lost in thought while examining a Calder sculpture." Whether it was a mobile or a stabile we cannot be sure. Stabile artist Robert Harrison has written: "The most engaging aspect of Calder's sculpture [is] its interaction with space. Mobiles participate in lively dialogues with their own environs.…[S]tabiles enfolded and incorporate spatial volumes.…The stabiles, even though they are stationary, have an implied lyrical movement."

Composed of five intersecting steel forms of one curve and four planes, *La Grand Voile* (The Big Sail), all thirty-three tons of it, is poised delicately on four legs. Catherine Stratton, the wife of Julius Stratton (no relation to Samuel), remarked that its installation attracted wide attention: "Crowds of faculty and students watched the superb demonstration of aesthetic engineering" that transpired as the great sculpture was set in place before Pei's skyscraper. Calder, like Lipchitz, had trained as an engineer before turning to sculpture, and the dynamic interplay between art and engineering remains breathtaking a half century and more later.

Neither the Jewish aspect on the one hand nor the scientific on the other was anything but reinforced by the striking contrast between the extremes of the twentieth century: the horror of the Holocaust and the glory of Einstein's breakthrough, and what Picasso—and Calder—did with it. MIT, Kline makes a point of saying, was unique among the "museums and university galleries in the Greater Boston area, none of which at the time were actively collecting contemporary art." It was truly a case of "Einstein come among the daffodils."

30 *Transparent Horizon*
Louise Nevelson, 1975

A dark sensibility, its sources not so easily found, also suffuses this work, which has not been universally admired. One outraged admirer of this distinguished artist made the rebuttal: "*Transparent Horizon* is charged with dream, shadow, and mystery. Nevelson considers herself 'an architect of shadows' and maker of spectral shapes and primordial images.…*Transparent Horizons* stands like a totem: somber, enigmatic, and magical." It remains so today.

It was also one of the first works paid for by the MIT "per cent per art" policy established in 1968, providing that in every instance of construction or remodeling of

Louise Nevelson's *Transparent Horizon* projects a darker sensibility than Calder's. Nevelson spoke of herself as "an architect of shadows." This was one of the first works of MIT's notable collection of outdoor sculpture funded by the "per cent per art" program that mandates a certain percentage of all funding for construction on campus be dedicated to the fine arts.

a university building, a percentage of the funds must be set aside for artwork in and around the architecture. In an April 28, 1985, article in the *New York Times*, the critic John Russell wrote:

> It is difficult to exaggerate the near-frenzy of identification with which MIT in the 1960s was regarded by people in many parts of Europe....This was the place of all places, we thought, in which superior intellectual power could go to work....It would follow, as day follows night, that the new forms of art would be generated at MIT as soon as new kinds of artists became aware of its potential....MIT turned to the Modern movement in architecture in the late 1930s and early '40s with an openness of mind that was to turn it, over the next 30 and more years, into a living museum of the Modernist idiom.... Large-scale works began to be collected....By the 1960s, public art at MIT was getting to be a pioneering activity...with particular attention to sculptures by Picasso,...Louise Nevelson, Henry Moore.

Russell's article was headlined "Art Breathes Freely at MIT's New Center," by which was meant the new List Visual Arts Center. List succeeded the original Hayden Library art gallery, expanding its mission, which was already nationally known. In 1985 MIT's arts crusade reached perhaps its culmination in the design and erection of I. M. Pei's Wiesner Building, on the first floor of which the List Center, which curates MIT's public art collection, is located.

By then Wiesner was no longer president. It says a good deal for how strongly he identified with this modern art crusade and made it his own that he was not yet president during the early stages of the movement for art detailed here. Much credit is also due to Julius Stratton and Howard Johnson, who served successively as MIT presidents during the 1960s.

31   Wiesner Building

List Visual Arts Center
Settee, Bench, and Balustrade: Scott Burton, 1985
Upper Courtyard: Richard Fleischner, 1985

Here-There
Kenneth Noland, 1985

According to Wiesner's autobiography, this charismatic leader was determined to make MIT a home "in Boston for the best, the newest, often the most contemporary art," a cause in which Albert and Vera List, important modern art collectors, were happy to enroll. The couple established several List centers in the northeastern United States. Of these, according to Judith Champa, writing in *Art New England* in 2013, the one at MIT stands out as a place "where art and science are mutually informative, rather than competitive." MIT's List, Champa feels, is "a collecting and exhibiting museum without rival among contemporary institutions."

Curator Patricia Fuller's mission statement for the List says it all: its task is to be "continually updating the notion of what is art by adding new pieces that keep the dialogue alive on campus…an important part of the educational experience." Henry Moore was recruited, and soon, Picasso's work appeared as well on the MIT campus. It was the first large-scale monumental sculpture by that master in New England.

32 Figure découpée (Cut-Out Figure)
Pablo Picasso, 1975

It is something of a trek from McDermott Court to the Sloan School of Management at the extreme eastern end of MIT's East Campus, but going to see any work of Picasso is never a side trip, and MIT's rare cast-concrete sculpture of 1958 by the artist (cast five years later and installed in 1975) is worth the effort. Eleven feet high, *Figure découpée* (*Cut-Out Figure*) (representing a great bird, head and beak to the right, outstretched wings above) illustrates well the dialogue between painting, sculpture, and drawing that preoccupied Picasso all his life. This is one of three casts of the sculpture, and the only one in the United States. Writes Kline: "Picasso had long desired to make monumental sculptures; *betongraveure* [concrete engraving] made available to him a technique suited to the translation of his recent planar sculptures into durable materials on a monumental scale." Picasso entrusted the Norwegian artist Carl Nesjar, who introduced him to this process, "with the enlargement and fabrication of his sculpture in concrete. Their collaboration began in 1956.…In 1963 the first of three concrete casts of *Figure découpée* was made [from a wooden maquette by Picasso]."

33 Three-Piece Reclining Figure: Draped
Henry Moore, 1975

The Henry Moore work is in the other direction from McDermott Court, but much closer, just past Eastman Court to the west in Killian Court. We are again in the Great Court of MIT.

Howard Johnson, then president, recounted in his memoir, *Holding the Center*, how he and Wiesner (then provost) showed the British artist around the Great Court, hoping to secure from him a work for the collection. Moore was not overly enthusiastic at first, even though it was "a bright sunny day," but suddenly, "when he saw the place we had in mind, on the edge of DuPont Court, he became excited by the prospect." The result was *Three-Piece Reclining Figure: Draped*, a large bronze whose monumentality lends gravity to the grandeur of Bosworth's Great Court.

Thus has MIT begun to redeem itself for decades of ignoring its architect's repeated plea that his Great Court was designed to find its focus in sculpture. Bosworth specifically was imagining a statue of Minerva, the Roman goddess of wisdom, three stories high. He had "never so far succeeded in getting the MIT of Boston to spend a cent on sculpture," he wrote a friend. He wanted to give the

MIT commission to his friend Paul Manship, who later made the famous golden *Prometheus* of 1933 at New York's Rockefeller Center, a sculpture that makes clear the loss to MIT. To some extent the Moore figure makes up for it.

The establishment and evolution of the List Visual Arts Center, which maintains and curates all the Institute's outdoor sculpture, was really a reintroduction of a system used in the nineteenth century when MIT was first responsible for another famous outdoor collection of sculpture, the public art of the Back Bay. It all began in the controversy of the 1880s and 1890s over the issue of sculpture in Copley Square. An effort to place a statue of Christopher Columbus of very modest artistry—the statue has now been banished to the suburb of Revere—caused progressive forces to rally around the establishment of a Boston art commission that would ensure a higher quality of public art. Enter Arlo Bates, MIT senior professor of English. The story is told by the historian Thomas J. Brown in *Hope and Glory* (2009):

> Elites lashed out.... Arlo Bates satirized the corruption of public art in his novel, *The Philistines* (1889).... A lobbying campaign to...establish a Boston Art Commission, a state agency that entrusted the chief officers of the Museum of Fine Arts, the Boston Public Library, the Boston Society of Architects, and the Massachusetts Institute of Technology [architecture school], together with the city's mayor, with veto power over the placement of art works on city property. The trend-setting legislation contributed to a sharp decline in the number of [proposed] monuments.... In one of its most important decisions, for example, the Art Commission provided Copley Square with permanent protection.... No statues would be allowed.

34   *Alchemist*
Jaume Plensa, 2010

Continuing westward, this peregrination among outdoor sculpture in MIT's present-day campus reaches a meaningful conclusion in *Alchemist* by the Catalan sculptor Jaume Plensa. Given to MIT to mark its sesquicentennial in 2011, it stands, or rather sits, just opposite the great columned portico of the second Rogers Building. I like the commentary of an otherwise anonymous contributor by the name of Margaret to the website Art for Breakfast in October: "White, emotive, anonymous. Alchemy is the magical side of science.... Surrounding oneself in numbers until they become more than numbers—metaphors, surrogates of complex theories of the order of the universe. The symbols...become the form. From a distance the piece is of a thinking man, seated—but up close [the symbols] are an abstraction....The public is pulled

This giant bird is a rare example of the cast-concrete sculpture of Picasso. *Figure découpée (Cut-Out Figure)* of 1958 was cast five years later and installed in 1975. It was made from a wooden maquette by Picasso, and he entrusted Carl Nesjar with its enlargement and fabrication in concrete.

Henry Moore is widely regarded as the greatest twentieth-century sculptor. He confirmed the location for his work, *Three Piece Reclining Figure, Draped,* when President Johnson and Provost Jerome Wiesner showed him Killian Court.

into the mind of a scientist." She adds, "This piece specifically addresses the communication of mathematics—which at MIT is not only a science but an art."

35 Collier Memorial
J. Meejin Yoon, 2015

While this book was being written, it became clear that another outdoor sculptural work—a memorial to the MIT policeman who was shot dead by the Boston Marathon bombers during their escape on the night of April 18, 2013—must rightly be included. The artist is J. Meejin Yoon, principal of the Boston-based architectural firm Höweler + Yoon and an associate professor of architecture at the Institute.

Erected on the actual site where the officer's murder took place, the design is inspired, Yoon has said, by the "gesture of the open hand." The metaphor is as powerful as the design is evocative: representing, on the one hand strength—the five radial walls of solid American granite—and, on the other, thoughtfulness—the series of "reflection gardens" the walls define. These walls, eloquently pierced by openings that disclose significant campus vistas, meet in a central vaulted void intended as an intimate space for contemplation, shielded somewhat from the busy world. Therein is this inscription, cut into the granite: "In the line of duty, Sean Collier, April 18, 2013." The entire design stands, Yoon says, as a "physical form of strength and

Alchemist, the 2010 work of Catalan sculptor Jaume Plensa, was given to MIT to mark its sesquicentennial. The sculpture was placed on the lawn in front of the Student Center between the MIT Chapel and the portico of the second Rogers Building, MIT's main entrance today.

connectedness" reflective of Collier's own character. A window cut through the wall of the central arch focuses on the spot of the attack.

The structure is made of gray Virginia granite and is held together without concrete or steel reinforcing elements. The enormous stones of the walls serve as buttresses for the compression arch, the keystone weighing some seven tons. Compression arches have not been made since the Middle Ages. The engineering was the work of MIT professor John Ochsendorf, who, using sophisticated computer models, had to prove to skeptical authorities that there is a reason that the great vaults of the ancient cathedrals have lasted longer than all modern vaults. The structure represents the perfect coming together of art, architecture, and engineering.

The Collier Memorial by associate professor of architecture J. Meejin Yoon commemorates the murder of MIT police officer Sean Collier by the Boston Marathon bombers on the night of April 18, 2013.

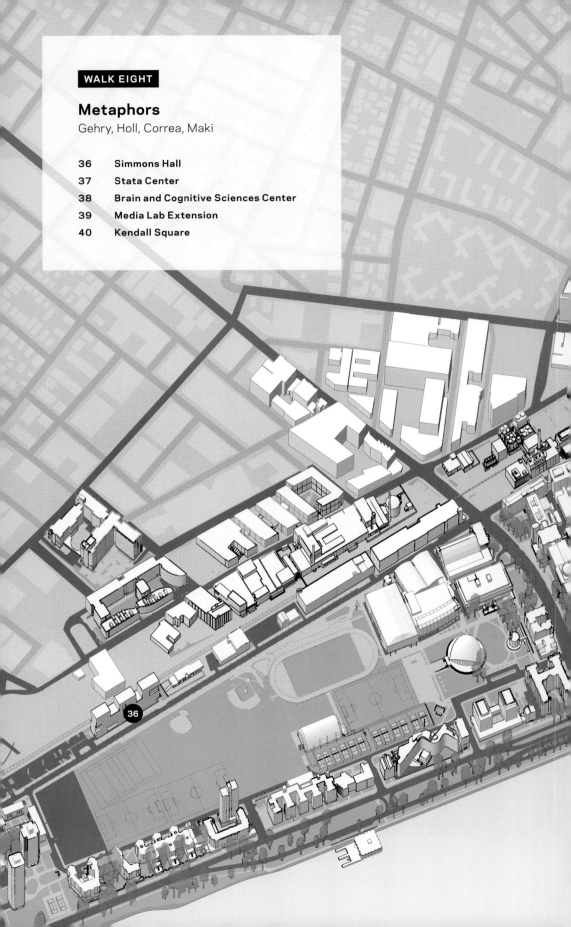

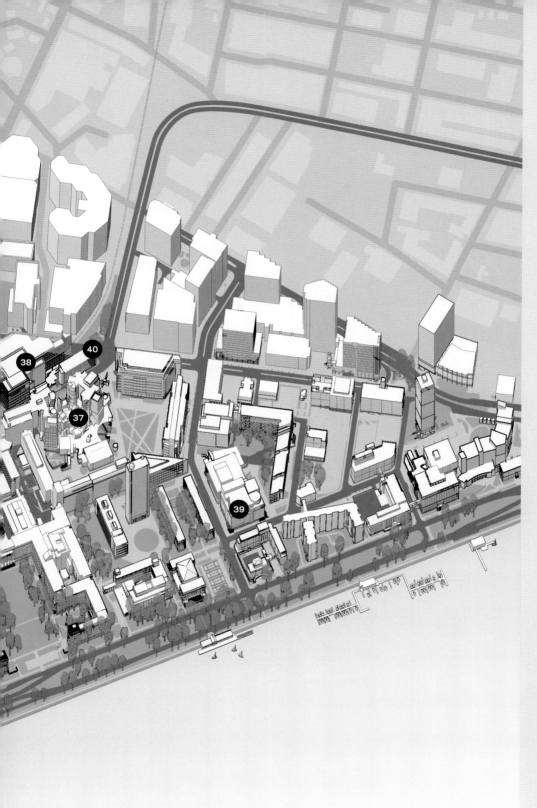

Metaphors

Gehry, Holl, Correa, Maki

"Frank Gehry is the most staggeringly talented architect this country has produced since Frank Lloyd Wright." So declared Ada Louise Huxtable, dean of American architecture critics, in the *Wall Street Journal* in her column of June 12, 2001. I wonder if among her readers that day was Charles Vest, who three years before had written in "The Path to Our Future" of his vision of the role architecture should play in positioning MIT for the twenty-first century.

Vest, MIT's president in the last decade of the twentieth century and nearly half of the first decade of the twenty-first, was famously open-minded and creative. According to then provost L. Rafael Reif, it was President Vest who, in his OpenCourseWare initiative, had "the simple, elegant, and unprecedented idea that MIT should make available all its course materials online to anyone in the world, for free." The same spirit drove Vest's MIT architectural vision at the dawn of the new century. "I believe that the buildings at this extraordinary university should be as diverse, forward-thinking, and audacious as the community they serve," he once said. "They should stand as a metaphor for the ingenuity at work inside them." Vest's idea, Mark Jarzombek has pointed out, was not entirely new in MIT's history. The design by I. M. Pei's office of the first Media Lab in 1984 was a fulcrum for the Institute's architecture with respect to a building's exterior design being an explicit reflection of its (interior) function.

Six years after Vest's essay and three years after Huxtable's declaration, the *CBS Evening News* on May 13, 2004, reported that "the campus of MIT is undergoing an astonishing transformation under the courageous leadership of university president 'Chuck' Vest." The star architect at the heart of the transformation: Frank Gehry. Vest confessed in his afterword to William J. Mitchell's *Imagining MIT*, "I knew in my heart I wanted to go with Frank Gehry."

The walk that follows is a sort of dialogue between president, architect, and critic. None of the chief players were natives of the area. All were drawn to New England's metropolis by its academic repute. Gehry, Canadian born and based in Los Angeles, was an alumnus of Los Angeles City College and the University of Southern California School of Architecture who later studied at Harvard's Graduate School of Design. MIT recruited its fifteenth president from the University of Michigan, where Vest, a West Virginia native trained as a mechanical engineer, had been educated and after a distinguished teaching career had turned to educational administration and risen to the rank of provost. The chief voice on the critical side, the *Boston Globe* architecture critic Robert Campbell, was from Buffalo, New York, and came to study at Harvard as an undergraduate. He received advanced degrees there and at Columbia in both architecture and journalism, teaching widely as well. He was also a published poet, at his height in this decade, as were Vest and Gehry. In 1996 he

Detractors railed against Steven Holl's Simmons Hall as the "Big Sponge on Campus," but it is arresting architecture, especially inside.

earned the Pulitzer Prize for criticism, only the third given for architectural criticism since Huxtable. It is the equivalent of the Pritzker Prize in architecture, which Gehry had won seven years earlier. By the late 1990s both men were in their sixties.

36 Simmons Hall

Steven Holl, 1999–2002

The transformation began to unfold on the West Campus in 1999–2002 with the design and erection of Simmons Hall. The work of the New York architect and Columbia professor Steven Holl, this building—ten stories high and 330 feet long—"was partly inspired, Holl has said, by the sponge he was bathing with one morning." So *Technology Review* reported in 2002. Susan Nasr explained: "When Steven Holl set out to design a dormitory that looked like a sponge, he wanted holes. Lots of holes. So, huge gaps that double as terraces separate Simmons Hall's three aluminum towers. Volcano-shaped lounges push through the floors. And thousands of two-foot-square windows indent the facade. The result is an undeniably sponge-like edifice." Pressed for a concept, the architect mentioned "porosity." The image proved captivating enough that Pagan Kennedy ventured in the *New York Times* the following year in a piece titled "Big Sponge on Campus": "The building is shot through with sinuous grottos that reach several stories high…. I gaze up at walls that curl like smoke towards a vast skylight. 'Wow. Wow. Wow,' is all I can say. Holl's inspiration

Simmons Hall
by Steven Holl,
interior

suddenly makes sense. We could be standing in a giant sea sponge. The room is way too gorgeous for undergrads. A supermodel named Inge should live here, posing against the undulating walls with a wine glass half-forgotten in her hands." For very different reasons—there are nine small windows (two feet by two feet) to every student room—many undergrads would have agreed with Kennedy.

Robert Campbell, like Kennedy, was impressed. Simmons, he wrote in his review, is "unlike any building you've ever seen…daring, serious, memorable." In 2005 it won the J. Harleston Parker Medal of the City of Boston and the Boston Society of Architects for the most beautiful building of its year of completion in Greater Boston. Some disagreed. But no one doubted it was the most daring. Vest was off to a good start. But the issue would really be pressed on the East Campus at Gehry's Stata Center when it opened in 2004. Stata's design astounded one and all, pro and con. All the more so because it replaced a legendary older building, about which people held such strong opinions that its replacement spawned a kind of generational civil war.

37   Ray and Maria Stata Center
Gehry Associates, 1998–2004

Garage start-ups are an American tradition. So are basement start-ups. The Wright Brothers come to mind; so do Disney, Amazon, Apple, and Google. All global empires now, all begun in garages. And the better for it, the tradition insists. Spartan works; grunge inspires.

MIT itself, of course, did not begin in a garage, nor a basement, but—after a brief stay in a prosperous downtown Boston commercial building—in an elegant, stately building by one of Boston's first Paris-trained architects on the north-east-corner block of what would become Copley Square. Myran Pierce reported in his 1903 article in *Technology Review* that "an eminent French architect has pronounced [the first Rogers Building] the finest building in Boston," by no means eclipsed as the Acropolis developed. Yet no one, I think, has yet suggested that MIT's elegance in 1874 inspired Alexander Graham Bell's creativity. It was the lab equipment Bell craved, but it was the building's stately exterior that first struck the inventor. It is a mystery why so many (philistines?) think this way, privileging ugliness, so wary of the power of beauty. But tell that to the disciples of MIT's Building 20, a "temporary" structure erected during World War II when resources and time were short, and the need for space urgent in the Allied crusade.

It was a three-story, wood-frame, gray, asbestos-shingled "plywood palace" whose ramshackle grimness, to hear these disciples talk, not only reflected the true, practical, Spartan MIT aesthetic (they were conveniently forgetting Copley Square and the Great White City on the Charles). Its inhabitants succeeded in "the creation of radar, the construction of the world's first atomic clock,…the start of the modern school of linguistics…[and the building of] one of the earliest atomic particle accelerators." World War II may have been won in Building 20, the subject

Ray and Maria Stata Center by Frank Gehry, exterior (OPPOSITE), interior (ABOVE)

of this much-quoted article of 1998 in the *New York Times* by Philip Hilts: "The British under siege…shipped over the 'magnetron,' a device that could produce just the needed waves. The first radar image produced from the British machine and the ensuing American research was obtained from the roof [meaning the pinnacle of the dome] of the Christian Science temple across the Charles River. They conveyed the good news to their colleagues across the Atlantic by inserting a single cryptic sentence into a commercial short wave broadcast: 'We have seen Mary Baker Eddy with one eye.'"

Understandable that such a building, forced like its occupants to urgent tasks in wartime, would become legendary, a veritable "magic incubator." Magic, however, is not usually so grim, nor the buildings the object of such dark romance. No more, declared Charles Vest. Not in peacetime at the dawn of the twenty-first century. As he put it in his afterword to *Imagining MIT*, his purpose was to "transform" the Institute's campus. "Without diminishing the intensity and rigor," wrote Vest, he was determined "to make MIT a brighter place." Building 20 was not a bright place. Instead Vest saw visions of Frank Gehry's new Guggenheim Museum Bilbao in Spain. In his afterword, he was candid:

> The selection of Frank Gehry to design a new home for computer sciences, the Ray and Maria Stata Center, was pivotal. Some twenty architects were invited to propose designs.…I met with the [selection] committee when it was ready.…Lo and behold, there was a 50/50 split between the architects.…I wanted to go with Frank Gehry, because we had to do something big, bold, exciting, and different to lead into the new century. I resolved that if I could convince Bill [Dickson, who had led MIT construction almost since he had graduated] that this was the thing to do, I would know that it was the right decision. We chatted for a while, and I told Bill my thinking. "Well, let me tell you something. When our chapel was designed by Eero Saarinen, it was considered so radical that the sponsoring foundation pulled its funding from it. Well, look at how proud we are of it today." I said, "You make the call."

The result was all Vest could have wanted, and a good deal more he surely didn't. Boston University president John Silber, whose sole architectural credential seems to be that his father was said to have been an architect, took the extraordinary step of making the Stata Center a centerpiece—and the cover photo—of his book *Architecture of the Absurd*, pronouncing it a "disaster." No more encouraging was William Morgan, an architectural historian writing in the Hartford, Connecticut, *Courant*: "[Stata's] design has as much staying power as a Mickey Mouse telephone." Even the *New York Times* felt bound to point out that many "likened [Stata's] jumble of yellow and white aluminum, polished stainless steel, and orange brick towers, tubes, cubes, and cones to a Disney animation." It only sounds like a compliment *now*.

Even Campbell seemed to rise to the bait, writing at various times of Stata's "jazzy and cartoonish aesthetic" and declaring that "it looked like it had been hit by an earthquake. Its parts tilt and crash drunkenly into one another." In the same column he described the building's aesthetic as "manic and delirious." These judgments were invariably tempered, however, by a much more ambiguous context, which on the one hand acknowledged the widely askew aspects of the design, but on the other remained interested in what it all might mean.

This ambiguity, if that's the right word, continued in Campbell's year-end review of world architecture in 2004. Although he gave Stata pride of place everywhere, he also noted an important aspect of its origins: "Boston had its Stata Center at MIT," he wrote, going on to remark pointedly how it reflected that year's Venice Biennale's emphasis on buildings "made possible by the computer," before moving on to other buildings in London and New York. But he also wrote in his column of April 25 that year: "The Stata is an act of serious architecture. Coming off two world triumphs—the Guggenheim Museum in Bilbao, Spain, and the new Disney Hall in Los Angeles, Gehry, 75 and a Pritzker Prize winner, is riding higher than any other architect of his generation....Everything looks improvised [at Stata], as if thrown up at the last minute. That's the point. The Stata's appearance is a metaphor for the freedom, daring, and creativity of the research that's supposed to occur inside it."

Vest's perspective exactly, practically word for word. Indeed, when Campbell first encountered Vest's concept in 2002—that each of MIT's buildings "should stand as a metaphor for the ingenuity at work inside them"—the *Globe* critic found it "a compelling concept." Campbell's 2004 review of the completed Stata was in a similar vein. But a year later came the turn: Now he found Vest's concept "worrisome" and within a paragraph escalated to a strident and personal condemnation. "To me... Vest's premise is an absurd fallacy."

Vest retired from the presidency in 2005, and—not least because of the economic crash—MIT pulled back on *starchitecture*, as it was coming to be called. But Campbell clearly remained fixed on Vest's concept, returning to it with unusual vehemence as late as 2011, when he wrote in a review praising the sort of "background building" that had returned to fashion at MIT. "Years ago, when Stata and Simmons were being created, MIT's president was Charles Vest. Vest made a statement I'll never forget. Said he"—and then Campbell repeated what had by then become Vest's mantra about the building as metaphor, concluding by asking: "Should a building really be an audacious metaphor? I don't think many would claim that today." He then went so far as to caricature Vest's concept: "Put it this way: Should Albert Einstein have worn an inventive hat, one that could stand as an audacious metaphor for the ingenuity at work inside his brain?" His answer was to prefer the sort of building "that's here to do its job rather than flaunt its aesthetics."

The architect's efforts to weigh in on the debate, it should be noted, very much echoed Vest's ideas. "What I want is to make some kind of magic and take people someplace they've never been before," Gehry wrote in his part of *Building Stata*, elaborating:

> The building reflects the culture of the people inside it. They are all going to be colliding with each other intellectually over time. That's what it's all about....I am happy that this

building expresses what's going on inside. My interpretation is that it reflects the different groups, the collision of ideas, the energy of people and ideas. They each have their
own sorts of vectors and they will all be colliding with each other, some accidentally
and some by contrivance. That's what will lead to the breakthroughs and the positive
results. I think that's really going to work. I can't wait to see everybody in there—to see
the beehive buzzing.

I wonder if that way of putting it—more down-to-earth and practical—did
not strike a chord with Campbell, who, before Stata was completed, reviewed in
2003 Gehry's other major new work of the period, his spectacular Disney Hall in Los
Angeles. There were no complaints of flaunting its aesthetics. Instead, Campbell
found Disney Hall "unforgettable" and "flabbergasting," comparing it to the Sydney
Opera House. And the next year, he had seemingly resolved the Building 20 / Stata
issue as well: "Building 20's greatness was its absence of architecture," he wrote
on April 18. "The Stata Center is the opposite. It tries to do with architecture what
Building 20 did by not having any."

By 2007 Vest and Gehry had both moved on, and Campbell was very personal
in his praise of Stata: "Stata is an amazing and, on the whole, excitingly successful
place. For me, every visit was a spatial, visual, and social pleasure. Whatever you
think of this building's aesthetics, it is doing its job," Campbell asserted, reiterating
his highest praise of the moment.

If President Vest's chief architectural adviser, Dean William J. Mitchell, is to
be believed, there was one aspect of what Stata was expected to stand for that
Campbell might have taken more alarm at than worrisome presidential metaphors.
It was an aspect that was not made much of at the time of the building's design and
erection, but that emerged after its completion in Mitchell's *Imagining MIT*, his record
of his role in the MIT building program. Even then Mitchell chose his words carefully
when he asserted that for some "ideologically attuned urbanists"—including, one
suspects, himself; why else raise the issue at all?—"Stata's intricacies, surprises,
and refusal of rigid systems are…*a standing rebuke* [emphasis added] to the Main
Group's too easy assumption of the architectural language of authoritarian power,
as it was deployed from Versailles to Albert Speer."

To associate Bosworth's serene and regal Main Group with Speer's strident
Nazi aesthetic is absurd, rooted in a total misunderstanding of the neoclassicism
of the Great White City; this sort of attitude is obnoxious. We all know what author
Kenneth Clark meant when he declared in *Civilisation* that he "wonder[ed] if a single
thought that has helped forward the human spirit has ever been conceived or written
down in an enormous room"—and proceeded to walk the length of Versailles's Hall of
Mirrors. But note Lord Clark's addendum: "Except, perhaps, in the reading room of
the British Museum." Significant exception. Does anyone think the Lincoln Memorial
stands for "authoritarian power"? Or the Boston Public Library?

Mitchell's sly association of Hitler's iconic architect with MIT's iconic architect
is particularly dangerous because Bosworth's work, and the work of Bulfinch and

ABOVE: "Frank Gehry," Ada Louise Huxtable once wrote, "is the most staggeringly talented architect this country has produced since Frank Lloyd Wright," and Gehry's Stata Center is certainly MIT's most important architecture of our own era. These photos offer several bold, even provocative, perspectives.

Jefferson and McKim regarded as standing behind it, is more widely admired today for its flexibility than for its stately beauty. That smacks, of course, of "faint praise" and has particular pertinence in the area of historic preservation at MIT. One of the most captivating aspects of Stata, for example, is "Student Street," an imaginative twenty-first-century version of Bosworth's Infinite Corridor of 1916, Stata being a much more open design that reflects student opinion that closed doors are isolating. Behold, the 1916 original has been in places remodeled to reflect the twenty-first-century version. But care must be taken to preserve significant stretches of the original, the character of which remains compelling—especially in the way the parade of doors blurs departmental distinctions in favor of research-oriented groups.

38   MIT Brain and Cognitive Sciences Complex
Charles Correa, lead designer; Goody, Clancy and Associates, laboratory and research space designer, 2003–5

All the time these issues were roiling around MIT and beyond, across the street a hugely different building—in every way a protest against the Stata Center, according to Gehry's foes—was rising higher and higher: the Brain and Cognitive Sciences Complex. The largest neuroscience research center in the world, it is in many ways the heart of the East Campus, which is dominated by biotechnology and the life sciences. The dedication of this complex in 2005, the year after Stata's opening, coincided with the appointment of a new MIT president, Susan Hockfield, also a professor of neuroscience in the Department of Brain and Cognitive Sciences. She was the first biologist to head an institution better known for leadership in the physical sciences—engineering, electronics, physics, and chemistry. Her appointment signaled the increasing importance of biomedical research.

Equally important in the long sweep of MIT's history, Hockfield was also the first woman to serve as president. Vest had launched a landmark "Study on the Status of Women Faculty in Science at MIT" in 1998, which prompted the Institute at the time of his death in 2013 to issue an unusually frank exposition of Vest's handling of this issue, an exposition that Emma Savage Rogers and Ellen Swallow Richards would doubtless have been interested to read: "The public examination of MIT's troubled history on issues relating to gender equity ultimately proved a high point of [Vest's] tenure. In 1998 Vest forthrightly acknowledged serious gender-equity problems…[and] supported corrective measures to address long-standing imbalances." His action stimulated action across the country, and resulted at MIT in: the first woman head of the School of Science, the university's first five female vice presidents, and in a very real sense, surely, Vest's successor. Nor was Vest slow in other areas of diversity: he appointed the first African American chancellor in the Institute's history.

To design the new Brain and Cognitive Sciences Complex, Vest had turned to another Asian alumnus of MIT, a 1955 graduate of MIT's School of Architecture

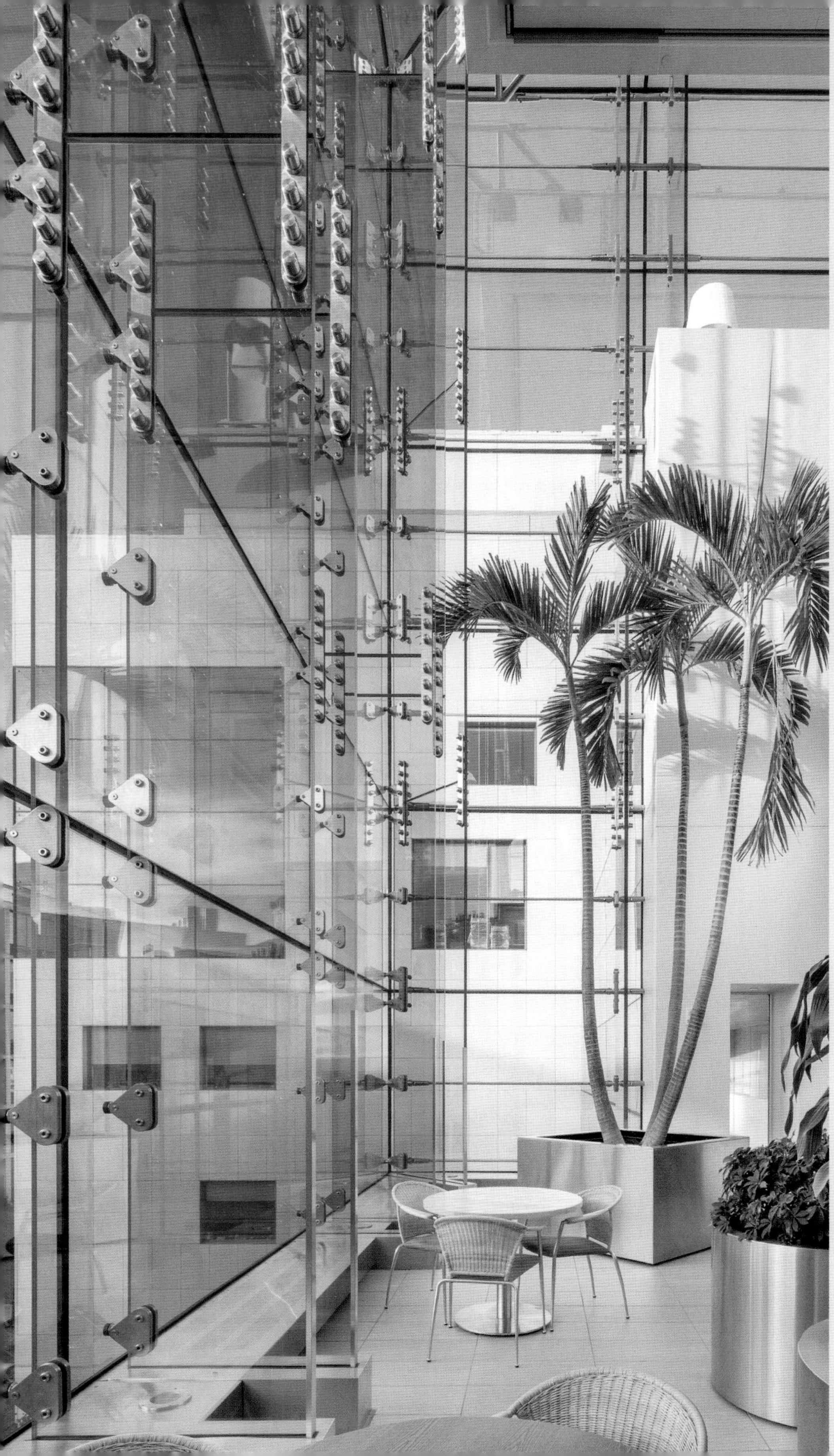

and Planning, Charles Correa. After his studies in the United States, Correa did not become an American citizen but returned to India, where he began his practice in 1958, subsequently becoming India's greatest living architect. Mumbai-based, he has done most of his work in India. But his reputation is worldwide, and some sense of his work emerges in this 2014 online report of his appearance before a group of Indian architects:

> "Architecture should speak of its time and place but yearn for timeliness."…Architect's Guild in Marigalore on Thursday offered thunderous applause to Correa.…His design grandeur is visibly evident in [the] Mahatma Gandhi Memorial Museum, Mumbai's popular Kanchanjunga Apartments, Jaipur's Jawahar Kala Kendra, Boston's Brain and Cognitive Science Center [sic], and the ever popular Champalimaud Centre for the Unknown, Lisbon, Portugal. [Correa also believes that] "architecture should be city-centric."…He also presented a slide show, highlighting the evolution of architecture. He advised budding architects to derive ideas from ancient monuments.

ABOVE AND PREVIOUS: Charles Correa's Brain and Cognitive Sciences Complex is the largest neuroscience research center in the world. Standing across Vassar Street from the Stata Center, the buildings are described by one critic as respectively "like a cop and a drunk," insisting this dialogue between "a clown and straight man" was "as close as architecture gets to street theater."

To this it is interesting to add that in an interview in *Design and Architecture* in May 2013, when asked about his years at MIT, Correa remembered chiefly that "we learnt principles there, we went back to Louis Sullivan." It is one of the few times that the most illustrious alumnus of MIT architecture, too often forgotten today, has been cited by a modern master.

In many ways more traditional than Vest, Gehry, or Campbell, Correa insists that "just as there is writing and there is architecture, there is construction and then there is architecture," and it is hard to imagine him in any situation privileging Building 20's aesthetic or lack of same. In his writings on the MIT science complex, Campbell seized at once on the striking contrast with the Stata Center. "The two buildings, both of them huge, face each other [across Vassar Street] like a cop and a drunk," he wrote in as memorable a line as he has ever composed. Nor could he help saying it again, noting that Correa's complex was as "logical and understated as Stata is manic and delirious." And then again: the game it sets up, the classic one of "clown and straight man," the *Globe*'s critic asserted, was "as close as architecture gets to street theater." A face-off of such dimensions between two of the world's greatest contemporary architects is bound to compel thought, all the more so in the face of the fourth and final of MIT's foursome just down the street, a building that is arguably the most thought provoking of them all.

39 Media Lab Extension
Fumihiko Maki, 2007–10

"There was no competition, no string of interviews.... [The] dean of the School of Architecture and Planning,... acting [for] MIT President Charles Vest, went directly to Maki and asked if he'd do it." That's Fumihiko Maki, the legendary Pritzker Prize–winning Japanese architect. Educated at the University of Tokyo and then trained in architecture at the Cranbrook Academy in Michigan and the Harvard Graduate School of Design, from which he received his master's in 1954, Maki practiced and taught in America—for SOM in New York and Sert Jackson in Boston—then returned to Japan in the 1960s and has been based there ever since. In 2010, when this MIT commission was completed, he was eighty-two.

According to the School of Architecture and Planning's online report of a conference held at the time of the complex's opening, at Maki's first meeting about the project at MIT in 1998, he emphasized the effect of two things on his thinking: the spectacular views of Boston he remembered from a reception he once attended while at Harvard (in the neighborhood of the MIT complex he was now to design), and "the student-made mezzanines in the MIT architecture department of the 1970s, a lively complex of joyously crude ad hoc structures. Maki said he aimed for a similar scenario, but elegant, without the slum-like quality of those grass-roots rabbit warrens."

It was another variation on the theme of Building 20, and this time the only presidential guidance was Hockfield's emphatic injunction that "this building cannot

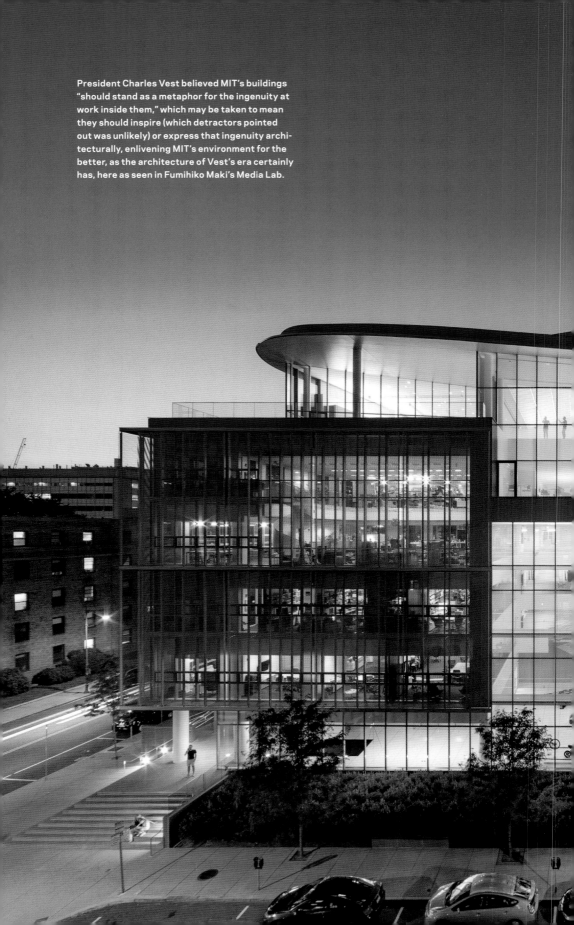

President Charles Vest believed MIT's buildings "should stand as a metaphor for the ingenuity at work inside them," which may be taken to mean they should inspire (which detractors pointed out was unlikely) or express that ingenuity architecturally, enlivening MIT's environment for the better, as the architecture of Vest's era certainly has, here as seen in Fumihiko Maki's Media Lab.

A graduate of Harvard's Graduate School of Design, Fumihiko Maki was in his late seventies when he designed the Media Lab building in 2007, and in his early eighties when he completed it in 2010. "This delicate white-and-silver butterfly of a building," in the words of *Boston Globe* architecture critic Robert Campbell, is certainly the most exquisite architecture at MIT.

leak." Campbell was thus finally incited to address the question that had haunted MIT's entire era of "starchitects," a decade-long project that he acknowledged was "probably bigger and riskier than anything of its kind in the nation today." It was a question that more than acknowledged the importance of MIT's achievement, not to mention that of Maki, who endowed the Institute with a masterpiece to crown its decade of building. Campbell framed his question very provocatively: "What happens when some of the world's messiest occupants move into the world's most exquisite building?"

Tech people are more at home, many think, in a mess—in basements and garages and ramshackle structures such as Building 20. Were MIT's architects casting too many pearls, so to speak, in an effort to yank the techies out of "grandmother's attic"—Campbell's words—into elegant atria, spacious labs, and rooftop terraces?

Insofar as Maki's building was concerned, its beauty trumped everything, bringing out the poet in Campbell. In 2009 he writes: "Almost everything in the building's exterior is white. You sometimes feel, as daylight sifts through the transparent walls, that you've been caught in a magical snowstorm." Four years later, he adds a variation on the same theme: "The Media Lab is magical. Wrapped in glass and transparent metal mesh, it appears, in certain kinds of light, to be made entirely of misty air." He waxes poetic over "this delicate white-and-silver butterfly of a building."

But what about the messy people? One has to read closely, as Campbell trod carefully. "[The Media Lab] is the classic marriage of form and content," he wrote in 2009, noting it was "an exercise in transparency.... It's in the atrium spaces—there are two—that the building really sings.... It's as spatially exciting as any modern building I know. But beyond that, it serves the purpose of teasing researchers to explore and peek everywhere." The operative word is "teasing." In 2013, "The windowed lab spaces seem to lock eyes with one another across an open atrium, thus becoming a metaphor for the hope that each researcher is aware of what the others are up to."

In a very real sense there is no resolution here. If Einstein and Michelangelo did not do their work in buildings that inspired them or expressed their ideas, Plato, by contrast, seems to have been much activated by the Athenian Stoa. Besides, one very important element in all this is quite new. Creativity, as we have come to understand it in modern times, is a new phenomenon in human history: more about groups than individuals, more social than solitary, interactive, and above all self-conscious, driven by whatever ideas about "innovation" spark youthful ambition. In this discourse architecture naturally plays its own, more active, role. It's another example of inventing the future.

A little history. "Since its founding...the Massachusetts Institute of Technology... nurtured close relationships with the region's industrial concerns. In 1886, MIT graduate Arthur D. Little established the first 'industrial consulting' firm in Boston.... In 1922, MIT engineering professor Vannevar Bush founded the American Appliance Company, which produced refrigerators in Kendall Square....The small company eventually became Raytheon," Elihu Rubin wrote in *Insuring the City: The Prudential Center and the Postwar Urban Landscape*. "Bush was crucial to the establishment of President Franklin D. Roosevelt's National Defense Research Committee on the eve of World War II."

More recently, an example of how Kendall is evolving is the new research center dedicated three years after Maki's building. It is modest enough architecturally, but hugely significant to the future of MIT: five floors of research labs at 400 Technology Square for the Ragon Institute of the Massachusetts General Hospital, MIT, and Harvard, dedicated in 2013 by the heads of those three institutions.

MIT President L. Rafael Reif, writing in the *Boston Globe* later that year, filled in the backstory, remarking that while William Barton Rogers moved to Boston in the first place because of its "knowledge-seeking" character and that the region was indeed famous for "great colleges, universities, and hospitals," there was today a whole new dimension to the matter. "We have not had anything," Reif continued, "like today's innovation economy. A place long admired for its educational excellence has branched out in exciting ways. We now hear Greater Boston called 'the bio-tech capital of the world.'"

The place Ragon chose to settle in, Technology Square, was brought into being on the northern edge of Kendall Square by President Killian in 1960 through Cabot, Cabot & Forbes, the venerable Boston developers, of which the prominent MIT alumnus and benefactor Edward H. Linde was an official. Then in 1978 Boston Properties, cofounded by Linde and Mortimer Zuckerman, was selected by the Cambridge Redevelopment Authority to mastermind the overall Kendall Square area: "[Linde] and Zuckerman went on to redevelop much of East Cambridge into the area now known as Kendall Square, home," the *Boston Globe* suggested, "to one of the world's deepest supplies of brain power and innovation."

Andrew Lo, a professor at the MIT Sloan School of Management, and Tom Rutledge, a Sloan graduate, go further, pointing out in 2014 in the same newspaper that "Boston might not be in the global top 10 in population, wealth, or industry, but it has a strong claim to being the innovation capital of the world in asset management, life sciences and medicine, technology, and other R&D-intensive disciplines. Leaders around the globe know that. In fact, many of them proudly display diplomas from Boston-area institutions in their offices."

Visitors today would do well to focus on what might be called the ever-lengthening vista across Longfellow Bridge at Kendall's southern edge. The most immediate view across the bridge, of Massachusetts General Hospital at Charles

This aerial photograph by David L. Ryan shows a powerful axis of MIT's historical development: MIT's Kendall Square in the foreground, the Massachusetts General Hospital in the middle, Boston's Financial District in the distance, and beyond that Boston Harbor (and now, Logan International Airport).

Circle, speaks to the example of the Ragon Center. According to the MIT News Office, the Ragon Center came to Kendall because it is "within a short bus or subway ride of some of some of the largest research hospitals in the world," not just Massachusetts General at bridge's end, but also those of the Longwood area around the Back Bay Fens. Then beyond the vista across the bridge are the towers of the downtown Government Center, where the JFK Federal Building is a symbol of the source—the National Institutes of Health—from which most of MIT's research support comes today. Beyond that view, the longest vista of all and the oldest for MIT is toward the densely clustered skyscrapers of the downtown Financial District overlooking Boston Harbor, which has fueled MIT for its entire history.

All the while—have you noticed it?—MIT's campus has been inching closer and closer to the sea, to Boston Harbor, where the dominant feature today is no longer the crowded wharves and piers of Victorian times but the runways and terminals of Logan International Airport. People forget that the huge railroad yards adjoining Copley Square and Back Bay Station in the Victorian era made the New World Acropolis a hub of transcontinental train traffic. MIT has always sought these kinds of portals, at first national, then—very quickly—global. Once it was the clipper ship; today it is the direct flight from Logan to Beijing, Dubai, or Istanbul.

The reader will recall here our second portal in "Part One"—"The Boston Money Tree"—in which the visitor was introduced to MIT's Hart Gallery at 77 Massachusetts Avenue. There we found a model of that great example of nineteenth-century New England entrepreneurship, the clipper ship, specifically the model of the legendary *Flying Cloud*, built in East Boston by Donald McKay. Remember how Russell B. Adams begins MIT's history not in 1861 but in 1790, in the triumphant return to Boston Harbor from "its great voyage of merchant adventure," and how Adams insisted that when MIT was founded, the very "spirit of Boston" came to be invested in the young Institute. And what a symbol of that Adams found in what I have been calling the Great White City on the Charles. He continued:

> From the start MIT had been generously supported by Boston's merchant and capitalist grandees, who saw the value of hard-nosed technical education in a rapidly changing world....As MIT became a national institution, support poured in [more widely, finally, from] George Eastman...[whose gift to build the new campus on the Charles River Basin] came to some $20 million [in 1912]. For the nation, for the world, and for Boston, this support for technology would yield a fruitful harvest....When Boston's decades of maritime and industrial prosperity had receded into dim memory, MIT would become a catalyst....While much of Boston slept [in the first half of the twentieth century], its spirit of earlier days was sustained in the classrooms and laboratories of the Massachusetts Institute of Technology, ready to rise again.

Lest this seem an unduly romantic interpretation of MIT's history, remember that the last building considered here—the Brain and Cognitive Sciences

Complex—is the largest neuroscience center in the world. Pundit Paul McMorrow wrote in an article of April 29, 2013, in the *Globe*:

> The MIT plans for remaking Kendall Square in Cambridge are stuffed full of huge numbers and huge ambition. The ten-year, $1 billion plan covers 20 acres...creating a new gateway into both the school and the city....But more than anything, they represent a microcosm of the Boston economy....Boston punches above its weight because its economy is built around huge institutions that don't ride business cycles. The region's universities and hospitals feed off proximity to each other....MIT is the most important institution in a region of highly important institutions."

Nor is this only a regional story. Adds McMorrow: "The nation's economy revolves around the kind of knowledge-intensive products—pharmaceuticals, biotech, computer technology—that Boston's institutions trade in."

And have been trading in since Rogers was drawn here in the mid-nineteenth century. With the exception of Tufts College (as it was then), a conventional liberal arts school founded in the Boston suburb of Medford in 1852, MIT was the first institution of higher learning to be founded in Boston's orbit in modern times—ahead of Boston University, Boston College, all of them—the first of anything like the radical importance of the founding of Harvard in 1636. Rogers broke Harvard's monopoly in decisive and (because so overtly technological) timely fashion, never challenging—as who would wish to?—the stature of the pioneering American seat of learning, but making of MIT something more: the icebreaker of a new world.

Russell B. Adams has been all along the most insightful pundit about MIT, the author of that seemingly crassly titled book, *The Boston Money Tree*. He wrote of the dedication pageant of the new campus in 1916 that "a lone searchlight on the newly consecrated cathedral of technology knifed across the sky until it touched the one bright beam still lofting from the brick Victorian pile that had housed MIT for nearly half a century. Briefly, the two lights stood locked in the night; then the beam from the old Back Bay building faded and disappeared, leaving the newer light pointing to the stars, a pale herald of things to come."

One wonders if the Reverend Theodore H. Ferris, rector of Trinity Church, Copley Square, knew of this when in 1954 he presided at the funeral of one of MIT's greatest presidents, Karl Compton. Ferris shared his thoughts with Compton's friends and colleagues. Like his famous predecessor at Trinity, Saint Philips Brooks, since canonized—MIT had a saint on its first governing board!—Ferris knew whereof he spoke when he declared of MIT that "the kind of human being we are trying to educate [is a person] with one eye continuously and honestly on the facts and the other on the stars."

When Theodore H. Ferris, rector of Trinity Church, eulogized President Karl Compton in 1954, he may have had the institution's historical memory of its Charles River Basin campus inauguration in mind: the goal of an MIT education, Ferris asserted, was a student with one eye on the facts, the other on the stars.

In 2011 MIT celebrated its sesquicentennial with a great river pageant reminiscent of the one that marked the passing of its original campus and the dedication in 1916 of its present Charles River Basin campus. Still, however, nearly a century after the move, the relationship remained so intimate with the historic Copley Square campus that it fell to the Prudential Center, the Back Bay's second-tallest skyscraper, to render the most dramatic salute amid bursting fireworks.

Sources

Abercrombie, Stanley. "Happy Anniversary, Baker House." *Architecture Plus* (July 1973).

———. Review of *Designing MIT: Bosworth's New Tech*, by Mark Jarzombek. *Journal of the Society of Architectural Historians* 64 (2004).

Abraham, Karl, Ernst Falzeder, and Sigmund Freud. *The Complete Correspondence of Sigmund Freud and Karl Abraham, 1907–1925*. London: Karnac, 2002.

Adams, Russell B., Jr. *The Boston Money Tree*. New York: Crowell, 1977.

Alcott, Bronson. *Conversations with Children on the Gospels*. New York: James Munroe, 1836.

———, Elizabeth Palmer Peabody, and Alice Howell. *How Like an Angel Came I Down*. Hudson, NY: Lindisfarne Press, 1991.

Alexander, Philip A. *Widening Sphere*. Cambridge, MA: MIT Press, 2001.

Allston, Margaret. *Her Boston Experiences*. Boston: Page, 1899.

"A Man and a Principle." *Boston Evening Transcript*, n.d.

Anderson, Stanford. "Introduction." In *Aalto in America*, edited by Stanford Anderson, Gail Fenske, and David Fixler. New Haven, CT: Yale University Press, 2010.

Anjulo, A. J. *William Barton Rogers and the Idea of MIT*. Baltimore: Johns Hopkins University Press, 2009.

Anwarruddin, Sardour. "Reading Emerson and Tagore in the Age of Religious Intolerance." *Asiatic/Journal of English Language and Literature* (June 2013).

ArmenianHouse.org. "Alice Stone Blackwell Biography," compiled by Mary M. Hoogasian. Accessed October 23, 2015. http://www.armenianhouse.org/blackwell/biography-en.html.

Atkinson, William P. "Liberal Education of the Nineteenth Century." In *English and Engineering*, edited by F. Aydelotte. Charleston, SC: Nabu Press, 2012. First published November 1873 in *Popular Science Monthly*.

Auxier, Randall E. "George Howison." In *Dictionary of Modern American Philosophy*. Bristol: Thoemmes Continuum, 2005.

Backus, Joseph. "Gelett Burgess, a Biography of the Man Who Wrote the Purple Cow." PhD diss., University of California, Berkeley, 1961.

Bacon, Mardges. *Le Corbusier in America*. Cambridge, MA: MIT Press, 2003.

Bailyn, Lottie. "Putting Gender on the Table." In *Becoming MIT*, edited by David Kaiser. Cambridge, MA: MIT Press, 2010.

Baltzell, E. Digby. *Puritan Boston and Quaker Philadelphia*. New Brunswick, NJ: Transaction, 1996.

Bartlett, Truman H. "Auguste Rodin, Sculptor." *American Sculptor* (January 26, 1889).

Bassett, Ross. "MIT-trained Swadeshis." *Osiris* (2009).

Bates, Arlo. *The Philistines*. Boston: White Dog, 2010. First published in 1888.

Bellamy, Edward. *Looking Backward*. New York: Houghton, 1888.

Beluschi, Pietro, to Eero Saarinen. January 1955. MIT Archives.

Bendix, Reinhard. *Max Weber: An Intellectual Portrait*. Garden City, NY: Doubleday, 1960.

Bergmann, Harriet. "The Silent University." *New England Quarterly* (September 2001).

Bermúdez, José Luis, and Sebastian Gardner, eds. *Art and Morality*. New York: Routledge, 2003.

Berring, Henrik. Review of *How the West Won*, by Rodney Stark. *Wall Street Journal*, March 30, 2014.

Bliss, Marshall. *Harvey Cushing: A Life in Surgery*. New York: Oxford University Press, 2005.

Blumenfield, Samuel L. *Is Public Education Necessary?* Old Greenwich, CT: Devin-Adair, 1987.

Boddy, Trevor. "I. M. Pei." *Architectural Review* (August 28, 2010).

"Boston Provides Free Education." *Boston Globe*, September 15, 1907.

Bosworth, William Welles. "New Buildings for the Massachusetts Institute of Technology." *Architectural Review* (September 1913).

————, to Miss Schillabes. April 19, 1954. MIT Archives.

Bourne, Frank. "Huntington Hall Frieze." *MIT Technology Review* 7 (1905).

Bowers, Andy. "What's a Boston Brahmin." *Slate* (March 1, 2004).

Brandeis, Louis, interview with Richards Livy. "Up from Aristocracy." *Independent* (July 27, 1914).

Brayer, Elizabeth. *George Eastman*. Baltimore: Johns Hopkins University Press, 1996.

Brooks, Van Wyck. *New England: Indian Summer*. New York: Dutton, 1950.

Brown, Milton. *The Story of the Armory Show*. New York: Abbeville Press, 1988. First published in 1963.

Brown, Thomas J. "Civic Monuments." In *Hope and Glory*, edited by Martin Blatt, Thomas J. Brown, and Donald Yacovone. Amherst: University of Massachusetts Press, 2009.

Brunton, Paul. *Indian Philosophy and Modern Culture*. New York: Dutton, 1939.

Budd, Louis. "Twain, Howells and the Boston Nihilists." *New England Quarterly* (September 1969).

Buell, Lawrence. *Emerson*. Cambridge, MA: Belknap Press of Harvard University Press, 2009.

Bunting, Bainbridge. *Houses of Boston's Back Bay*. Cambridge, MA: Harvard University Press, 1967.

———— and Margaret Henderson Floyd. *Harvard: An Architectural History*. Cambridge, MA: Belknap Press, 1998.

Burgess, Gellett. "Wild Men of Paris." *Architectural Record* (May 1910).

Buse, Peter, ed. *Benjamin's Arcades: An Unguided Tour*. Manchester, NJ: Manchester University Press, 2006. First published in 1905.

Cambridge Historical Commission. *Cambridgeport* 3. Cambridge, MA: MIT Press, 1971.

Campbell, Robert. "A Mural Creates a Secret Garden at MIT." *Boston Globe*, December 8, 2007.

————. "Breuer Brand of Modernism." *Boston Globe*, April 26, 2009.

————, and Jeffrey Cruikshank. *Artists and Architects Collaborate: Designing the Wiesner Building*. Cambridge, MA: List Arts Center, 1985.

Cannel, Michael. *I. M. Pei: Mandarin of Modernism*. New York: Carol Southern Books, 1995.

Canty, Donald, and Bernard Spring, "Concrete: The Material That Can Do Almost Anything." *Architectural Forum* (September 1962).

Casson, Herbert. *History of the Telephone*. Chicago: McClure, 1911.

Cederholm, Theresa Dickason. *The Battle to Bring Modernism to New England*. Madison, CT: Falk Art Reference, 2005.

Champa, Judith Tolnick. "MIT: A High-Powered Contemporary Art Lobby." *Art New England* (January–February 2013).

Chewing, J. A. "William Robert Ware at MIT." Unpublished manuscript, MIT Archives.

Chhapia, Hemali. "Singapore: Not Quite Boston." *Times of India*, March 21, 2010.

Chomsky, Noam. Interview. *Boston Globe*, August 8, 2010.

"Class Reunion Gifts." *Vassar Miscellany* (July 1, 1912).

Coburn, Frederick W. "An American City's Shopfronts." *Arts and Progress* (November 1910–October 1911).

————. "Restoring Paul Nefflen's Murals." *Brush and Pencil* (June 1906).

Cochran, Robert F., Jr. Review of *Louis D. Brandeis's MIT Lectures on Law*, by Louis Brandeis. *Pepperdine Law*, Fall 2012.

———, ed. *Louis D. Brandeis's MIT Lectures on Law*. Durham, NC: Carolina Academic Press, 2012.

Collins, C. C. *Werner Hegemann and the Search for Universal Urbanism*. New York: Norton, 2006.

Coolidge, John. "Introduction." In *Old Cambridge*, by Bainbridge Bunting and Richard Nylander. Cambridge, MA: Cambridge Historical Commission, 1973.

———. "Introduction." In *Boston Architecture*, by Donald Freeman. Cambridge, MA: MIT Press, 1970.

"Commencement" and "Dome Appears in Many Colors." *The Tech* (June 8, 1923).

Conway, F. S., and Jim Siegelman. *Norbert Wiener: Dark Hero of the Information Age*. New York: Basic Books, 2004.

Cooke, George W. *Unitarianism in America*. Boston: American Unitarian Association, 1902.

Le Corbusier, *Quand Les Cathedrales Etaient Blanches*. Paris: Plon, 1937.

Crunden, Robert M. *American Salons*. New York: Oxford University Press, 1993.

Curtis, William J. R. *Boston: Forty Years of Modern Architecture*. Boston: Institute of Contemporary Art, 1980.

Damon, S. Foster. *Amy Lowell: A Chronicle, with Extracts from Her Correspondence*. New York: Houghton Mifflin, 1935.

Deb, Siddhartha. "Sins of the Brothers: Jhumpa Lahiri's 'Lowland.'" *New York Times*, September 29, 2013.

Dickens, Charles. *American Notes for General Circulation*. New York: Harper & Brothers, 1842.

DiMaggio, Paul. "Cultural Entrepreneurship in 19th Century Boston: The Creation of an Organizational Base for High Culture in America." *Media, Culture and Society* 4 (1982).

Dini, Jane. "Sargent's Michelangelo." In *Sargent in Italy*, edited by Bruce Robertson. Princeton, NJ: Los Angeles County Museum of Art, with Princeton University Press, 2003. Exhibition catalog.

Domish, Mona. *Invented Cities*. New Haven, CT: Yale University Press, 1998.

Dougherty, Conor. "U.S. Cities with Bigger Economies Than Entire Countries." *Wall Street Journal*, July 20, 2012.

Douglas, Deborah. "MIT and War." In *Becoming MIT*, edited by David Kaiser. Cambridge, MA: MIT Press, 2010.

Durant, Elizabeth. "A Lab of Their Own." *MIT Technology Review*, August 8, 2006.

———. Review of *Designing MIT*, by Mark Jarzombek. *MIT Technology Review*, October 27, 2012.

"Eero Saarinen." *Time*, July 2, 1956.

Eliot, Charles W. "The New Education." *Atlantic*, February/March 1869.

Elling, George. "The New Buildings at the Massachusetts Institute of Technology." *Architectural Forum* (1917).

Ellis, Rufus. "Funeral Services of Prof. Wm. B. Rogers" *The Virginias* (June 1882).

Emerson, Ralph Waldo. "Brahma." *Atlantic*, November 1857.

———. *Journals*. Vol. 3. Temecula, CA: Reprint Services Corp., 1998.

Etzkovitz, Henry. *MIT and the Rise of Entrepreneurial Science*. London: Routledge, 2002.

"The Extremists: An Interview with Jo Davidson." *Arts & Decoration* 3, no. 5 (March 1913).

Fenske, Gail. "Aalto, Wurster, and the 'New Humanism.'" In *Aalto and America*, edited by Anderson Stanford, Gail Fenske, and David Fixler. New Haven, CT: Yale University Press, 2012.

Filler, Martin. *Makers of Modern Architecture*. New York: New York Review of Books, 2007.

Findlay, Nancy. *Artists of the Book in Boston 1890–1910*. Cambridge, MA: Dept. of Printing and Graphic Arts, Houghton Library, Harvard College Library, 1985.

Fitzgerald, Desmond. *Dodge MacKnight: Water Color Painter*. Brookline, MA: privately printed, 1916.

———. Papers 1868–1930. Archives of American Art, Smithsonian Institution, Washington, D.C.; Boston Public Library, Boston.

Fixler, David N. "Appropriate Means to an Appropriate End: Industry, Modernism and Preservation." *Journal of Preservation Technology* 39, no. 4 (2008).

Florida, Richard. "Where the Brains Are." *Atlantic*, October 2006.

Floyd, Margaret Henderson. *Architectural Education and Boston*. Boston: Boston Architectural College, 1984.

Forbes, H. A. Crosby. Interview with D. J. Minor. *Oklahoman*, July 12, 1987.

Ford, Edward R. *Details of Modern Architecture*. Cambridge, MA: MIT Press, 2003.

Gage, Lawrence. "'You Shall Be as Gods'?" *Real Physics* (blog), February 15, 2008.

Gelb, Barbara. "Theatre: Concealing While Revealing." *New York Times*, April 4, 1999.

Gelfand, Mark. *Trustee for a City: Ralph Lowell of Boston*. Boston: Northeastern University Press, 1998.

Gerdts, William. *The Color of Modernism: The American Fauves*. New York: Hollis Taggert Gallery, 1997.

Gibian, Peter. *Oliver Wendell Holmes and the Culture of Conversation*. Cambridge Studies in American Literature and Culture. Cambridge, MA: Cambridge University Press, 2001.

Glackens, William J. "The American Section: The National Art," *Arts & Decoration* 3, no. 5 (March 1913).

Glick, Thomas. *What About Darwin?: All Species of Opinion from Scientists, Sages, Friends, and Enemies Who Met, Read, and Discussed the Naturalist Who Changed the World*. Baltimore: Johns Hopkins University Press, 2010.

Goldberger, Paul. "Alvar Aalto Is Dead at 78, Master Modern Architect." *New York Times*, May 13, 1976.

———. *New York: The City Observed*. New York: Random House, 1979.

Goldhagan, Sarah Williams. *Louis Kahn's Situated Modernism*. New Haven, CT: Yale University Press, 2001.

Goodman, Paul. "Ethics and Enterprise: The Values of a Boston Elite, 1800–1860." *American Quarterly* (Autumn 1966).

Goodrich, Lloyd. "The Decade of the Armory Show," *Art in America* (1963).

Goodyear, William Henry. *Greek Refinements: Studies In Temperamental Architecture*. Oxford: Oxford University Press, 1912.

Gordon, Robert C. *Emerson and the Light of India: An Intellectual History*. New Delhi: National Book Trust, 2008.

Gordon, Susan. *Neurophenomenology and Its Applications to Psychology*. New York: Springer, 2013.

Gray, Paul. "Memorial Tribute to James R. Killiam." In *Memorial Tributes*, by the National Academy of Engineers. Washington, D.C.: National Academies Press, 1992.

Greenslet, Ferris. *Under the Bridge: An Autobiography*. New York: Houghton Mifflin, 1943.

Gregg, Frederick J. "The Attitude of the Americans." *Arts & Decoration* 3, no. 5 (March 1913).

Grinley, Chris, Michael Kubo, and Mark Pasnik. *Heroic: Concrete Architecture and the New Boston*. New York: Monacelli Press, 2015.

Gupta, Kumar. *The Great Encounter: A Study of Indo-American Literary and Cultural Relations*. New Delhi: Abhinav, 1986.

Haglund, Karl. *Inventing the Charles River*. Cambridge, MA: MIT Press, 2002.

Hale, Nathan G. *Freud and the Americans*. New York: Oxford University Press, 1971.

Hale, Phillip Leslie. "Nude Descending." In *The White Blackbird*, by Honor Moore. New York: W. W. Norton, 2009.

Hall, Peter. *Cities in Civilization*. New York: Pantheon, 1998.

Hall, Peter Dobkin, "Learning to Be Civic: Higher Education and Student Life, 1890–1940," paper read at Panel on Educating Leaders: Higher Education and Civic Elites, 1870–1970, Annual Meeting of the Social Science History Association, Chicago, IL, November 2001.

Hamlin, Oscar. *Boston Immigrants, 1790–1880: A Study in Acculturation.* Cambridge, MA: Belknap Press, 1991.

Hapgood, Frank. *Up the Infinite Corridor: MIT and the Technical Imagination.* Reading, MA: Addison-Wesley, 1993.

Hasselbach, Kurt. In discussion with the author, 2013.

Hegemann, Werner. *American Vitruvius: An Architect's Handbook of Civic Art.* New York: Architectural Book Publishing, 1922.

Hilliard, George S. "Memoir of the Honorable James Savage, LL.D." Boston: Massachusetts Historical Society, 1878.

Hilts, Philip J. "Last Rites for a 'Plywood Palace' That Was a Rock of Science." *New York Times,* March 31, 1998.

Hinsdale, B. A. *Horace Mann and the Common School Revival in the United States.* Norwood, MA: Norwood Press, 1898.

Hitchcock, Henry-Russell. *Architecture: Nineteenth and Twentieth Centuries.* New Haven, CT: Yale University Press, 1989.

Hockfield, Susan. "Fighting For the Nation's Future: The Founding of MIT in a Time of War." Boston Public Library Lowell Lecture on MIT Sesquicentennial, February 7, 2012.

Hoffman, Donald. *The Architecture of John Wellborn Root.* Chicago: University of Chicago Press, 1988.

Holmes, Oliver Wendell. *The Autocrat of the Breakfast Table.* New York: Houghton, 1899. First published in 1853.

———. "The Professor's Story." *Atlantic,* December 1859.

Horowitz, Joseph. *Classical Music in America: A History of Its Rise and Fall.* New York: W. W. Norton, 2005.

Howe, M. A. DeWolfe. *Boston: The Place and the People.* New York: Macmillan, 1903.

Hutchinson, William R. *The Modernist Impulse in Protestantism.* Durham, NC: Duke University Press, 1992.

Huxtable, Ada Louise. "The Bold and the Beautiful: A Tale of Two Franks." *Wall Street Journal,* June 12, 2001. Reprinted in Ada Louise Huxtable, *On Architecture.* New York: Walker, 2008.

———. "Looking Back in Boston." *New York Times,* September 28, 1980.

———. "The Tall Building Artistically Reconsidered." *New Criterion* (November 19, 1982).

"Institute of Technology." In *Bacon's Handbook of Boston,* by Edwin M. Bacon and George Edward Ellis. Boston: Houghton, Mifflin and Company, 1886.

Iyer, Pico. "The 'Transcendent' Dali Lama," *Radio Open Source* (April 11, 2008).

"James Savage Obituary." *Boston Globe,* March 10, 1873.

James, William. *Pragmatism and Other Writings.* New York: Penguin, 2000.

———. *Pragmatism: A New Name for Some Old Ways of Thinking.* New York: Longmans, Green, and Co., 1907.

———. *Essays, Comments, and Reviews.* Cambridge, MA: Harvard University Press, 1987.

Jarzombek, Mark. "Corridor Spaces." *Critical Inquiry* (Summer 2010).

———. *Designing MIT: Bosworth's New Tech.* Boston: Northeastern University Press, 2004.

"John Osborne Summer obituary." *Pencil Points* (May 1938).

Jones, Caroline. *Modern Art at Harvard.* New York: Abbeville Press, 1985.

Jordy, William. *American Buildings and Their Architects.* Vol. 4, *Progressive and Academic Ideals at the Turn of the Twentieth Century.* New York: Oxford University Press, 1986.

Kaiser, David. "Introduction: Moments of Decision." In *Becoming MIT,* by David Kaiser. Cambridge, MA: MIT Press, 2000.

Karso, Kerry Dean. "Boston." In *Encyclopedia of 20th-Century Architecture,* edited by Stephen Sennott. New York: Taylor and Francis, 2004.

Kazanjian, Victor, and Peter Laurence, eds., *Education as Transformation*. New York: Peter Lang, 2000.

Keller, Morton. "The Personality of Cities: New York, Boston, Philadelphia." *Proceedings of the Massachusetts Historical Society* (1985).

Kennedy, Pagan. "Big Sponge on Campus." *New York Times*, May 18, 2003.

Kennedy, Richard S. *Dreams in the Mirror*. New York: Liveright, 1980.

Kermes, Stephanie. "To Make Them Fit Wives for Well Educated Men: 19th-Century Education of Boston Girls." Online paper at New England Women's Club Fellowship, 2004.

Killian, James R., to E. L. Brooks. June 1956. MIT Archives.

———. *Education of a College President*. Cambridge, MA: MIT Press, 1985.

———. "That Those Do Not See May See." Speech, June 24, 1960.

———. *Walker Memorial Murals*. Cambridge, MA: MIT Press, 1935.

Kline, Katy. *Art and Architecture at MIT: A Walking Tour of the Campus*. Cambridge, MA: List Visual Arts Center, 1985.

Kramer, Peter D. *Freud: Inventor of the Modern Mind*. New York: HarperCollins, 2009.

Kuhn, Walt. Kuhn Family Papers. Archives of American Art, Smithsonian Institution, Washington, D.C.

Kuklick, Bruce. Introduction to *Pragmatism*, by William James. Indianapolis: Hackett, 1981.

LACMA. "Calder and Abstraction: From Avant Garde to Iconic." Accessed October 25, 2015. http://www. lacma.org/art/exhibition/calder-and-abstraction-avant-garde-iconic.

Lahiri, Jhumpa. *The Namesake*. Boston: Houghton Mifflin, 2004.

Lawson, Alan. "Freud in New England." Accessed October 25, 2015. http://www.heretical.com/freudian/ lawson.html.

Leonard, Thomas C. "Eugenics and Economics in the Progressive Era." *Journal of Economic Perspectives* (Fall 2005).

Leslie, Stuart W., and Robert Kargon. "Exporting MIT." *Osiris* 21 (2006).

Lucas, John. "A Centennial Retrospective: the 1889 Conference on Physical Training." *Journal of Physical Education Creation and Dance* (November/December 1989).

MacCauley, Hugh J. "Visions of Kykuit." *Hudson Valley [Regional] Review* (September 1993).

Macquarrie, John. *Christian Hope*. New York: Seabury, 1978.

Malloy, Vanij. "Non Euclidian Space...Alexander Calder's Mobiles." *EDPS Sciences*, September 5, 2013.

Mann, Arthur. *Yankee Reformers in an Urban Age*. Cambridge, MA: Belknap Press of Harvard University Press, 1954.

Martin, Reinhold. "The MIT Chapel with an Interdiscursive History." In *A Second Modernism: MIT Architecture and the "Techno-Social" Movement*, edited by Arindam Dutt. Cambridge, MA: MIT Press, 2013.

Matusow, Allen. "The Mind of B. O. Flower." *New England Quarterly* (December 1961).

McCord, David. *About Boston*. Boston: Little, Brown and Co., 1948.

McCoy, Garnett. "The Post-Impressionist Bomb." *Archives of American Art Journal* (1980).

McCullough, Diarmaid. *Christianity: The First Three Thousand Years*. New York: Penguin, 2010.

McElroy, Wendy. "Benjamin Tucker, Liberty and Individual Anarchism." *Independent Review* (Winter 1988).

———, ed. "The Life of Benjamin R. Tucker Disclosed by Himself." Accessed October 26, 2015. http://www. wendymcelroy.com/articles/tuckerauto1.html.

McKitterick, David. *New World of Learning 1873–1972*. Vol. 3 of *A History of Cambridge University Press*. Cambridge: Cambridge University Press, 2004.

"Memorial to Eastman." *Boston Globe*, October 23, 1934.

Menand, Louis. *The Metaphysical Club*. New York: Farrar, Strauss and Giroux, 2001.

Miller, Arthur. *Einstein, Picasso: Space, Time, and the Beauty That Causes Havoc*. New York: Basic Books, 2001.

"MIT's Great Court." *Boston Sunday Herald*, October 21, 1917.

MIT LIST Visual Arts Center. "Loohooloo." Accessed October 26, 2015. http://listart.mit.edu/
    public-art-map/loohooloo.

MIT Society of Arts. *In Memory Of William Barton Rogers*. Cambridge, MA: MIT Society of Arts, 1882.

Mitchell, Jack W. *Listener Supported*. Westport, CT: Praeger, 2005.

Mitchell, William. *Imagining MIT*. Cambridge, MA: MIT Press, 2007.

Morgan, Ann Lee. "French, Daniel Chester." In *Oxford Dictionary of American Art and Artists*. New York:
    Oxford University Press, 2007.

Morgan, Keith. Introduction to *Charles Eliot, Landscape Architect*, by Charles W. Eliot. Amherst: University
    of Massachusetts Press, 1999.

Morgan, William. "The Thinking-Man's Science Complex." *Hartford Courant* (May 14, 2006).

Morison, Samuel Eliot. *Three Centuries of Harvard*. Cambridge, MA: Harvard University Press, 1936.

———. *Maritime History of Massachusetts 1783–1860*. Boston: Houghton Mifflin, 1922.

Mueller, Merrill. "The Death of Winston Churchill." *NBC Special Report* (January 24, 1965).

Munch, Charles. Interview in *The Tech* (October 14, 1956).

Munroe, James P. "Mrs. William Barton Rogers, 1824–1911." *MIT Technology Review*, January 1911.

Nefflen, Paul. *American Architect* (September 24, 1898).

———. "Convictions: The Destroyed Frieze of the Mass. Institute of Technology." *American Architect*
    (October 15, 1898).

Neville, Robert. *Boston Confucianism: Portable Tradition in the Late Modern World*. Albany: State University of
    New York, 2000.

Nuland, Sherwin. *Harvey Cushing: A Life in Surgery*. New York: Oxford University Press, 2005.

Numbers, Ronald L. *Darwinism Comes to America*. Cambridge, MA: Harvard, 1998.

O'Donaghue, David. "America's Socrates." *Concord Magazine* (March/April 2001).

O'Gorman, James. *Living Architecture: A Biography of H. H. Richardson*. New York: Simon and Schuster, 1997.

"Old School Tie-Up." *Time*, November 25, 1946.

Passantino, Erika D., ed. *The Eye of Duncan Philips: A Collection in the Making*. New Haven, CT: Yale
    University Press, 1999.

Pearson, Henry G. *Richard Cockburn Maclaurin*. New York: Macmillan, 1937.

Perry, Ralph Burton. *The Thought and Character of William James*. Cambridge, MA: Harvard University Press,
    1948.

Peterson, Mark. *The City-State of Boston: Ebb and Flow in the Atlantic World 1630–1865*. New Haven, CT: Yale
    University Press, forthcoming.

Pfiefer, Edward J. "United States." In *The Comparative Reception of Darwinism*, by Thomas Glick. Chicago:
    University of Chicago Press, 1974.

Philpott, A. J. Review of the Blashfield murals, *Boston Globe* (January 1928).

Pierce, Myron E. "The Institute and the Commonwealth." *MIT Technology Review*, January 1903.

Pierson, George W. *Tocqueville in America*. New York: Oxford University Press, 1938.

Pritchett, Henry S. "Memoir of William Barton Rogers." In *Later Days of the Saturday Club 1890–1920*, by M.
    A. DeWolfe Howe. New York: Houghton Mifflin, 1927.

Prochnik, George. *Putnam's Camp*. New York: Other Press, 2006.

"Prospect/ Foreign Affairs Top 100 Public Intellectual Results." *Prospect* (October 15, 2005).

Rajghatta, Chidannand. "America's Tech Brahmins." *Times of India*, May 13, 2007.

Rand, Ayn. *The Fountainhead*. New York: Plume, 1994. First published in 1943.

Randall, Mercedes M. *Improper Bostonian: Emily Green Balch, Nobel Peace Laureate, 1964*. New York: Twayne, 1964.

Rasmussen, Steen E. *Experiencing Architecture*. Cambridge, MA: MIT Press, 1959.

Reed, Helen Leah. *Miss Theodora: A West End Story*. Whitefish, MT: Kessinger, 2007. First published in 1898

Reif, L. Rafael. "The Innovation Deficit." *Boston Globe*, December 29, 2013.

Rewald, John. *Cezanne and America: Dealers, Collectors, Art*. Princeton, NJ: Princeton University Press, 1989.

Richards, Simon. *Architect Knows Best: Environmental Determinism in Architectural Culture*. Farnham, UK: Ashgate, 2012.

Richardson, Robert. *William James: In the Maelstrom of American Modernism*. Boston: Houghton Mifflin, 2007.

———. *Emerson: The Mind on Fire*. Berkeley: University of California Press, 1996.

Roach, Mary. *Gulp: Adventures in the Alimentary Canal*. New York: Norton, 2013.

Roberts, Edward B., and Charles Easley. *Entrepreneurial Impact: The Role of MIT*. Cambridge, MA: MIT Entrepreneurship Center, 2009.

Rogers, Emma Savage, and William T. Sedgwick. *Life and Letters of William Barton Rogers*. Boston: Houghton, 1896.

Ronda, Bruce. *Elizabeth Palmer Peabody*. Cambridge, MA: Harvard University Press, 1899.

Rosenblith, Judy. *Jerry Wiesner, Scientist, Statesman, Humanist*. Cambridge, MA: MIT Press, 2003.

Roth, Leland. *Understanding Architecture*. Boulder, CO: Westview, 2006.

Rothenberg, Marc. *The History of Science in the United States*. New York: Taylor and Francis, 2001.

Rowe, Kathleen. "MIT Hurdler." *MIT News*, July 18, 1996.

Rubin, Elihu. *Insuring the City: The Prudential Center and the Postwar Urban Landscape*. New Haven, CT: Yale University Press, 2012.

Russell, John. "Art Breathes Freely at MIT New Center." *New York Times*, April 28, 1985.

Ryan, Dennis P. *Beyond the Ballot Box*. Amherst: University of Massachusetts Press, 1989.

Samuels, Ernest. *Bernard Berenson: Making of a Connoisseur*. Cambridge, MA: Harvard University Press, 1979.

Sandborn, F. B. *Recollections of Seventy Years*. Boston: R. G. Badger, 1909.

Sargent, William R. "H. A. Crosby Forbes: A Career and Legacy Born of the China Trade." *Orientations*, June 2003.

Sarna, Jonathan. *The Jews of Boston*. New Haven, CT: Yale University Press, 2005.

Sassen, Saskia. *The Global City: New York, London, Tokyo*. Princeton, NJ: Princeton University Press, 2001.

Schlesinger, Arthur M., Jr. Interview with Robert van Gelder. *New York Times*, March 10, 1946.

Schultz, Stanley. *The Culture Factory*. New York: Oxford University Press, 1973.

Schuman, Seth. "A Game of Telephone." *MIT Technology Review*, October 20, 2008.

Sedgwick, William T. "Emma Savage Rogers," obituary in *Boston Evening Transcript*, May 19, 1911.

Seggler, Stephen. *Nerds: A Brief History of the Internet*. New York: TV Books, 1999.

Selz, Peter. *Dimitri Hadzi*. New York: Hudson Hills, 1996.

Seshagiri, Urmila. "Jhumpa Lahiri's Real America: On the Lowland." *Los Angeles Review of Books*, October 9, 2013.

Shand-Tucci, Douglass. "Beethoven in Granite." *Open Letters Monthly*, July 4, 2012.

———. *Ralph Adams Cram: An Architect's Four Quests*. Amherst: University of Massachusetts Press, 2005.

———. "The Boston Religion: First American Modernism." Accessed October 25, 2015. http://www.backbay-historical.org/blog/archives/1145.

Shapin, Stephen. "Ivory Trade." *London Review of Books*, September 18, 2003.

Shephard, Odel. *Pedlar's Progress*. New York: Greenwood, 1968. First published in 1937.

Shoemaker, Howe. *Jacques Villon and His Cubist Prints*. Philadelphia: Philadelphia Museum of Art, 2001.

Silber, John. *The Architecture of the Absurd*. New York: Quantuck Lane Press, 2007.

Simon, Linda. *William James Remembered*. Lincoln: University of Nebraska Press, 1999.

Simon, Rita. *In the Golden Land*. Westport, CT: Praeger, 1997.

Sinclair, Upton. *Boston*. Rockville, MD: Wildside, 2010. First published in 1928.

Siry, Joseph. "Frank Lloyd Wright's Unity Temple and Architecture for Liberal Religion in Chicago, 1885–1909." *Art Bulletin* 73, no. 2 (June 1991).

Slaton, Amy. *Reinforced Concrete and the Modernization of American Building*. Baltimore: Johns Hopkins University Press, 2001.

Slavicek, Louise. *I. M. Pei*. New York: Chelsea House, 2009.

Smee, Sebastian. "More Than Numbers." *Boston Globe*, September 4, 2009.

Smith, Bruce, and Alexander Vertoff. *Greene and Greene: Masterpieces*. San Francisco: Chronicle, 1998.

Smith, Earl L. *Yankee Genius*. New York: Harper, 1954.

Smith, Merrit Roe. "God Speed the Institute" and "Elephant on the Charles," in David Kaiser, *Becoming MIT*. Cambridge, MA: MIT Press, 2010.

Smith, Richard Norton. *The Harvard Century: The Making of a University to a Nation*. New York: Simon and Schuster, 1986.

Solomon, Barbara. *In the Company of Educated Women*. New Haven, CT: Yale, 1986.

Speck, Lawrence. "Baker House and the Modern Notion of Functionalism." In *Aalto and America*, edited by Stanford Anderson, Gail Fenske, and David Fixler. New Haven, CT: Yale University Press, 2010.

Stahl, Frederick. "Educational Highlights." In *Architectural Education and Boston Centennial Publication of the Boston Architectural Center 1889–1989*, by Margaret Henderson Floyd. Boston: Boston Architectural Center, 1989.

Stark, Rodney. *How the West Won*. Wilmington, DE: ISI Books, 2014.

Stern, Madeline. *The Life of Margaret Fuller*. New York: E. P. Dutton, 1942.

Stone, Edward Durell. *Evolution of an Architect*. New York: Horizon Press, 1962.

Story, Ronald. *The Forging of an Aristocracy*. Middletown, CT: Wesleyan University Press, 1980.

Stratton, Julius, and Loretta H. Mannix. *Mind And Hand: The Birth of MIT*. Cambridge, MA: MIT Press, 2005.

Strong, Janet Adams, and Philip Jodidio. *I. M. Pei: Complete Works*. New York: Rizzoli, 2008.

Sullivan, Louis. *Kindergarten Chats and Other Writings*. New York: Dover Publications, 1968. First published in 1901.

———. "The Tall Building Artistically Considered." *Lippincott's Magazine* (1996).

Summerson, John. *The Classical Language of Architecture*. Cambridge, MA: MIT Press, 1966.

Swallow, Pamela L. *The Remarkable Life and Career of Ellen Swallow Richards*. Hoboken, NJ: Wiley, 2014.

Swope, Gerald. *Lecture Notes: Brandeis MIT Law Class*. MIT Archives.

Taylor, Eugene. "Professor James at the Podium." *New York Times*, April 16, 1969.

Taylor, Robert. "Making Spaces Human." *Boston Globe*, November 8, 1970.

"The Relation of Classic Examples to Architectural Design with Particular Reference to the Work of Welles Bosworth." *American Architect* (July 5, 1922).

Thomas, Robert McG. "Thomas Cabot, 98, Capitalist and Philanthropist, Is Dead." *New York Times*, June 10, 1995.

Tichi, Cecelia. *Civic Passions*. Chapel Hill: University of North Carolina Press, 2010.

Tilley, J. Michael. "Living Forward and the Development of Radical Empiricism." In *Kierkegaard's Influence on Philosophy: Anglophone Philosophy*, edited by Jon B. Stewart. Burlington, VT: Ashgate, 1912.

Troyens, Carol. "Unwept, Unhonored and Unsung." In *The Armory Show at 100*, by Marilyn S. Kushner, Kimberly Orcutt, and Casey Nelson Blake. New York: New-York Historical Society, 2013.

"Tucker, Noted Anarchist, Dies." *Boston Globe*, June 23, 1939.

Turner, James. *The Liberal Education of Charles Eliot Norton*. Baltimore: Johns Hopkins University Press, 2002.

Turner, Paul. *Campus: An American Planning Tradition*. Cambridge, MA: MIT Press, 1987.

"Unveiling the Portrait of Mrs. Rogers: Addresses Made by President Maclaurin and Professor Sedgwick at a Convocation of Students on the Anniversary of Mrs. Rogers' Birthday." *MIT Technology Review*, 1912.

Vallye, Anna. "Design and the Politics of Knowledge." PhD diss., Columbia University, 2011.

Volpe, Christopher. "The Seeing of the Thing: The Art and Teaching of Charles Woodbury and the Ogunquit Art Colony." Accessed October 25, 2015. http://christophervolpe.com/wp-content/uploads/2014/07/woodbury-presentation-chris-volpe.pdf.

von Eckardt, Wolf. "MIT Chapel." *Time*, May 7, 1984.

Vonnegut, Kurt. *Palm Sunday*. New York: Delacorte Press, 1981.

Wainwright, Oliver. "Architecture Has Become Too Mundane Says Correa." *Guardian*, May 15, 2013.

Walker, Frederick. Review of *Looking Backward*, by Edward Bellamy. *Literary Digest*, March 1890.

Walton, Christopher L. "Words Are Not the Only Language." *Philocrites Blog*. April 5, 1997. Accessed October 26, 2015. http://www.philocrites.com/archives/003143.html.

Watkin, David. *A History of Western Architecture*. London: Laurence King, 2005.

Weeks, Edward. "Kresge Auditorium." *Architectural Record* (October 3, 1956).

———. *The Lowells and Their Institute*. Boston: Little, Brown, 1966.

Weiner, Mina. *Edwin Howland Blashfield: Master American Muralist*. New York: W. W. Norton & Co., 2009.

Weiss, Ellen. *Robert Taylor and Tuskegee: An African-American Architect Designs for Booker T. Washington*. Montgomery, AL: New South Books, 2011.

Weisskoff, Victor, and Philip Morison. "Forty Years After: MIT, Los Alamos and the Bomb." The Karl Taylor Compton Lecture Series, Cambridge, MA, April 17, 1985.

Whitehill, Walter Muir. *Boston: A Topographical History*. Cambridge, MA: Harvard University Press, 1968.

———. *Boston in the Age of John Fitzgerald Kennedy*. Norman: University of Oklahoma Press, 1966.

Wilde, Karl, and Nilo Lindgren. *A Century of Electrical Engineering and Computer Science at MIT, 1882–1982*. Cambridge, MA: MIT Press, 1985.

Williams, Alexander. *A Social History of the Greater Boston Clubs*. Barre, MA: Barre Publishers, 1970.

"William Barton Rogers Obituary." *Boston Evening Transcript* (May 31–June 3, 1882).

Williams, William Carlos. *Letters of William Carlos Williams to Edgar Irving Williams, 1902–1912*. Madison, NJ: Fairleigh Dickinson University Press, 2009.

———. "St. Francis Einstein of the Daffodils." In *The Complete Collected Poems of William Carlos Williams, 1906–1938*. Norfolk, CT: New Directions, 1938.

Wilson, Richard Guy. "I. M. Pei." In *Macmillan Encyclopedia of Art*, by Bernard L. Myers and Trewin Copplestone. London: Macmillan, 1977.

Wiseman, Carter. *I. M. Pei: A Profile in American Architecture*. New York: H. N. Abrams, 1990.

Witham, Larry. *Where Darwin Meets the Bible*. Oxford: Oxford University Press, 2005.

Wolfe, Alexandra. "Weekend Confidential: Harvard President Drew Faust." *Wall Street Journal*, January 31, 2014.

Wood, Deborah, ed. *Marion Mahoney Griffin: Drawing the Form of Nature*. Evanston, IL: Mary and Leigh Block Museum, with Northwestern University Press, 2005.

Wylie, Francis. *MIT in Perspective*. Boston: Little, Brown, 1975.

Yaeger, Dan. "Vita: Francis Lowell Cabot." *Harvard Magazine* (September/October 2010).

Image Credits

Index

Page references for illustrations appear in *italics*